LIFE AND FAITH
Psychological Perspectives
on Religious Experience

LIFE
AND
FAITH

Psychological Perspectives
on Religious Experience

W.W. MEISSNER, S.J., M.D.

GEORGETOWN UNIVERSITY PRESS
Washington, D.C.

Library of Congress Cataloging-in-Publication Data

Meissner, W. W. (William W.), 1931-
  Life and faith.

  Bibliography: p.
  1. Psychology and religion--Addresses, essays,
lectures.   I. Title.
BF51.M45   1987   201'.9   87-8026
ISBN 0-87840-429-5
ISBN 0-87840-423-6 (pbk.)

CONTENTS

PREFACE   xi

Section I. **Grace and the Psychology of Grace**   1

  Chapter 1. Grace and Nature   3
      The Need for a Psychology of Grace   3
      Inquiry   4
      Grace as Psychological   6
      Grace and the Nature of Man   8

  Chapter 2. The Nature of Grace   9

  Chapter 3. Toward a Psychology of Grace   20
      Grace as Ego Energy   23
      Grace as Object Relation   27
      The Development of the
        God-Representation   28
      The Nature of the Relationship to God   38
      Transitional Phenomena   38
      Transition   40
      Transitional Phenomena in Religion   43
      The Capacity for Object Love   44
      Grace as Relational   51
      Toward Spiritual Identity   53

  Chapter 4. The Development of Spiritual Identity   61
      Trust/Hope, Faith   64
      Autonomy/Contrition   68
      Initiative/Penance   70
      Industry/Fortitude   73
      Identity/Humility   74
      Intimacy/Love of Neighbor   76
      Generativity/Service, Zeal   77
      Integrity/Charity   78
      Grace and Spiritual Identity   80

Section II.   **Dimensions of Religious Experience**   85

PART 1.   FAITH   87

Chapter 5.   Faith and Subjectivity   89
               The Problem of Faith   89
               Faith and Reason   91
               Belief and Subjectivity   93
               Despair versus Faith   101
               The Pathology of Despair   105

Chapter 6.   Faith and Experience   112

Chapter 7.   Faith Development   120
               Stage 0. Undifferentiated   121
               Stage 1. Intuitive-Projective   123
               Stage 2. Mythic-Literal   127
               Stage 3. Synthetic-Conventional   128
               Stage 4. Individuating-Reflexive   130
               Stage 5. Paradoxical-Consolidative   131
               Stage 6. Universalizing   134
               Discussion   135

Chapter 8.   Psychology and Faith   137
               Regression in Faith   137
               Instinctual Bases of Faith   139
               Faith and Trust   141
               Faith and Fidelity   144
               Integrative Function of Faith   147
               Faith and Grace   148

Chapter 9.   Faith and Identity   150
               Luther's Quest   150
               The Inner Turmoil   151
               Power and Victimhood   153
               Negative Identity   155
               Conflict and Ideology   157
               The Psychology of Faith   158
               Faith versus Ideology   161
               Beyond Ideology   163
               Faith and Spiritual Identity   165

PART 2.   HOPE   169

Chapter 10.   The Theology of Hope   171
                Traditional Approach   172
                Recent Approaches   173

Chapter 11. The Psychology of Hope 179
Psychodynamics 179
Development 183

Chapter 12. The Psychopathology of Hope 189
Role of the Superego 190
Hopelessness 192

Chapter 13. The Psychotherapy of Hopelessness 194

Chapter 14. Hope and Faith 203

Section III. **Toward an Understanding of Religious Values** 207

Chapter 15. The Place of Values 209
Values in Social Science 210
Values in Anthropology and Sociology 211
Individual Values 212
Values and Psychic Function 212
Ethical Relevance 213
Value-Theory and Ethics 214
Sexuality 215
Ethical Neutrality 216

Chapter 16. Values as Psychological 218
Components of Values 218
Recapitulation 222
Values and Psychic Organization 227

Chapter 17. Values as Cultural 231
Views on Culture 231
Values in Culture 234
Culture and Personality 235
Culture and Values 237
The Notion of Cultural Values 239
Variations and Variability in Values 242
Values as Integrative 244

Chapter 18. Ethical Identity 245
The Life Cycle 246
The Ethical Dimension 247
Religion and Trust 248
Ethical Sense and Virtue 249
The Golden Rule 250
The Ethics of Generativity 251
Religion and Identity 252

Chapter 19. The Place of Religious Values 254
 The Nature of Religious Values 254
 Religious Values as Internalized 257
 Religious Values and Identity 265
 Values and Grace 273

Chapter 20. Alienation and the Crisis of Values 276
 The Context of Alienation 276
 Approaches to Alienation 277
 The Alienation Syndrome 280
 Adolescent Alienation 283
 Alienation and Dissent 286
 Religious Alienation 288
 Recapitulation 295
 The New Romanticism 296
 Conclusion 301

REFERENCES 303

Veni, Creator Spiritus

Infirma nostri corporis,
Virtute firmans perpeti,
Accende lumen sensibus,
Infunde amorem cordibus.

Hostem repellas longius
Pacemque dones protinus,
Ductore si te praevio
Vitemus omne pessimum.

Da gaudiorum praemia,
Da gratiarum munera,
Dissolve litis vincula,
Adstringe pacis foedera.

Preface

The psychoanalytic approach to the understanding of religious phenomena has a brief but unfortunate history. The argument began, of course, with Freud. It is little more than half a century since he put forth his views on religion and religious faith in *The Future of an Illusion* (1927). While the corpus of Freud's writings has served subsequent generations of students of psychoanalysis as a rich mine of provocative insights and richly intuitive ideas, his writings on religion have proven more problematical and controversial.

Freud's view was straightforwardly and avowedly agnostic and materialistic. He regarded religious beliefs as illusions, forms of powerful wish-fulfillments, and the phenomenon of religion itself as a form of universal neurosis based on the model of the obsessional neurosis that he had defined with such admirable insight and clarity.

Freud presents himself in this argument as the implacable, determined, remorselessly logical man of science who sets his face against all illusions, all beliefs, all myths that are not supported by hard scientific evidence and reason. Such illusions are only the infantile residues of the past and have no place in the world of adult rationality and the unavoidable need to face the demands and constraints of reality. Freud saw himself as a crusader, a destroyer of illusions, a slayer of neurotic dragons that inhibited mankind's potential for psychic growth and maturity. In his dialogue with an imaginary opponent who proposes the validity of religious ideas and the necessity of illusion, Freud replies (1927:49):

> I must contradict you when you go on to argue that men are completely unable to do without the consolation of the religious illusion, that without it they could not bear the troubles of life and the cruelties of reality. That is true, certainly, of the men in whom you have instilled the sweet—or bitter-sweet—poison from childhood onwards. But what of the other men, who have been sensibly brought up? Perhaps those who do not suffer from the neurosis will need no intoxicant to deaden it. They will, it is true, find themselves in a difficult position. They will have to admit to themselves

the full extent of their helplessness and their insignificance in the machinery of the universe; they can no longer be the center of creation, no longer the object of tender care on the part of a beneficient Providence. They will be in the same position as a child who has left the parental house where he was so warm and comfortable. But surely infantilism is destined to be surmounted. Men cannot remain children forever; they must in the end go out into 'hostile life'. We may call this 'education to reality'. Need I confess to you that the sole purpose of my book is to point out the necessity for this forward step?

Freud had in effect thrown down the gauntlet, and Oskar Pfister, the Lutheran pastor and long-time friend and follower of Freud, took up the challenge as a member of the loyal opposition. Pfister was the right man for the job, since he was not only deeply committed to and absorbed in religious matters as part of his own career and life commitment, but also had been engaged in an ongoing debate with Freud about the psychoanalytic approach to religion—a debate that lasted over thirty years of their friendship. There is good reason to believe that Pfister was the fictitious opponent with whom the argument of *The Future of an Illusion* was carried out. Freud was, in fact, responding to arguments that had been raised to him by Pfister (Meissner 1984).

Pfister's response was in the form of a lengthy article, which he entitled *The Illusion of the Future* (1928). His argument rested on three major points: first, that Freud's view of religion was a particularly limited one insofar as it focused exclusively on aspects of religious phenomena that were essentially neurotic in character. Pfister argued that Freud had had little or no experience of the broader reaches of religious experience, and that he had little knowledge of the importance of religion as a sustaining force in human affairs, as well as little familiarity with the more scientific and intellectual aspects of theological discourse.

Second, Pfister attacked Freud's understanding of culture, which he felt Freud saw too exclusively from the clinical and psychoanalytic perspective. The phenomenon of human culture, including religious culture, is considerably richer, more complex and derived from higher-order capacities and functions of the human psyche than were accounted for by Freud's instinctual theories.

And third, Pfister defended the role of illusion in human experience. Where Freud saw illusions as reflections of neurotic and infantile residues and set himself to eliminate them, Pfister saw such illusions, particularly religious ones, as essential food without which the human soul would wither and die. He argued that, while the scientific purview gave little room for such illusions and offered no basis for their validation, that did not mean that such illusions were not valid in their own right or that they did not reflect and express important dimensions of human existence, particularly the moral and spiritual dimensions essential for human civilization and existence as we know it.

However controversial and radical Freud's views may have seemed, they set the direction for psychoanalytic thinking for many years to come. Only gradually and with the shifting emphases in psychoanalytic theory itself did the psychoanalytic understanding of religious phenomena begin to shift. Perhaps the most important development was the emergence of an ego psychology which made it possible for analysts to conceptualize higher-order psychic functions in terms other than the derivation from instinctual energies. Other important advances in psychoanalytic thinking came from the emergence of an object relations theory, particularly that developed by the genial and intuitive Donald Winnicott. That current has continued to evolve and is today concerned with questions of an emerging psychology of the self, further increasing the range and explanatory power of psychoanalytic understanding.

Winnicott (1971) had staked a claim for an intermediate area of experience, the area of illusion, which was neither exclusively subjective nor objective but was in some degree both. This middle ground, which he referred to in terms of "transitional phenomena" or the area of illusion, was the realm in which illusion and reality not only touched but became inextricably intermingled. In the language of daily life, the arena of public discourse, the illusory and the real are mutually opposed and exclusive. What is illusory is held to be not real, and what is real is similarly regarded as not illusory. But in the realm of transitional experience, where the illusory and real dimensions intermingle and interpenetrate in such a way that they cannot be disentangled without destroying the essence of the experience, such a dichotomous opposition does not obtain. In terms of Winnicott's analysis of the transitional object, it is impossible to divorce the mother created subjectively by the child from the real mother he finds in reality (Winnicott 1971). Rizzuto (1979:227–28) has put the argument in the following terms:

> The risk in understanding psychic life is to apply to it the separation of subject and object indispensable in science and philosophy. Freud has shown beyond doubt that man's needs and wishes color whatever he does and whatever he sees. Man is always playing with reality, either to create himself through illusory anticipation, to sustain himself by illusory reshaping of what does not seem bearable, or simply to fool himself through illusory distortion of what he does not like. If the illusion, the playing with available reality, goes beyond immediate need, pathology and delusions ensue. Illusory transmutation of reality, however, is the indispensable and unavoidable process all of us *must* go through if we are to grow normally and acquire psychic meaning and substance.

Thus, the debate over the role of illusion in human experience has taken a decided turn—for all practical purposes a 180-degree turn—from that taken by Freud (Meissner 1984). The changed perspective, following both the lead originally given in Pfister's reply to Freud's diatribe against religion and also the course sketched out by Winnicott's subsequent suggestions, has brought the phenomenon of illusion and the related capacity for cultural experience into the very heart of the human phenomenon. Rizzuto once again puts the argument in decisive terms. She writes (1979:209):

> Reality and illusion are not contradictory terms. Psychic reality—whose depths Freud so brilliantly unveiled—cannot occur without that specifically human transitional space for play and illusion. To ask a man to renounce a God he believes in may be as cruel and as meaningless as wrenching a child from his teddy bear so that he can grow up. We know nowadays that teddy bears are not toys for spoiled children but part of the illusory substance of growing up. Each developmental stage has transitional objects appropriate for the age and level of maturity of the individual. After the oedipal resolution God is a potentially suitable object, and if updated during each crisis of development, may remain so through maturity and the rest of life. Asking a mature, functioning individual to renounce his God would be like asking Freud to renounce his own creation, psychoanalysis, and the "illusory" promise of what scientific knowledge can do. This is, in fact, the point. Men cannot be men without illusions. The type of illusion we select—science, religion, or something else—reveals our personal history and the transitional space each of us has created between his objects and himself to find "a resting place" to live in.

Spurred on by the broadening framework of conceptualization and understanding and by the shifting perspectives generated by a deepened comprehension of such phenomena, the psychoanalytic approach to religion has undergone considerable evolution. Where only a few short decades ago doors and minds were closed, both from the side of the psychoanalysts approaching religious experience and from the side of religious scholars and thinkers in their attitude toward psychoanalytic contributions and understanding, the climate of thought and conceptualization has changed dramatically. I have attempted to trace some of these conceptual shifts and to delineate the inherent conceptual bases on which the dialogue between psychoanalysis and religious thinking might take place (Meissner 1984). This advancing and changing climate of opinion was put very succinctly by Loewald when he wrote (1978:73):

If we are willing to admit that instinctual life and religious life both betoken forms of experience that underlie and go beyond conscious and personalized forms of mentation—beyond those forms of mental life, of ordering our world, on which we stake so much—then we may be at a point where psychoanalysis can begin to contribute in its own way to the understanding of religious experience, instead of ignoring or rejecting its genuine validity or treating it as a mark of human immaturity.

By the same token, if theologians and religious thinkers can begin to reflect on essentially religious and spiritual phenomena specifically as human experiences, as embedded in the vicissitudes, conflicts, and motivational turmoil of the human psyche, then a common ground for more meaningful mutual understanding and dialogue may be at hand. It is the supposition that the conceptual frames of reference have moved to such a point that motivates the studies in this volume.

The material which follows is divided into two major sections, both reflecting facets of a major common theme and attempting to bring the resources of psychoanalytic methodology to the understanding of core religious issues.

The first section is given over more directly to a study of the psychology of grace and the implementation of such a perspective, particularly in reference to faith and hope as essential elements in the Christian religious experience—as well as in the experience of other religious traditions. Theologians have long taught that grace exercises effects on the human psyche, and to that extent it becomes possible to speak of a psychology of grace. How that psychology might be envisioned and what it might entail in terms of a psychoanalytic frame of reference—or even more generally of any psychology—are matters of considerable controversy.

The approach I have taken represents only one attempt rooted in a psychoanalytic orientation to address the complexities of this problem. Within the Christian religious tradition, the psychological action of grace is potentially both profound and far-reaching. The resources of any psychology (psychoanalytic or other) for plumbing the depths of such profoundly meaningful religious experiences are quite limited. Psychoanalysis does not explain everything—indeed, it cannot explain everything. Within its own proper and limited perspective, however, the psychoanalytic approach offers the potentiality for generating certain insights and for deepening our understanding of the phenomena of grace, faith, and hope insofar as they impinge on, influence, and shape the psychic organism.

The methodology of psychoanalysis is by its very nature reductive. To the extent that its method is that of natural science, it must be so, since the approach of any science is inherently reductive. This does not mean, however, that psychoanalytic understanding is necessarily reductionistic. The methodology requires that analytic explanations be cast in terms of the theoretical concepts of the models of the mind with which analysis works. Analytic understanding is formulated in terms of the economic, dynamic, genetic, structural, and adaptive perspectives—the basic metapsychological assumptions that form the essence of any analytic conceptualization. Such an account becomes reductionistic only when the formulation is taken as exclusive or as an exhaustive rendering of the intelligibility of the object. No scientific account can make such a claim, nor, in terms of our contemporary epistemology, would it. The history of science, however, has not been unmarred by such misapprehensions.

In his recent work on the epistemology and hermeneutics of psychoanalysis, Ricoeur has focused the function of psychoanalysis thinking vis-à-vis religious understanding in terms of the destruction of idols. He writes (1970:230):

> It is difficult to pinpoint what is properly psychoanalytic in Freud's interpretation of religion. However, it is essential to put into sharp focus those elements of his interpretation that merit the consideration of both believers and unbelievers. There is a danger that believers may sidestep his radical questioning of religion, under the pretext that Freud is merely expressing the unbelief of scientism and his own agnosticism; but there is also the danger that unbelievers may confuse psychoanalysis with this unbelief and agnosticism. My working hypothesis, . . . is that psychoanalysis is necessarily iconoclastic, regardless of the faith or nonfaith of the psychoanalyst, and that this "destruction" of religion can be the counterpart of a faith purified of all idolatry. Psychoanalysis as such cannot go beyond the necessity of iconoclasm. This necessity is open to a double possibility, that of faith and that of nonfaith, but the decision about these two possibilities does not rest with psychoanalysis.

The inherent iconoclasm of psychoanalytic methodology may lead to the destruction of idols—but what then? What is left? Does psychoanalysis have anything to say about the rest, about the truth or belief-value of religious conviction or reality beyond mere idolatry? Ricoeur answers (1970:235):

> The relation of religion to desire and fear is, of course, an old theme: the peculiar role of psychoanalysis is to decipher that relation qua *hidden* relation and to relate the deciphering process to an *economics* of desire. The enterprise is both legitimate and necessary; in conducting it psychoanalysis does not act as a variety of rationalism but fulfills its proper function. The

question remains open for every man whether the destruction of idols is without remainder; this question no longer falls within the competency of psychoanalysis. It has been said that Freud does not speak of God, but of god and the gods of men; what is involved is not the truth of the foundation of religious ideas but their function in balancing the renunciations and satsifactions through which man tries to make his harsh life tolerable.

But one must add to this that psychoanalysis, as we have already noted, no longer finds it so necessary to be iconoclastic. If Freud was the destroyer of illusions, present-day psychoanalysis not only finds room for illusions in human experience, but has moved to the more authentically scientific position of appreciating their value and setting itself the task of exploring and understanding that value and its place in the psychic economy. Even the idols may not, indeed need not, reflect merely infantile and neurotic needs.

The second important focus of this study is on the understanding of religious values. Religious values form a central arena within which the influence of religious convictions and orientations can be suitably identified. The place and function of values within a psychoanalytic perspective is by no means convincingly or unequivocally determined or articulated. Values have long been associated with the nature and functioning of the superego, but as the framework of analytic understanding evolves, the theory brings with it a more complex, more meaningful understanding of values and their roles in human psychic functioning. Insofar as they can be conceptualized as psychic structures which direct and guide human behavior, values have a much more complex involvement in the organization of the psychic apparatus. Undoubtedly, the superego plays a central role, but not to the exclusion of other aspects of psychic functioning. Like these other aspects, values cannot be claimed as the exclusive domain of any one of the psychic agencies; rather, all of the psychic agencies have their proportional and collaborative role to play in the shaping and forming of values, as well as in their day-to-day operation. Consequently, the considerations presented here begin with a fundamental conceptualization of the nature of values and their role in psychic functioning.

Values play a particularly important and central role in the shaping of the adult personality and form a core element in the integration of what Erikson has referred to as a "sense of identity". The direction and intention of these essays is to bring into focus the role of values, particularly religious values, in forming and maintaining a sense of identity which can serve as the basis not only for psychological maturity but for an enlarged sense of ethical and spiritual identity. The place of religious values in such a process must be central, and our understanding of values must be adequate to carry the burden of such a formulation.

There is a common thread that winds its way—at some times tortuously, at other times more openly and explicitly—through the whole of the following material, and that is the theme of the development of spiritual identity. The theme is enunciated initially in terms of the role of grace, and is particularly focused in terms of the virtues of faith and hope, and in the progressive development of spiritual identity; but it is also refocused and reformulated in terms of the core element of such spiritual identity, namely, a spiritual value system.

I hope that these few comments may help the reader in making his way through what follows. The burden of the volume is one psychoanalyst's attempt to bring the resources of the psychoanalytic discipline to a deepened understanding of religious experience. I hope that the reader will not look for more than is offered nor feel that more has been promised than the author can deliver. The matters at hand are of considerable complexity and controversy. If this effort can serve to advance the dialogue even a small step, or can stimulate or challenge others, who are better equipped to plumb these depths than I, to respond, I shall feel it has been worthwhile.

I would like to express my gratitude to my teachers, supervisors, and friends who have not only encouraged the preparation of this study but have helped provide the inspiration behind it. In particular, I would thank the Reverend John Courtney Murray, S.J. (now deceased), who gave me rich counsel and encouragement in thinking along these lines; and Dr. Gregory Rochlin, whose psychoanalytic wisdom has helped me to keep an open, receptive mind. The teachers and friends whose conversations and reactions have been both stimulating and informative are too many to mention. I would like to thank the Reverend John H. Wright, S.J., and the Reverend Harvey D. Egan, S.J., for critical reading of parts of the manuscript. And I would like to express my special appreciation to Miss Elfriede Banzhaf, whose assistance and devotion through all stages of the writing, preparation, and editing of this work have been invaluable.

Grace and the Psychology of Grace

Grace and Nature

The Nature of Grace

Toward a Psychology of Grace

The Development of Spiritual Identity

CHAPTER 1

Grace and Nature

The Need for a Psychology of Grace

We live in curious times. Our age has been called the age of anxiety, the age of automation, the atomic age. It is an age in which technology has become a dominant influence in shaping the course of history. At the same time, it is an age in which our finest instincts for truth, justice, and charity have been activated on a scale never before witnessed in human civilization.

Ours is also, very decidedly, an era of psychological concern. Mental health is a primary public health problem. Psychological testing in all its forms is big business. Beyond these superficial facts of contemporary life, there is a growing awareness and concern with the inner self. Insatiable human curiosity has become introverted, has turned in upon itself, seeking to know more adequately, precisely, and scientifically what man is and why he behaves, thinks, and experiences as he does.

In the religious sphere, the anguish of soul that accompanies the modern predicament often finds an answer in faith. The priest, in the confessional and outside of it, is confronted with the whole gamut of problems and emotional disturbances. It is not a matter of deciding on the morality of this or that situation. Rarely, even in the confessional, is a priest unable to reach a moral decision. His problem is basically and universally pastoral. He must have a fundamental understanding of human motivation and the roots of behavior, and of the role that man's religious existence plays in his life adjustment. He needs to understand, as he attempts to help individual penitents, what influences the way they behave and believe.

The influences are multiple. They are psychological, sociological, and theological. If the Christian life means anything, it means that God is presently active in the souls of his flock. This presence and activity presumably make a difference. But the technical theological understanding of trinitarian processes and divine indwelling may tell us little or nothing about the impact of these realities on the inner workings of the individual soul. The priest, then, cannot rely much on theological knowledge in his efforts to understand the influence of grace and to help the soul become more receptive to that influence.

Inquiry

The inquiry into the psychic nature of grace involves consideration of the methodology of the psychology of grace, and the lines of thought along which such a psychology can be developed. The suggestions and indications offered here regarding the shape of this psychological understanding and the lines of thought it might follow are advanced only tentatively. They are intended to demonstrate merely that the psychology of grace can be structured in meaningful terms; I do not maintain that these particular terms are necessarily the right ones.

First, we must determine what the psychology of grace is *not*. Christian tradition has constantly concerned itself with the life of grace. Over the centuries, the doctrine of grace has undergone extensive development, and Christian reflection has arrived at a profound understanding of the nature of grace. But this understanding has been couched primarily in ontological terms. The questions which have been asked, and to a large extent answered, concern the existence of grace, and the conditions of its possibility, its ontological nature, and the nature of its theological effects on the human soul. In recent years, however, the emphasis has shifted from these predominantly ontological concerns to focus on the phenomenology of religious experience. This change in emphasis from the objective to the subjective leads the inquiry toward an explicitly psychological perspective, yet the formal discussion remains philosophical and theological rather than psychological. Christian thought has also been concerned with the theological dimensions of the relationship between grace and the person of Christ, the incarnation, the redemption, the sacraments, and the church. Guided by revelation, Christian theology has developed a theology of grace which has far-reaching implications for the meaning and understanding of our relationship with God. With this theological elaboration have come many insights on the impact of grace on human nature.

In theological perspective, a *vulnus* or "wound" was inflicted on human nature in the Fall, and the action of grace is directed to healing

that wound. If the *vulnus naturae* resulting from original sin can be regarded as a loss of integrity, then the action of grace is directed toward
the reintegration of our nature. If the effects of sin can be spelled out in
terms of a disordered concupiscence, then the influence of grace can be
conceived of as contributing to an increasingly ordered concupiscence.
Implicit in such formulations is the presumption that grace is psychologically relevant, that it has an influence on our psychological life.
But this consideration remains more or less latent and implicit in the
development of the theological meaning of the life of grace.

Even antecedently to the *vulnus naturae*, man was a creature whose
creaturehood involved both finitude and fallibility. He became a sinner
both by his own efforts and because of original sin. Despite these impediments, he is the creature whom God has summoned, through his
free disclosure and communication of himself, to share in his own inner
life. This is not merely a relationship of love and intimacy, but a call for
the creature to participate in the divine nature and ultimately to share
with the Son in the Beatific Vision of God's own essence (Rahner
1965).

Until recently, there was little concern with or extended attempt to
penetrate within human reality and determine what changes were to be
found there. But this is precisely what the psychology of grace must try
to do. Grace not only alters our theological condition, changing us in
reference to the supernatural, but it delves into our very nature and
makes contact with the depths of our psychic reality.

The question that the psychology of grace poses is the question of
human nature and of what changes may occur in it under the influence
of grace. It is important to realize that the inquiry into the psychology of
grace, therefore, is not a theological inquiry. It is specifically a psychological inquiry and must be carried out in psychological terms. The
psychology of grace, then, does not imply a transposition of theological
insights into psychological language. The inquiry is an independent one
and must work its way to its own conclusions and state them in terms
that are psychologically relevant. The psychology of grace must be
definitively a valid psychology. Its language must be the language of psychology and its formulations must establish its connections with existing
psychological theory. Moreover, its methods must be basically psychological. Its questions must be directed to our inner subjective experience. It must explore the relations between grace and our behavior,
attitudes, emotional experience, values, and ideals. This is in no sense a
theological or ontological investigation. It is rather an inquiry into the
concrete and existential dimensions of the Christian life.

While the psychology of grace must remain methodologically independent from theology lest it lose its scientific autonomy and become

less than an authentic psychology, it nonetheless retains a specific and necessary dependence on theology. Grace is, after all, a divine activity, not immediately open to human observation. Further, whatever may be the reverberations of the action of grace in human experience, there seems to be no graced experience that cannot be duplicated or mimicked apart from grace. Even in the loftiest mystical experiences of the great saints, the supernatural origin of what happens is ascertained on other grounds than the experience itself. The experience of "divine presence" which is frequently associated with the effects of grace is not of such quality that it could not be simulated by psychological mechanisms operating independently of the action of grace. Consequently, the question of whether it is grace which is operative in a particular instance cannot be answered on psychological grounds alone. The elaboration of theological norms is necessary.

On another level entirely, the psychology of grace cannot exist in a vacuum. What grace is, what the conditions of its operation are, and what are its effects, are all questions that require theological orientation. Thus the basic lines of inquiry, the directions of thinking about the psychological effects of grace, must be derived from theological reflection. Only theological reflection can answer these questions—not that the answers are going to be psychological, but they direct the course of psychological inquiry. It makes a great difference, for example, whether grace is considered to be a sort of extrinsic force that coerces our will, or an inner process that depends on the exercise of our free will. It makes a difference whether it directs its effects to the will or to the imagination. Thus, the theology of grace must set the guidelines and indicate the proper focus of investigation, but from there on the investigation must be psychological. Nevertheless, while the methods and concepts are psychological, the validity of any conclusions may be established only by crosschecking with theological insights into the nature and operation of grace.

Grace as Psychological

We are generally persuaded that the operation of grace in the human soul carries with it certain definite psychic effects. Yet, throughout the history of the Christian reflection on the revealed reality of grace and the experience of the life of grace, there has emerged no clear concept of what the precise psychic effects of grace are and how those effects are achieved.

The fundamental objective of the historical Christian reflection has been to define the ontological nature of grace and the complex relation between grace and nature. Such an understanding cannot be complete, because it deals with the mystery of divine action and existence, specifically with the relation between the created and uncreated gift of grace. However successful such a reflection may be, as an ontological reflection it remains on a level of exterior and objective analysis. The analysis consequently fails to throw light on the effect of grace upon the inner life of the soul, or its meaning in human life and experience.

Unquestionably, a rich fund of data dealing with the effects of grace is to be found in the sources of the Christian tradition. Reflection on the life of grace runs through the Scripture, particularly in the writings of St. Paul. It was extended in the patristic tradition and found its most sublime expression in St. Augustine. These reflections are essentially phenomenological and descriptive, however. The experiences and reflections of the saints have added a wealth of data about the life of grace. Yet nowhere, to my knowledge, has the reflection on this experience been articulated on the level of scientific analysis.

What, then, are we concerned with in the inquiry we are proposing? We are concerned with the action of grace, with the psychological dimension and effects of that action in the human soul.

First, I wish to state clearly what is being attempted and what is not being attempted. The influence of grace on human existence is so profound and far-reaching that it is difficult to isolate one aspect of the complex reality without becoming involved in related problems on other fronts. An attempt to formulate a specifically psychological theory of the effects of grace inevitably raises important questions for the analysis of scriptural data, and other questions regarding the complementarity between the psychological anaylsis and traditional theological formulations. Each of these aspects demands extensive consideration, which I shall not undertake here. Nor shall I try to develop the scriptural foundations or to link the psychological formulation with a strictly theological formulation of the nature and action of grace. These matters belong to the theological dimension of the problem of grace and lie beyond this study. Rather, attention and intention are focused on the psychological dimension of the action of grace.

My basic conviction in this regard is that the action of grace must make a difference to the living of the Christian life. It must alter our experience and the course of our life cycle. This does not mean that the action of grace is itself immediately experienced, but it does mean that we are somehow changed and presumably spiritually assisted and advanced by its influence. This is, of course, where the basic problem begins. For all the elaborate theological teaching on grace and its effects, we have not yet achieved a meaningful understanding of its action on the human psychic structure and functioning.

The analysis of the psychology of grace begins with a major presumption of a theological order, namely, that the order of grace is perfective of the order of nature. Implicit in this presumption is the conviction that there is a basic correlation and interaction between a variety of elements in which the growth of each is dependent on and integral to the growth of others. The elements concerned are the life of grace, the habit of charity, human freedom, perfection of self, and personal autonomy.

Grace and the Nature of Man

Man is a concrete existent who is brought into being by a specific act of creation. He emerges into a reality that is permeated by the supernatural and governed by the primacy of the supernatural. Man's nature is directed to the further and higher perfection of the supernatural order. *Gratia perficit naturam.* Man's elevation to the level of supernatural existence and function is more of a fulfillment and enrichment of his nature than an extrinsic accretion to that nature. Grace, then, raises man to a new level of existence which cannot be fragmented into atomic parts, even though distinctions can be made between the levels of existence. Under grace, man becomes a unified, integral existent whose existence becomes specifically supernatural. Thus, grace not only elevates man to a new level of being, but is simultaneously perfective of man's nature itself (Rahner 1961).

CHAPTER 2

The Nature of Grace

Over the last twenty years, the theology of grace has shifted from an older ontological and causal analysis, based on essentially Thomistic principles, to an approach that is much more phenomenological, personalist, and even psychological in emphasis; from a concern with the ontological nature of grace to a concern with the relationship between God and man and the role of grace as a gift from God to man.

A number of important thinkers have contributed to this progression. Rahner, for example, has moved from his analysis of obediential potency and the supernatural existential (1961) to an understanding of grace in terms of personal relations. In this latter analysis, grace emerges as a form of God's free self-communication, which is both healing and elevating, drawing us to a personal union with God (1968).

A similar approach had been suggested by Alfaro (1960). Man is regarded as a finite spirit, a created person, whose fulfillment can be found only in his relationship with an infinite, uncreated person. In this context, grace is God's free gift of himself to man, bringing forth created grace in man by which he is called to a personal union with God.

A third contributor to this movement, on a more popular level, is Fransen (1962, 1964, 1969). In his treatment, grace becomes an invitation to a loving relationship with God. Grace comes to represent the presence within man of the persons of the Trinity, Father, Son, and Holy Spirit. In this chapter, we review some of the important aspects of this evolving view of grace, as a necessary framework for our consideration of the psychology of grace.

From the standpoint of the divine initiative, grace implies the infinity of God's love enfolding and embracing not only mankind, but each individual human being. That loving initiative flows from the Trinity itself, reflecting man's eternal election by the Father, his redemption by the Son, and finally his sanctification by the Holy Spirit. Man is called in history to share in God's own intimate life through God's own free self-communication and self-disclosure. Moreover, God's loving initiative is not merely a giving of creative gifts as a token of his love; rather, God communicates himself. His action on the soul is not a form of creative activity only, or of omnipotent causality, but of loving self-communication (Rahner 1965).

From the human perspective, grace comes to represent a summoning to man's destiny, to a transcendence that fulfills man's deepest longings and brings to completion the work of his creation. As Fransen (1962:xiii–xiv) observes:

> ... grace signifies rebirth in Christ. It denotes a mysterious but nonetheless eminently real stream of life which wells up from the deepest stratum of our being where it rests securely in the creative hand of God, up through all the slowly developing stages of our personality, irrigating and permeating the innumerable areas of our complex psychology, yet never ceasing to be a divine life, a purely gratuitous gift, God's constantly renewed and freely bestowed love.

This view of grace is rooted in the Old Testament and the books of the Pentateuch. It is related to the concept of the covenant, in which God extends his favor and love to his children and they are called to a fellowship with God in love, justice, and truth. Similarly, in the New Testament, the notion of grace emerges as an expression for God's loving intervention in the history of salvation, particularly in the Christ event. The notion of God's grace emphasizes his freely bestowed love and his entering into a salvific relationship with us. Hence, God's grace makes us children of God and calls us to union with God in Christ through filial love. God truly becomes our father in a deeply personal, meaningful sense (Berger 1968).

God's loving self-communication is totally gratuitous. His gift is totally undeserved, not only because the creature can lay no claim to anything before God, but even more because, tainted with the evil of concupiscence and original sin (the *vulnus naturae*), we have lost all privilege and status. As Rahner (1968) points out, even our acceptance of grace must have its ground in God in the same way as the gift itself. Even our ability to accept God's gift of himself is itself a supremely free grace. As Rahner (1965:193) puts it, "The self-communication as such effects its own acceptance, so that the actual and proximate ability to accept it is the sheerest grace."

The effect of God's self-communication is to bring about the created gift of grace within the human soul. It is a driving force within us, the influence of the Holy Spirit conjoined with the human spirit and giving life and vitality to the theological virtues within the human soul. Grace thus flows from within and not from without. As Fransen (1962:51–52) observes:

> This grace flows from within us and not from outside. For God is more truly within us than we ourselves, and His inward driving and urging, natural or supernatural, is closer to us and more interior than our own deeds. And therefore, God works in us from inside outwards, while all creatures work from outside inwards. And because of this, grace and all divine gifts and God's inspirations come from within the unity of our spirit, and not from without through the senses and its images.

This gratuitous self-communication and its free acceptance on our part through faith, hope, and love brings about a living presence, an indwelling, of the Trinity within our soul. The effect of grace is the creative presence of God in the soul. Through grace then, we are united with the Father, Son, and Holy Spirit, drawn into the intimacy of divine trinitarian life. This is the mystery of God's presence, the divine indwelling (John 14:23–26).

We thus acquire an interior divine image which completes and elevates our nature. In this sense, the divine self-communication is a supernatural action which is above and beyond our inalienable nature. Insofar as it implies a participation in the reality of God himself, it is beyond merit. It is possible only insofar as the capacity to receive it is freely bestowed by God.

The mediator of grace, of course, is Christ, and it is his image that is imprinted on us through grace. Through our union with him we become children of God together with the Son of God. And it is through this union that our fallen nature is restored and the wounds of sin are healed. In this restoration is the healing aspect of grace, the *gratia sanans*, by which the sinful wound of our fallen nature is healed. Grace is healing insofar as it provides a capacity for observing the natural moral law. Similarly, our union with Christ as the Son of God reflects the elevating aspect of grace and signifies its supernatural character. Grace is thus elevating to the extent that it enables us to perform truly salutary acts, i.e., acts that contribute to justification (Rahner 1965).

Through union with Christ we are drawn into union with the Father and the Holy Spirit as well. All grace is due to free election by the Father, and belongs to his initiative in granting it. Not only does his election initiate the call of grace, but by it we are summoned to union with him as the final goal of all grace. He adopts us as his children, unites us with his son, and extends to us his loving fatherhood. The doctrine of union with Christ is symbolized in the parable of the vine and the branches (John 15:1–9).

This same symbolism can apply to the connection of Christ and his church. Paul speaks of the church as the "mystical body" of Christ. While the preoccupations with the effects of grace in the individual soul belong to a psychology of grace, the giving and receiving of grace is not simply a personal, private matter. It bears a collective reference and impact. It has reference not only to the community of believers, but is reciprocally reinforced through that community. The community of believers is the church, so that God's loving communication of himself must have particular reference within the body of the church which is Christ's body. Thus theologians teach not only that grace is received through the church, in particular sacramental and liturgical forms, but that the giving and receiving of grace more generally must have implicit ties with the church's function in the economy of salvation. But God's loving initiative is extended to all men and women, who are created in his image, so that, in accepting his grace, they are joined with him and to the body of his son. Consequently, the theological implications of grace and the presence of God within man would seem to transcend mere juridical boundaries.

The history of grace has not been without its vicissitudes. One important focus of difficulty has been the relationship between uncreated and created grace. Uncreated grace refers to God himself insofar as he communicates himself to us in love. Created grace represents the result of this divine self-communication. Thus God's free self-communication, as uncreated grace, provides the basis for our justification. Justification through grace is a new birth, producing a new creature, the dwelling place of the Spirit of God, re-created by the divine self-communication (Rahner 1965). Any way of thinking about grace that would tend to make it a thing or treat it as an object and put it within reach of our autonomous capacity is unacceptable. The concept of created grace implies that we are genuinely and interiorly transformed by the divine self-communication so that something is created within us that is beyond the realm of our own inherent nature. But theologians have not reached any agreement about the relationship between created and uncreated grace, nor any understanding of how created grace is brought into being.

Theological reflection on these questions has suffered greatly from the Lutheran controversy over justification. Luther held that we are justified only through grace, and that no merit or right of ours can lay claim to that grace. Consequently, the idea of created grace or any interior justification is meaningless. We are justified exclusively through grace, that is, through God's love and nothing further. The only grace that matters is uncreated grace. Thus, the problem of the connection and relationship between created and uncreated grace was solved by simply eliminating created grace.

The response of the Council of Trent, meeting the challenge of Luther's teaching, was to bring created grace back into the picture. The Council insisted that the formal cause of justification is the justice of God, not as an inherently divine attribute, but rather the communication of that justice to us by which he makes us just. By this communication we are not merely said to be or reputed to be just, but are in fact just by reason of the justice we receive through the Holy Spirit. The Council did not use the term "created grace," even though it is by created grace that we are justified, but settled for a less technical emphasis that the justice by which we are justified is in fact inherent in ourselves.

The emphasis of post-Tridentine theology fell primarily on created grace, so that for several centuries the efforts of Catholic theologians were directed to substantiating and defending the existence of created grace and to understanding its nature. As Fransen (1962) complains, the historical direction of theological thinking left relatively undeveloped any understanding of the ultimate root of man's interior sanctification and justification, namely, the living indwelling of the Blessed Trinity. The notion of created grace became somewhat disconnected from its roots, the only connection with God being the causal link, the appreciation of grace as a gift given by God as an exercise of his creative power. In consequence of this development, created grace received a greater emphasis and a more central place in the understanding of the theology of grace than it deserved. Recent efforts to develop a more scripturally authentic and theologically meaningful understanding of grace have been subsumed within the larger theory of the mystery of trinitarian indwelling. Grace is thus seen as coming into being by reason of God's uniting himself to us, and the divine indwelling takes place without intermediary or medium. Created grace arises from our immediate union with God, in God's loving communication of himself.

One of the major problem areas in the theology of grace is the relationship between grace and freedom. Participation in a supernatural order demands a free response, such that participation on any other grounds would constitute a violation of the structure and dynamism not only of man's nature but of the supernatural (Rahner 1961).

The theological concept of freedom implies certain qualities of the self. Theologians would maintain that the human being as a free agent is rooted in the ground of being that transcends any particular human agent, but without which that agent is nothing and has no meaning. Human existence derives from a source beyond itself, and human activity reveals ultimately the effects not only of the immediate finite agent, but of an infinite agent as well. Second, the human self cannot be realistically and meaningfully conceived only in terms of an atemporal idea of man abstracted from either personal or human history. And finally, human history cannot be adequately encompassed by an understanding of man alone. Human history takes on a fuller meaning only when it is contemplated within a vision of the human person in relation to an ultimate author of history. This particular vision is achieved only through the exercise of divine graciousness in the form of a personal self-revelation that invites us to faith.

This divine action goes by the name of grace, the gracious intervention of God in a limited and imperfect world that prompts us toward the fulfillment of divine purposes, the enrichment of God's kingdom in this world, and the achievement of the Christian vision of the human. Thus, there is a constant tension in the Christian dialogue between weakness and limits of human freedom, on the one hand, and the power and majesty of God at work in human beings and human history to bring about God's purposes in this world, on the other. Such doctrine is not delusion, nor does it leave open only the path of passivity and resignation. If it accepts suffering, disappointment, and loss, it does not pretend that they can be transformed into satisfactions or pleasures. It does not deny the role of the human agent in forgiving his own destiny or the course of history. It is, in fact, an affirmation that history is more a divine comedy than a Greek tragedy.

A second notion, that of self-affirmation, is fundamental to the notion of freedom. Freedom is an act of self-affirmation. The description of freedom as a choice between certain limited and nonessential goods represents a behavioral and rather superficial level of analysis. Much more profoundly, freedom involves an affirmation of the self that is essential to integral human existence. The self needs affirmation, or else it withers, and becomes less and less an authentic self. Affirmation is necessary to the maintenance and growth of a spiritual life.

Let me carry this notion a step further. The self is a structured reality, regardless of how the terms of its structure are defined. I have attempted to indicate some of the psychological aspects of that structure, but these constitute only one dimension of it. The essential point is that self-affirmation is in and of itself self-construction. The structure of the self is dynamic, evolving, and always in the process of attainment. The affirmation of self in and through freedom may also be defined in terms of structural organization. Freedom is thereby the *via regia* for self-organization, self-structuralization, and self-perfection. We can crystallize the psychological dimension of this aspect of freedom in the term "self-synthesis." The free act, therefore, is an act of self-definition by which the ego shapes and elaborates the reality of the self's structure. It involves a transition from potency to actuality, from imperfection to perfection, from indetermination to determination.

It is equally true, without contradiction, that from another point of view human freedom is always a limping, fragile affair. The affirmation or structuralization of self is always incomplete and tenuous. It achieves its objectives, if at all, in a painfully partial and piecemeal fashion. Perhaps man's hardest task is to become a fully autonomous, total and authentic self. Yet, this is precisely the task we are called to by the dynamisms inherent in our own nature. In fact, the goal of liberty—perfect self-affirmation—is beyond our capability. Herein lies the most perplexing and mysterious, yet the most essential facet of human existence: man, who is compelled by the most profound dynamisms of his nature to seek the perfection of his own self-affirmation, carries within himself obstacles to that achievement. His very affirmation is an affirmation of a torn and divided reality.

Our situation is not desperate, however. The self-affirming and creative aspects of human freedom are an integral part of the divine plan. The dynamisms inherent in man's freedom are contiguous with the dynamisms of God's salvific intervention. The fulfillment of our self-affirmation is made possible only through the action of grace. But one cannot say that our self-affirmation is completed by grace. That is an impossible statement because it destroys the reality of our self-affirmation and distorts the nature of grace. Affirmation of self must remain an active process we carry out ourselves, or else it is not in any real sense self-affirmation. Further, it is essential to the nature of grace that it exercise no effect independently of our natural capacities. Rather, we must say that our self-affirmation becomes more perfect through the action of grace.

In a theological perspective, then, freedom is not so much a quality as an enterprise demanding intense activity and setting objectives as severe as any man proposes to himself. The enterprise is to become fully oneself. But the vision of what we are to become is itself beyond our capacity. The goal of self-affirmation must be seen in the light of revelation: there, the complete vision of ourselves and our nature is set forth. Theological reflection tries to bring that vision into focus. Christian theology stresses the profound reality of freedom and emphasizes its significance in the Christian life.

The general picture of human freedom that emerges from this theological perspective is complex and ambiguous. By way of contrast, the psychoanalytic view of man's limited freedom sets a realistic constraint on the extent to which the theological vision of the meaning of freedom can be realized in the actual human condition. The theological presumption that freedom is a necessary condition for a life of grace, and indeed for any meaningful religious life, is not absolute or itself unconditioned. The theological assessment asserts no more than a defect in man's nature—a *vulnus naturae*. Its concern, therefore, centers on the struggle to overcome the defect and thereby to achieve a full expression of human existence. A basic postulate of Christian theology claims that man's nature does not in itself possess the potentiality to overcome its own intrinsic limitation and defect. The loving and gratuitous power of God through grace is required.

The psychoanalytic perspective, on the other hand, has no interest in theological suppositions or implications. It is concerned with the actual conditions and constraints of the exercise of human freedom. Its business is the discovery of the nature of the impediments, both intrinsic and extrinsic, to the individual's realization of a sense of autonomy. In a way, then, theology takes up where psychoanalysis leaves off.

While the divergence and differences of the psychoanalytic and theological perspectives must be respected, the important and enlarged areas of mutual reinforcement and dialogue should not be ignored. If psychoanalysis sets limits on the realization of the theological ideal, it nonetheless addresses the terms on which the theological dimension defines itself. By the same token, the theological endeavor can no longer make an unquestioned presumption of the presence or exercise of freedom without taking into account the actual extent of realized freedom in individual humans. Insight into the human conditions of freedom is the preserve of psychoanalysis and its related disciplines. Theological reflection, then, cannot take place in a vacuum, as has too often been the case in the past. It requires fundamental and significant information from the basic human sciences, among which psychoanalysis has its appropriate place.

While Christian theology stoutly maintains and defends man's inherent freedom, it also maintains that grace is a free gift of God and that even our capacity freely to respond to and accept God's grace is itself a grace from God. Rahner (1968) would have us speak of "cooperation," but even so, the saving action remains in God's hands. Rahner points out that not only the capacity for salutary action but also our free consent itself is the result of God's grace. It was, in fact, the unvarying assumption of this theological truth that was taken for granted on both sides of the controversy over grace between the Thomists and the Molinists, so that neither doctrine had to be abandoned. In Rahner's terms, "it is therefore grace itself which sets free our (formal) freedom in capacity and in act for saving action, and heals it in itself" (1968:420). Thus, our capacity to say no to God's gracious initiative is itself a God-given quality. If we say no, it is in virtue of our own autonomous capacity; if we say yes, our response is in part attributable to God's gift.

Fransen (1962:169) puts the matter in these terms. If God, working through grace, creates whatever is good in us, how can we be free? Fransen answers as follows:

> Faith has already provided us with the main answer. If grace is indeed love, then it means freedom. There is nothing so personal, so spontaneous, so free as love. Love is the soul of freedom. But we are able to grasp this only when we do not conceive of grace as a "thing" in us, some sort of directionless energy. Neither may we think of it apart from the divine indwelling. Grace originates from the indwelling, is bred in the indwelling and leads to a more complete indwelling. Grace signifies the personal relations of love.

The mystery is that God can exercise his profound and meaningful influence at the very core of our existence. Yet, it is God who has created our nature, and by his providence and concursus sustains it in existence. His action then works from within, from the very origins of our being. Fransen writes (1962:172):

> God, then, does not work in us from the outside, violently imposing Himself on us, binding and determining us to do what is good. As Creator, He stands at the wellspring of our existence, at the point where it flows uninterruptedly from His creative hand. He alone can reach our freedom right at its source and yet do it no violence. On the contrary, He renews it and endows it with true freedom .... We must freely become what in fact we are. God does that for us by His grace.

To complete this discussion of the theology of grace, I would like to focus on certain qualities of grace that may be useful or significant in discussing the psychology of grace. Grace can function in several contexts. The first of these has to do with the fact that, as a result of the Fall, we are trapped in a state of concupiscence, the *vulnus naturae*, which deprives us of the capacity to observe even the law of nature. That defect can only be overcome by a special helping gift of God, which provides us with the capacity to observe the moral demands of the natural order. God's gift in this context is referred to as a healing grace (*gratia sanans*). By his indwelling, God heals our sinfulness at its very root, by attacking the origins of pride and self-glorification. Thus, God's indwelling love sows in us the seeds of love.

I would note in passing that this emphasis points to an important psychological root of our disordered nature and our concupiscence in the pathology of narcissism, which is the source of pride and self-glorification.

By this healing gift, we are no longer simply sinners trapped in the coils of concupiscence and fallen nature. But the healing is a process that takes time, even a lifetime. God's grace does not transform nature, but operates in and through it. We require time to grow, to develop slowly, and to become increasingly ourselves. Grace must respect in its healing impact the inherent laws of human psychological development and change.

But we are also called to a share in the life of God, and it is this supernaturally uplifting capacity of grace that is reflected in the term "elevating grace" (*gratia elevans*). Through grace, we are invited by the Father to participate in the very life of the Trinity. We thereby become the children of God in union with the Son of God. Through this elevating aspect of grace, a truly supernatural life is born within us. It is no longer a question of releasing us from the chains of sinfulness, for through elevating grace we are raised to a new level of being, a level of supernatural participation in the life of God.

Another distinction that comes into play is that between sufficient and efficacious grace. The church's teaching regarding sufficient grace arose in the face of the Jansenist propositions to the effect that some of God's commandments were impossible for those in the state of grace to observe and that God's grace, which might make such observance possible, was wanting; that in the state of fallen nature, grace is irresistible when it is given; and that in this fallen state, merit or sin was merely a matter of freedom from external coercion. Contrary to these views, the church proposed that in the state of fallen nature, which is the actual state of our human existence, God always gives sufficient grace to observe his commandments. But that grace does not violate our free capacities. Sufficient grace does not prevent us from committing sin, but offers the necessary help that we require to gradually achieve an acceptance of and obedience to God's will. Our freedom is not a given, but a task and a challenge. God's gift calls us to greater growth and development in freedom, leading to the freedom of his sons and daughters. Thus, sufficient grace carries with it a dynamic meaning in that it is present in the soul as a force which enhances and enlarges our natural capacity for free choice and decision.

It was also in the Jansenist context that the notion of "efficacious grace" (*gratia efficax*) arose. Even the use of the term, once dangerously close to the Jansenist notion of "irresistable grace," demands clarification. It means that when we perform a good action, we owe it ultimately to God's grace. But God's grace cannot be antecedently efficacious, since this would seem to violate our essential freedom. However, it can be regarded as consequently efficacious, that is to say, when we perform a good action that is in accordance with God's will and law, that action is due to God's grace.

CHAPTER 3

Toward a Psychology of Grace

We can turn now to some considerations that might provide a basis for a theory of the psychological effect of grace. This undertaking imposes certain limits. The first is that it can deal with grace only to the extent that grace can be conceived as having a psychological correlate. Consequently, although sanctifying grace is the basis for our spiritual existence, my analysis is not directly concerned with it because there is no consensus regarding specifically psychological effects that can be attributed directly to sanctifying grace as such. The possible psychological effects of such sanctifying grace, at least as I would see it, would be more reasonably regarded as secondary (actualizing) effects of grace, rather than as specifically sanctifying.

I am more concerned with the effects of actual grace but not, even here, with the effects of actual grace as elevating. Elevating grace may also be considered as having healing effects, which would imply psychological effects. My consideration is limited to the healing effects of grace because the psychological correlates can be more clearly determined. Consequently, I am concerned here only with actual grace as healing, whether such graces be merely healing or also elevating. According to the demands of this theory, I shall regard all actual graces as having a healing effect.

In attempting a psychology of grace, I have been forced to adopt a theoretical orientation. No one theory dominates modern psychological thought; one must pick and choose. Within the last half-century, there has emerged within psychoanalysis a gradually clarifying body of knowledge dealing specifically with the psychology of the ego and the self. The theory is still in flux, but with certain clarifications and reservations I have found it to be the most useful for my purposes. At this stage, I am concerned to show that there are basic principles upon which a psychology of grace can be constructed.

In trying to build a bridge between two areas of thinking, one has to start on both sides of the chasm and work toward the middle. One runs the risk that the two structures may not join perfectly when they meet, particularly when the visibility to the other side of the chasm is not altogether clear. I accept the supposition that the ego has energies available to it independent of libidinal energies and that it is capable of organizing and directing its own proper functions independently of non-ego influences. This does not deny the operation and effect of such non-ego forces, but it does postulate a radical, independent capacity for self-determination within the ego.

From another point of view, the complete development of the implications of a psychology of grace cannot adequately deal with the healing function of grace without formulating in psychological terms the psychological correlate of the *vulnus naturae*. Perhaps the *vulnus naturae* deserves priority in the development of a psychology of grace, but in this formulation the psychological aspects remain implicit in the analysis of the therapeutic function of grace.

This account attempts to provide a theoretical construct in terms of which we can anchor the psychological correlates of the action of grace. But it is clear that even the ultimate psychological implications of grace within the human soul have reverberations that affect the whole of the psychic organization, and thus grace has a total impact on the functioning of the human personality in general. Even though we are able to describe separately functioning psychic entities or systems, there is no implication in the theory that such systems operate in isolation from one another. Rather, they are part and parcel of the integrated functioning of the human personality.

Current theological perspectives on grace emphasize the interpersonal dimension, the gratuitous self-communication and presence of the triune God within the soul elevated by grace. The psychoanalytic approach to personal relationships and interiority is cast in terms of a theory of object relations and a correlative theory of internalization (Meissner 1979, 1980). These perspectives bear on the nature and quality of object relationships and the manner in which the derivatives of such objects are assimilated to the subject's inner world and are woven into the fabric of his self-organization.

We can remind ourselves that grace is a divine action that exercises a causal and motivational influence on the receptive psyche. It is this aspect that preoccupied earlier theological thinking on grace. Its focus was on the ontological characteristics of grace as an action initiated by God and producing effects of a created order in the human subject. While that mystery remains unresolved, theological reflection has added a more phenomenological and personalist dimension that treats grace as well in terms of personal relationship and communication. The theological problem is to comprehend both of these dimensions sufficiently; the theory of grace suffers if either side is neglected. We need therefore to develop a context that will enable us to put forward an integrated theory of grace as both ontological-causal and relational-interpersonal. The theological risk involved would be a compromising of the transcendence of the divine giver and the gratuity of his gift.

There is an interesting parallel in this to recent developments in psychoanalytic theory. Freud's early thinking, following the scientific model of his day, was cast in terms of causal influences and effects. Within the rigidly deterministic framework of scientific causality, he described intrapsychic forces, based on the theory of the instincts—at first libidinal, later libidinal and aggressive—that played themselves out in complex patterns to give rise to dreams, parapraxes, symptom formation, neuroses, character formation, and so on. These forces operated almost completely intrapsychically, with little external input. Subsequent developments of the theory created more evolved and elaborate accounts of the intrapsychic structural apparatus, but still in the objectified, causal framework of a natural science.

More recent theoretical developments have led in quite a different direction. Appreciation of the influence of other people on the growth and functioning of the human personality led to the development of object-relations theory and an increasing focus on interpersonal dynamics, with all that implies for the formation and integration of the self. The parallels to the evolution of the theology of grace are striking: from the ontological, objective, and causal to the relational and personal. Theology and psychoanalysis have been treading parallel paths.

The failure to keep such theoretical distinctions in mind has often resulted in a tendency to substantialize or reify the respective psychic entities, with a resulting parcelization or splitting up of the functions of the mind into more or less separate categories. The tendency to anthropomorphize such reifications has been vigorously attacked in recent years by Roy Schafer (1976). Schafer's critique of psychoanalytic theory is that it tends to split the mind up into a series of minds, and that in this process the unity and integrity of the human personality is destroyed. Schafer himself argues for the abandonment of all such categories and an insistence on the unity of the human agent as the sole source of psychic activity. While the construction I am attempting here focuses the specific relevance of the action of grace primarily in terms of the ego itself, there is no intention to isolate those effects within the ego as though it were a separate entity. Rather, the modifications that the actions of grace may bring about within the ego and its functions have reverberations which play themselves out in all psychic systems, affect the integration and functioning of the personality as a whole, and give a certain cast and character to object relationships and involvements. Some of these secondary effects and ramifications could perhaps more aptly be described in the contemporary psychoanalytic frame of reference provided by the notion of the self and its correlative object-relations.

Grace as Ego Energy

With these reservations and qualifications in mind, then, we can proceed to the tentative construction of a psychological theory of the operation of grace. Our first approach is in terms of the natural science model of the psychic apparatus, specifically in terms of the structures and forces that compose the functional psychic systems. This part of the analysis is objective and causal, and envisions grace as a form of psychic energy or energization. This metaphor reduces grace to its least common denominator as a psychologically relevant entity.

The basic principle is that grace works in and through the resources of the ego. Its influence is manifested in the vital capacity of the ego to perform its proper and autonomous functions. In this framework, therefore, grace can be regarded as a dynamizing activation of the energy resources latent within the ego. Its effect is to reinforce, support, and energize the ego in the exercise of proper ego functions. Consequently, the functions in question lie within the range of the ego's natural capacity. Anything beyond this would carry us beyond the scope of a psychological theory and into the realm of theology. Grace does not force the ego to act, nor does it replace the ego's proper function with a divine activity. Its healing effect is precisely to enable the ego to mobilize its own latent resources and direct them to purposeful action.

It is important at this juncture to keep before the mind's eye the essential distinctions drawn above between the theology and the psychology of grace. Our concern here is solely and specifically psychological, that is, the formula we are constructing is relevant only to those specific psychological functions within which the natural correlates of grace can be recognized. Theology itself and the theology of grace are not concerned with such functions. The language of the psychological consideration, including both its concept of "nature" and its emphasis on the healing aspects of grace, has nothing to do with the theological dimensions of the action of grace, namely, the elevating or perfecting of man's nature in a specifically spiritual order that enables him to posit spiritually meaningful and relevant acts. The emphasis and implication of that analysis are quite different and independent from the analysis suggested in this study.

Grace, then, stands on the side of the ego and supports its proper functioning. It is important to have some understanding of the nature and extent of the ego's functioning in order to form some appreciation of the psychological effect of grace on the soul. The basic conception of psychic structure with which we are dealing is that provided by the structural model of psychoanalytic theory. The psyche is structurally composed of three entities: id, ego, and superego. The function of the ego in the interaction between these structural components is to arbitrate between the forces of the id, the demands of the superego, and the demands of external reality to which the organism must adjust. The ego is, therefore, the agent of intrapsychic harmony and adjustment to external reality.

Reality has a certain predetermined structure into which the ego must learn to fit itself harmoniously. Failure to make such an adjustment brings a high cost in terms of conflict, tension, frustration, etc. The ego has the alternative, vis-à-vis reality, of adjustment or withdrawal as possible means of resolving the tensions resulting from the failure to achieve integration. The reality in question is a complex order of things that includes not only the world of physical existents, but other people in complex social and cultural interaction. Beyond these experienceable aspects of reality, there is the profoundly meaningful reality that is known through revelation. Man lives and moves and has his being in a reality that is supernatural and spiritual; his adjustment to reality cannot be regarded as complete unless the ego has been able to integrate its functioning harmoniously in relation to the order of spiritual realities and values.

Consequently, the ego's basic and essential orientation is toward reality: ego-functioning is determined by the reality principle. This is the basic norm of adjustment for the ego, even in its relation to the id and its instinctual drives. The energies of the id are based on and derived from primarily biological instinctual drives. Under the stimulus of the child's experience of things and people, these drives become attached to certain objects, an attachment called "cathexis." Chiefly through cathexis, the growing organism is related to the world of its experience. Governed by the pleasure principle, such cathexis of the libidinal drives can be directed either to external objects ("object-cathexis") or to the self ("narcissism"). The libidinal energies are organized in terms of the immediate achievement of self-gratification. As such, they inevitably come into conflict with the reality orientation of the ego. The ego's functions of sensory awareness and organization provide an initial contact with physical reality. By its functions of apprehension and understanding, the ego becomes increasingly aware of the complex demands and limitations imposed by physical and social reality. The ego's task is to integrate the pleasure-dominated striving of libido with the demands of that reality.

The aggressive drives are also subject to distribution and regulation, but the aggressive vicissitudes are not synonymous with those of the libido. Directed toward the outside world, aggression can serve important functions in the service of mastery, competence, and the achievement of purposeful goals. As we all know, it can also be turned to the uses of hostility and destruction. It is not clear what a parallel concept to libidinal cathexis might be for aggression. The aspect of "attachment" does not seem to apply. But like libido, aggression can be turned within and directed toward the self, as happens when superego aggression is directed against the self—in guilt, for example. With aggression as well as libido, the ego is the agency of modulation, direction, and regulation which brings aggressive impulses into line with the demands of reality and the adaptive intentionality of the ego itself.

The ego has at its disposal several means for attaining this objective. The original conception presented a picture of the ego defending itself from the disruptive and destructive forces of the id, and consequently the ego's techniques for controlling the instinctual energies were called defense mechanisms. But the term can be misleading. Actually, the problem for the ego is the assertion and maintenance of its proper control over instinctual forces. Proper ego control seeks a harmonious middle ground between extremes that is determined by the basic reality orientation of the ego. At one extreme, the ego can repress instinctual forces, thus driving them into the unconscious. At another extreme, the ego can capitulate to instinctual demands and accept the pleasure principle or immediate discharge as its norm of ajustment. Either extreme is undesirable: repression lays the foundation for subsequent neurotic domination of unconscious instinctual drives, and capitulation merely intensifies the problems of adjustment to reality demands.

The ego, however, is an independent and autonomous psychic structure. It has energies proper to itself that it can use to control the forces of the libido. The problem arises not out of libidinal object-cathexis or aggressive release, which may be essential for good emotional adjustment, but out of the excess of object-cathexis or destructive aggression. The pleasure principle of itself knows no limits; limits must be imposed by some extrinsic source. The ego must, therefore, either assert its own countercathectic energies (in the normal course of development) or mobilize and direct them toward the control of instinctual forces. Thus, countercathexis is an essential ego function, used to establish and maintain appropriate ego-control over libidinal and aggressive energies. The norm of appropriate control is the basic reality orientation of the ego; control can be considered established when instinctual energies are no longer disruptive of ego-functioning and adjustment, and when the particular instinctual drive can be accepted as ego-syntonic (rather than as ego-dystonic, as would be the case in excessive and uncontrolled attachment). In a well-integrated and maturely functioning psyche, ego energies and instinctual energies are mutually supportive and coordinated. This means that libidinal and aggressive energies remain effectively in operation, but their operation is directed and controlled by the reality-oriented ego. It is clear, therefore, that the meaning of countercathexis advanced here is much broader than the classical Freudian concept.

Where ego-control was not effectively established in the developing organism, establishment of such control can be most difficult. The energies of the id offer stiff and sometimes extremely subtle forms of resistance to such control. Every psychotherapist has seen the stubborn conflict between the neurotic ego and the forces of the id. Libidinal resistance and the continued uncontrolled attachment of libido are an obstacle to the effective operation of grace. The effect of grace here is to support the ego in the exercise of its countercathectic function, thus helping the ego to mobilize its own energies and effectively organize them for its attack on the id.

Ego-id interaction is one of the most important areas of consideration in analytic theory. Considerably more complex than indicated here, it involves the whole range of ego defense mechanisms. I have attempted merely to point out a basic principle of the operation of grace in relation to this area of intrapsychic conflict.

Another important area of ego-functioning and adjustment lies in the interaction between ego and superego. The superego is the part of the psychic structure that is organized out of the introjected attitudes and norms of behavior imposed from the social reality. The most important source of such introjections was thought to be the prohibitions and norms laid down by parents, which were incorporated by the child into his own psychic structure, thus becoming "internalized" norms of behavior and judgment. In the normal course of development, the internalized norms of the superego are realistic and therefore do not come into conflict with the basic reality orientation of the ego. Where the developmental process is defective, usually because of defective functioning of parental figures, the superego tends to impose unrealistic demands on the ego, demands that are usually moralistic in tone and, if excessively rigid and severe, cause difficulty in the adjustment of the personality. When such demands assume the ascendancy in psychic functioning, the cost is paid in the form of guilt feelings, obsessions, compulsivity, depression, etc. The operation of grace supports and energizes the ego in its struggle to assert priority over the unrealistic demands of the superego. Because the defect in the ego is often severe, the struggle is difficult to win. The difficulty is compounded by the fact that many people with ego defects lead moral lives; in fact, they are ultramoral. But the norm of ego-control remains reality, and the realistic moral response does not traffic in excessive, severe demands. There is a radical opposition between the prescriptions of a realistic morality and the obsessive rigidity of the superego.

These considerations come to a specific focus in the understanding of religious values and value systems (see Section III of this study). The modifications of ego functioning, as one aspect of the psychological impact of grace, have specific implications both for the integration of ego and superego functioning and for the overall development and functioning of the self-organization.

Thus, the changes in psychic systems that we can hypothetically connect with the psychological action of grace have their determinable correlates and expression within the realm of values. Specifically at question are the organization and development of religious values which become the core cognitive and affective structures around which, in psychological terms, the human agent integrates his spiritual existence. Only within recent years has psychoanalysis begun to come to terms with the importance of value systems in numerous areas of significant psychological functioning and personality development, and has thus begun to provide the basis in theoretical understanding whereby the formation and functioning of such systems can be effectively conceptualized.

By implication, therefore, spiritual growth, or the development and deepening of the spiritual identity, ultimately can be translated into terms of the formation, maintenance, deepening and, in a strictly technical sense, internalization of such religious value systems in the personality organization and life experience of the human agent. These questions, which are central to the understanding of the psychology of grace, are taken up more in detail in the section on religious values (pp. 254–301). Let us return to our more immediate concern with the effects of the operation of grace within the psyche.

Grace as Object Relation

The developments in the theology of grace that I have traced in Chapter 2 enunciate a specifically relational theme in terms of an understanding of grace as the divine self-communication to man in a loving relationship, resulting in the divine presence and divine indwelling within the soul. When we search for a set of natural categories in terms of which the relational implications of this teaching can be understood, we turn naturally to psychoanalytic object relations theory. Object relations theory attempts to provide an account of the history and development of the human individual's capacity to be related to and to have relationships with significant human objects. It is thus a theory of the development of our capacity for such relationships and of the nature and quality of those relationships as they play themselves out in the course of our life experience. It should be noted here that the term "object," which the theory employs for technical reasons, does not refer merely to inanimate objects, but more specifically to other human beings. Object relations is, therefore, a theory of interpersonal relationships (Greenberg and Mitchell 1983).

From the point of view of the argument we are developing here regarding the psychology of grace, the resources of an object relations theory must be regarded as fairly limited. The capacity for object relationships is without question an integral part of man's natural capacity, but we are dealing here in the context of a theology of grace and a specific human capacity to be related to the divine object. Consequently, from a merely natural perspective our understanding of our capacity to relate to God as an object is limited by our understanding of our capacity to relate to other human beings as objects. But from a supernatural perspective, the capacity to enter into a divine relationship must be given as a special gift out of God's loving initiative. The capacity itself would have to be congruent with and in some sense integrated with the natural human capacity for object relationships. In this sense, the supernatural capacity given through grace could be understood as building on, enhancing, and elevating our natural capacity for object relationships. In this connection, I would argue that all of the principles I will develop regarding the influence of grace on man's natural capacity and functioning (see below) will also be applicable in the present context.

The question that poses itself for our present consideration builds on the issue of what can be said about the divine relationship proposed by the theology of grace in terms of its natural correlates. We must ask, then, what is the nature of this relationship with God, and to what extent can it be envisioned as an object relationship? The argument hinges on the question of whether or not such a thing as a God-representation can be conceived of, and if so, what is its nature and what role does it play in our psychological development?

The Development of the God-Representation   My objective is to sketch out a developmental typology or schema based on psychoanalytic parameters within which the full range of religious behavior and experience may be conceptualized. Before proposing the schema, it may be useful to specify some of the implications of such an approach. An appeal to a developmental framework makes the assumption that the phases of the process are in some sense related to the normal and general experience of children. Thus, the phases of the schema would have to be tested against aspects of development in children, particularly in religious ideation and experience. The phases follow an epigenetic sequence: successive phases of the process create, work through, and resolve certain developmental issues that provide the basis for maturational potentialities. The developmental achievements of each phase contribute to the potentiality for growth, maturation, differentiation, integration, and stabilization of elements of the adult personality. At the same time, the success of this process depends on the resolution of the conflicts arising in previous phases. Thus, when the process is considered as a whole, the developing personality is a composite of its successive developmental achievements and their more or less successful integration, on the one hand; and, on the other hand, specific residual deficits and archaic remnants reflecting earlier developmental difficulties and the persistence of unresolved elements from one or more developmental strata.

Certain aspects of the child's development seem particularly relevant for the shaping of his religious experience and ultimately for his experience of relationship to God. At the most rudimentary level, the child's early experiences of "mirroring" in relationship to the mother provide the basis for important elements in the structuring of his concept of God. In his experiences of the mother as a loving and caring presence, in nursing, and in the mother's participation in the act of mirroring by which the child finds himself narcissistically embraced, admired, recognized, and cherished, he discovers a symbiotic union with the mother that can serve as the basis for an evolving sense of trust, acceptance, and security.

The need for this kind of narcissistic mirroring is never entirely lost but rather evolves during the course of life. The rudiments of the mirroring phase of infantile experience may be distilled into the person's experience of his relationship to God. If the mirroring has been defective, he may enter further stages of life with a basic sense of being cut off or lost, or may defensively elaborate a sense of his own omnipotence, a feeling of being *like* God that substitutes for the lost sense of being *with* God (Rizzuto 1979).

To the extent that the child is able to pass beyond the mirroring phase to a stage of dependence on an idealized image of the mother, his notion of God can be gradually shaped around this idealizing experience and further elaborated with fantasy. These aspects of the child's emerging religious experience are both derivative of and intertwined with the child's ongoing experience of the real mother.

> At the moment of their encounter it becomes clear that the child is small and needs the adult and that the adult is powerful and "knows" the child internally. Now the fate of the child and the God representation alike depend on how the two characters—mother and child, God and child—are seen and the real and fantasied nature of their interaction. (Rizzuto 1979:188)

The parents' influence continues to play a role in the development of the child's religious thinking. There is little doubt that the family in general plays an important part in the development of religious experience. The close relationship between family and religious structure has been frequently noted (Vergote 1969). The family is ultimately the model for both religious relationships and values. The parents' religious attitudes, behavior, and even language are immediately transmitted to the child. In addition, the patterns of protection, well-being, and authority inherent in family structure find their natural extension and elaboration in religion.

The child's earliest images of God are cast almost exclusively in the image of the parents. However, it should be noted that additional representational components may derive from other significant objects in the immediate family (grandparents, siblings) or from extrafamilial social and cultural influences (priests, nuns, ministers, rabbis). The confusion between parental and divine images is at first almost total. From about the age of three or four years, the child has no difficulty in imagining a God. But the images of the divine are full of fantasy and fascination, not unlike the world of fairly tales. And from the beginning, the child's image of God is colored with ambivalence: while there may be feelings of trust and dependence on a kind, loving, and protecting God, there are also elements of awe and fear.

This ambivalence can reflect the child's ongoing experience with the mother. With considerable variability, the child experiences the mother more or less ambivalently. She is experienced on the one hand as good—as providing love, protection, and nurturing, the mother with whom the child feels a sense of security and trustful reliance. But there is also the bad mother, who withholds, punishes, and is not available to satisfy the child's infantile wishes and needs; she becomes an object of fear. In the child's infantile fantasy, the fear is often of destruction or being devoured. These fantasies are highly oral in character, whether positive (nurturing) or negative (being devoured). The history of religion provides numerous examples of this split in the image of the mother: benign, loving mother-goddesses opposed to threatening, devouring goddesses.

To the extent that the child's early experience with the mother has tipped the balance in the direction of more positive and gratifying experiences, a sense of trust is laid down that provides a foundation for the later development of a sense of trusting faith in the relationship with God. Where early infantile experience is discolored by insecurity, uncertainty, or anxiety, the foundation is laid for a mistrust that can contaminate and distort the later experience of God (see Chapter 4).

The succeeding phase of development (described by Freud in libidinal terms as the anal phase, particularly its latter, anal-sadistic portion) is a time for the conjunction of numerous important developmental parameters. Besides the familiar struggles over anal control and the related issues of autonomy and independence, there are problems of separation and individuation, as well as the dawning of Piaget's symbolic function and the emergence of emotional object constancy. Sometime during this phase the child discovers that objects in the world are made by people, giving rise to a rudimentary notion of anthropomorphic causality. Soon the endless questions begin about how things are made or where they came from. The answer that God made the world or the sky can be envisioned only in anthropomorphic terms—God is a person who is big enough and powerful enough to make very large things. But this line of inquiry soon leads to the notion of God as the uncaused cause, the cause that nobody has made, but that simply is. The child's mind is set abuzz with theories, imaginings, and fantastic ideas. God becomes a problem in that he looms as someone powerful and important, to whom adults pay great respect and reverence, but who cannot be seen, talked to, or touched. Yet he rules everything and everywhere. The child is left little recourse but to imagine this God in terms of the most formidable human beings he knows, his parents. At first he tends to use both father and mother for this purpose, but later, increasingly, the father more than the mother; this tendency is reinforced by the extent to which the father becomes the more powerful, aggressive, or punitive parental figure.

As the child begins to move beyond the age of oedipal concerns and involvements, he gradually becomes aware of the distinction between God and his parents. His view of his parents becomes more realistic, more aware of their limitations and incapacities as human beings. He begins to experience with some disappointment the erosion of his narcissistic ideals. He learns that his parents do not know everything and cannot do everything; their power to influence the world around them seems to him to be increasingly tenuous and limited. The child becomes more and more aware of the faults and contradictions of his parents, both father and mother. At this stage, he tries in some sense to salvage the narcissistic investment in an omnipotent ideal by resort to a heavenly Father, who promises to be all-powerful and perfect, as his earthly parents are not. This is also the period for emergence of the family romance, with its investment of idealized empowerment and perfectibility in the imagined parents of the romanticized mythical family. As with the idealized picture of God, the romanticized parents are imagined as embodying characteristics of strength and virtue that contrast dramatically with the looming imperfections of the real parents.

The object relations that provide the basis for the child's representation of God can shift their positions in regard to the relation to God in a variety of ways. There may be direct continuity between the parental image and the God image, so that they can be used more or less equivalently or as substitutes in the face of defensive pressures. Or they may be directly opposed, so that they become antagonistic, usually reflecting underlying processes of defensive splitting. God in this scenario may be utterly good and protecting, while the parents are regarded as mean, ungiving, or unloving. The opposite—idealized parents and devalued God—can also happen. Or the good and bad qualities of both God and parents may be seen in various combinations (Rizzuto 1979).

However important these growing realizations are in the child's mind, the transition to a heavenly Father is strongly influenced by the attitudes and behavior of his parents. Their own religious faith and conviction about God's existence, and their lived sense of personal relationship with a transcendent God play an important role in the child's evolving conceptions. To a child of four to five it is a significant revelation, for example, that his own father and mother had fathers and mothers of their own, just as he has. The dissolution of the myth of the absolute or omnipotent parent can be disillusioning or disconcerting to the child's mind.

With the dissociation of the image of the father from the image of God, the child's notion of God acquires more universal and pragmatic connotations. God is the maker of everything in the world, or he is in the protective power of good, fighting against the evil personified by the devil. To a child of this age, God is envisioned in terms of his relationship to the everyday world and in terms of specific and practical questions. The child asks what God looks like, whether he is a man, what he does, and where he lives. He wants to know if God can be called on the telephone, or whether he makes cars. Some children are at the same time very aware of God's presence and are even afraid that God watches them and sees whatever they do (Gesell 1947).

To the child of six, God is the creator of the world, of all the animals and the beautiful things in it. He is able to accept these ideas even though he soon becomes more skeptical. He likes to listen to Bible stories over and over. God has become more real, and the child begins to develop a relationship with him. Consequently, prayers become more important, particularly insofar as he feels a growing sense of confidence that God will listen to and answer them. At the same time, God's evil counterpart also takes shape in the child's mind in the form of the devil. In an earlier era, the notion of the devil loomed longer in the minds of Christian believers and thus became a much more vivid and dramatic focus for the child's nameless anxieties and phobic concerns.

The child's notion of God at this stage is essentially anthropomorphic. He sees God as a magnified human agent and envisions his actions in and on the world as forms of human action. But his notion of God's activity, and his representation of God are increasingly transformed. Early on, the anthropomorphism is direct and specific: God lives in a house, he eats, sleeps, and so on. During latency, children still tend to think of God in anthropomorphic terms, but even so, God is regarded as somehow different from other people in that he lives with the angels in heaven and cannot be seen or touched by ordinary humans. However, as the child approaches puberty, more spiritualized notions of God predominate. Certainly, by this time, children's notions of God seem to lose the fairytale, magical, and fantastical qualities common to oedipal-age children.

The anthropomorphic characteristics of the child's view of God are also expressed in his fantasy of how God acts in the world. As Piaget has described, children between the ages of six and eleven tend to explain nature and the world by an appeal to animism or to some human form of technology. When the child begins to question the perfection and omnipotence of his parents, some of the qualities formerly attributed to adults can be transposed to the divine being. The child first imagines God along the lines of a specifically human model and thinks of God in human terms. However, from time to time the dissociation between God and all others breaks this pattern, so that the child's view of God is increasingly cast in symbolic terms. This symbolic quality of the child's thinking reaches operative expression only in adolescence.

In general, the child's ambivalence toward the God-representation, expressed particularly in terms of reverence, awe, and fear, increases with age. God is viewed not simply as one who is benevolent and good; his almighty power is to be both revered and feared. The child progresses from a naive trust in God to a fuller understanding of his majesty, transcendence, and power, which are to be approached only with fear and reverence.

Piaget has emphasized the essentially egocentric quality of the young child's thinking. It is only with the emergence of object relationships, the establishment of object constancy, and the working through of oedipal involvements that reality increasingly impinges on the child's awareness and draws him away from this egocentricity to an involvement with objects. Only gradually does the child come to accept the existence of other people as centers as activity and influence. To the child, the concept of God remains for a considerable time more or less immersed in affective self-centeredness. The persistence of this infantile self-centeredness, together with its narcissistic components, can have profound effects on the development of his representation of God, and can give rise in adult life to severe religious conflicts or even to religious rebellion in the form of agnosticism or atheism. The religious truth of the child appears as mere infantilism to the eyes of the adult, so that the adult who has not been able to grow beyond this level of religious experience is left with little recourse but to renounce these infantile residues.

The same narcissistic trends that give rise to infantile egocentricity are also at the root of the forms of magic so often seen in infantile religiosity. Piaget has studied the child's sense of immanent justice. A child of six, for example, believes that a wrong deed will be punished automatically by some catastrophe. This belief in immanent justice is reinforced by his animistic belief in humanlike intentions behind events in the world. This animistic sense of intentionality is often directly translated into religious terms, particularly in children who have received enough religious education to have a sense of the immanence of God. They would attribute immanent justice to the will of God and relate this to their belief in God and his providence. The belief in immanent justice diminishes with age, so that by the time of puberty it is practically nonexistent, at least in children raised in Western cultures.

It is worth noting that belief in immanent justice nonetheless persists on an unconscious level in many religious believers. Under certain forms of stress or anxiety, there may be a revivification of intense unconscious guilt and a regression in superego functioning that will influence an individual's attitude toward God. This dynamic is recognizably pathological, although Freud tended to regard this form of pathology as typical of religious dynamics. In a child's mind, however, these attitudes merely represent a mixture of emerging religious beliefs with magical beliefs.

Similar manifestations of religious attitudes can be found in primitive religions, but in the child they remain open to gradual transformation and modification during the rest of the developmental sequence. Persistence of such beliefs can be found in animistic beliefs in divine protection or divine punitive intentions. They may also find expression in belief in the causal efficacy of prayers, particularly in the expectation that God will hear and answer the petitioner's prayers. Sacramental signs and rituals in particular provide an arena in which such magical expectations may play themselves out. A child often believes that the sacraments have some automatic, magical effect that is produced independently of the recipient's consciousness. The residues of such magical belief can be identified even in adolescence. This trend in religiosity can be reinforced by the natural obsessionality of latency-age children, particularly in obsessional practices—for example, repeating certain numbers, counting groups of objects, avoiding cracks in the pavement, and so forth. These are more or less secular forms of magical ritualistic behavior that are easily translated into a magical religious form of ritualism.

Adolescence is one of the most crucial periods in the development not only of personality but also of religious attitudes and experience. In this regard, Rizzuto (1979:201) has observed that

> . . . adolescence confronts the growing individual with a need to integrate a more cohesive and unified self-representation which will permit him to make major decisions about life, marriage, and profession. That developmental crisis, with its intense self-searching and reshuffling of self-images in the context of trying to find a niche in the world of oneself, brings about new encounters with both old and new God-representations. They may or may not lend themselves to belief.

At about the age of twelve or thirteen, there is a shift from thinking about God in more or less attributional terms to increasing personalization of the God image. God is specifically God the Savior, God the Father. The notion of God is increasingly interiorized, and God is regarded in primarily subjective attitudes of love, obedience, trust, doubt, fear. This development follows the natural course of affective adolescent development. The themes and corresponding God-representations that express the adolescent's experience of religion are heavily influenced by his affective needs. Frequently, this highly personalized and subjective God-representation is difficult for the adolescent to integrate with the more objective attributes proposed by organized religion.

The personalized adolescent image of God most often takes the form of a providential father who watches over and guides the adolescent along life's uncertain path. Often adolescents attribute to God the qualities they would seek in special and intimate friends—that is, emphasizing understanding and affective communication. Moreover, the increased measure of narcissism in adolescent development influences the ego-ideal and plays a part in the religious sphere as well. The adolescent idealizes his companions and friends as well as the adult figures whom he seeks to imitate and with whom he ultimately wishes to identify. The components of his inner, idealizing narcissism are thus transferred to the object in whom the adolescent seeks the perfection that he himself wishes to possess by identification.

This idealization affects the God-representation insofar as God is cast in the role of a pure and perfect being. Adolescent boys tend to emphasize these objectively idealized qualities of the God-representation more than girls, who tend to emphasize qualities of loving relationship in the God-representation. God becomes the ideal confidant, who understands everything and responds to the girl's most intimate wishes and needs. The frequent waning of religious experience toward the end of adolescence reflects the diminishing intensity of the narcissistic idealizing process with the adolescent's gradual assimilation of more mature and adult life patterns and commitments. Among Christian groups, the figure of Christ in particular becomes an important object for this form of narcissistic idealization and attachment. Where adolescent idealization is not tempered by a greater maturity of judgment and discretion, the figure of Christ can become a superhuman model and a repository for fanatical tendencies.

Adolescence is also a period of increased sexual conflict and guilt. The degree of superego repression and guilt can be reinforced by religious prescriptions and ideals. This inherent moralism then carries a sense of sinfulness, which can become such a burden and a narcissistic impediment that it results in a rebellion against religious standards and values. Frequently, adolescents find themselves caught between standards of moral laxity on one side and hyperrigid moralism on the other.

Along with these tendencies to moralism and internalization of religious experience, adolescence is also a time for intensifying religious doubt. Doubt is often an expression of the adolescent's need for autonomy in the face of the regressively reactivated pull to dependency on parental objects. For some adolescents the quest for independence can be pursued only through overthrowing and rejecting parental norms and standards. Religion in such cases may become the symbolic repository for parental authority and the corresponding conflicts of continuing dependence. The adolescent who needs to reject authority may find this need perverting his religious experience and his relation to God as well.

This doubt may be reinforced by adolescent affective turmoil, particularly by conflicts over sexuality. Plagued by sexual conflicts and feelings of guilt, the adolescent may be overwhelmed by shame and insecurity over his inability to live up to lofty religious standards of conduct. Consistent with the continuing influence of parental figures and family milieu, the adolescent's religious crisis often reflects conflicts and tensions between his parents or between them and their children. The result may be a form of rebellion and alienation that not only impedes the adolescent's growth to maturity but corrupts and subverts his further religious development as well.

The resolution of adolescent issues only leads the young believer to the threshold of a religious struggle that he must carry on for the rest of life. In this regard, Vergote (1969:300) writes:

> But after adolescence the young believer thinks more freely about the meaning of existence. He must make his mental synthesis of the world. He has come to be less centered on himself and is more deliberately committed to human society. This leads him to query the different theories of life with which he meets; he also reflects on the human necessity of having some religious belief and on the significance of institutionalized religion. This new questioning is more objective than earlier doubts had been, and is part of the effort which the adolescent makes to assume personally the religion he has inherited. Man does not acquire true religious faith, that is, a really personal faith recognized in its transcendent finality, before the age of thirty years. Experience has shown that after adolescence the whole religious formation apparently has to undergo revision—not because the child or the adolescent has not hitherto been authentically religious, but because man does not acquire sufficient maturity to make a real personal choice and to recognize reality before he has become adult.

In terms of the understanding of religious experience, the experience of the adult may reflect the more or less satisfactory integration of derivatives of all developmental phases. Primitive experiences from archaic developmental levels may be successfully transformed and integrated with later developmental achievements—and thus take on a different significance and a more differentiated symbolic reference. This transformation of function and significance allows us to identify both the original relevance of the archaic symbol and its more evolved, symbolically differentiated and enriched context without reducing their connection to an identity or resorting to the developmentally obtuse formula of repetition. The essence of development lies in the "overcoming" and differential superseding of origins, not in their simple repetition.

At the same time, an epigenetic schema recognizes that development does not take place in linear or blocklike progression. The individual's emerging religious experience may achieve developmental resolution in varying degrees, so that the result is a heterogeneity of relatively mature and relatively archaic elements, stemming from any of the developmental levels and phases. As Rizzuto (1979:201) comments:

For the rest of the life cycle the individual will again find himself in need of
critical changes in self-representation to adapt to the inexorable advance of
the life cycle as well as to new encounters with peers and parental representatives. God—as a representation—may or may not be called in to
undergo his share in the changes. Finally, when death arrives, the question
of the existence of God returns. At that point, the God-representation,
which may vary from a long-neglected preoedipal figure to a well-known
life companion—or to anything in between—will return to the dying person's memory, either to obtain grace of belief or to be thrown out for the
last time.

The Nature of the Relationship to God

Insofar as the nature and quality of the God-representation has its
roots in human experience and psychology, we can infer that the divine
relationship which meets and permeates man's capacity for relationship
must be cast in terms of this basic representation and its implications. At
this juncture in the development of the argument, I would want to press
a few steps further the analysis of the God-representation, and by implication the questions related to our capacity for relationship to God.
We would want to ask about the nature of the God-representation and
what we can discover about the psychological processes involved in its
organization and functioning. This inquiry leads us into the murky area
of transitional phenomena and the place of illusion in our religious experience. Freud saw illusions as the product of neurotic wish-fulfillments and drew the conclusion that religious beliefs were cast in opposition to reality, so that the adherence to religious beliefs through faith was
in fact a form of neurotic distortion of reality (Freud 1927).

Transitional Phenomena   Despite Freud's unremitting onslaught a-
gainst illusion in many areas of human experience, recent years have
brought a shift of attitude within psychoanalysis; the current perspective
not only finds a place for illusion but defines it as a powerful, necessary
force in human psychic development and in the continuing nourishment
and health of the human spirit. This change in perspective regarding illusion has largely resulted from the thinking of Donald Winnicott. Winnicott has proposed that illusion is an important aspect of man's capacity
to involve himself in the world of his experience, a capacity that ultimately finds expression in his creativity and ability to shape a human
and meaningful environment and to achieve what Piaget describes as accommodation and assimilation.

Winnicott's contribution to our understanding of illusion was his analysis of "transitional objects" and the development of other transitional phenomena derived from the use of such objects. In Winnicott's (1971) view, the child's use of transitional objects begins with his early use of his fist, fingers, or thumb to stimulate his mouth and oral mucosa, thus satisfying his oral instinctual needs. Within a few months, infants become fond of playing with some special object to which they become attached, even addicted.

The dynamics of this process are intimately connected with the pattern of the earliest mother-infant interaction. Mother and child are caught up in a form of undifferentiated unity created out of their dual participation. The participation of the "good-enough" mother in this union serves to preserve the infant's sense of continuity in his existence. The mother's empathic abilities to meet the baby's emerging need and to harmonize with his biological rhythms are crucial ingredients. If the infant's hunger becomes extreme, the sense of union with the mother may be disrupted. Good-enough mothering includes a capacity for holding that provides the infant with a sense of union and security that, in turn, lays the foundation for basic trust. Conversely, where the mother's holding fails to meet the infant's needs, the basis may be laid for distrust and a sense of deprivation or, in the extreme, for more chaotic, rageful discharge reactions that may approach the experience of fragmentation or panic.

In the face of these risks, which are part and parcel of any mother-child interaction, the child seeks to maintain the sense of security and quiescence that he associates with the mother's soothing ministrations. He seeks a substitute object that can fill in for the mother's lapses or failures in fulfilling his needs. In this sense, the infant's hand becomes a substitute for the mother's breast; gradually the infant's interest turns to some other object, often part of a sheet or blanket that joins his fingers in his mouth. The object chosen for this soothing varies considerably, but the important point is that it serves a vital function for the infant, usually when going to sleep. It provides a defense against the anxiety connected with the loss of the mothering figure. The adopted object acquires crucial importance and must be available at all times. Moreover, it cannot be altered in any significant way. If it gets dirty and smelly enough, the mother may feel compelled to wash it for hygienic purposes. But she then learns that this introduces a disruption in the continuity of the infant's experience of the object—a disruption, in fact, that may destroy the objects meaning and value to the infant.

Winnicott is thus staking a claim for an important aspect of human life that takes its place along with involvement in interpersonal relationships and the inner world of psychic functioning. He is defining an intermediate area that he calls "experiencing", to which both the inner psychic reality and external relationships contribute. He comments, "It is an area that is not challenged, because no claim is made on its behalf except that it shall exist as a resting-place for the individual engaged in the perpetual human task of keeping inner and outer reality separate yet interrelated" (1971:2). He asserts (1971:3) the importance of illusion in human psychological development and functioning:

> It is usual to refer to "reality-testing", and to make a clear distinction between apperception and perception. I am staking a claim for an intermediate state between a baby's inability and his growing ability to recognize and accept reality. I am therefore studying the substance of *illusion*, that which is allowed to the infant, and which in adult life is inherent in art and religion, and yet becomes the hallmark of madness when an adult puts too powerful a claim on the credulity of others, forcing them to acknowledge a sharing of illusion that is not their own. We can share a respect for *illusory experience*, and if we wish we may collect together and form a group on the basis of the similarity of our illusory experiences. This is a natural root of grouping among human beings.

The original fit of need and adaptation provides the stage for the child's illusion of magical omnipotence. The mother's task as the child matures is gradually to disillusion the infant. If the primary illusion has been reasonably well established, the way to successful disillusionment then lies open. The gradual disillusionment and the increase of the titer of frustration set the stage for the frustrations of weaning.

Essential to Winnicott's view is the notion that the dialectic and the tension between illusion and disillusionment continues through the whole of human experience and human life. The task of coming to know and accept reality is never finished. No human being is ever free from the tension of relating inner to outer reality. Relief from this unending tension is gained only in the intermediate area of illusory experience, which remains unchallenged even in the life of the adult, and provides the dominant mode of experience in the arts and religion. Winnicott (1971:14) comments:

> Should an adult make claims on us for our acceptance of the objectivity of his subjective phenomena we discern or diagnose madness. If, however, the adult can manage to enjoy the personal intermediate area without making claims, then we can acknowledge our own corresponding intermediate areas, and are pleased to find a degree of overlapping, that is to say common experience between members of a group in art or religion or philosophy.

Transition   The vicissitudes of transitional phenomena also lay the basis for the child's emerging capacity for symbolism. In a sense, the piece of blanket can be taken as symbolizing the mother's breast, but, as Winnicott suggests, its actual transitional function is as important as its symbolic value. He observes (1971:6), "Its not being the breast (or the mother), although real, is as important as the fact that it stands for the breast (or mother)." The use of transitional objects, then, is a step toward the symbolic function more than an actual use of symbolism. When the capacity for symbolism is achieved, the infant has already gained the capacity to distinguish between fantasy and fact, between internal and external objects, between primary creativity and perception, between illusion and reality.

However, the capacity to use transitional objects points in the direction of later symbolic capacities. In a loose sense, symbols can be regarded as an *unio oppositorum*, in the sense that some extrinsic object or form is used to express something from the subjective realm. Dream symbols, for example, would be one form of conjunction or intrinsic and extrinsic elements. Manifest objects, or even persons in the dream content, are transformed and come to express subjective affects, meanings, and significances. A symbolic dimension is added to the explicit content of the dream by allowing it to be a channel for the expression of a latent content (Grolnick 1978).

Similarly, real external objects and experiences can become vehicles for the expression of subjective intentions and significances and thus take on an added, symbolic dimension. The symbolic dimension of such experiences and objects takes part in the intermediate realm of illusion, which is compounded from objective elements intermingled with subjective attributions expressing the human capacity to create meaning. Thus, even though the dream takes place entirely within the intrapsychic realm, it can be regarded as a form of transitional experience.

The basic notion of transitional phenomena has been extended in a variety of directions and applied to various aspects of adult experience. Modell (1968) has developed the notion of a transitional object relationship. As is the case with the child's transitional object, the transitional human object stands midway between the inner and outer worlds. Modell comments (1968:35):

> The transitional object is not completely created by the individual, it is not a hallucination, it is an object "in" the environment. It is something other than the self, but the separateness from the self is only partially acknowledged, since the object is given life by the subject. It is a created environment—created in the sense that the properties attributed to the object reflect the inner life of the subject.

Winnicott's notions of the transitional object and transitional phenomena extend into the realm of cultural experience. Here Winnicott's approach to illusion separates itself from that of Freud. Freud's emphasis on the distortion or contradiction of reality in the service of wish-fulfillment is basic to his view of illusion. But what Freud sees as distortion and contradiction of reality, Winnicott sees as part of man's creative experience. What Freud sees as wish-fulfillment dominated by the pleasure principle and in opposition to the reality principle, Winnicott views as human creativity.

Rizzuto (1979:227–28) articulates the tension in these positions:

> In ordinary language, the language of everyday life where we all meet publicly, *illusory* and *real* are antithetical, mutually exclusive concepts. This is not so in the private realm of transitional reality where illusory and real dimensions of experience interpenetrate each other to such an extent that they cannot be teased apart without destroying what is essential in the experience. It is impossible to separate the mother created by the child from the mother he finds . . . . Reality, on the other hand, can take for the experiencing individual all the shapes that his psychic defenses need to attribute to it, to make it bearable . . . . The risk in understanding psychic life is to apply to it the separation of subject and object indispensable in science and philosophy. Freud has shown beyond doubt that man's needs and wishes color whatever he does and whatever he sees. Man is always playing with reality, either to create himself through illusory anticipation, to sustain himself by illusory reshaping of what does not seem bearable, or simply to fool himself through illusory distortion of what he does not like. If the illusion, the playing with available reality, goes beyond immediate need, pathology and delusions ensue. Illusory transmutation of reality, however, is the indispensable and unavoidable process all of us *must* go through if we are to grow normally and acquire psychic meaning and substance.

In Winnicott's view, illusion becomes a developmental form of transition to reality: without the capacity to utilize transitional objects and to generate transitional forms of experience, the child's attempts to gain a foothold in reality will inevitably be frustrated. Illusion in this view is not an obstruction to experiencing reality but a vehicle for gaining access to it. If Freud sought to rule out illusion and destroy it, Winnicott wishes to foster it and to increase man's capacity for creatively experiencing it. Illusion is an important part of human experience, in that it is not by bread alone that man lives. Man needs to create, shape, and transform his environment; to find meaningful channels for expressing his inner life, or rather the constant commerce between the ongoing world of his external experience and his inner psychic reality. Winnicott's standard of psychic health is not the separation of the real and the wishful, as Freud might have had it, but rather their creative and adaptive intermingling and exchange.

It is through illusion, then, that the human spirit is nourished. Freud would have us live in the harsh world of cold facts and realities, ruled by reason. Reason has its place for Winnicott, of course—and its place is not a small one. But the life of the imagination, the life of creative expression, whether wishful or not, is for him a vital part of human experience. To be without imagination, without the capacity for play or for creative illusion, is to be condemned to a sterile world of harsh realities without color or variety, without the continued enrichment of our creative capacities.

Transitional Phenomena in Religion   The thesis we are pursuing here is that religion partakes of the character of transitional phenomena or the transitional process, and as such achieves its psychological reality and its psychic vitality in the potential space of illusory experience. While it shares this participation in the illusory with other aspects of human culture, it is unique among them because of the extent to which it impinges on what is most immediate and personal in man's psychic life, namely, man's sense of himself—his meaning, purpose, and destiny.

An essential aspect of the faith experience is the individual's representation of the figure of God. The idea of the representation of God as a transitional object has been presented elsewhere (Meissner 1977, 1978b), but perhaps the single most important contribution to its understanding has come through the recent work of Rizzuto (1979), who offers extensive documentation of her conclusions, based on the study of a series of patients and on the analysis of in-depth data of a number of them. She concludes that God is a special kind of object representation that the child creates in the intermediate psychic space where transitional objects achieve their powerful and illusory existence. Like other transitional phenomena, the experience of God or the God-representation is neither a hallucination nor is it beyond the reach of subjectivity; rather, it is located, in Winnicott's terms, "outside, inside, at the border" (Winnicott 1971:2). Unlike the teddy bear or the blanket, God is created out of representational derivatives from the child's experience, particularly of primary objects.

As a transitional object, God is also of a special order in that he does not follow the usual course of such objects—that is, he is not gradually decathected, ultimately to be forgotten or relegated to psychic limbo. Rather, the God-representation is cathected with increasing intensity during the pregenital years, reaching a peak during the high point of oedipal excitement. The representation that survives the oedipal crisis depends on the manner of the child's oedipal resolution and the resulting psychic compromises. Rather than losing force, the meaning of the God-representation is intensified by the oedipal experience. Even when the outcome is loss of meaning or rejection, God as a transitional object remains available for further processing, for further acceptance or rejection. Even in a state of relative abandonment or repression, the God-representation maintains the potentiality for revivification and further integration. As Rizzuto (1979:179) puts it, "Often, when the human objects of real life acquire profound psychic meaning, God, like a forlorn teddy bear, is left in a corner of the attic, to all appearances forgotten. A death, a great pain or intense joy may bring him back for an occasional hug or for further mistreatment and rejection, and then he is forgotten again."

The psychic process of creating and finding God continues through the course of the human life cycle. Thus, the characteristics of the God-representation are shaped following the epigenetic and developmental laws that we have attempted to describe. By the same token, the God-representation is the object of other psychic processes having to do with defense, adaptation, and synthesis, as well as with the need for meaningful relationship.

While God shares the transitional space with other cultural representations, the God-representation has a special place in that it is uniquely connected to our sense of ourselves, of the meaning and purpose of our existence and ultimate destiny. Once this transitional object representation is created, whether it is dormant or active, it remains available for continuing psychic integration. The God-representation participates in the ongoing process of exchange that develops in relation to the individual's evolving self-representation. This process is an authentic dialectic insofar as the God-representation transcends the subjective realm. As Rizzuto (1979:180) notes, "The transitional object representation of God can be used for religious purposes precisely insofar as he is beyond magic." And as Winnicott (1971:10) says, "The transitional object is never under magical control like the internal object, nor is it outside control as the real mother is."

The capacity for object relationships expresses itself in the capacity for object love. An exploration into the psychological components of the capacity for loving other human beings may serve us to understand better the elements of the loving relationship involved in the giving and receiving of grace.

The Capacity for Object Love   Two developmental achievements form the necessary building blocks for the capacity to love others. The first is the integration of early capacities for erotic stimulation, particularly oral and tactile stimulation, with later capacities for loving another as a human person in his or her own right. The second is the union of such body surface stimulation with full genital satisfaction in relationship to a specific love object, including the capacity to accept and integrate complementary sex roles and gender identity. The first task is normally accomplished during the preoedipal years and is related to the gradual emergence of an integrated sense of self and identity as a separate, independent entity. Various forms of narcissistic and more primitive character organizations demonstrate the failure of this process. The second task normally is accomplished through the successful resolution of the oedipal situation and its inherent conflicts, including the unconscious prohibitions against sexual activity. Failure in accomplishing this developmental task usually results in a variety of neurotic syndromes and sexual inhibitions.

Kernberg (1976) has provided a schematic analysis of levels of developmental achievement which affect the capacity for loving relationships. This developmental continuum can be described in five configurations.

(1) The first configuration represents a total lack of capacity for establishing meaningful genital and loving relationships with another human being; this incapacity is characteristic of the more severely narcissistic and borderline personalities.

(2) The second configuration expresses itself in sexual promiscuity, usually heterosexual but always polymorphously perverse, and is found in less severely disturbed narcissistic personalities.

(3) The third configuration expresses itself in primitive idealizations of the love object, often with a clinging infantile dependence; usually the capacity for genital gratification is preserved. This configuration is typical of certain types of borderline personality.

(4) The fourth configuration includes the capacity for establishing stable and meaningful object relations, but without the capacity for full sexual gratification; it is usually found in the less severe forms of character pathology and the neuroses.

(5) The fifth configuration represents the normal integration of genitality with the capacity for tender, loving, and meaningful object relationships.

A detailed discussion of these configurations follows.

Configuration 1. Many patients with severely disturbed narcissistic personalities have never been in love. This basic inability may often be masked by a behavioral promiscuousness, but despite their capacity to engage in fleeting sexual encounters, they lack the capacity to really fall in love with another human being. Kernberg (1976) notes that narcissistic personalities lacking this capacity may show a type of sexual promiscuity quite different from patients with less severe forms of narcissistic pathology. Promiscuity on a neurotic level—for example, in women having hysterical personalities with masochistic features—usually is motivated by unconscious guilt over gratifying love relationships with a man. Such neurotic conflicts would represent on an unconscious level the forbidden oedipal incestuous connection with the father. At the same time, such hysterical and masochistic patients enjoy a capacity for stable, meaningful object relationships in other areas of their life beyond the sexual. For them, meaningful, productive relationships with men are possible as long as no sexual element is involved. Any movement toward sexual intimacy simply stirs unconscious resentments over submission to the male phallus and unconscious guilt regarding forbidden sexual desires.

In contrast, the promiscuity of narcissistic personalities is connected with the sexual excitement in which the desired and attractive body of the mother stirs unconscious envy, the wish to possess, and an unconscious need to devalue and despoil that which is envied. The sexual fulfillment satisfies the need for conquest and leads to the inexorable devaluing of the loved object, so that both sexual stimulation and interest in the other rapidly subsides. The result of such involvements is that narcisstic personalities often spend their lives devoid of any meaningful loving relationships and become isolated, lonely and empty human beings.

Configuration 2. In somewhat less severely disturbed narcissistic disorders, these patients, who are often the victims of a driven narcissistic promiscuity, also reveal an underlying desperate search for human relatedness and love. But their search is magically connected with parts of the body (breasts, penises, buttocks, vaginas) without any capacity to advance to a level of being able to establish a loving relationship to another human being as a separate and whole person.

Often in such narcissistic males, there is a considerable degree of envy and hatred of women, clinically matching the intensity of penis envy in women. These elements are accompanied by a pathological need to devalue women, ultimately a devaluation of the mother as the primary object of infantile dependency. There is consequently a denial of any dependency on or any need for women. In the face of such neurotic and narcissistic needs, any capacity for deep personal relationships or meaningful sexual involvement with women is out of the question. This configuration may turn to a homosexual form of expression, often linked to a frantic search for sexual gratification and expressing itself in multiple promiscuous relationships. For other patients, fleeting infatuations may in fact reflect initial efforts in the direction of establishing a love relationship, but often it is limited by an idealization of the physical and sexual attributes of the object to be conquered. However, such narcissistic men are unable to accomplish a more normal form of idealization in which the individual woman, her personality and character, is idealized along with her female genitality, so that in conjunction with the valuing of her sexual capacity there is an increasing tenderness and concern for her as a separate human being.

Configuration 3. The intense love attachments of this configuration are accompanied by forms of primitive idealization, although these involvements tend to be somewhat more lasting than the transitory infatuations of narcissistic patients. This form of pathological falling in love is found most frequently in women having infantile personalities with borderline structure, who tend to cling desperately to an idealized object so that it is practically impossible to maintain any realistic perception of the man. In such patients there is also a predominance of splitting mechanisms in which the primitive idealization makes the object into an all-good object in order to defend against the projection of aggressive all-bad components. This process is more primitive than idealizations in which the capacity to integrate the good-and-bad aspects of ambivalent object relationships—that is, the good and bad aspects of objects— provides the basis for the development of a capacity for guilt, concern, depression, and the need for reparation. Paradoxically, Kernberg regards this form of love relationship as representing a higher point on the developmental continuum than the more severely narcissistic incapacity to love, even though such personality structures seem to be operating generally at a more primitive and disturbed level. When more severely disturbed narcissistic personalities can be brought to a higher level of idealization in which the capacities for guilt, depression, concern, and reparation can be generated, an important developmental step has been accomplished.

Configuration 4. This next level combines an increased capacity for romantic idealization along with underlying unconscious sexual conflicts and genital inhibition. For such cases, usually neurotic in character, the overcoming and resolution of infantile sexual conflicts are necessary before the individual can enter into any more total or meaningful relationship to a love object. This means the overcoming of oedipal conflicts, usually for men the overcoming of castration anxiety, and for women, penis envy.

In terms of the narcissistic dynamics, this level of idealization represents a distinct advance over previous forms of more primitive idealization. Here the idealization pertains not only to the physical, bodily attributes of the person, or even the person himself, but more significantly to the values which are inherent in this individual's personality structure. Kernberg (1976:210) comments:

> Intellectual, esthetic, cultural, and ethical values are included here; and I think this represents, in part, integration of the superego on a higher level,

one linked to the new capacity for integrating tender and sexual feelings and to the definite overcoming of the oedipal conflict. At the same time, in this establishment of identifications with the loved object involving value systems, a movement from the interrelation of the couple to a relationship with their culture and background is achieved, and past, present, and future are thereby linked in a new way.

We can also note that the capacity for successful sexual intercourse and orgasm is not by any means synonymous with the capacity for mature love relationships. Moreover, even though sexual passion is usually expressed in orgastic sexual intimacy, it is not limited to this focus. Rather it expresses itself in other forms of sensuality, longing for the object, with a deepened sense of appreciation of the attributes of the object, extending even to the human values of the object. Such passion in human beings is more than merely excitement in its more explicit and narrowly focused sexual implications. In its best sense, it implies a subtle yet deep, even self-critical sense of loving another person, as well as a sense of toleration and appreciation for the mystery which separates one person from another and which, in the face of longing, limits and frustrates the wish to possess and unite.

Psychoanalysts have generally come to appreciate that the older instinctual theory, which linked maturity with genitality, cannot be unequivocally maintained. In fact, genital primacy does not guarantee sexual maturity, nor does it necessarily represent a higher level of psychosexual development (Lichtenstein 1970). Kernberg (1977:98) relates the extension of sexual passion to a crossing of the boundary of the self. He writes:

> Sexual passion integrates this simultaneous crossing of the boundary of the self into awareness of biological functioning beyond the control of the self and the crossing of boundaries in a sophisticated identification with the loved object while yet maintaining the sense of separate identity.

Thus the experience of shared orgasm implies an empathic openness to the sexual partner, a certain transcendence of the experience of the self, an abandonment of oedipal attachments, and an engagement in a new object relationship that reconfirms one's own separate identity and autonomy. The time-limited boundaries of the self are transcended so that the past context of infantile object relations is transformed into a new and personally recreated involvement.

Configuration 5. We can ask what is involved in the capacity for mature love relationships. Balint (1948) had suggested that over and above genital satisfaction, such a capacity required a form of mature idealization, a capacity for tenderness and concern, and a particular form of identification. This identification implied that the desires, wishes, feelings, sensitivities, attitudes, interests, limitations, and strengths of the sexual partner should be given the same degree of importance as one's own. The resolution of oedipal conflicts and the more complete integration of genitality into the love relationship allows for a deepening of the sense of mutual identification and empathy. In this sense, full sexual identity implies the clarification and establishment of reciprocal sexual roles and leads the way to a full awareness of implicit social and cultural values. Normal sexual identity does not depend on successful identity formation, but rather is an important contributing and consolidating element of identity formation.

The emergence of these processes allows the experience of falling in love to be transferred into a state of being in love. The integration of genitality provides for full sexual gratification, which implies the requisite integration of pregenital sexuality with genital trends. The idealization at this level reaches beyond the more conflictual implications of guilt, concern, and reparation toward an idealization in terms of the sublimation of oedipal attachments into the new love relationship and an integration of value systems corresponding to the ideal of the object.

Kernberg (1976) emphasizes the different forms of idealization that play themselves out in both normal and pathological patterns. He suggests three levels of idealization. (1) The first is a primitive level, dominated by splitting mechanisms in which the love object is made into an all-good, all-perfect object, while the negative bad side of the ambivalence is attributed either to other objects in the environment or to the individual's own self. Such primitive idealizations reflect a form of falling in love that cannot be sustained; it usually leads to destructive forms of disruption and acting-out, and thus fails in any attempt at transition toward being in love with the object. (2) Then there is a form of idealization, related to the capacity for mourning and concern, in which empathy for the object is generally more realistic but still lacks meaningful genital features. Such states of falling in love are common in neurotic patients and allow for the establishing of a more stable love relationship. Nonetheless, these relationships are usually conflict-ridden and less than satisfying. (3) Finally, there is normal idealization, usually achieved developmentally toward the end of adolescence or in young adulthood, which reflects the attainment of a stable sexual identity and a realistic perception and appreciation of the love object.

Kernberg (1977) has cast additional light on the complexities of love relationships by advancing the notion of the crossing of boundaries of the self in such relationships. Such an involvement with the love object should be contrasted with more regressive merger phenomena in which the distinction between the self and the object becomes blurred, and the object and subject become psychically amalgamated in some fashion, whether by incorporation (obliteration of the object) or by projective identification (obliteration of the subject). Such states are obviously quite primitive and pathological.

The crossing of boundaries in more mature love relationships, however, involves the persistent experience of the self as separate, individual, and discrete. Such a consolidation of the experience of the self and its correlative identity allows for the possibility of meaningful identification with the loved object. This crossing of the boundaries of the self in terms of object love and the potentiality for meaningful identification provides a basis for the experience of transcendence of the self. Consequently, psychotic identifications in which the boundaries between self and object are weakened or obliterated represent a diametrically opposite phenomenon. At this crossing point, the loved object is no longer merely a neurotic object but becomes a beloved person. As Kernberg notes, this point of transition is always fraught with pain and frustration because the other is present only in a limited sense as available for physical communication and contact; the inner life of the other remains elusive, unavailable, and impenetrable. Object love carries within it the revelation of the other as other—as unique, separate, and individual, and as preserving the inherent autonomy and personal freedom of the object.

The notion of boundaries and the crossings of boundaries has important ramifications for large areas of our understanding of human experience. Crossing of boundaries involves a persistent experience of a discrete self containing its own inherent integrity and cohesiveness, yet allowing a further progression in the direction of an identification with structures beyond the self. However, the capacity of the human personality for identification with structures beyond the limits of the self has profound implications for our ultimate understanding of the nature of human relatedness.

These implications, it seems to me, extend not simply to the acme of human love relationships, but also shed significant light on other poorly understood phenomena, such as certain forms of mystical ecstatic experience and profound religious phenomena. In these contexts we may not be dealing with regressive merger phenomena in any sense, but rather with a capacity to transcend the usual limits of object relationship in the direction of a consummate union with a loved object. Even if such phenomena involve elements of regressive narcissistic symbiotic wishes, they are subsumed in a process of quite a different order, which bases itself not only on the maturity and integrity of psychic structure and the capacity for relationship, but leads even further to the transcendence of the boundaries imposed in the ordinary context of such relationships.

Grace as Relational

Any attempt to understand the psychology of grace in terms of its relational dimension must build on the complex understanding of object relationships. From the foregoing discussion, it is clear that the development of the capacity for object relatedness is a lifelong process that begins immediately after birth and continues on through the life cycle. The question we must confront is how grace, envisioned in terms of divine self-communication, loving relationship, presence and indwelling, intersects with the structure of object relationships as we are able to define them in psychological terms.

The focal point for such a consideration is the God-representation. The individual's relationship to God will be cast in the form set by the God-representation, to whatever extent that representation functions at a conscious and/or unconscious level. Moreover, the God-representation, as we have already discussed, reflects the vicissitudes of the child's emerging capacity for object relationships through the course of his development (see the section dealing with this development, pp. 28–38). It can be fairly stated that the God-representation itself reflects a variety of the influences of that development and has its own unique history for each human individual. It is perfectly consistent with our understanding of grace and its operation that the very process by which this representation is formed and sustained is itself subject to the effects of grace. It is in terms of the form of the God-representation that the individual shapes the pattern of his attitudes toward, feelings about, and the quality of his relationship to God.

In addition, the God-representation shares in the peculiar qualities of a transitional object relationship. As such, the relationship to God has its own distinctive characteristics that mark it off from other such transitional involvements. In this relationship, God is not experienced as a distinct and separate object, although it can be argued that the effects of the relationship through grace can be experienced as they operate in the human psyche. In terms of the transitional structure of this relationship, the subjective component is contributed through the inherent creativity of the free human response to the initiative of grace. But the objective component cannot be itself experientially identified, and rests upon the vitality and actuality of divine initiatives which can be known only through faith.

Clearly, the response to the initiative of divine love is the formation of a sense of loving relatedness to God. What, then, does it mean in psychological terms to love God—an object transcending the capacities of human experience? Here I would argue that the terms of the love of God are related to and derive from the capacities for loving attachment that are organized and expressed through the God-representation. As with any form of love of an object, the representation provides a medium for the intentionality of the loving act. Thus it is not the God-representation which is loved; rather it is through the quality of the God-representation that the image of the God who is loved comes to express itself. Man cannot love an abstraction, but must translate this into psychologically meaningful terms relevant to his own human experience. God is not loved in His essence, but through a medium that translates that love into terms of human experience. The image of God must be anthropomorphized in some fashion in order for the experience of the love of God to become humanly possible. In the Christian dispensation, that image is provided in part in the person of Jesus Christ.

The question of the experience of the presence or indwelling of the divine Trinity is a much controverted subject about which little can be said from the perspective of psychology. Some mystical accounts are very suggestive, but unfortunately there is nothing in the phenomenology of these experiences that could not be mimicked, one way or another, by purely psychological forces and mechanisms of a suggestive, illusory, or even delusional character. This does not mean that accounts of lofty mystical experiences or ecstatic union can simply be discounted. Rather they must be treated with respect and as sources of important data about the more advanced, elevated reaches of man's capacity for spiritual existence and experience. At the same time, they cannot serve as unequivocal sources of evidence to demonstrate the effects of grace and divine presence.

Nonetheless, where the phenomenological and experiential aspects of the effects of grace fail us in offering a firm basis for any cogent argument, the theology of grace offers an alternative platform. The loving initiative of God's self-communication through grace is both an invitation and an inner urging of the soul toward union with God. From one point of view, the gist of the argument I have been developing here would suggest that to the extent the individual psyche had developed meaningful capacities for mature love relationships, receptivity to the effects of grace would be correspondingly enhanced. In this sense, grace enlarges on and elaborates the mature capacity of the soul for loving relationship. It amplifies to the highest sublimated level the capacity for idealization and the desire for consummated union with the ultimate loved object (a desire that in human terms and for human objects is always permeated with limitation and frustration). In addition to this enhancing of loving absorption, grace also raises the sense of spiritual identity and autonomy to a new level.

Toward Spiritual Identity

Under the influence of grace, the human soul undergoes a process of development which corresponds to the psyche's long and continual process of development on the natural psychological level. If that process is successfully accomplished, the mature personality evolves a sense of self-cohesiveness and a personal identity of its own. Achieving a conscious sense of identity, one becomes aware of the continuity of his personality as a satisfactory integration of the structural subsystems composing his body and mind. He experiences solidarity with a set of realistic values embedded in a certain social and cultural matrix. I shall have more to say about the course of this development later on, but here it must be said that the ultimate source of this integration and unity within the personality must be the self-conscious ego itself. The ego is the executor of its own development, a development achieved through the exercise of its functions of execution and synthesis. The maturely functioning personality, with a secure sense of identity and self-integration, responds to his life situation in a realistic manner. His response to the stimulus factors, particularly emotional stimuli, that impinge upon him is appropriate and proportioned to the intensity and quality of the real stimulus.

The person with a mature identity and a fully formed sense of self, being adequately adjusted to the whole complex of reality, recognizes and accepts realistic norms of behavior according to which he acts. The complex of these norms makes up a value system that is an essential component of the mature personality. The fully formed identity possesses a realistic and comprehensive value system, which functions as an effective determinant of the activity of the ego. The realistic value system of the Christian (as I have already suggested) is constituted in part by values inherent in the objective, ontological structure of reality and in part by values derived from and based on revealed truth.

The concepts of psychological identity and self-organization, reflecting the level of functioning proper to the mature personality, can be extended and adapted to the spiritual level. The ego develops under the influence of grace to a certain level of maturity and appropriate spiritual functioning. The psychological correlate of such spiritual growth is the development of a spiritual identity. Just as psychological identity implies a sense of awareness of the continuity of self and of solidarity with

naturally accepted values, so spiritual identity implies a sense of awareness of one's spiritual existence as a son or daughter of God and a sense
of solidarity and oneness with a set of supernatural, divinely revealed
values. The emergence of spiritual identity bespeaks a continually
deepening awareness of the realm of spiritual realities, the presence of
God, the promptings of grace, etc. The development of spiritual identity
is the central notion of a psychology of grace, the psychological correlate
of the life of grace within the soul.

Awareness of divine "presence" is closely linked to the elevating effects of grace and to the giving of the uncreated gift of the Holy Spirit.
Even though, for purposes of analysis, we must separate and distinguish
levels of influence and effect, we are still dealing with an integral reality.
Consequently, the demands of a more synthetic view must be kept in
mind. Spiritual identity is only one aspect of the complex reality of the
life of grace. The problems of the relations of "presence" and the action
of grace are more strictly theological concerns, but they are not without
relevance to a more complete consideration of the psychology of
grace.

Under the influence of grace, therefore, the resources of the ego are
extended and activated, and the sense of self enriched and sanctified.
The understanding is clarified and deepened, the organization and
direction of energies are made more effective and secure, the establishment of ego-control is stabilized and extended, and the whole range of
ego-functions is made more effective. The effects of grace, however, are
subject to the laws of ego-functioning. From the perspective of the energic hypothesis, I have suggested that the action of grace is directed to
the formation through ego-activity of a spiritual identity, and that
spiritual identity can be regarded as an enlargement, development, or elevation of personal identity.

At the same time, the action of grace takes place within a context in
which the divine self-communication is both loving and eliciting love,
and providing a matrix of loving acceptance and intimate union. Spiritual identity is that level of inner organization and structure of personality which we attain when we are functioning on a spiritual level;
that means acting in accord with the demands and commitments as well
as the spiritual values inherent in that order of existence and derived
from it. Through grace, that spiritual identity is defined in relation to
another, in a relationship of loving attachment, devotion, and reciprocal
self-communication.

The ego is the engineer of its own growth in spiritual identity. This
does not imply that the ego is capable of spiritual growth without the
help of grace, since it is specifically and exclusively the energizing force
of grace that makes possible this development at the psychological level.

The growth of spiritual identity is a dynamic and continual process involving certain identifiable ego-functions. The process is one of progressive and deepening awareness of the moral and theological structure of the order of spiritual existence and an assimilation of the inherent values proper to the spiritual order. The primary orientation in which the spiritual reality is comprehended and appraised is effected by the ego's cognitive functions. By its functions of perception and comprehension, the ego is brought into initial contact with reality and to a recognition of the value structure of that reality. The comprehended values must be realized, accepted, internalized, made a part of the ego's own evolving value system, accepted as functional norms for the direction and organization of the ego's vital activity and existence. Recognition and comprehension are therefore followed by internalization as part of a sequence of ego activity.

An important part of the process of internalization of values is the mechanism of identification. The ego fashions a sort of ego-ideal for itself, which becomes the guiding norm for the subsequent organization and direction of its activities. The child's most significant identifications are normally those formed with parental figures. But the process of identification is prolonged at less intense levels through the rest of life; it is a major mechanism of adjustment. Throughout the course of psychological development, fragmentary identifications with admired or loved persons are internalized by the ego, assimilated to the emerging self-ideal, and built into the fabric of a developing self-structure. In the Christian experience and in the growth of spiritual identity, the most significant identification is with the person of Christ. Here again, however, identification is chiefly a matter of the internalization of the value system embodied in Christ's words and actions and a realized acceptance of that value system as the norm of personal activity.

But the mechanism of internalization or identification does not exhaust the complexity of the process of spiritual growth. Even the emerging psychological identity is never merely an additive product of the fragmentary identifications. It is something wholly new and unique. There is an active engagement of the ego in the process of identity formation, in which the ego is continually caught up in the process of synthesizing each new fragment of internalization into an integrated personality.

In the formation of a spiritual identity, internalized spiritual values are integrated into a constantly evolving synthesis. The process is dynamic and continuous, since the realm of spiritual reality, unlike the realm of physical reality, is capable of endless penetration and ever more profound comprehension and realization. The process of spiritual growth, then, is a continually renewed activation of the ego's capacities to penetrate more deeply into supernatural truths, to refine and deepen the understanding of the values inherent in those truths, and to internalize and synthesize these elements into an integrally functioning ego-structure. At all levels of the process, each step taken is a dynamic preparation for succeeding steps. Each new realization is an orientation and preparation for subsequent realizations. Each new synthesis develops the structure and capacity of the ego to a level at which it becomes capable of the subsequent synthetic effort. Each new synthesis incorporates, intensifies, reinforces, and prolongs the whole series of preceding syntheses, but at the same time brings to them a new perception and penetration.

Grace, of course, would be the energizing, dynamizing principle that makes this spiritual growth possible. It also provides the meaningful context of object relatedness that makes the process human—since the intentionality of the ego and its growth is always relational. Even if its affects on the merely psychological level can be regarded as a mobilization of the latent resources of the ego, and even if the psychological correlates of spiritual growth can be spelled out in terms of specific ego-functions, grace itself remains a much more profound reality, exerting effects far beyond any psychological manifestation. Grace is by its nature a gratuitous gift of divine love; consequently, the gift must be freely received and accepted. Moreover, grace works through nature and, therefore, through human freedom. God does not force grace on us, even when it is efficacious. The exercise of human freedom is an essential part of human cooperation with grace. The internalization and synthesis of values represent an engagement, a commitment on the part of the ego, in which the ego is in effect shaping and determining its internal structure, determining the course of its own existence. At each new synthetic progression, the ego achieves a new level of internal development, a new stage of self-formation and self-realization. It has actualized a further segment of its own potentiality; it has made a progression from indetermination to self-determination, from unfulfillment to self-fulfillment, from nonbeing to being, from imperfection to an emerging perfection. The person achieves a veritable *position du soi par soi*. This ongoing self-determination represents an exercise of radical human freedom. At each progressive synthesis, the ego is confronted with a choice: either to project itself into a new commitment to the internalized values of the new level of synthesis or to withhold itself from that basic engagement. Insofar as ego-synthesis seems to imply such a self-commitment, the process of synthesis seems to depend on and imply such an exercise of freedom. It can be seen from this point of view, which is psychological rather than ontological, that human spiritual development and cooperation with grace are achieved through the exercise of human freedom.

Consequently, there can be no opposition between the operation of grace and the exercise of freedom. The progressive synthesis of a spiritual identity involves an increasing orientation to spiritual values. Implied in this development, then, is an ever increasing responsiveness to the influence of grace, a responsiveness that is not possible without a corresponding increase in the ego's capacity for autonomous self-determination. Each new level of synthesis brings with it a broadening of the ego's proper function of autonomous self-determination, i.e., an increase in its radical freedom. Real and authentic freedom is the measure of the ego's success in establishing its proper control over the non-ego psychic structures and in achieving its own proper autonomy. Each new synthesis represents a development of the ego, and ipso facto implies a new and higher capacity for the exercise of freedom as well as an intensified capacity for response to the continued influence of grace.

Consequently, as the ego progresses along the path of spiritual development, its response to grace becomes ever more spontaneous and complete. Increasing ego-autonomy implies a parallel increase in the effective control of libidinal energies and a gradual overcoming of libidinal resistances. The mobilization of ego-energies and ego-resources becomes progressively more facile and complete. The ego grows apace in self-realization, self-determination, spontaneity, and responsiveness to grace. Spiritual growth implies a growth in the glorious freedom of the children of God, which was taught by St. Paul and expanded in the teaching of St. Augustine.

Attention can be called here to the Ignatian understanding of the "times" of election. In the first time, God so moves and attracts the will that, without doubting, the one making the election follows a course of action. In the second time, the soul is led by the experience of consolation and desolation, and through the discernment of spirits is led to follow a given course of action. In this third time, by a laborious process of purification, the soul achieves indifference and then by step-by-step reasoning and reflection, determines on the course of action that seems to represent God's will. These times seem to represent different levels in the spontaneity of the ego in responding to the impulse of grace—the first time representing a more advanced stage, the second less, and the third least. In the first time, the ego is capable of mobilizing its resources and committing itself to God's will with an evident spontaneity that contrasts with the labored and prolonged effort required to achieve a corresponding effect in the third time. (See Rickaby (1923) and Meissner (1963–1964).)

Thus far, I have been concerned merely with the mechanisms of psychological development under the influence of grace. It is possible, however, to attempt some understanding of the process of growth itself. To begin with, we have to deal with the articulation in functioning between two levels of development, the psychological and the spiritual. The basic principle guiding this formulation is, as stated in the beginning, the psychological operation of grace. Grace is the energizing and relational principle on the spiritual level for the proper functions of the ego. Development of a spiritual identity, then, is achieved through the same ego-functions that are involved in the natural psychological identity. The relation between these two levels is based on the operation of common functions: in terms of psychological identity, these functions operate on their own, but in terms of spiritual identity, there is an added component supplied through grace.

Consequently, it is possible to lay down a principle of interaction: the *principle of reciprocal influence*. The principle is that where the operation of given function or combination of functions is impeded by a defect in natural development of the personality, the energizing influence of grace upon that function enables the ego to exercise that function in a more effective fashion than it could otherwise have done. On the other hand, the principle would also say that where there is a developmental defect in a particular ego-function, the capacity of the function to utilize available ego-energy is impeded and that therefore its capacity to utilize ego-energy made available through the influence of grace is decreased. Thus, the effectiveness of grace is always conditioned by the current capacity of the ego to function autonomously. At the same time, it is obvious that the giving of grace is not limited by the status of the ego: an extraordinary grace can bring about extraordinary effects, even in a relatively weak ego. But this would be an exception to the rule. Normally, there is a proportion between the effects of grace and the capacity of the ego to respond to it. The implications of the principle of reciprocal influence will be seen in greater detail further on.

There is an immediate implication which stems directly from these considerations and conclusions. The action of grace not only operates through the proper functions of the ego, but it depends to some extent on the functioning of that ego in order to produce its effects. Further, the specific character of its effects (from a psychological perspective) reflects the unique characteristics of each individual ego. But the force of these conclusions represents merely a psychological explication of a solidly established theological principle, namely, that the action of grace perfects nature. The perfecting of nature is reflected on the psychological level in the parallel development of the ego in autonomy, control, freedom, and maturity of function, together with the emergence of a sense of spiritual identity. We have seen that as spiritual identity evolves, personal freedom evolves concurrently. Thus, not only is human freedom required for cooperation with the action of grace to begin with, but under the action of grace the ego grows apace in its capacity for freedom. And reciprocally, as the ego grows in freedom or the capacity to exercise its inherent freedom with increasing spontaneity, it develops in its inherent receptivity to the action of grace.

A second principle I would propose is the *principle of compensatory activation*. The essential impact of the action of grace is the energization of ego-functions. As a consequence, where a given ego-function is impaired by the defects encountered in the course of its development, the energizing influence of grace makes the effective operation of that function possible in a manner which would otherwise be psychologically impossible. The compensatory action of grace, therefore, can serve a sanating function insofar as it makes possible the recouping of losses experienced all through the course of development. This is no magic transformation since by hypothesis it depends on the cooperation and effective effort of the ego. Grace cannot force the ego's functioning. The response is entirely free. Consequently, there is implicit in this view a certain plasticity in the ego which enables it, through the exercise of the same synthetic and executive functions which presumably operate in the formation of personality at each stage of development, to reconstruct itself in a process of positive development.

It is also possible to lay down a developmental principle: *the principle of epigenesis*. The process of psychological development is one of organic growth (accepting a biological model for the moment), in which at any stage of the total organism's development particular organs or organ systems pass through periods of maximal development. Each system has its own developmental rhythm, so that the intensities of development of the separate systems do not coincide. One can map out various stages, then, in which the development of particular systems reaches particular intensity. The fact remains, however, that the total organism *and* its subsystems are developing continuously. If such an epigenetic analysis designates the development of a particular system as characteristic of a given developmental stage, it does not imply that the system undergoes no development in the other phases of growth; rather, it implies that there has been such a development but that its intensity, dictated by the inherent developmental rhythm of the system in its integrated interaction with the whole complex of subsystems composing the total organism, has been significantly lowered during the other phases and reaches its maximal level only during the appropriate phase. This is merely a general norm for organic development that applies equally well to the understanding of psychological development. The growth of the personality to mature identity can be described in terms of the epigenetic principle. I suggest that a similar analysis of developmental stages can be applied to the growth of a mature spiritual identity.

Implicit in this development, then, lies the issue of the interaction and interrelation between personal identity and spiritual identity. The specific dimensions which we wish to bring together can be conceptualized as "ego-strengths," those inherent strengths of the ego which enable it to function effectively in the face of duress and stress, of inner conflict and turmoil. Erikson (1964) has taken the bold step of calling such strengths "virtues." The insight he proposes establishes the link between the classic analysis of the virtues as based ultimately on the Stoic schema of virtues and as elaborated by the Christian theological tradition and the modern psychological concern with ego-strength or, as White (1963) would put it, ego-competence.

We are concerned, then, with the relation between the qualities of a mature sense of personal identity and the dimensions of a spiritual identity. The essential difference between them, from the perspective I have been developing here, is that the former owe their emergence to the native power of the ego in its normal course of development while the latter owe theirs to the action of grace. Both levels of personality organization are tied together, however, by the common ground of evolution from the same ego and the identically same ego-functions. The crucial question has to do with the specific nature of the action of grace in energizing the native capacities of the ego.

This principle implies that there is a law of intrinsic development which governs the evolution of spiritual identity, just as there is a law of development which governs the emergence of personal identity. Certain stages of spiritual development must be passed through and completed before others can be experienced. This principle has been operative in the traditional treatments of spiritual growth in which development has been divided into stages: purgative, illuminative, and unitive, as an example. This principle has psychological relevance since the relations and interactions between the natural levels of personality development and spiritual development link the course of spiritual development to that of natural development. The specific terms of the analysis into periods of development and phases of selective organization on the spiritual level must remain for the moment highly tentative and problematic.

CHAPTER 4

The Development of Spiritual Identity

With these principles in mind, I shall now attempt a tentative reconstruction of the developmental process of spiritual identity. The analysis of the development of psychological identity has been provided by Erikson (1959, 1963), and the analysis presented here derives from his conceptualization. Erikson bases his formulation on the fundamental schema of personality development provided by psychoanalytic theory. Freud had formulated his theory of personality development in terms of certain psychosexual stages. Erikson broadens this basically biologically oriented consideration and adds a parallel development in terms of psychosocial stages. The developmental process is the outcome of the complementary interaction of intrinsic biologically based forces and crucial object-related experiences. Just as the psychosexual development is determined largely by the child's reaction to his own developing biological organism and its needs, there is a concurrent developing social interaction between the child and the significant figures around him. The pattern of this interaction depends to a certain extent on the pattern of psychosexual adjustment, but there are now additional significant factors that are specifically interpersonal and social, and even cultural.

The analysis is unquestionably more complex than the presentation given here. But I shall try to indicate its outlines so that the relations between the growth of psychological identity and that of spiritual identity can be clarified. Chart 1 has been designed to help keep the complex relationships in view, and the explanation follows the basic schema of the chart. Such a chart has some disadvantages. The reality and dynamic process of the organic development of a complex living reality can never, of course, be adequately reduced to a chart.

First, a word of explanation. Column 1 indicates the chronological stages of physical growth. These stages provide the context of biological development in which psychosexual and psychosocial development are realized. Column 2 indicates the phases of psychosexual development, which correspond to the stages of physical growth. The first two columns are closely linked insofar as psychosexual development is determined by and depends on the rhythm of biological development in the organism. Column 3 indicates the phase of psychosocial development, which typically parallel the phases of psychosexual organization. At each phase of psychosexual development, the emerging personality meets a crucial problem in adjusting itself to the interpersonal and cultural matrix in which the individual lives. The characteristics of the particular phase of psychosexual development set up and condition the crisis. Its successful resolution will determine the normal emergence of the personality. Each such success builds a foundation for a further progression to the subsequent phase and crisis. Where the resolution of a particular phase fails, there is a defect in personality development that adversely affects the successful resolution of subsequent phases. Moreover, the successful resolution of each phase contributes an essential element in the construction of a mature identity. It must be remembered that the entire process at this level is subject to the law of epigenetic development. The resolution of each crisis and the differential development of the personality in relation to that crisis represent a period of maximal development in this particular area of function. This does not mean that the same elements do not undergo important modifications in the other phases of psychosocial development. The tension between trust and mistrust remains significant from the first moment of life to the last, but the primary confrontation with this basic dimension of interpersonal relations occurs in infancy. The infant whose interaction with the significant other has been resolved along the lines of basic trust has accepted a fundamental position to approach subsequent relations with other people similarly. Achieving a basic sense of trust likewise creates an interpersonal climate and a personal disposition that make the successful resolution of the subsequent crisis of autonomy all the more likely. Conversely, if the infant resolves the crisis of trust vs. mistrust along the lines of basic mistrust, the likelihood of resolving the subsequent phase of basic autonomy will be much diminished.

Another important point is that the course of each phase is not an "all or nothing at all" affair. The crisis is resolved through the emergence of an attitude that incorporates elements of each basic alternative. Successful resolution implies that the positive disposition predominates in the composite orientation of the personality. Each individual, however, carries elements of both the positive and the negative poles of psychosocial adjustment. Achieving an integration of these polar elements enables the mature identity to function positively in the various tribu-

CHART 1. Comparative Development of the Psychosocial
and Psychospiritual Organism

Stages of growth	Psychosexual phases	Psychosocial crises	Psychospiritual crises
Infancy	Oral-respiratory (incorporative mode)	Trust/mistrust	Faith, hope
Early childhood	Anal-urethral (retentive-eliminative mode)	Autonomy/shame, doubt	Contrition
Play age	Infantile-genital (intrusive mode)	Initiative/guilt	Penance, temperance
School age	Latency period	Industry/inferiority	Fortitude
Adolescence	Puberty (genital maturity)	Identity/identity diffusion	Humility
Young adulthood	Genitality	Intimacy/isolation	Love of neighbor
Adulthood		Generativity/ self-absorption	Service, zeal self-sacrifice
Maturity		Integrity/despair, disgust, self-contempt	Charity

lations of life. The level of maturity any individual attains depends on the extent to which he has successfully resolved each crisis toward the positive polarity and the extent to which he has harmoniously integrated these basic personality dispositions into an adequately functioning, realistically oriented totality.

Column 4 indicates the phases of development of a spiritual identity. Great caution is called for in advancing such a schema, and flexibility is required in interpreting it. Psychosexual development is closely linked to the stages of physical growth, since the psychosexual phases depend on the emergence of physical subsystems of the biological organism. Psychosocial development, while still closely linked to psychosexual factors, enjoys a more flexible course of development because of the influence of interpersonal and sociocultural factors that cannot be regularized as fully as purely biological ones. Still greater flexibility characterizes psychospiritual development, where a completely gratuitous factor must be taken into account. Consequently, no parallel can be established between the course of physical, psychosexual, and psychosocial development and the course of psychospiritual development. The latter may not begin until late in life, depending on the disposition of grace.

There seems to be an epigenetic development, however, that comes into play even in psychospiritual development. The arrangement presented in column 4 of Chart 1 is an attempt to designate the relevant phases of this development. It should be obvious that the development on this level of organization of the human psyche cannot be reduced to hard and fast laws. The life of the spirit enjoys a flexibility and spontaneity deriving from its essentially self-determinative character. Identity formation, whether psychosocial or psychospiritual, is a process of active engagement of the ego in which the ultimate product bears the mark of individuality that transcends the additive elements of any summary analysis. This is particularly true at the level of psychospiritual organization, where extra-ego sources of determination diminish in importance. The whole process of development on the psychosocial level, and even more on the psychospiritual level, is a constantly renewed and ongoing process of dynamic synthesis.

The psychospiritual crises reflect aspects of spiritual identity as they function on a more mature and evolved level. They are distributed according to the tentative hypothesis that each aspect of spiritual identity has its point of connection and finds its potential psychological roots in one or other aspect of the development of psychological identity.

With this brief consideration of the individual columns of Chart 1, I turn now to the interrelation among the various levels and phases of development. I shall discuss each row and each set of psychosexual, psychosocial, and psychospiritual crises separately.

Trust/Hope, Faith

The crisis of trust-mistrust is the first psychosocial crisis the infant must face. It takes place in the context of the intimate relationship between infant and mother. The infant's primary orientation to reality is erotic and centers on the mouth. The typical situation in which the infant's oral eroticism is experienced is the feeding relationship. Depending on the quality of the child's feeding contacts, he learns to accept what is given to him by the warm and loving mother; he learns to depend on that mother and to expect that what she provides will be satisfying. The child's oral orientation is largely biologically determined; the mother's feeding orientation is a product of biological factors, but also of a complex process of personal development in which her sense of identity as a woman and as a mother plays a vital part. Any defect in her identity will thus have important consequences for the quality of the interaction between herself and her child.

The quality of the child's experience in social interaction with the significant others in his environment extends to a whole complex of interactions and experiences that are characteristic of this stage of development. The successful resolution of this initial phase of interaction entails certain orientations and dispositons that will determine the subsequent course of his interpersonal interactions. They include a dispositon to trust others, basic trust in himself, a capacity to receive from others and to depend on them (to entrust oneself), and a resulting sense of self-confidence. The unsuccessful resolution of this crisis, on the other hand, will result in the defect of these same qualities and the relative dominance of their opposites: mistrust, lack of confidence, etc. Consequently, the designations "basic trust" and "basic mistrust" stand for a complex of personality factors characterizing the successful or unsuccessful resolution of this first crisis.

The dimensions of spiritual identity which seem to parallel the dimension of basic trust are faith and hope. Faith implies a receptivity, a willingness to accept the word of God, a fundamental trust and confidence in God, a sufficient confidence in and trust of self to make the commitment of self that is required in bridging the chasm between the security of reason and the darkness of faith. Hope, likewise, implies a basic confidence in the power and goodness of God, an entrusting of self to His fidelity to His promises. Hope implies a capacity to receive promised rewards.

Here we are concerned with faith as a basic orientation of the ego toward the fundamental realities of the spiritual life. Faith is fundamentally a commitment of oneself to God, a disposition of trusting acceptance toward the will of God, an entrusting of oneself to God's providential care. In the face of the revealed and revealing word, faith responds with receptivity and acceptance, trusting in the trustworthiness of God's revelation as representing fundamental religious truths. The fundamental issue of faith is the capacity to relate oneself in a trusting orientation toward the revealing God.

It is obvious in the light of these reflections that there is an intrinsic relation between the openness of faith on a religious and spiritual plane and the openness of a basic trust on a purely interpersonal plane. In a more profound sense, it is difficult to separate respective planes of this nature since faith for the Christian is itself a relation between the believer and the person of Jesus Christ. Faith can be understood, then, as a psychological disposition of those same ego-functions which are involved in basic trust, a prolongation of basic trust to the spiritual level.

Basic trust provides a preliminary disposition of faith. Thus faith is psychologically more-possible for the individual with this basic disposition than for someone unable to trust.

But there is more to it than that. Faith stands beyond reason. Human reason can carry a man up to a critical point where faith becomes possible, but not beyond it. The line between the assent of reason and the assent of faith is not continuous. Reason is the great resource of the natural ego. But the natural ego cannot come to faith without the dynamics of grace to enable it to bridge the dark chasm that yawns between the reasoned assent to religious propositions and the total commitment of faith. Faith becomes impossible, then, for the intellect which cannot trust beyond the limits of its own reasoned certitude. Psychologically speaking, the energizing effect of grace makes faith possible. Faith demands that trust project itself into the darkness beyond. But there must be a certain basic self-trust, a certain confidence of judgment and of valuation based on the trustworthiness of the ego's own perceptions and convictions. Faith is, after all, a reasonable if not reasoned judgment, at least in one dimension.

If it is fair to say that faith is facilitated by a basic sense of trust, it is likewise fair to say that faith is impeded by the opposite disposition, basic mistrust. The inability to confide oneself in a trusting relation to anything outside of oneself as an impediment to faith. It is here that the sanating action of faith inspired by grace comes clearly into focus. Faith is, after all, a basic dimension of spiritual identity, one that more or less sets the direction of the ego toward the spiritual level of existence. Granted that faith is more readily established where basic trust has already prepared the preliminary psychological dispositions, faith does not demand trust as a necessary foundation. Where faith becomes independently possible through the action of grace, it establishes a fundamental openness of soul which cannot fail to have a reciprocal effect on the psychological orientation of the ego. By a kind of reciprocal influence, then, we can say that faith induces trust. It must be so, if faith itself embodies trust as an integral part of its own internal structure.

Moreover, it is the initiative of grace that makes the response of faith possible. In the language of the analogy of personal relationship, God's loving self-communication draws the soul to himself. Man is drawn to, loved, and accepted by the most trustworthy of objects.

Hope is a second dimension of spiritual identity which seems to bear an intrinsic relation to basic trust. Erikson (1964) explicitly relates hope to the infant's first encounter with trustworthy maternal persons. Hope derives from an expectation, a desire that God in his goodness and love will respond to spiritual needs and longings. It is ultimately an expression of a wish for the definitive satisfaction of salvation. This expectation originates (psychologically at least) in the warmth and satisfaction of the trusted mother. Her trustworthiness is the foundation which shapes and stabilizes hope. Hope is a basic quality of experience which is made firm by the satisfaction of desires, from the infant's primitive desire for nourishment and affection to the adult's deepest, most soulful cry for strength and spiritual consolation. Karl Menninger (1959) has written: "Unconcerned with the ambiguity of past experience, hope implies progress; it is an adventure, a going forward, a confident search." On the spiritual level, hope is the driving and motivating force behind our efforts to live life fully and integrally. It is a dynamizing force in spirituality, rooted in our trust and in the trustworthiness of God and His fidelity to His promises.

Erikson (1964) offers us a synthetic conception of hope. "Hope is the enduring belief in the attainability of fervent wishes, in spite of the dark urges and rages which mark the beginning of existence. Hope is the ontogenetic basis of faith, and is nourished by the adult faith which pervades patterns of care." Confidence in the attainability of our wishes rests on the same foundations as faith, namely, a trusting relation to others and a reliance on their trustworthiness. The spiritual dimension of hope is perhaps the most profoundly enduring belief in the attainability of a wish that man can experience. Hope, like faith, is a theological virtue; its realization as a dimension of spiritual identity is the fruit of grace. Despite this fundamental independence from natural desires and wishes, hope is both psychologically relevant and rooted in psychological development. The emergence of hope and faith is thus facilitated by the basic disposition of the primitive strata of infantile development which opens the psyche to reciprocally rewarding relations with its environment through basic trust. Hope's emergence through the action of grace in the ego elicits a fundamental psychological orientation within the ego which vitalizes and expands the capacity for trust that was undercut in the natural course of development. Basic trust, then, is not only at the root of faith and hope, but is a necessary component of these dimensions of spiritual identity. Where faith and hope emerge under the action of grace in the formation of a spiritual identity, the integral relation between personal identity and spiritual identity demands a sanating and reciprocal education of basic trust.

It seems, then, that both faith and hope build upon the capacity of the personality for trust and confidence. If the person has developed this capacity, his spiritual disposition through faith and hope is more secure, and the extension of basic trust to an infinitely loving Father and God is thus made easy. Where the initial crisis has been resolved in favor of basic mistrust, however, the capacity for entrusting oneself to God through faith and hope is impeded. Conversely, by reason of the principle of reciprocal influence (see Chapter 3), the implied disposition of trust and confidence in God through faith and/or hope will exercise a reciprocal influence on the orientation to basic trust in the personality. The extent to which the sanating influence of trust in God will be realized depends on the intensity of the energizing effect of grace and on the degree to which the ego mobilizes its resources in responding to grace.

The parallel between basic trust and faith seems to be a legitimate extension of Erikson's (1959:64–65) notion of basic trust. He remarks that

> the psychological observer must ask whether or not in any area under observation religion and tradition are living psychological forces creating the kind of faith or conviction which permeates a parent's personality and thus reinforces the child's basic trust in the world's trustworthiness . . . . All religions have in common the periodical childlike surrender to a Provider or providers who dispense earthly fortune as well as spiritual health; the demonstration of one's smallness and dependence through the medium of reduced posture and humble gesture; the admission in prayer and song of misdeeds, of misthoughts, and of evil intentions; the admission of inner division and the consequent appeal for inner unification by divine guidance; the need for clearer self-delineation and self-restriction; and finally, the insight that individual trust must become a common faith, individual mistrust a commonly formulated evil, while the individual's need for restoration must become part of the ritual practice of many, and must become a sign of the trustworthiness of the community.

Autonomy/Contrition

The second stage of psychosexual development is anal eroticism. Biologically, this stage is marked by the formation of a fuller stool and sufficient maturation of the neuromuscular system to allow control of sphincter muscles governing retention and release of waste materials. The anal zone becomes a source of erotic stimulation through the pleasurable sensations of retaining or releasing. On the psychosocial level, the child becomes aware of himself as a separate and independent unit. Growing muscular control is accompanied by an increasing capacity for autonomous expression and self-regulation, typically centering on problems of sphincter control of the so-called anal period. The ego begins to interact assertively with other wills in the social environment, particularly with parents in the toilet-training situation. Successful resolution of the crisis of autonomy lays the foundation of a mature capacity for self-assertion and self-expression, a capacity to respect the autonomy of others, to maintain self-control without loss of self-esteem, and for rewarding and effective cooperation with others. Conversely, failure to resolve the crisis lays the foundation of a false autonomy that feeds on the autonomy of others by domination and excessive demands, or of an excessive rigidity than can be identified in the fragile autonomy of the compulsive (anal) personality. Failure to achieve basic autonomy implies a lack of self-esteem that is reflected in a sense of shame, a lack of self-confidence that is implied in self-doubt. This is generally characteristic of the scrupulous penitent.

The psychospiritual complement of basic autonomy is contrition. I suggest this connection hesitantly, since a more exact statement of the relationship between the two would require a careful phenomenological analysis of contrition. But it seems that true contrition provides an extension in the spiritual order of the fundamental dispositions of basic autonomy. Contrition is a complex state of mind, but essential to it is a return to a true sense of self-esteem, a realization and revaluation of the true dignity of self in the wake of a prior capitulation and self-debasement before inferior forces. Contrition for sin implies a conversion within the ego by which the ego comes into possession of its own basic autonomy; but this repossession is specifically spiritual in that it constitutes a recognition of self as the ultimate source of personal responsibility and the self-determining source of the moral response. The ego assumes responsibility for its own deviation from the internalized schema of spiritual values; it thereby implicitly asserts its autonomy and rejects external domination. Similarly, the purpose of amendment, which the Council of Trent insists on as an integral part of true contrition, is a natural consequence of such self-possession in which the ego directs itself toward its own internal reorganization and development.

Consequently, contrition is an expression of spiritual autonomy. If the personality has attained a measure of basic autonomy, the prolongation of that same basic orientation in the spiritual realm is facilitated. But if basic autonomy has not been achieved, emergence of the essential dispositions of true contrition becomes all the more difficult. Thus, shame and doubt are radically opposed to true contrition. Shame is the reaction of the guilty soul trying to hide its face from God, while true contrition is the reaction of the soul that turns to God in sorrow and seeks forgiveness. Shame is negative, but contrition is positive. The negative disposition of doubt is a condition of insecurity and irresolution, while contrition is a clear and humble self-appraisal with a determination to self-amendment. The scrupulous person's anxious self-doubting impedes the capacity for true contrition and probably reflects a basic failure to resolve successfully the crisis of autonomy.

Initiative/Penance

When the child enters the play age, the maturing organism reaches a developmental stage in which the subsystem serving the functions of locomotion and language is adequately organized to permit facile use. Motor equipment has developed sufficiently to permit not merely the performance of motions, but a wide-ranging experimentation in locomotion. The child begins to "test the limits" of his new-found capability. His activity becomes vigorous and intrusive. A similar crystallization occurs in the use of language, which becomes an exciting new toy calling for experimentation and the satisfaction of curiosity. Intrusion characterizes the child's activity: intrusion into other bodies by physical attack, into other people's attention by activity and aggressive talking, into space by vigorous locomotion, and into the unknown by lively curiosity. All this is accompanied by growing sexual curiosity and development of the prerequisites of specifically masculine or feminine initiative, which is conditioned by the development of a phallic eroticism.

In the psychosocial sphere, the child's experience is governed by an expanding imagination that must begin to mesh with the world's real structure, both physical and social. The child's fancy meets the nonfanciful demands of reality. Especially in the area of phallic activity and sexual curiosity, the conflict takes on serious proportions. Excessively severe rebuke or prohibitions can bring about unnecessary repressions and can restrict the play of the child's imagination and initiative. If the crisis of initiative is successfully resolved, positive residues are provided for the development of conscience, a sense of responsibility and dependability, self-discipline, and a certain independence in the mature personality. This is therefore a crucial stage for the formation of the superego, based on the introjection of authoritative, and especially parental, prohibitions. Unsuccessful resolution of the crisis provides a basis for the harsh, rigid, moralistic, and self-punishing superego that is the dynamic source of a sense of guilt.

The interplay of parental prohibitions and identifications can work against the emergence of that sense of initiative which lends a certain spontaneity and freedom to the child's inquiring intrusions. The child assimilates an internalized system of parental norms and prohibitions which guide the course of behavior and serve as the roots for development of a mature value-system. If the assimilated elements are fundamentally realistic in foundation and orientation, they can be synthesized into the evolving structure of the mature ego. In this instance, the pattern of identifications is well defined and supported by mature parental identities, and parental prohibitions are balanced and reasonable. Much of the development of superego at this level is a function of parental adjustment and maturity level. If, however, parental role functions are disturbed in one or another degree or dimension, the child's successful resolution of this psychosocial crisis is threatened.

The child's emerging phallic interests need the support and formative influence of secure, stable identifications in order that the foundations of a mature sense of sexual identity and role function can be established. The inability of parents to provide models of sexual functioning impairs the child's identification in this essential area of self-awareness. This dimension of superego formation is important for the evolution of a guilt-free sense of sexual adjustment.

Moreover, the assimilation of parental prohibitions and demands sets the stage for the future integration of ego and superego functioning. If parental demands are reasonable and realistic, the conjoint functioning of ego and superego are made possible. But if demands and prohibitions become the vehicle of parental immaturities, superego formation is impaired by assimilation of these immature elements and the ground is laid for future conflict and guilt feelings. Guilt, then, arises from the disparity between the activity of the ego and the value-dependent prescriptions of the superego. Where the internalized norms of the superego are based on unresolved infantile conflicts (oedipal conflicts in Freud's terms), this primitive unreasonableness of the superego underlies guilt feelings which are unrealistic and therefore neurotic. The defect in this case is the superego. If the value-system is realistically based and oriented, guilt is still a possibility, not because of the inherent punitiveness of the superego but because of the defection of the ego.

The sense of initiative seems to extend itself to the spiritual level through the fundamental orientation of penance. Penance is a prolongation and consequence of the basic attitudes generated in contrition; in this prolongation, the awareness and realizations found in contrition are followed by a more or less permanent disposition to take effective means. Penance, then, represents the ego's self-assertion in the face of forces that tend to inhibit its autonomous functioning. Through penance, the spiritually oriented ego assumes responsibility for its own regulation and discipline, particularly with regard to libidinal attachments. The ego assumes the active role in establishing and maintaining ego-control. In the growth to spiritual identity, the development from contrition to penance marks a progression in the autonomous, effective functioning of the ego and implies a more effective mobilization of its resources.

The basic dispositions essential to authentic penance reinforce the dispositions proper to basic initiative; in addition, one who has achieved a sense of that initiative in his personality development thereby finds the disposition of penance more congenial. At the same time, the lack of basic initiative can operate to inhibit the ego's capacity to achieve true penance. Where the natural capacity for true initiative is absent, one cannot expect a facile response to the more demanding initiative inherent in true penance. But where the individual is enabled through the dynamic impulse of grace to achieve some measure of true penance, the implicit exercise of spiritual initiative in the ego can produce an effect on the basic disposition to initiative itself.

It is important to distinguish true penance from false forms that are occasionally expressed in a religious context. True penance is an ego function, and is therefore guided by a sense of balance and realistic proportion. It is difficult to establish norms of judgment, but in general true penance does not lean toward excess. The saints sometimes seem to indulge in penitential extremes, but the authenticity of their penance can ultimately be judged only by the extent to which it is at the service of the ego. The ultimate distinction between true and false penance lies in the source of the initiative for self-discipline: the ego or the superego. More accurately, one must know whether it is authentic self-discipline (and therefore an effort to achieve and establish ego-control) or self-punishment (which would stem from the excessive severity of the superego).

Penance is thus a form of spiritual initiative. It stands in radical opposition to neurotic guilt because it opposes the latter's mechanisms, and it resolves realistic guilt by restoring the balance of appropriate ego-activity and drawing it back into congruence with the real value-system.

It should be obvious that the principle of reciprocal influence is operative in this dimension of spiritual identity as well as in others. Penance is more readily achieved in the ego which already has a strong sense of initiative, precisely because initiative stands in opposition to neurotic guilt, with which true penance is incompatible. The punitive self-doubt of the scrupulous penitent is a form of neurotic guilt and thus an impediment to the sense of real penance which is essential for spiritual growth. A basic sense of guilt derived from the unsuccessful resolution of this psychosocial crisis of initiative stands in the way of true penance. Where real penance can be elicited through the action of grace, however, the emergence of such spiritual initiative would seem to have an inductive influence on basic orientation, even on the natural psychological level.

True penance is, therefore, incompatible with a basic sense of guilt. Penance stands for an assertion of ego-control over libidinal and aggressive energies; the sense of guilt represents the failure of ego-control and the domination of the superego. Guilt feelings have no place in the authentic disposition of penance. This does not mean that there is no such thing as real guilt, i.e., responsibility for violation of the moral order; but the mature and positive response to the guilt situation is not guilt-feelings, but contrition. Where guilt dominates the picture, true contrition and penance are impeded.

Continuation of the basic dispositions of penance is expressed in temperance, insofar as the exercise of the functions of the ego proper to penance is directed toward establishing a balance between the ego and other psychic structures. The same functions are brought into play in preserving the balance, once it has been struck. Maintenance of ego-control and regulation of psychic impulses according to the inherent values of reality are what characterize temperance.

Industry/Fortitude

The period of infantile (phallic) sexuality and the period of adult sexuality (puberty) are separated by the so-called latency period, in which the child's interest is generally diverted to other matters. The child steps up from the level of imaginative exploration and play to a level in which his participation in the adult world is foreshadowed. In our culture, the child is sent to school, where he begins to learn the skills that will equip him one day to take his place in adult society. His interest turns to doing things and making things—in general, he becomes involved in developing the necessary technology for adult living. He is drawn away from home and its close association, and is plunged into the matrix of the school system. He learns the reward systems of the school society and assimilates the values of application and diligence. He also assimilates the implicit cultural values of work and productivity. He achieves a sense of the pleasure of work, of the satisfaction of a task accomplished, and of the merit of perseverance in a difficult enterprise. In other words, the normally developing child adds to his evolving personality a sense of industry. There is a danger at this stage that a lack of success in meeting the demands of the school society will produce in him a sense of inadequacy and inferiority. It must be remembered, of course, that failure to achieve a sense of industry may indicate a defect in the resolution of previous crises. Excessive dependency on the emotional support of the family setting can impair the child's ability to enter successfully into the atmosphere of competiton and cooperation with peers in the school society. In any case, the sense of inferiority can issue from the child's failure to find rewards in meeting the demands of the school setting.

The basic sense of industry implies a certain capacity within the ego not only to direct its energies to a goal, but also to maintain that mobilization of resources until the goal is achieved or the task completed. The spiritual analogue of industry is fortitude, which implies not merely ego-control, but the emerging capacity of the ego to sustain its constant effort to establish and maintain that control in the face of strong opposition and resistance. In this sense, fortitude represents an advance over previous phases of psychospiritual development in that the capacity for prolonged effort implies a deepening and closer organization of the entire psychic structure. The ego, which has realized in itself a basic sense of industry, will all the more readily be enabled to prolong the same ego-dispositions into the disposition of fortitude. The defect of industry will make that prolongation all the more difficult.

Conversely, where the ego achieves spiritual fortitude with the support of grace, the sanating effect becomes feasible. A sense of inferiority is a fear of failure or of an incapacity to compete on the same footing with others. If the ego is rooted in such inadequacy, the intensification of spiritual ego-strength through fortitude becomes more difficult. But if the individual mobilizes his resources through fortitude, the groundwork is laid for at least a partial sanating influence which can mitigate the results of the initial developmental failure to resolve the industry crisis successfully.

Identity/Humility

The passage to adolescence is marked by intense physiological growth and sudden maturation of genital organs in both sexes. The psychosexual phase of puberty is accompanied on the psychosocial level by an organization or crystallization of the residues of the preceding formative phases. Preparations for participation in adult life must now begin to take a more or less definitive shape; the adolescent must begin to establish his future role and function with adult society, including the consolidation of gender identity as male or female. He must develop a confident self-awareness predicated on his ability to maintain inner sameness and continuity, and on the expectation that this awareness is matched by the sameness and continuity of his meaning to others. This particular psychosocial crisis is therefore peculiarly vulnerable and sensitive to social and cultural influences. The context of the crisis is specifically interpersonal, and thus its successful resolution becomes all the more tenuous and problematic. Achieving a sense of personal identity requires an awareness of the context of relations to reality within which the self forms and maintains its own proper identity.

Who and what I am cannot be divorced from the interaction that both links my self to reality and separates it from the non-ego reality. Self-awareness, therefore, goes hand in hand with awareness of the other, whether that other be merely physical or personal or spiritual. Identity implies a duality of awareness that underlies an acceptance of both poles of the experience of personal continuity. The failure of this psychosocial crisis implies a defect in awareness both of the self and of the non-ego reality, a failure in the recognition and acceptance of the self and the real; it implies an unclarity and permeability of ego-boundaries that have been described as "identity diffusion." Identity diffusion and self-alienation (Meissner 1978) lie at the root of many, if not most, of the adolescent problems in our culture.

On the spiritual level, the basic elements of self-knowledge and self-acceptance are realized in humility, which implies a sense of personal continuity, and a realization and acceptance of one's own creatureliness and basic dependence upon God for continued existence. True humility is based on an awareness of the real context of existence, in relation to God and to one's fellowmen. Through humility we become aware of our own spiritual identity, and achieve an operative acceptance of our relation and subjection to the influence of grace.

Realization of one's own inherent dignity as a child of God is inseparable from appreciation of the inherent dignity of all persons. This dimension of self-awareness and self-acceptance implicit in humility sets its face against pride. Pride puts the individual before others because doing so is somehow necessary to compensate for the failure to achieve that awareness and acceptance of self which perceives one's place before God as creature, as contingent, as dependent, as derivative in its own existence. True humility results in a gracious acceptance of and resignation to God's will, for it recognizes in that will the ultimate determinant of its own position within the structure of reality.

Humility is directly opposed to that excessive valuation of self which is pride. Where the one is, the other cannot be. (One is reminded of the old quip that one can be humble and proud of it.) Humility in its authentic roots is neither a social pose nor a pattern of behavior. It is a quality of the ego which reaches into the most fundamental levels of the personality. It is in this sense a dimension of the person and not a quality of his acts. Let us not mistake the superficial for the fundamental. One who continually demonstrates initiative may not necessarily have a-chieved that dimension of personal development implied in basic initiative, but may, in fact, be driven by a sense of guilt or personal worthlessness. So, too, one who displays humble demeanor and actions need not have achieved a true sense of humility as a dimension of an authentic spiritual identity.

It is fairly obvious that an underlying defect in the sense of identity hinders the achievement of true humility on the spiritual level. Similarly, the dispositions inherent in a secure sense of personal identity are an apt groundwork for the realistic orientation of self in the spiritual realm that is implicit in true humility. The sanating influence of humility upon the diffusion of identity, however, is more tenuous, if nonetheless real. Achievement of self-realization and self-acceptance in the spiritual order would serve as a crystallizing element in the otherwise unstructured diffusion. The question would be whether true humility were possible without an underlying structure of self-possession and ego-integrity. From this point of view, we might conceive of pride as a form of defense against the threatening insecurity inherent in identity diffusion.

Intimacy/Love of Neighbor

Adulthood is marked on the psychosexual level by the achievement of genital maturity. To Freud, genital maturity meant the adequate functioning of a mature, well-adjusted personality. On the psychosocial level, this development is paralleled by the establishment of significant interpersonal relationships that complement the previously formed identity in the social sphere. Typically, the emerging sexual drive focuses on another individual of the opposite sex as its object. The elements of sex identification, which are essential to personal identity, are naturally expressed as established by the standards of intersex behavior of society and culture. The intimate association of male and female in a close interpersonal union is thus an extension of their own identities as well as a culturally approved institution (marriage). This does not mean that the sexual act is the only path to a sense of intimacy. From the standpoint of personality development, the crucial element is the capacity to relate intimately and meaningfully with others in mutually satisfying and productive interactions. The pattern of such self-fulfilling relations depends in large measure on the identity one has accepted as his or her own. The religious vocation, for example, is a primary path to achievement and expression of a sense of intimacy without sex. Such intimacy, however, is not possible unless the religious person has gained a secure sense of his or her own identity as a religious.

Failure to resolve successfully this psychosocial crisis results in a sense of personal isolation. The incapacity to establish warm and rewarding relationships with others is but a reflection of the failure to realize a secure and mature self-acceptance. Interpersonal relationships become strained, stiff, formal. Even if a facade of personal warmth can be erected, there is a rigidly maintained inner wall that is never breached, a wall defended by intellectualization, distanciation, and self-absorption. On the psychospiritual level, the basic sense of intimacy seems to find its complement in the second great commandment of the law: love of neighbor. In the course of epigenetic development, this psychospiritual phase is crucial. Up to this point, the analysis has been concerned with the intrinsic emergence of the spiritual organism itself. At each phase, the whole previous development has undergone a vital resynthesis, in and through which the emerging spiritual identity achieves a new level of realization and growth. When the ego realizes within itself an authentic love of neighbor, the spiritual identity achieves a new synthesis in which the self-realization of its humility is deepened and intensified. The ego reaches a level of development in which its control of intrapsychic dynamisms permits diversion of its energies outside itself. This extension implies an enlargement and growth to a new level of interior organization within the ego.

While love of one's neighbor is spiritually motivated and directed, its affinity to the sense of intimacy is striking. It is not difficult here to see the principle of reciprocal influence at work. For the person who has achieved a basic sense of intimacy, the spiritual love of neighbor is much more congenial. Conversely, one can readily comprehend the sanating influence of true love of neighbor upon an ego that has failed to grow in a sense of intimacy.

Generativity/Service, Zeal

The term "generativity" points to a primary concern with establishing the succeeding generation (through genes and genitality) and guiding it. However, other areas of altruistic effort cannot be excluded. Perhaps "productivity" or "creativity" would be better terms. Erikson (1964:131–132) remarks:

> Generativity, as the instinctual power behind various forms of self-less "caring," potentially extends to whatever a man generates and leaves behind, creates and produces (or helps to produce). The ideological popularization of the Western world which has made Freud the century's theorist of sex, and Marx that of work, has, until quite recently, left a whole area of man's mind uncharted in psychoanalysis. I refer to men's *love for his works and ideas as well as for his children,* and the necessary self-verification which adult man's ego receives, and must receive, from his labor's challenge. (Italics in the original.)

What is involved here is a fuller realization of self in terms of expressing utilizing the individual's maximum creative capacities. Such creativity can assume a myriad of forms, depending on one's native endowment; but the realized generativity is also largely determined by the identity the individual has accepted and by the extent to which he is capable of interacting maturely and cooperatively with others. Consequently, success in this area depends closely on the satisfactory resolution of the two preceding phases of identity and intimacy. Moreover, true generativity has as its goal the enrichment of the lives of others; it involves direct concern with the welfare of others exclusive of any concern for the welfare of self. Enrichment of one's identity is a necessary by-product of generativity, but it cannot be its direct objective. Failure to achieve a sense of generativity promotes a certain self-absorption that expresses itself in self-indulgence, self-love, and selfishness.

The basic dispositions of generativity are expressed on the psychospiritual level in the motif of service, which is an essential element of Christian perfection. Both generativity and service require a social commitment based on a realization that each individual has a responsibility to his fellow human beings whether it be to advance and preserve the well-being of the species through propagation and training of children; to work for the improvement of humanity's social, cultural, and economic situation; or to commit oneself to the betterment of its spiritual condition and attainment of its ultimate end. This conviction is most fully expressed in the spirit of zeal, particularly apostolic zeal.

Commitment to the service of others or the expression of a true spirit of zeal would be impaired by the kind of self-absorption and self-indulgence that comes from the failure to achieve a sense of generativity. Commitment to service calls for self-sacrifice and unselfishness, both of which are implied in basic generativity. Where the development of the personality has failed to reach generativity, however, grace can enable the ego to achieve an unselfish giving of itself to the service of others. In some measure this can help to sanate the original failure in the ego.

Integrity/Charity

Integrity marks the culmination of the development of the personality. It implies and depends on successful resolution of all the preceding crises of psychosocial growth. It means acceptance of oneself and all aspects of life, and integration of these elements into a stable pattern of living. It implies experience of and adjustment to life's trials and troubles, as well as to its rewards and joys. Consequently, existence holds no fear; the ego is resigned to acceptance of life and to acceptance of life's end in death. Integrity thus represents the fully developed personality in its most complete and mature self-realization. Failure to achieve ego-integration often results in a kind of despair and an unconscious fear of death: the one life cycle, given to every man as his own, has not been accepted. One who fails in integrity lives in basic self-contempt.

The effort toward integration which is called forth in this last fundamental crisis of the life cycle is directed in terms of ultimate issues. It involves—as it must for the questioning and understanding animal that is man—a confrontation with the fundamental issue of meaning and meaningfulness. If man has the innate capacity to bring meaning into his existence, in this last crisis ultimate meaningfulness must be found or not found. Ultimate lack of meaning issues in profound despair. Ultimate meaning can be either accepted or rejected.

The need for meaning finds a variety of responses, depending on where one seeks for an answer. The irreligious person can arrive at ultimate meaning in a form of wisdom. Erikson (1964:133) describes such wisdom in these terms:

> Wisdom, then, is detached concern with life itself, in the face of death itself. It maintains and conveys the integrity of experience, in spite of the decline of bodily and mental functions. It responds to the need of the on-coming generation for an integrated heritage and yet remains aware of the relativity of all knowledge.

Whether such wisdom is ultimate or provides the fundamental sense of integration that man seeks is beside the point. It represents a resolution of this crisis in terms which answer to basic needs of human nature. For the religious person, however, a more profound and far-reaching answer is provided from the resources of revelation and faith. The wisdom achieved presents itself as an understanding of the meaningfulness of existence in relation to a spiritual order governed and directed by God's will and loving providence. Within that framework, the individual has a meaning and an inherent value which fit him into a larger structure and divine purpose. The wisdom by which he understands the significance of his spiritual existence makes his acceptance of his life cycle and his confrontation with death both easier and integral to the totality of his existence.

Just as integrity completes and integrates the natural personal identity, so on the psychospiritual level charity subsumes, assimilates, and integrates the whole psychospiritual development. Spiritual identity thereby achieves its fullest expression and highest realization in and through charity. Similarly, charity intensifies and elevates each of the prior elements, perfecting each and integrating all into an increasingly perfect synthesis. The emergence of charity as the epitome of spiritual perfection is a striking instance of the epigenetic principle at work. Charity was rudimentary in the primitive orientation of the ego through faith and hope. At each succeeding phase of spiritual synthesis, charity has assumed a more significant role and has developed in intensity. Finally, at the culmination of the process of spiritual development, charity becomes the dominating factor. Charity, therefore, is the yardstick of the development of spiritual identity and responsiveness to grace. One's capacity, under grace, to love God depends upon the degree to which the ego is in complete, autonomous control of its proper functioning. Ego-autonomy is possible only to the extent that the ego has reached a high level of inner development. Love of God implies complete surrender of self to God. In that surrender, we achieve the highest expression of our freedom, because our surrender is an act of unrestrained autonomy—the giving of ourselves.

Insofar as the ego achieves this autonomy, charity has a unique unifying and synthetic effect on the ego. Through such a level of autonomous function, the ego has reached a high level of synthesis. The interdependence of autonomy, ego-synthesis, and charity seems to suggest that a defect in basic integrity would inhibit the ego's capacity to achieve charity on the sprirtual level. There is always a question of degree, particularly since charity itself has an almost infinite range of expression. The less the mature personality has attained a sense of identity, the greater the internal obstacle to its love of God; but to the degree that charity is realized with the help of grace, the reciprocal integrating effect asserts itself.

Grace and Spiritual Identity

The notion of spiritual identity, like that of personal identity, is an integrative one. Over and above the question of the individual's capacity for personal maturity, there is a basic incapacity to lead a supernaturally oriented life without the assistance of grace. From the very first moment of spiritual rebirth in baptism, man becomes a *nova creatura*. Through the divine indwelling, he takes on a new existence which is specifically supernatural, and that existence is nourished and developed by the power of grace. Implicit in such a view of man's supernatural existence is the realization that this existence is subject to development. The life of the Spirit is like a seed that begins in the simplest manner and undergoes a slow, sometimes painful advancement.

Spiritual identity involves an awareness and acceptance of spiritual values which are derived from a prior acceptance of a supernatural order of existence. The basic disposition for such an acceptance comes through faith. There is a maximal development of the basic strengths of temperance, fortitude, justice, and prudence; and then there is the full complement of the virtues, crowned by the theological virtue of faith, hope, and charity. In short, a fully developed spiritual identity signifies the full flowering of Christian virtue and saintliness.

We need not catalogue the elements of such a picture here, but several points should be made. Spiritual identity depends on grace for its growth and achievement, and is related to psychological qualities of a distinctly different order from those associated with personal identity. This does not mean that there cannot be a broad overlap between these two identities. It is difficult, if not impossible, to conceive of a person motivated by supernatural charity not being at the same time capable of trust and of intimate relations with others. But it remains true that without grace supernatural charity is not possible, and, although it presumes intimacy, it involves much more.

Further, it is not enough merely to indicate that spiritual identity encompasses the Christian virtues. Our understanding of these virtues must be set down in psychological terms. The hardest work for a future psychology of grace must be done precisely on this level. One cannot presume that we have any meaningful psychological understanding of the Christian virtues. Although Erikson has opened the way for us to conceptualize the Christian virtues in psychologically relevant terms, we do not know whether development will in time be rewarding and fruitful for the psychology of grace and for the understanding of the ego's functioning. In indicating the virtues here, we are simply indicating the direction of a future program of study and understanding.

From the psychological point of view, it is important to stress that the achievement of spiritual identity, to whatever degree this is realized in the individual person, is an achievement of the ego itself. Grace does not change us, but gives us the power to change ourselves. We grow to spiritual maturity under grace through our own activity. If the development of the virtues is to have any meaning psychologically, it must be in terms of the synthetic activity of the ego. The development of such virtues implies growth, restructuring, organization, and integration within the ego.

The achievement of spiritual identity involves a right ordering of behavior and internal impulses and the integration of psychic energies under the ego's direction and control. This is akin to what theologians have called an ordered concupiscence. The rebelliousness of our lower nature through disordered concupiscence is one of the unfortunate consequences of original sin. But the effect of grace is to reestablish the control of our higher nature and bring about an internal integration. This is achieved psychologically through establishment and maintenance of ego-control over the energies of the instinctive part of our psychic structure. Consequently, spiritual identity implies such ego-integration, but I hasten to add that personal identity implies the same thing. In other words, spiritual identity builds upon personal identity.

It should be evident, from this partial analysis, that there is a reciprocal relationship between personal identity on the natural level and spiritual identity on the supernatural. In psychological terms, then, spiritual identity builds upon personal identity. There are two consequences of this relationship. First, the degree of spiritual identity which one can achieve may be limited by, or related to, the degree of prior personal identity achieved. Second, spiritual identity is in some sense perfective of personal identity.

An explanation of these propositions will clarify their relationship. If spiritual identity is dependent on the ego's capacity to exercise its synthetic function autonomously, then the extent to which the ego has contributed to a sense of identity is a measure of that capacity. Therefore, the mature ego is more autonomous, more in control of the energies at its disposal, and so more capable of bringing about self-modifications motivated through grace. Putting it another way, the higher degree of ego-control in the mature ego permits it to utilize more effectively the energies put at its disposal through grace.

Spiritual identity is perfective of personal identity in the sense that the added energizing activity of grace enables the ego to function more perfectly due to the greater energy resources at its disposal. Furthermore, the structures and functions associated with spiritual identity are identical with those associated with personal identity, but are raised to a higher level of activity and relationship. This underlines the point I have already made—that grace is operating in and through ego functions. The increase of energy which the ego can channel into these functions underlies the ego's capacity to engage in the divine relationship and to form a spiritual identity.

This analysis of the development of a spiritual identity has had one objective: to demonstrate that a psychological analysis of the process of spiritual growth under the influence of grace is feasible. The details of the analysis are secondary. Erikson's conception of the development of personal identity is not complete and in time will undoubtedly yield to a better analysis. The development of spiritual identity as I have described it may also be inadequate; it, too, will yield to a better understanding and more refined analysis. But I hope that the basic principles of analysis, particularly those governing the integration of natural psychic functions with the psychological effects of grace, may serve as guidelines for the formulation of any theory of the psychological aspects of grace.

The implications of this analysis are clear. The psychological preoccupations of our times have sometimes led us away from an appreciation of the meaningfulness and pertinence of God's grace for those very concerns. But in terms of the foregoing analysis, our highest potentiality for effective and mature psychological functioning, our greatest capacity for self-realization, for the achievement of true personal autonomy and freedom, lie specifically in our cooperation with and responsiveness to the promptings of grace.

Dimensions of Religious Experience

FAITH

Faith and Subjectivity

Faith and Experience

Faith Development

Psychology and Faith

Faith and Identity

HOPE

The Theology of Hope

The Psychology of Hope

The Psychopathology of Hope

The Psychotherapy of Hopelessness

Hope and Faith

PART 1

FAITH

CHAPTER 5

Faith and Subjectivity

The Problem of Faith

Faith has been a major problem at all stages of religious history. Abraham was the archetype of faith in the old dispensation, and Paul, standing at the threshold or the new, made faith a major theme of his preaching. At the birth of the Reformation, the rending of Christendom centered on the issue of faith. The preoccupation throughout this long history has been primarily ontological—within the limitations of multiple variations and approaches. There are ontological questions concerning the nature of faith, the metaphysical definition of faith, the relation of faith and grace, etc. There are also epistemological questions: What is the proper object of faith? How is assent possible without evidence? How do we achieve certitude, or what kind of certitude do we achieve, in the act of faith?

The intention in this study is quite different from the concerns that have dominated traditional approaches. Here, our approach is specifically psychological, focusing on the motivational, genetic, topological, structural, dynamic aspects of faith. We seek to explore its relations to the vital structure of the mind, and to examine its functions within the psychic economy. Faith is, after all, a human response to a revelation. It therefore has a psychology that relates it to the spectrum of human psychological functioning. By exploring and asking questions about the psychology of faith, we can further illumine its structure and intelligibility.

Although the psychological consideration of faith is formally distinct and independent from traditional approaches, it depends in many ways on those approaches. The rich content of traditional formulations provides the basis for the psychological consideration. It also provides insights than can direct the psychological inquiry. Thus, a true psychology of faith cannot be worked out in isolation from a theology and ontology of faith. It depends on them and seeks their guidance through an uncharted country.

Another emphasis can be profitably made in distinguishing the psychological from more traditional perspectives. Psychology is fundamentally an empirical science. Its formulations are in the form of generalizations, and its perspective is that of extension rather than intention. It is concerned with the full spectrum of expression of the phenomena it studies, and with the varieties of interindividual variation. It focuses on human beings rather than on human nature. The more traditional philosophico-theological approaches work with abstractions, natures, universals, formally stated in terms of natures and properties, intention rather than extension. Thus, where tradition can speak of the nature of faith and the nature of man as substantial and universal concepts, the psychologist can speak only of faith as a phenomenal range of experience having an inner diversity as well as generality. It is a shared experience involving shared meanings and symbolic elements, but it is an experience that is unique to each person. Within the context of diversity the psychologist seeks the more common elements and tries to relate them to known psychological principles.

Moreover, the term, faith, can have a diversity of referents. The theological and philosophical history of the arguments over faith is a saga of diversity in definition and concept. Here, we are concerned with faith as a disposition in the human psyche. The problem is to clarify what is encompassed in such a disposition. There has been a tendency in the Christian tradition to intellectualize faith—to conceive of it as an intellectual act, an assent to the revealed truth, an assertion of the revealed truth as true. Other apsects of the human response are regarded as preparatory or consequent to this central intellective act, but they are not faith. The Lutheran argument over faith and works seems to have been fundamentally an issue of whether faith was only the central act, or whether it included more.

From a psychological point of view, to isolate a central element (an intellectual element at that) and consider it alone is to invite sterility. There can be little argument with the centrality of the intellectual dimension in faith, but as a human response it embraces the totality of our psychic life. Our intellect does not function as a disembodied phantom. Our intellectual response, particularly in the act of faith, is an expression of the whole person—of the rich complexity, drives, needs, instincts, defenses, and capacities, and the constellation of these that is uniquely personal. Faith, then, even if one seeks to isolate and analyze the intellective element, derives from and reflects other aspects and levels of the psychic organization.

When we speak of "faith," therefore, we are referring to an organized sequence of acts that derives from various levels of the mind and integrates the diverse functions of these structures into a unified, organized whole. We can call this organized sequence a "process," thereby emphasizing that the organization involves sequence; it cannot be conceived as a static organization, frozen in a moment of time, but is a dynamic activity.

Faith and Reason

The problematic of faith has always been cast in terms that set off the act of faith as being in a different order from the ordinary run of human experience. It involves a firm assent to and acceptance of a truth and a reality without the usual props of intellectual conviction. One cannot ascribe reasons or provide arguments or point to compelling evidences; the believer is rationally vulnerable. As a consequence, faith is set off from and opposed to "reason." Reason arrives at its convictions and certitudes by a process of investigation, argument, and proof. Faith appeals to nothing outside itself. Believers believe because they have faith, and disbelievers disbelieve because they have no proof.

No thinker has better captured the absurdity of faith than did that remarkable preanalytic psychoanalyst, Kierkegaard. His ruminations on the faith of Abraham and the challenge to that faith in the directive to kill Isaac (his only son and the fruit of his old age, the promise of his heritage) reveal to us the complexities of faith and its place in the broader context of human existence (Kierkegaard 1941).

Abraham's faith was a paradox, because his belief was a belief in the absurd, "He believed by virtue of the absurd; for all human reckoning had long since ceased to function" (Kierkegaard 1941). One is reminded of the Tertullian *credo quia absurdum*. Faith reaches beyond the illumination of reason into the darkness of paradox. Abraham is in no sense a tragic hero, because tragedy is mediated and calculable. One can understand tragedy, but one cannot understand faith.

The last outpost of reason was what Kierkegaard called infinite resignation. Faith presupposes the resignation of all finite goods and dissociation from all wish-fulfillments. One who has not made this resignation does not have faith. Only in such an infinite resignation does man begin to catch a glimpse of his true validity, and only then does it become possible for him to grasp his existence by virtue of faith. One must stand at the edge of the precipice if he is to leap into the dark chasm. Thus, faith is not an emotion precisely because it requires resignation. It is not an instinct of the heart, but a paradox of life and existence. Faith is not a suspension of reason, but a reaching beyond it.

The paradox is rooted in the antithesis of God and man. Faith is a submission to God that requires ethical maturity and the capacity for resignation, which leaves man with no recourse but the impossible. At this point the absurd begins. The paradox is that man, by reaching through the veil of dread into the emptiness of the absurd, finds a relation to God that is stripped of all the trappings of the finite; in this relation man finds the highest realization of himself. The further paradox is that beyond resignation man lives again in the finite, but by virtue of a faithful relation to God that derives in no sense from understanding. Faith is, therefore, the highest human passion—touching life at every point of our essential existence, transcending the calculations and illusions of worldly wisdom, grasping and immersing itself in the finitude of life (beyond withdrawal from the finite in resignation), triumphing over the dread that permeates man's finite existence.

The process of faith, then, embraces both resignation and belief, loss and restitution. The psychological insight into this sequence is profound. It pivots around the issue of the absurd, for this constitutes in a sense the borderline between resignation as a function of reason and the movement beyond resignation in faith. It is important to emphasize that faith does not dissolve or resolve the absurdity. If the absurd ceases to be absurd, faith ceases to be faith.

Psychologically speaking, the significant aspect of faith is its uncertainty. Faith is a category of life and existence rather than of thought. Human life is filled with uncertainties and conflict. Faith provides illumination, direction, and meaning to life; it is an affirmation of encounter and relation between God and man. But within this affirmation, which is a human one, there lie the shadows of self-deception, projection, denial, illusion, doubt—in short, uncertainty. In Kierkegaard's terms, however, these are categories of the finite, and they must be resigned before true absurdity and authentic faith can be achieved. But the resignation does not eliminate the shadows, nor does faith, in passing beyond resignation, eliminate them.

Faith is not a static position at which one arrives and into which one then settles comfortably. It is a dynamic, living process, a vital reality always in flux. Its grasp upon the certainties of its assertion is unstable and precarious. Abraham believed in virtue of the absurd, but his belief did not once and for all dispel the absurdity. The continuance and persistence of faith are impossible without the persistence of the absurd. And while faith in a sense triumphs over dread, it cannot annihilate that dread. Rather, the dread persists—modulated and surpassed, to be sure, but nonetheless remaining as a constant reminder of human fragility.

It is not surprising that the act of faith should be set off from reason and contrasted with it. But when we focus rather on the process, it is reasonable to shift the emphasis in two ways. Rather than conceiving "reason" in narrowly intellective terms, we can think of it in terms of all of the levels of psychic structure and organization that determine, in a loose sense, the process of faith. It becomes possible, therefore, to explore faith less in terms of its divergence from or contrast with reason, and more in terms of its continuities with reason. This is no more than to insert faith back into the living reality of human existence and to try to see it as it really is—not as a static abstraction of an ideal, but as an imperfect and fragile, dynamic and vital process that is (as Kierkegaard would have it) our highest passion.

Belief and Subjectivity

The discussion in Chapter 3 has brought us to the conclusion that religious belief has its proper place within the realm of transitional phenomena. Faith is neither a form of objective knowledge nor a form of purely subjective understanding—as Freud might have assumed. Transitional phenomena are neither subjective nor objective; they cannot be objective without sharing in human subjectivity, nor subjective without touching and including the realm of objectivity. Faith participates in illusion (Winnicott 1971; Meissner 1984).

No one has struggled more tellingly with the ambiguities of faith than Kierkegaard. He declared the relevance of subjectivity against the claims of objective systematic thinking. Reacting against the sweeping systematic rationalizations of Hegel, he laid the ground for the claims of individuality. Without discounting or devaluing the need for objective scientific accounts, he was exquisitely sensitive to the risks and limitations of an exclusively objective approach. He sought another approach, another kind of truth about man. Beyond the realm of objective reflection, there were fundamental questions about the meaning of existence, the nature of man, and the uses of freedom, which could not be addressed by scientific methods and could be approached only by "subjective reflection" or "existential thinking."

For Kierkegaard, subjectivity implies an inwardness or existential attitude in the individual psyche. The Augustinian implications of his position have been noted (Collins 1953); he gives the notion of the *homo interior* a specifically religious connotation, such that significant truth gained through inwardness and subjectivity is primarily an ethico-religious truth. In this sense, subjectivity implies a personal inward embrace of morality and religious life, an aspect of the reality of human nature that is not open to scientific inspection. Kierkegaard's understanding of subjectivity and individual reality culminates in his concept of faith.

In the face of the reductive claims of objectivity, he proclaimed (1846) a bold fundamental thesis, namely, that truth is subjectivity. He shifts the focus of the inquiry from the object of apprehension, the "what" of thinking, to the nature of the subject's relationship to what he thinks, the "how." Truth, in this view, becomes a question more of the individual's relationship to the object rather than of the validity of the object itself. It is this more decidedly ethical and personal kind of truth that Kierkegaard has in mind when he joins it to subjectivity.

There is, moreover, something unique and special about being a subject. There is also something special about being a lover or even a hero: "And yet, being a lover, a hero, and so forth, is precisely a prerogative of subjectivity; for one does not become a hero or a lover objectively" (1846:117). The same can be said of religious devoutness: devoutness inheres in subjectivity and no one ever becomes devout objectively. Kierkegaard comments (1846:178):

> When the question of truth is raised in an objective manner, reflection is directed objectively to the truth, as an object to which the knower is related . . . . When the question of the truth is raised subjectively, reflection is directed subjectively to the nature of the individual's relationship: if only the mode of this relationship is in the truth, the individual is in the truth, even if he should happen to be thus related to what is not true.

The knowledge of God is an example. Objectively, the question is whether the object of knowledge is, in fact, the true God. But subjectively, the question has more to do with whether the nature of the individual's knowledge reflects a relationship which is, in fact, a God-relationship. Here, the emphasis is less on what is known than on the individual's relationship, cognitively and personally, to what is known.

Kierkegaard does not abandon the realm of objectivity, but rather envisions the role of subjective truth as taking its point of departure from the point at which objective uncertainty arises. It is as though the process of understanding had reached a fork in the road at which objective knowledge must be placed in question. At such a point, there is objective uncertainty, but it is precisely this which increases the tension of subjective inwardness. The truth, then, takes on a special meaning: "An objective uncertainty held fast in an appropriation-process of the most passionate inwardness is the truth, the highest truth attainable for an existing individual . . . . The truth is precisely the venture which chooses an objective uncertainty with the passion of the infinite" (1846:182).

The commitment to individual truth and meaning must take place in relation to the residual objective uncertainty which can never be totally eliminated or absolved. This aspect is given poignant expression (1834–55:15):

> The thing is to understand myself, to see what God really wishes me to do; the thing is to find a truth which is true for me, to find the idea for which I can live and die. What would be the use of discovering so-called objective truth, or working through all the systems of philosophy and of being able, if required, to review them all and show up the inconsistencies within each system; what good would it do me to be able to develop a theory of the state and combine all the details into a single whole, and so construct a world in which I did not live, but only held up to the view of others; what good would it do me to be able to explain the meaning of Christianity if it had no deeper significance for me and for my life; what good would it do me if truth stood before me, cold and naked, not caring whether I recognized her or not, and producing in me a shudder of fear rather than a trusting devotion?

In other words, what does it profit a man if he gains the whole world of objective knowledge, and suffers the loss of himself? For Kierkegaard, existential truth is practical, never completed, and basically paradoxical. It is concerned with human actions and self-development rather than with the making or transformation of external objects; with individual human existence rather than with general laws and impersonal processes. Its ultimate aim is the cultivation of the self, especially in its free relationships with other human selves, and utimately with God. For the human subject, this remains unfinished business since man cannot be regarded as a completed reality, but rather as evolving in a continuing, dynamic process of becoming and striving. Existential truth is less a body of truth than the manner in which the subject applies this truth to himself and his inner life. Human life is a continual process of adaptation, change, loss, and unremitting striving.

A fundamental dimension of Kierkegaard's thinking is his notion of the individual—for him, specifically, the notion of an individual before God. In order to be a human being, one must also be an existing individual. There are two ways in which one can be such an individual (and this becomes a fundamental option, a basic either-or, in Kierkegaard's thinking): *either* he can forget that he is such an existing individual and so he becomes a comic figure, since man must exist whether he wills it or not; *or* he can focus his entire energy on the realization of the fact that he is such an existing individual. The primary concern, then, is not what it means to be human in some general or abstract sense, for this would be an objective question, but rather "what it means that you and I and he are human beings, each one for himself" (1846:109).

Ethical choice is central to the notion of the individual and subjectivity. For Kierkegaard, the manner of choice, not its object, is of primary importance. Ethical choice is absolute, that is, the choice is made in some unlimited way so that the individual assumes complete responsibility for it: "If you will understand me aright, I should like to say that in making a choice, it is not so much a question of choosing the right as of the energy, the earnestness, the pathos with which one chooses. Thereby the personality announces its inner infinity, and thereby, in turn, the personality is consolidated" (1843a, part 2:171). Such an act of choice is unavoidably an expression of the ethical.

The only absolute either-or is the choice between good and evil, and that is an ethical choice. Ethical choice is opposed to aesthetic choice, which Kierkegaard describes as either entirely immediate or as losing itself in the multifarious. Again, it is not a choice of good as opposed to evil, but a choice between good and evil or their exclusion:

> It is, therefore, not so much a question of choosing between willing the good *or* the evil, as of choosing to will, but by this in turn the good and the evil are posited. He who chooses the ethical chooses the good; but here the good is entirely abstract, only its being posited, and hence it does not follow by any means that the chooser cannot in turn choose the evil, in spite of the fact that he chose the good. Here you see again how important it is that a choice be made, and the crucial thing is not deliberation, but the baptism of the will which lifts up the choice into the ethical. (1843a, part 2:173)

Through the medium of ethical choice the individual becomes an individual; he is detached from the crowd, he is made aware of himself as a vital personal center of responsibility and selfhood.

Kierkegaard undoubtedly saw the risk in his emphasis on subjectivity and individuality, especially the danger of self-isolation and withdrawal from human society. The *Journals* contain frequent references and cautions regarding the overextension of his thesis. He compared his own vocation to that of the spy in enemy territory or the sentry on the lonely battlefield—circumstances which amplify the need for inner resourcefulness and the emphasis on the individual. He reviled any appeal to public opinion or mass movements as criteria of truth. He was troubled by the tendency to adopt a herd mentality as the result of social forces which led toward egalitarian ideals and the consequent engulfment of the individual in the political mass—the democratic majority, the race, the class, the nation, or even humanity itself.

Human existence loses all inherent value when it is absorbed into the totality, gaining its meaning and purpose not from itself but as a part of the whole. Public opinion then takes precedence over individual judgment, and men become "cipher-men," demoralized and unhuman. Individual values and responsibility are diminished and decisions are made by an appeal to numbers and impersonal factors. Kierkegaard found no truth in the masses; the crowd was untruth.

Although the spectre of the mass man is a threat to human existence and value, Kierkegaard insisted that every person in the crowd has the inner power to become an individual, a true and authentic self. His *Christian Discourses* are addressed to individuals, that is, to every human being precisely as an individual. For him, the call of Christianity to mankind is for each and every human being to become an individual.

The culmination of existential truth and the highest act of man's individual subjectivity take place in the act and assent of faith. For Kierkegaard, faith is man's supreme passion and his highest, most meaningful act of existence, in which his entire self is engaged in a temporal and historical process which is a synthesis of the temporal and the eternal, and in which the believer becomes identified with Christ. Faith implies an act of the will, a fundamental choice in which man not only radically expresses his subjectivity, but also posits himself in his choosing to will the infinite.

The paradox is that faith does all this by virtue of the absurd and not by virtue of human understanding. The paradox of faith is cast in terms of the contrast between the knight of faith and the knight of infinite resignation. The knight of infinite resignation is like the ancient Stoic or the modern romantic hero who renounces everything in life without any hope of getting it back. He therefore denies himself the finite, the world and everything in it, and lives in the infinite. In contrast, the knight of faith undergoes an infinite resignation as well: he gives up everything, as his companion knight has done, but at the same time he believes by virtue of the absurd that he will gain it back in the end. So, he goes about living his life in a manner consistent with this assumption. His is a double movement—both of infinite resignation and of continuing to live in the finite.

The model of the knight of faith was Abraham, whose profound faith and obedience to God's command to slay his son Isaac is the subject of Kierkegaard powerful discourse on faith, *Fear and Trembling* (1843b). The first movement in Abraham's faith was infinite resignation. Kierkegaard writes (1843b:48):

Abraham I cannot understand, in a certain sense there is nothing I can learn from him but astonishment. If people fancy that by considering the *outcome* of this story they might be moved to believe, they deceive themselves and want to swindle God out of the first movement of faith, the infinite resignation. They would suck worldly wisdom out of the paradox. Perhaps one or another may succeed in that, for our age is not willing to stop with faith, but with its miracle of turning water into wine; it goes further, it turns wine into water.

But the movements of faith lie beyond infinite resignation. In faith man chooses and commits himself "in virtue of the absurd":

> For the movements of faith must constantly be made by virtue of the absurd, yet in such a way, be it observed, that one does not lose the finite but gains it every inch.... Hail to him who can make these movements, he performs the marvelous and I shall never grow tired of admiring him, whether he be Abraham or a slave in Abraham's house; whether he be a professor of philosophy or a servant-girl, I look only at the movements. But at them I *do* look and do not let myself be fooled, either by myself or by any other man. (1843b:48–49)

Kierkegaard's dialectic on faith, then, turns around the two poles of infinite resignation and choosing in virtue of the absurd. Of the knight of faith he writes (1843b:51):

> And yet, and yet I could become furious over it—for envy, if for no other reason—because the man has made and in every instant is making the movements of infinity. With infinite resignation he has drained the cup of life's profound sadness, he knows the bliss of the infinite, he senses the pain of renouncing everything, the dearest things he possesses in the world, and yet finiteness tastes to him just as good as to one who never knew anything higher.... And yet, and yet the whole earthly form he exhibits is a new creation by virtue of the absurd. He resigned everything infinitely, and then he grasped everything again by virtue of the absurd.

Infinite resignation leads to the threshold of faith and is the last stage prior to faith. Those who have not made this movement have not faith, "for only in the infinite resignation do I become clear to myself with respect to my eternal validity, and only then can there be any question of grasping existence by virtue of faith" (Bretall:125).

Thus, faith in a fundamental way participates in a paradox, in that it places the particular (that is, the individual) above the universal: "Faith is precisely this paradox, that the individual as the particular is higher than the universal, it is justified over against it, is not subordinate but superior ... " (1843:66)

In faith there is a suspension and transcending of the ethical as universal. The story of Abraham contains what Kierkegaard calls a "teleological suspension of the ethical," a suspension of the basic principle that a father should love his son and not kill him. The difference between Abraham, who suspends the ethical and goes beyond it, and the tragic hero is that the tragic hero remains within the ethical. The tragic conflict is between one expression of an ethical *telos* and another.

Abraham went beyond the ethical entirely, but he did so in terms of a higher *telos* outside and beyond the ethical. Abraham's action cannot be brought into relation with the universal; it is a purely personal and individual action. Kierkegaard (1843b:77) sums up the story of Abraham:

> The story of Abraham contains therefore a teleological suspension of the ethical. As the individual, he became higher than the universal: this is the paradox which does not permit of mediation. It is just as inexplicable how he got into it as it is inexplicable how he remained in it. If such is not the position of Abraham, then he is not even a tragic hero, but a murderer. To want to continue to call him the father of faith, to talk of this to people who do not concern themselves with anything but words, is thoughtless. A man can become a tragic hero by his own powers—but not a knight of faith. When a man enters upon the way, in a certain sense the hard way of the tragic hero, many will be able to give him counsel; to him who follows the narrow way of faith no one can give counsel, him no one can understand. Faith is a miracle, and yet no man is excluded from it; for that in which all human life is unified is passion, and faith is a passion.

In driving a wedge between the finite and the infinite, between infinite resignation and faith, between the universal and the individual, and between the ethical and faith, Kierkegaard sets up a radical (perhaps even too radical) dissociation of faith from any form of reason or rational process (Edwards 1971). He writes (1846:116):

> In this way Christianity protests every form of objectivity; it desires that the subject should be infinitely concerned about himself. It is subjectivity that Christianity is concerned with, and it is only in subjectivity that its truth exists, if it exists at all; objectively, Christianity has absolutely no existence. If its truth happens to be in only a single subject, it exists in him alone; and there is a greater Christian joy in heaven over this one individual than over universal history and the system, which as objective entities are incommensurable with that which is Christian.

The task of becoming a subject is extremely arduous since it must work against so many ingrained resistances in human nature and in society. It runs counter to the admired wisdom of the age that sets before the subject the task of increasingly divesting himself of his subjectivity so as to become more and more objective; Christianity teaches that the way is to become subjective, that is, to become a subject in truth.

But faith asserts itself only in virtue of the absurd. With this, logic and objective inquiry cannot grapple. Hear Kierkegaard (1846:189):

> Suppose a man who wishes to acquire faith; let the comedy begin. He wishes to have faith, but he wishes also to safeguard himself by means of an objective inquiry and its approximation-process. What happens? With the help of the approximation-process the absurd becomes something different: it becomes probable, it becomes increasingly probable, it becomes extremely and emphatically probable. Now he is ready to believe it, and he ventures to claim for himself that he does not believe as shoemakers and tailors and simple folk believe, but only after long deliberation. Now he is ready to believe it; and lo, now it has become precisely impossible to believe it. Anything that is almost probable, or probable, or extremely and emphatically probable, is something he can almost know, or as good as know, or extremely and emphatically almost *know* but it is impossible to *believe*. For the absurd it is the object of faith and the only object that can be believed.

Thus, to return to an earlier formula, becoming and being a Christian are not defined objectively in terms of the *what* that is believed (*fides quae*), nor subjectively by an approximation to probabilities. They are defined in terms of the *how* of belief (*fides qua*). They are not determined by what has gone on in the individual, but by what the individual has undergone. Kierkegaard summarizes this sentiment and perspective as follows (1846:540):

> Subjectively, what it is to become a Christian is defined thus:
> The decision lies in the subject. The appropriation is the paradoxical inwardness which is specifically different from all other inwardness. The thing of being a Christian is not determined by the *what* of Christianity but by the *how* of the Christian. This *how* can only correspond with one thing, the absolute paradox. There is therefore no vague talk to the effect that being a Christian is to accept, and to accept, and to accept quite differently, to appropriate, to believe, to appropriate by faith quite differently (all of them purely rhetorical and fictitious definitions); but to *believe* is specifically different from all other appropriation and inwardness. *Faith is the objective uncertainty along with the repulsion of the absurd held fast in the passion of inwardness, which precisely is inwardness potentiated to the highest degree.* This formula fits only the believer, no one else, not a lover, not an enthusiast, not a thinker, but simply and solely the believer who is related to the absolute paradox.

Despair versus Faith

One of the most powerful aspects of Kierkegaard's argument regarding subjectivity and existential truth comes in his analysis of despair, the radical converse of faith. The man in despair is essentially double-minded: he has two wills, such that he is unable to will one thing; specifically, he is unable to will to be himself. In *Sickness unto Death*, Kierkegaard writes (1849:153):

> A despairing man wants despairingly to be himself. But if he despairingly wants to be himself, he will not want to get rid of himself. Yes, so it seems; but if one inspects more closely, one perceives that after all the contradiction is the same. That self which he despairingly wills to be is a self which he is not (for to will to be that self which one truly is is indeed the opposite of despair); what he really wills is to tear his self away from the Power which constituted it. But notwithstanding all his despair, this he is unable to do; notwithstanding all the efforts of despair, the Power is the stronger, and it compels him to be the self he does not will to be. But for all that he wills to be rid of himself, to be rid of the self which he is, in order to be the self he himself has chanced to choose. To be the *self* as he wills to be would be his delight (though in another sense it would be equally despair), but to be compelled to be *self* as he does not will to be is his torment, namely, that he cannot get rid of himself.

The immediate man is immersed in the earthly and finite; he has no infinite consciousness of the self or of the nature or fact of despair. His despair is passive. Kierkegaard says of him (1849:184):

> The *immediate* man (insofar as immediacy is to be found without any reflection) is merely soulishly determined, his self or he himself is a something included along with "the other" in the compass of the temporal and the worldly, and it has only an illusory appearance of possessing in it something eternal. Thus, the self coheres immediately with "the other", wishing, desiring, enjoying, etc., but passively.

Such a man acquires some slight understanding of life by learning to imitate others around him, seeing how they live their lives, and by mimicry he, too, manages to live after a fashion. Kierkegaard (1849:186) focuses this form of despair specifically in terms of a pathology of the self:

> This form of despair is: in despair at not willing to be oneself; or still lower, in despair at not willing to be a self; or lowest of all, in despair at willing to be another than himself. Properly speaking, immediacy has no self, it does not recognize itself, so neither can it recognize itself again; it terminates

therefore preferably in the romantic. When immediacy despairs, it possesses not even enough self to wish or to dream that it had become what it did not become. The immediate man helps himself in a different way: he wishes to be another.

If the immediate man has some degree of self-reflection, his despair may be somewhat modified. There may be some degree of consciousness of himself and of his despair: but the despair is essentially a matter of weakness and passivity. It is a form of not wanting to be oneself. His degree of self-reflection allows him to become aware of himself as essentially different from his environment and its external aspects. But when such a soul comes to the point of accepting himself, he runs afoul of one or another difficulty. He finds himself without perfection, and this frightens him away. He is left in a state of despair—the despair of weakness, of passive suffering of the self which he can only do his best to defend. Kierkegaard says of him (1849:188–189), "So then he despairs, and his despair is: not willing to be himself. On the other hand, it strikes him as ridiculous to want to be another; he maintains the relationship to his self—to that extent reflection has identified him with the self."

If man may despair about the earthly, he may also despair about the eternal or about himself. As Kierkegaard observes (1849:195):

> This despair represents quite an advance. If the former was the *despair of weakness,* this is the *despair over his weakness,* although it still remains as to its nature under the category "despair of weakness".... This difference consists in the fact that the foregoing form has the consciousness of weakness as its final consciousness, whereas in this case consciousness does not come to a stop here, but potentiates itself to a new consciousness, a *consciousness* of its weakness. The despairer understands that it is weakness to take the earthly so much to heart, that it is weakness to despair. But then, instead of veering sharply away from despair to faith, humbling himself before God for his weakness, he is more deeply absorbed in despair and despairs over his weakness.

Ultimately, there is despair over oneself, for despair about the eternal is impossible without some concept of self. If a man is to despair over himself, he must in some degree be conscious of having a self. But it is precisely this over which he despairs—not over something earthly, but over himself. With this greater consciousness, there is a greater knowledge of what despair is, that it is a loss of the eternal and oneself. This despair too is despair at not willing to be oneself.

Beyond this despair of weakness, Kierkegaard places a further form of despair which becomes conscious of the reason why it does not want to be itself; this is the despair of willing despairingly to be oneself—namely, defiance. Kierkegaard comments (1849:201):

> First comes despair over the earthly or something earthly, then despair over oneself about the eternal. Then comes defiance, which really is despair by the aid of the eternal, the despairing abuse of the eternal in the self to the point of being despairingly determined to be oneself. But just because it is despair by the aid of the eternal, it lies in a sense very close to the true, and just because it lies very close to the true, it is infinitely remote. The despair which is a passage way to faith is also by the aid of the eternal: by the aid of the eternal the self has courage to lose itself in order to gain itself. Here on the contrary it is not willing to begin by losing itself, but wills to be itself.

This despair is conscious of itself since it comes not from something external as a form of suffering, but directly from the self. This willing of oneself in despair requires a consciousness of what Kierkegaard calls the infinite self, the self man despairingly wills to be. As he puts it (1849:201–2):

> By the aid of this infinite form the self despairingly wills to dispose of itself or to create itself, to make itself the self it wills to be, distinguishing in the concrete self what it will and what it will not accept. The man's concrete self, or his concretion, has in fact necessity and limitations, it is this perfectly definite thing, with these faculties, dispositions, etc. But by the aid of the infinite form, the negative self, he wills first to undertake to refashion the whole thing, in order to get out of it in this way a self such as he wants to have, produced by the aid of the infinite form of the negative self—and it is thus he wills to be himself.

But such a self can never become any more than it is in itself; hence in its despairing efforts to will to be itself, it ends up by becoming, in fact, no self. Rather than succeeding in becoming itself, in fact, it becomes no more than a hypothetical self:

> The self is its own lord and master, so it is said, its own lord, and precisely this is despair, but so also is what it regards as its pleasure and enjoyment. However, by closer inspection one easily ascertains that this ruler is a king without a country, he rules really over nothing; . . . . So the despairing self is constantly building nothing but castles in the air, it fights only in the air. (1849:203)

Thus, the despair of this despairing self is precisely a despair at willing to be oneself. If there is in this self any fault or flaw or form of suffering, the negative self, the infinite form of the self, will try to cast this away or pretend that it doesn't exist, and will want to know nothing about it. But this tactic has little success; like Prometheus, the self is chained to its servitude.

But this despair which wills desperately to be itself is not willing to hope. The individual offended at the whole of existence, and in spite of his suffering he wills not to be himself without it, for this would be to move in the direction of resignation. So he defiantly wills the whole of his existence, wills himself as suffering, almost defying his torment. He will not hope in the possibility of help, let alone seek help by virtue of the absurd, by virtue of the fact that for God all things are possible. Rather than seek help, he would prefer to be himself, with whatever tortures and torments that choice may entail. The more consciously such a sufferer determines in despair to be himself, so much the more does his despair become demoniac. Kierkegaard describes this process (1849: 205–6):

> A self which in despair is determined to be itself winces at one pain or another which simply cannot be taken away or separated from its concrete self. Precisely upon this torment the man directs his whole passion, which at last becomes a demoniac rage. Even if at this point God in Heaven and all his angels were to offer to help him out of it—no, now he doesn't want it, now it is too late, he once would have given everything to be rid of this torment but was made to wait, now that's all past, now he would rather rage against everything, he, the one man in the whole existence who is the most unjustly treated, to whom it is especially important to have his torment at hand, important that no one should take it from him—for thus he can convince himself that he is in the right. This at last becomes so firmly fixed in his head that for a very peculiar reason he is afraid of eternity—for the reason, namely, that it might rid him of his (demoniacally understood) infinite advantage over other men, his (demoniacally understood) justification for being what he is.

This does not explain faith in any sense, but it does set the stage for our further exploration of the implications and derivations of faith. In so doing, we are not so much reaching for an understanding of faith as relating it to processes and functions that we can understand. And if it is fair to say with Kierkegaard (who echoes a substantial Christian tradition) that faith cannot be understood because it transcends the categories of understanding, it is also fair to say that faith is after all a human process with a history and psychology that do not transcend understanding.

The Pathology of Despair

In clinical terms, Kierkegaard's formulations, despite his unique vocabulary, come close to a phenomenology of clinical conditions that can be easily recognized from a psychoanalytic perspective. The analysis of despair readily translates into more clinical terms. At the core of despair there is an inability to will onself. The clinician can recognize here a core disturbance that is found, with variations, throughout a broad spectrum of psychopathology. The inability to will oneself in an honest, authentic, and responsible manner lies at the core of many neurotic difficulties. For the sake of exposition, I will translate this difficulty into terms derived from the vocabulary of internalization, which may bring us closest to the implications of Kierkegaard's account.

From the perspective of internalization and its correlative context of object relationships, the individual human psyche develops through the progressive organization and integration of internalizations deriving in important ways from the ongoing experience of objects in the individual's human environment (Meissner 1979). The synthetic aggregation of these internalizations gradually gives rise to a self-organization within the psyche, which corresponds to a sense of self with varying degrees of autonomy and serves as the basis for the differentiation between the self and external objects. The important forms of internalization are introjections and identifications, both of which contribute in major ways to the self's organization and functioning.

The underlying motivation of identification is the wish to be like an object or model. The parallel motivation underlying introjection is based more on a wish to be the same as the object or to possess whatever quality or attribute the object possesses. Consequently, identification takes place at a more advanced and differentiated level of functioning than introjection. The attempt to be like a model takes a secondary process pattern of organization, and the object which the individual wishes to resemble is perceived, maintained, and tolerated as separate. Thus identification involves a reasonable approximation of selective characteristics which are relatively well integrated into the structure of the self-organization. The wish to be like the object stems from a relatively positive affective attachment to and involvement with the object; this would obviously include positive attitudes and emotional inclinations such as admiration, respect, love, friendship, and so on (Meissner 1972, 1981).

While identification seems to function more on a level of secondary process organization, introjection tends to be significantly more open to primary process influences. Consequently, introjection is more global and less selective in what it takes from the object, with the immediate result that what is derived from the object through introjection is not always easily integrated with the rest of the developing organization of the individual's ego. Introjection is more open and susceptible to the influence of drive derivatives, whether libidinal, aggressive, or narcissistic, so that it seems to be less reality based, more magical in its implications and consequences. It aims at identity with the object rather than mere similarity, tends to be more global and less differentiated, is less well structured and delineated in terms of the boundaries between subject and object representations, and is generally more vulnerable to regressive and instinctual pulls. Thus, the introjective configuration tends to be more defensively organized, more specifically responsive to underlying defensive needs (Meissner 1971, 1983).

The classic situation in which introjection predominates over identification is in the mourning of a lost object, particularly one which is narcissistically invested and ambivalently regarded. To defend against the sense of loss of such a significant object, the individual introjects aspects of the object and assumes them as an acquired part of the individual's own sense of self. Thus, in Freud's analysis of the dynamics of melancholia (1917), the withdrawal of narcissistic cathexis carries along the original ambivalence toward that object which now becomes directed toward the self. The self now begins to experience itself as having the characteristics of the lost object. Freud later applied this analysis to the internalization which gives rise to the superego in relatively normal development (1923). Thus, superego formation is one of the major classic loci in which introjection was a major contributing mechanism.

The sense of self, of what and who one is, arises out of the integration of these introjections and identifications. When the pattern of introjections acquired over the course of one's developmental history is affectively harmonious and positively tinged, it fosters a relatively unconflicted and positive sense of self which can serve as the basis for a harmonious and well-functioning internal psychic integration and for healthy adaptation to one's environment. However, when these introjective configurations arise out of situations of conflict, tension, or other forms of dysphoria or disharmony in relationships with significant objects, the introjective organization takes on a strongly defensive character and tends to be discolored by instinctual imbalances and pathogenic defensive organization. Phenomenologically, such an individual develops a sense of self characterized by a variety of pathogenic traits, such as feelings of inadequacy, vulnerability, worthlessness, extreme sensitivity and pride, grandiosity, excessive dependency, hostility and rage, shame—and a host of similar affect-ladened characteristics which derive from the internalization of elements that originated in distorted relationships with significant objects (Meissner 1978).

The man who despairs is unable to will himself, that is, his own true, authentic sense of self. Rather, he wills a self which is not himself: from the perspective of internalization, he wills that self-organization which has evolved around the core pathogenic introjects and which he has taken to be himself, but which essentially is not. As the configuration of pathogenic introjects has developed, it has given rise to a whole complex of feelings, attitudes, and fantasies which provide the substance of the sense of self by which the individual leads his life. This sense of self forms the internal regulating principle by which he integrates his internal reactions and provides the basis for patterns of behavior and expression. For example, the depressed patient, who considers himself worthless and unloved, will seek out situations, find the appropriate objects, and provoke reactions and circumstances that reinforce these feelings. His experiences, which by all counts are essentially no different from the ordinary range of good and bad human experiences, can be transformed by him, through imagination and fantasy, into experiences which reenunciate and confirm his inner conviction about himself.

The work of analysis entails stripping away aspects of this pathological organization, tracing their origins in the individual's life experience, unearthing the usually hidden and unconscious motivations which preserve and reinforce this pathogenic configuration; the aim is to enable the individual little by little to abandon his attachment to them and to open up inner possibilities and potentialities for some new configuration that will be healthier and more adaptive. But the man of despair who wills this pathogenic configuration and clings to it in the face of efforts to pull him away from it, can only will the self that he sees and senses; it is his misfortune that this pathogenic self is not his real self.

So Kierkegaard's immediate man does not inwardly possess an autonomous sense of self which he can affirm as truly his own. Rather, he lives by fitting in with the expectations and demands of his environment, or by attaching himself to others as if the power of existence lay in them and he could achieve it for himself only by his attachment to them. Thus, the immediate man lives a life of sorts, but it is a false life, a pseudo-life based on his need to comply and imitate; his life is truly not his own but is dictated by forces around him or imitates other lives. Thus, the self he wills is not truly his own.

Kierkegaard's description of this condition is reminiscent of some familiar schizoid variants in the clinical situation. The schizoid individual is caught on the horns of a need-fear dilemma: an intense need for and dependence on objects and an equally intense fear of engulfment, of being swallowed up and consumed by them. Such a patient complains of feeling isolated and cut off, of being shut out, strange; of an inner emptiness, a life which seems futile, meaningless, leading nowhere and accomplishing nothing. The schizoid person cannot effectively choose his own self as involved with and related to objects. External relationships are affectively empty and characterized by emotional withdrawal. The individual draws behind a defensive shell into a hidden inner world so that his conscious sense of himself is emptied of any real vital feeling and capacity for involvement, and so seems to have become unreal. His attitude to the world around him is one of noninvolvement and mere observation, without any real feeling, attachment, or participation.

Two prominent variants of this schizoid condition are the "false-self" organization, described by Winnicott (1960), and the "as if" personality, defined originally by Deutsch (1942). In the false-self variant, there is a turning away from interpersonal relationships out of a need to preserve the sense of inner autonomy and individuation. The false-self is related to and involved with the external environment and real objects, while the true self inhabits the inner core of the personality and remains hidden away from the scrutiny of outside observers. The false-self is erected essentially to protect and preserve the true self against losing its sense of subjectivity, vitality, and inner autonomy. The schizoid dilemma arises because the inner autonomy and authenticity of the true self is threatened by engulfment in its relationships to objects. The false-self, operating as a facade, manages to survive through compliance. This compliance forms a substitute way of relating to objects and of dealing with the demands of the external environment, but it is at once fallacious, unreal, and fragile. The behavior that derives from this false-self often seems empty and lacking in vitality or significance; it may also serve as a source of deep inner desperation and hopelessness.

Deutsch's account of the as-if personality focused on the impoverishment of emotional relationships which these character types manifest. These patients seem lacking in wholeness or genuineness, and yet their lives seem to move along as if they were complete. Deutsch (1942:263) commented:

> Outwardly the person seems normal. There is nothing to suggest any kind of disorder, behavior is not unusual, intellectual abilities appear unimpaired, emotional expressions are well-ordered and appropriate. But despite all this, something intangible and indefinable obtrudes between the person and his fellows and invariably gives rise to the question, "What is wrong".

For such individuals, relationships are devoid of warmth, emotions seem formal and stereotyped, like those of an actor who is well-trained in playing his part but lacks the necessary spark to make it come to life. The relationship to the world and the people in it is based on an almost child-like imitation. The result is a passivity to the demands of the environment and a plastic capacity to mold one's self and one's behavior to fit such external expectations. The attachment to objects can often be adhesive, but there is no real warmth or affection, and this creates such emptiness and dullness that the partner often breaks off the relationship precipitously. When he is thus abandoned, the as-if person may display a more or less spurious affective reaction or a total absence of such reaction. In any case, the object is soon replaced with a new one, and the process repeats itself.

Kierkegaard's immediate man, who manages to live a life based on compliance and mimicry, is left in despair—despair at not willing to be himself or even to have a self, or to be something other than himself. His is a false self. Clinically, the issues involved in this spectrum of alternatives can be recognized as fundamentally narcissistic. Such a despairing individual as the immediate man is unwilling to choose himself because he does not find that a satisfactory choice. It is not good enough. He is unwilling to accept himself with all of his weaknesses, imperfections, shortcomings, inadequacies, and limitations. He holds out for something better, nobler, more ideal, closer to the perfection he envisions and desires for himself.

Kierkegaard defines one extreme defensive posture in this context of narcissistic entitlement and adherence in terms of defiance, that is, the will to be oneself despairingly. Clinically, this is akin to the paranoid disorders. The paranoid patient stakes a defiant claim on his own individuality, specialness, and difference. Here, the self defiantly proclaims itself to be what it wills to be and rejects, often angrily and destructively, what it cannot accept within itself. It retreats to a sense of self embedded in grandiosity and often sets up against the rest of the world in embattled hostility. Such a person cannot accept his true self at all, but must substitute for it a hypothetical self, a self such as he wills it to be, not as he is.

What is entailed in the choosing of one's self? Kierkegaard answers that the choice involves resignation, followed by a gaining back of what has been lost by virtue of the absurd. These dynamics can be translated into a psychoanalytic perspective in terms of the dynamics of narcissism. When we speak of resignation of the self, we immediately recognize the momentousness of such a requirement. The individual has spent a lifetime shaping and constructing the self-organization which he identifies as himself and which has become the core of his experience of himself. How is it possible to resign oneself, to give up oneself? After all, we are talking about one's self, that which is most precious, most closely identified with our sense of who and what we are. The very idea of resigning oneself is threatening in the extreme, more threatening than the idea of resigning any other possession or quality that we can regard as extrinsic to ourselves. But it is this resignation which Kierkegaard requires for faith.

Moreover, from a dynamic point of view, this resignation is all the more difficult because the self has become the locus of intense narcissistic investments. It may seem paradoxical, since the pathogenic sense of self has become the source of so many psychological difficulties and other painful dysphoric affects that plague the individual's existence and cause unhappiness and maladjustment in so many dimensions of life. One would think that such a person would be only too eager to surrender this source of pathogenic dismay, but it is not so. He mobilizes powerful resistances to surrendering this precious sense of himself because it is *his* self, the only self he has ever known or ever had.

The situation, it seems to me, is quite analogous to Kierkegaard's infinite resignation leading to faith. The second step of the process is the choosing of oneself by virtue of the absurd, and by this choosing to gain back everything that has been lost, and more. The individual must come to see what is contained and involved in his pathogenic self, which he has chosen but which is not himself. The individual must be able to resign that self, particularly because of the narcissistic investments that it entails. The dynamics of narcissism display themselves in two decisive and polarized directions: in a superior direction, giving rise to a sense of specialness, of being different from and somehow superior to one's fellowmen; and in an inferior direction, giving rise to a sense of shame, inferiority, and inadequacy. These are parts of the pathogenic sense of self, organized around the narcissistically embedded and pathogenic introjects which the individual chooses and to which he clings desperately, but which are not authentically himself. He must resign these elements and in the face of what is unknown, in virtue of the absurd, he must come to choose that which is himself.

The argument I have been developing in this section, following Kierkegaard's lead, brings us to a basic orientation toward faith. The path toward faith lies in the direction of true selfhood, psychic integration, autonomy, authenticity, and freedom. The capacity to have a self that is autonomous, authentic, and real is intimately involved in the capacity for faith. By the same token, the inability to have a self, to choose one's authentic self and its attendant values, the embroilment in pathological fixations and deficits, set the stage for the organization of a false-self that can have little internal life of its own. This is the path that leads to despair and ultimately to defiance against man and God.

CHAPTER 6

Faith and Experience

In the effort to focus the psychological dimensions of the faith experience, our emphasis falls on the quality of that experience rather than on the nature of faith itself. We are interested in the implications and reverberations of faith within the human psyche. We want to know how it articulates with man's experience of himself, with his affective and cognitive life, and with the process by which he relates with and involves himself in the world around him. In this sense, faith is not only an action-event in the intrapsychic realm, but it also reflects important aspects of the individual's relationships with other human beings and his environment. Faith also permeates the organization and integration of one's own sense of self and identity. These strains are implicit in Kierkegaard's approach to faith (see Chapter 5) and are condensed in the definition of faith provided by Niebuhr (1960:16). Faith is:

> ... the attitude and action of confidence in, and fidelity to, certain realities as the sources of value and the object of loyalty. This personal attitude or action is ambivalent; it involves reference to the value that attaches to the self and to the value towards which the self is directed. On the one hand it is trust in that which gives value to the self; on the other hand it is loyalty to that which the self values.

Thus, faith entails a double movement: on the one hand, the giving of trust and loyalty to that which has objective value to oneself and, on the other hand, the receiving of meaning and value from that other.

This view of the relational character of faith is embedded in an object relations context, since the object of trust and valuing is always another person. On the human level, the experience of faith is always the self's response receiving recognition and valuing from another self.

Where that loyalty and value are invested in structures in the environment, the personalizing need is so great that these entities are experienced and reacted to in more or less personalized terms. For example, the response of an academic who has failed to achieve tenure and has been dismissed by his university is usually one of deep personal pain, disappointment, and disillusionment. Or an executive who has given years of loyal service to his company and is let go out of economic necessity, does not react to the corporate structure, but personalizes the experience and feels rejected and abandoned. Thus, the faithful commitment of one's self always carries with it, explicitly or implicitly, a sense of personal reference.

The faith experience, then, embraces man's total self and permeates his experience of himself. That experience is not merely cognitive but affective as well. As the younger Niebuhr (1972:47) expresses it: "Affective faith is an awakening, a suffering of a whole frame of mind that endows the individual with a resonance lying at the foundations of his existence. It qualifies all of his interaction with other men, with himself, and with his near and ultimate environment."

Emphasis on the experiential and affective aspects of faith has led to a focus on the active processing in both affective and cognitive terms that are involved in the human experience of faith. In these terms, faith is contrasted with belief (Smith 1979). Faith is regarded as a more personal element in man's religious experience, a basic orientation of his personality toward the world of his experience. At the same time, it reflects a capacity to live in more than worldly terms, to transcend mere worldly experience, to feel and act in terms of a transcendent reality. Belief, by way of contrast, has a more objective reference in terms of a religious tradition, a system of beliefs, or a set of doctrinal statements. As Fowler (1974, 1976) has noted, the noun "faith" has no corresponding verbal form in the English language; the comparable verbal term is "believing." But believing, or belief, does not provide an adequate synonym for faith. Consequently, the emphasis on faith as an activity (verbal) and as a personal and intrapsychically relevant process contrasts with the concept of faith or belief referring to a static collection of propositions or a system of beliefs. Faith in this sense embraces a sense of trust and commitment to someone or something. It implies a personal investment, a caring, and a communication of one's self.

Faith is thus essentially relational; it is an active mode of being in relation to others by which we invest in those others and make a commitment, which itself fulfills our deepest needs as human beings. Without such faithful relationships through the course of one's life experience, one cannot become a self and cannot maintain a meaningful human existence. Without involvement in and commitment to objects, in a more limited psychoanalytic perspective, no authentic sense of self is possible. But this interpersonal relatedness is not restricted to mere interpersonal contexts. Rather, it extends to the broader complex contexts of human connection and association, the organizations of personal and social groupings which form the fabric of human life and activity. Without this interpersonal commitment and fidelity, human groups could not maintain themselves, for such commitment and fidelity are essential to the life of the human family and the human community. Such a consideration leads Fowler (1974:3) to define faith as "that *knowing* or *construing* by which persons or communities recognize themselves as related to the ultimate conditions of their existence."

To carry the analysis a step further, the shared commitment implicit in faith includes adherence to the basic values which form the inherent and immediate culture of any given group. The faithful communication between members of any human group requires a commitment to truth as an inherent value. Fidelity to a marital relationship connotes not only a commitment to the marriage partner, but also a shared acceptance of and commitment to the ideal and the values of the marriage relationship. Political fidelity involves not merely loyalty to one's fellow citizens but also an implicit commitment to the ideals of justice and the common good (Fowler 1976). In a word, faith permeates the depths of human psychological structure and experience, and extends its formative capacity to the full range of human involvements and commitments.

One of the most important dimensions of the faith experience is its involvement in and expression through fundamental religious values. In this connection, Lonergan (1972) emphasizes not only the affectional aspect of the faith experience but its inherent sense of commitment to a system of values and the ultimate source of such values. Faith is thus a "value-knowing," which embraces the full range of meaningful human values but leads beyond them to the ultimate source of value. Lonergan writes (1972:114):

> To our apprehension of vital, social, cultural, and personal values, there is added an apprehension of transcendent value. This apprehension consists in the experienced fulfillment of our unrestricted thrust to self-transcendence, in our actuated orientation towards the mystery of love and awe.

The value-knowing, therefore, which is faith, involves a dynamic pressure toward the apprehension of transcendent value. For Lonergan, the dim apprehensions of the transcendent and ultimate reality as intelligible, reasonable, true, and real, provide the ground for inferring the transcendent as the absolute source of value.

The distinctions we are addressing here have their corresponding elements in the traditional Catholic theology of faith in the distinction between the *fides quae creditur*, which is equivalent to what we have called "belief," and the *fides qua creditur*, which comes closer to the notion of faith described here. The *fides qua creditur* describes faith as a personal encounter, the human response to relevation and the revealing God. Only gradually in the Catholic tradition has the emphasis shifted from the *fides quae* to the *fides qua*. The traditional Catholic view had long been concerned with the substance and content of faith, that is, faith as a body or a system of revealed truths, rather than with the phenomenology or psychological analysis of faith as a human process.

Perhaps the most decisive shift in emphasis and orientation took place in the Second Vatican Council, in the interpretation of the nature of revelation, which in effect led to an expansion of the understanding of faith in both a universal and personal direction (Baum 1966, 1969). In terms of a more universal perspective, the emphasis shifted from a concept of revelation as a fixed body of truths, which entered human history at a fixed point in time, to a more open view of revelation as a continuing process in history, which was completed with the coming of Christ. Rahner (1968:310) expresses this expanded understanding of faith in the following terms:

As a result of God's universal salvific will and the offer of the supernatural grace of faith as an abiding feature of man's mode of existence as a person, every human being, even previous to the explicit teaching of the Christian message, is always potentially a believer and already in possession, in the grace that is prior to his freedom, of what he is to believe (i.e., freely accept): God's direct self-communication in Christ.

Consequently, faith and revelation are not the privileged possession of a particular religious community. Moreover, the envangelical task can no longer be conceived in terms of a missionary function to impart the true faith in a manner that may be alien to the history and culture of a particular group, but rather to develop and elicit, out of an already preexisting faith, the full christological and ecclesiological implications of preexisting beliefs.

This universalizing dimension of faith is accompanied by a deepening of its personal dimension. The reality of faith precedes its explicit formulation in terms of a particular symbolic system. Thus, the roots of faith reach to the depths of personality and influence the sources of man's constitution as a unique self. The theologian of faith, then, must look for faith not only beyond the boundaries of his own community of belief, but within himself, in his own experience; he must seek within his earliest and most interior life in order to find the ground of faith (Rahner 1968).

Consideration of faith as an active process and as experience casts the approach to the understanding of faith in a more explicitly psychological mode. Faith unavoidably impinges on and influences the organization and structure of the personal self. Emphasis here falls on the inner multiplicity and division in the human personality that reaches out for healing. As McDargh (1983:28–29) puts it,

> The emphasis here is on the invisible loyalties which are distributed throughout the self-system so that there is not one coherent and cohesive self but rather the experience of many warring "selves" which withdraw from any central self the energies available for relationship and commitment.

The descriptions of such inner division and "personal manifoldness" (Niebuhr 1941) are reminiscent of forms of psychopathology found in the psychoanalytic literature in which splitting and self-fragmentation are phenomenologically observable. This self-divisiveness functions at both the conscious and unconscious levels. It involves a division in terms of conflicting loyalties to different centers of meaning and value in the individual's present life experience, but it also implies that elements of the self and its history remain dissociated and denied to conscious awareness insofar as the individual lacks the capacity to maintain them within a unified, meaningful sense of self (McDargh 1983).

While these descriptions seem strikingly parallel, I do not wish to infer that they are synonymous. The psychopathological description offers an account of the inherent structure of the personality which reflects a developmental history and a constellation of fixations and conflicts that prevent adequate development. These implications are lacking in the account of the inner division of man without faith. That division could certainly take place in an individual who has achieved a reasonable level of self-development and integration in psychological terms, but the divisiveness in question is more pertinent to issues of coherence and integration of value systems, and of a faithful commitment to the ultimate, transcendent source of values.

The distinction here must fall back on our earlier discussion of the relationship between grace and nature, in which it was determined that, while the sanating or healing effect of grace could have an important influence on the structure of the personality that had failed to achieve an adequate level of identity formation, there was nothing inherent in the structure and nature of human experience to prevent an individual personality from achieving meaningful psychological development quite independently and separately from any influence of grace. Similarly, in the present context, faith may have an enhancing, unifying effect on the integration and value orientation of the personality, but it is not essential to that process. By the same token, it can have an integrating effect on the self-system that suffers from one or other form of developmental deficit, particularly having to do with the fundamental issues of basic trust and the capacity for commitment. In this sense, then, it can be said that faith functions as an important element in the integration of the self-system and that it exercises an important influence on the self-organization, reflected in a patterned manner of processing, construing, and interpreting experiences. Faith, therefore, comes to play a more or less central role in shaping the responses and initiatives that determine the course of a human life.

Within this perspective, then, faith involves itself in the fundamentally human process of establishing and maintaining a sense of self and identity. Faith in this sense is a human achievement and human process that prepares the psychological ground for the transcendent experience of faith (Niebuhr 1963). McDargh (1983:74) expresses this aspect of the faith experience in the following terms:

> The world, and first and primally the interpersonal world of the parenting other(s), comes at the fledgling self as a reality that communicates in a myriad of spoken and unspoken ways its valuation of that newly emerged human being. The individual in turn responds with others but by extension towards the totality of that which is. The subsequent process then of the development of the self, the negotiation of oneness and separateness, is at every point founded upon and conditioned by this interpretation of the whole as good or evil, trustworthy or untrustworthy, deserving of loyalty or requiring a constant vigilance.

The question of the healing or integrating capacity of the development of faith has been focused in terms of the acceptance of and commitment in trusting loyalty to the revealing source of all existence and value. That commitment draws the individual soul beyond limited, mundane allegiances and values toward a higher, more embracing vision of a commitment of God. This higher vision finds its ultimate meaning in a life of dedicated responsibility to the inherent values of the religious belief system (Niebuhr 1963). Faith draws the individual on to a fullness of the Christian life, to intense Christian love modeled on the person of Christ, and to a vocational commitment whose purpose is the nurturing of the Kingdom of God (McDargh 1983).

But faith so conceived is Janus-faced: it not only faces the inner world of human self-organization and integration, but it turns another face outward and upward, as it were, toward relationship with God. The objects of our valuing and committing are always limited and finite. Consequently, our human commitments are permeated with disappointment and disillusionment. The human objects of our trust and ideals fail us, by their imperfection and limitations, their betrayals, their selfishness and cruelty, even by their abandonment of us in death. The causes and ideologies to which we look for support and strength, often prove to be illusory and imperfect. As McDargh (1983:27) comments:

> In the limit situations of our lives, preeminently in the encounter with suffering and death, all gods are tested and sooner or later found wanting. The second vexing difficulty with finite centers of loyalty and value is that they are multitudinous, not only sequentially but simultaneously. As a consequence we find ourselves organizing our lives in terms of a number of different gods, often with competing and conflicting claims upon our fidelity.

The element that draws us beyond these finite commitments and disillusioning loyalties is what Niebuhr (1941) calls the revelatory event, that is, an event of such a nature that we are enabled to respond in trust and fidelity to the ultimate source of life and value. The response to revelation gives new life and meaning to one's sense of self. It plays upon the fundamental level of the self which orients us to our environment and gives meaning and purpose to this self. As Niebuhr (1941:79) insisted, "The participating self cannot escape the necessity of looking for pattern and meaning in its life and relations." The revelatory experience elicits a personal response of commitment, trust, and loyalty that is pertinent to an encounter with the infinite. Moreover, the revelatory event involves not only knowing but being known, not only valuing but being valued, so that all values become transvalued in relationship to the commitment to ultimate values. For Christians, the encounter with God, the ultimate valuer, is mediated through the revelation of Jesus Christ, who unveils in the history of his life, death, and resurrection the enduring values of God the Father. Insofar as the individual responds to the ultimate reality, to the ultimately valued and valuable, he can be said to have faith in God. For Niebuhr, then, the human person strives consciously and/or unconsciously to seek and respond to the ultimate reality beyond mundane realities, the one beyond the many, and thus enters into a relationship with the transcendent object.

Fowler approaches this matter somewhat differently in his development of the connection between faith and the transcendent. He argues that the maintenance of a shared vision of reality in human communities must be based on interpersonal faith and faithfulness, which in turn rest upon a common awareness of relatedness to the transcendent. The continuation of human community and the meaningfulness of human life requires a shared vision of the excellence of being. Fowler (1974:7) writes:

> The maintenance of "reality" requires constant renewal and transformation. The trust and loyalty to each other—and to each other in a shared vision of excellence of being—must consistently be developing and revivifying. A principal contribution of institutional religions in cultures is their generation of renewing power and passion in the mainly tacit covenant which sustains a people's interpersonal trust and their shared visions of excellence of being. A society's covenantal maintenance and continual renewal of 'reality' requires faith in a transcendent source and center of being, value and power.

The patterns of faith give a sense of order, coherence, and meaning to the scattered forces and powers that impinge on human beings and communities. The sense of the ultimate goal and source of human existence provides a framework in which interpersonal, institutional, and vocational covenants can be maintained. The commitment of faith, then, gives direction and purpose to limited, mundane commitments; it permeates and determines relationships and commitments to the causes and contexts that form the pattern of one's life.

This view of faith as experience can be summarized succinctly. (1) The emphasis on faith as experience broadens the implications of the process of faith to universal dimensions. All persons share in faith to the extent that they find meaning for their human existence by placing trust and fidelity in certain objects or centers of devotion and value. Faith in this sense is neither equated with religion nor necessarily religious in any formal sense. It reflects rather the relatedness of a person or community to a transcendent reality whose nature is apprehended through faith, informs and influences the values and ideals of persons or groups. (2) In the personal sense, faith provides meaning and relevance for integrating and sustaining a cohesive sense of self. It involves a sense of self in relationship to others, a sense of self as valued and valuing. (3) Faith is an active, dynamic process, a mode of existence and relationship which gives form and coherence to human life and experience. (4) In its specifically religious sense, as faith in God, faith reflects the self's total integration in a relationship of trust and fidelity to the ultimate being who is the source and goal of all human life and value.

CHAPTER 7

Faith Development

To the extent that the preceding argument has successfully developed the notion of faith as experience—that is, as an affective knowing and an affective process—our inquiry draws closer to the concerns of psychological understanding. The understanding of faith as experience requires a developmental perspective and context within which the derivations of the inherent elements of the faith experience find their origins. For example, insofar as the element of trust is an inherent constituent of the experience of faith, such trust should not be considered simply as a form of infantile investment in and dependence on a need-satisfying object; rather, from a developmental perspective, it can be seen as spanning a continuum of levels of developmental experience in which the elements of trust emerge and are progressively modified as they enter into and participate in the integration of increasingly mature levels of personality organization and functioning.

Here I am presenting a complex overview of aspects of the development of the faith experience, building on an earlier schema (Meissner 1984) and leaning heavily on the empirical studies of Fowler (1974, 1976, 1981; Fowler and Keen 1978), whose work places the study of the empirical basis of the faith experience on a solid footing. As with all empirical undertakings, there are inherent limitations to his method; the interpretive categories arrived at may also be questioned and will undoubtedly be improved and modified by futher study. It is important to emphasize that Fowler's approach is basically structuralist in that he attempts to focus on the underlying structures and operations involved in human thought processes, particularly in faith-knowing. As he puts it (1974:1), his attempt is "to understand and define the *laws* or *patterns* the mind employs in constructing the ideas, concepts and beliefs that constitute the *contents* of thinking and valuing."

Fowler's study of the progressive development of faith builds on earlier developmental work by Piaget and Kohlberg. Piaget's (1977) study of cognitive development is well known, particularly with regard to the stages of sensory motor schemata and cognitive skills from the earliest levels of reflex action through the unfolding of formal operational thought capacities in adolescence. These stages are summarized in Table 1.

Even more important in Fowler's work has been the influence of Lawrence Kohlberg of Harvard University. Kohlberg's (1969) efforts had been directed to studying the development of moral thinking and moral evaluation. Like Piaget, Kohlberg has validated empirically six stages of moral development extending from the preconventional level of heteronomous morality to the most advanced postconventional level of universal ethical principles. These stages are summarized in Table 2.

With these extensive empirical findings as a basis, Fowler has endeavored to formulate, through his own empirical research, a parallel series of progressive stages in the development of faith experience. The following summary undertakes to integrate Fowler's observations regarding these stages in the structural-developmental understanding with a more specifically psychoanalytic perspective (Meissner 1984).

Stage 0: Undifferentiated

This phase involves a preconceptual and prelinguistic disposition toward the conditions of life. Faith knowing at this level is preselfconscious and involves the communication of meaning and purpose by caring environmental figures, usually the parents; included are nonverbal, often tactile, communications that influence the emergence of basic trust, autonomy, hope, and will. The developmental experiences also contain a potential for the opposite resolutions of doubt, shame, dread, and terror (see the discussion of infantile roots in the development of faith, Chapter 8).

From a psychoanalytic perspective, this earliest mode of religious experience is based on conditions of early archaic narcissism and must be regarded either as developmentally primitive or deeply regressive. The individual at this level has not achieved self-object differentiation, and the relation with significant objects is essentially symbiotic in character. Narcissistic experience is marked by unconditional omnipotence and absolute dependence. Religious experience at this level

TABLE 1.   Piaget's eras and stages of logical and cognitive development

Era I (age 0-2) The era of sensorimotor intelligence

Stage 1. Reflex action.
Stage 2. Coordination of reflexes and sensorimotor repetition (primary circular reaction).
Stage 3. Activities to make interesting events in the environment reappear (secondary circular reaction).
Stage 4. Means/ends behavior and search for absent objects.
Stage 5. Experimental search for new means (tertiary circular reaction).
Stage 6. Use of imagery in insightful invention of new means and in recall of absent objects and events.

Era II (age 2-5) Symbolic, intuitive, or prelogical thought

Inference is carried on through images and symbols which do not maintain logical relations or invariances with one another. "Magical thinking" in the sense of (a) confusion of apparent or imagined events with real events and objects and (b) confusion of perceptual appearances of qualitative and quantitative change with actual change.

Era III (age 6-10) Concrete operational thought

Inferences carried on through system of classes, relations, and quantities maintaining logically invariant properties and which *refer to concrete objects*. These include such logical processes as (a) inclusion of lower-order classes in higher order classes: (b) transitive seriation (recognition that if a > b and b > c, then a > c): (c) logical addition and multiplication of classes and quantities; (d) conservation of number, class membership, length, and mass under apparent change.

Substage 1. Formation of stable categorical classes.
Substage 2. Formation of quantitative and numerical relations of invariance.

Era IV (age 11 to adulthood) Formal-operational thought

Inferences through logical operations upon propositions or "operations upon operations." Reasoning about reasoning. Construction of systems of all possible relations or implications. Hypothetico-deductive isolation of variables and testing of hypotheses.

Substage 1. Formation of the inverse of the reciprocal. Capacity to form negative classes (for example, the class of all not-crows) and to see relations as simultaneously reciprocal (for example, to understand that liquid in a U-shaped tube holds an equal level because of counterbalanced pressures).

Substage 2. Capacity to order triads of propositions or relations (for example, to understand that if Bob is taller than Joe and Joe is shorter than Dick, then Joe is the shortest of the three).

Substage 3. True formal thought. Construction of all possible combinations of relations, systematic isolation of variables, and deductive hypothesis-testing.

(Table reprinted from Lawrence Kohlberg and Carol Gilligan, "The Adolescent as a Philosopher: The Discovery of the Self in a Postconventional World," *Daedalus* 100 (Fall 1971): 1063.)

would involve a merging of the boundaries between self-representation and God-representation. The sense of self lacks cohesion and remains in a state of undifferentiated diffusion or, in states of extreme (psychotic) regression, even severe fragmentation. Psychotic formations may take the form of delusions of omnipotence and God-like grandiosity, or even hallucinations.

A question can be raised regarding the differentiation between these primitive, regressive states of fusion and merger, and mystical, ecstatic experiences. Mystical experiences also involve a loss of boundaries, a diffusion of the sense of self, and absorption into the divine object. But a distinction must be drawn between regressive merger and the capacity to transcend the boundaries of the self, allowing for the self's immersion in the love object (see discussion of crossing of boundaries, Chapter 3). In mystical states, we are dealing with a condition in which the self is subsumed by the loving presence of a divine object, which calls on the soul's capacity to reach beyond the boundaries of self, and to empty out the self in a loving embrace and absorption into the object. This transcendent capacity of the psyche to immerse itself in such a loving object relationship need not be regarded as regressive; rather it may reflect one of the highest attainments of man's spiritual life and capacity (Meissner 1984). Such transcendent absorption in the love object stands in radical opposition to the psychotic self-absorption by which external objects are drawn into the omnipotent orbit of the primarily narcissistic psychotic process.

Stage 1: Intuitive-Projective

The first stage of faith-knowing occurs typically in the age range of four to seven or eight years. The child's world is fluid and novel. The awareness of self as a center of experience and as involved in relationships with others is rudimentary. The child's reasoning and judgment are preoperational, lacking the resources of inductive and deductive logic. Causal relationships are poorly grasped, and explanations of cause and effect tend to be merely descriptive. The child has difficulty in focusing on more than one dimension or aspect of a situation at one time, so that impressions tend to be partial, erroneous, and fragmented. This makes the differentiation between fact and fantasy difficult and gives the child's thinking a somewhat magical character.

Due to the relatively undeveloped sense of causal and temporal relationships, the child's experience has an episodic quality. Episodes

TABLE 2. The Six Moral Stages

Level and Stage	Content of Stage		Social Perspective of Stage
	What Is Right	Reasons for Doing Right	
LEVEL I—PRECONVENTIONAL Stage 1—Heteronomous Morality	To avoid breaking rules backed by punishment, obedience for its own sake, and avoiding physical damage to persons and property.	Avoidance of punishment, and the superior power of authorities.	*Egocentric point of view.* Doesn't consider the interests of others or recognize that they differ from the actor's; doesn't relate two points of view. Actions are considered physically rather than in terms of psychological interests of others. Confusion of authority's perspective with one's own.
Stage 2-Individualism, Instrumental Purpose, and Exchange	Following rules only when it is to someone's immediate interest; acting to meet one's own interests and needs and letting others do the same. Right is also what's fair, what's an equal exchange, a deal, an agreement.	To serve one's own needs or interests in a world where you have to recognize that other people have their interests, too.	*Concrete individualistic perspective.* Aware that everybody has his own interest to pursue and these conflict, so that right is relative (in the concrete individualistic sense).
LEVEL II—CONVENTIONAL Stage 3—Mutual Interpersonal Expectations, Relationships, and Interpersonal Conformity	Living up to what is expected by people close to you or what people generally expect of people in your role as son, brother, friend, etc. "Being good" is important and means having good motives, showing concern about others. It also means keeping mutual relationships, such as trust, loyalty, respect and gratitude.	The need to be a good person in your own eyes and those of others. Your caring for others. Belief in the Golden Rule. Desire to maintain rules and authority which support stereotypical good behavior.	*Perspective of the individual in relationships with other individuals.* Aware of shared feelings, agreements, and expectations which take primacy over individual interests. Relates points of view through the concrete Golden Rule, putting yourself in the other guy's shoes. Does not yet consider generalized system perspective.

Stage	What Is Right	Reasons for Doing Right	Social Perspective of Stage
Stage 4—Social System and Conscience	Fulfilling the actual duties to which you have agreed. Laws are to be upheld except in extreme cases where they conflict with other fixed social duties. Right is also contributing to society, the group, or institution.	To keep the institution going as a whole, to avoid the breakdown in the system "if everyone did it," or the imperative of conscience to meet one's defined obligations (Easily confused with Stage 3 belief in rules and authority; see text.)	*Differentiates societal point of view from interpersonal agreement or motives.* Takes the point of view of the system that defines roles and rules. Considers individual relations in terms of place in the system.
LEVEL III—POST-CONVENTIONAL, or PRINCIPLED Stage 5—Social Contract or Utility and Individual Rights	Being aware that people hold a variety of values and opinions, that most values and rules are relative to your group. These relative rules should usually be upheld, however, in the interest of impartiality and because they are the soical contract. Some nonrelative values and rights like *life* and *liberty*, however, must be upheld in any society and regardless of majority opinion.	A sense of obligation to law because of one's social contract to make and abide by laws for the welfare of all and for the protection of all people's rights. A feeling of contractual commitment, freely entered upon, to family, friendship, trust, and work obligations. Concern that laws and duties be based on rational calculation of overall utility, "the greatest good for the greatest number."	*Prior-to-society perspective.* Perspective of a rational individual aware of values and rights prior to social attachments and contracts. Integrates perspectives by formal mechanisms of agreement, contract, objective impartiality, and due process. Considers moral and legal points of view; recognizes that they sometimes conflict and finds it difficult to integrate them.
Stage 6—Universal Ethical Principles	Following self-chosen ethical principles. Particular laws or social agreements are usually valid because they rest on such principles. When laws violate these principles, one acts in accordance with the principle. Principles are universal principles of justice: the equality of human rights and respect for the dignity of human beings as individual persons.	The belief as a rational person in the validity of universal moral principles, and a sense of personal commitment to them.	*Perspective of a moral point of view* from which social arrangements derive. Perspective is that of any rational individual recognizing the nature of morality or the fact that persons are ends in themselves and must be treated as such.

(Reprinted from Thomas Lickona, ed., *Moral Development and Behavior: Theory, Research, and Social Issues* (New York: Holt, Rinehart and Winston, 1976), pp. 34-35.)

are experienced, but the narrative line of interconnection is weak. Consequently, the child's sense of coherence is largely related to the degree of sameness and continuity provided by the significant others in his environment.

The child's capacity for adopting the perspective of others is severely limited. His thinking and valuing are egocentric, oblivious to the experience of others and to the fact that their needs and interests may differ from his own. Empathy is limited to superficial behavioral impressions, with no capacity to experience imaginatively what the other may be feeling internally.

The child's sense of authority is governed largely by the nature of his attachments to parents or parent substitutes. His dependence on powerful parental objects and his attunement to parental expectations, reinforced by rewards and punishments, condition his responses to their authority. The child is also influenced by visible qualities of physical size and power or by external symbols of authority, such as a uniform. By and large, the significant others in the child's world are members of the family or others immediately related to the family. Friends and playmates can have an impact on the child's self-awareness, but the degree of their influence depends on the acceptance and approval of parental figures.

Generally speaking, the child's understanding of issues of good and bad, right and wrong, is premoral, putting it roughly at the level of Kohlberg's preconventional heteronomous morality (Stage 1). Ideas of right, duty, and obligation have not yet been formed. The goodness or badness of acts is not connected to intention and will, but rather is judged in terms of visible consequences, particularly punishment or praise.

In terms of the progression in narcissistic development, this stage involves a differentiation of the grandiose self from the idealized parental imago. These derivatives of primitive archaic narcissism express the relative location of narcissistic qualities of omnipotence and grandiosity, either in the self or in the recently differentiated objects, specifically the parents. This differentiation calls into play the mechanisms of introjection and projection, which operate to shape the child's emerging experience of the inner and outer worlds. The introjection of narcissistic qualities gives rise to the grandiose self, and the projection of those qualities serves as the basis for the idealized parental imago (Kohut 1971; Meissner 1978).

The idealization of and dependence on the parents are important for the child's establishing and maintaining a cohesive sense of self. A vulnerability to fragmentation of the self can result from an intensification of narcissistic defenses, particularly in the form of regression to grandiose and omnipotent fantasies. The God-representation can likewise reflect the projection of characteristics of omnipotence and omniscience to a perfect, idealized image. Moreover, the relationship to the God-figure is permeated with a sense of utter dependence on and fear of divine omnipotence, which is reflected in a need to placate the deity by means of superstitious rituals and magical ceremonials.

Religious experience tends to be largely animistic, reflecting the influence of projective mechanisms, defending against intense and unresolved ambivalence (usually toward parental figures), and the associated narcissistic perils of separation and abandonment. Generally, the predominance of projective and introjective processes, and the weakness in the cohesion of the self, weaken the lines of differentiation between fact and fantasy, and blur boundaries between the natural and supernatural. Affective and cognitive experiences tend to be fused or confused, so that religious experience is apt to be dominated by its affective aspects. God is pictured in animistic, magical terms as an omnipotent, omniscient deity. Imagery about God may have a somewhat unspecific, preanthropomorphic content (as in a pananimistic sense of God as a numinous presence in the universe), but is more likely to be cast in concrete, personalized, and anthropomorphic ways. The relationship to this idealized omnipotent God is usually conflicted and tends to be resolved by masochistic submission or superstitious subjugation.

Stage 2: Mythic-Literal

This stage is predominant from ages six or seven to eleven or twelve, although it may be found in some degree even at adolescent and adult levels. Cognitively, the child has begun to sort out the differences between the real and unreal on the basis of practical experience. In addition, there is a development in the inner world of speculative fantasy and imagination. In Piaget's terms, the child has reached the level of concrete operational thinking. This involves the capacity to observe a sequence of actions and to infer causal relationships. In consequence, thinking and reasoning are gradually freed up from the constraints of perception and feeling. But thinking patterns remain relatively tied to concrete sensory experiences and are not yet able to utilize the capacity for abstraction.

The emergence of concepts of time, causality, and the lawfulness of action gives rise to a capacity for narrative connection, which lends some coherence to the flow of experience. Stories or myths have considerable appeal, allowing the child to develop a sense of involvement in and relationship to his environment without needing to reflect on meaning or implication. This is accompanied by an increasingly flexible perspective, which allows the child to view situations from different vantage points and to appreciate that others, too, can do so. The skill of projecting oneself imaginatively into someone else's point of view begins to make real empathy possible.

In terms of authority, the child begins to form his own canons of judgment regarding everyday experience, but still looks to trusted adults, whether parents, teachers or older siblings, to validate his conclusions. The criteria for choices and preferences are not yet matters of conscious reflection. The broadened social world includes relationships with teachers, other school authorities, friends and their families, schoolmates, and perhaps even religious figures. Socially relevant characteristics, having to do with ethnic origin, racial heritage, religious affiliation, and social class begin to play a role in the child's own developing self-image. Identifications with specific reference groups begin to influence the child's sense of self, often in the context of stereotypical views of other groups and orientations.

The capacity for moral judgment reaches a new level of reciprocity and a sense of fairness. The child begins to take account of the needs and demands of others and expects others to make similar allowance for his own needs and demands. This is roughly equivalent to Kohlberg's Stage 2 of moral development.

The capacity to differentiate between a symbol and what is symbolized begins to emerge. The symbol is usually connected with a particular objectifiable referent. Although the symbol may refer to something imaginative or nonexperiential, this most often is translated by analogy into something concrete. Images or symbols for God tend to be anthropomorphic, and narrative and mythical accounts are preferred for communicating notions of transcendent meaning.

The child attains a cohesive sense of self. The primary narcissistic vulnerability is no longer that of dissolution of the self or loss of self-cohesiveness, but is rather focused more specifically on the maintenance of self-esteem. Mechanisms of introjection and projection continue to be used defensively for preserving the residues of infantile narcissism.

State 3: Synthetic-Conventional

This stage is largely an adolescent phenomenon, although for some persons Stage 3 characteristics persist well into adult life and even middle age. The achievement of formal-operational thinking allows for mutual role-taking in social relationships. Thus the individuals can construct a sense of self as they appear in the eyes of others, while at the same time maintaining the sense of other individuals with whom they may be involved, as functioning in the same way. This permits a more objective view of relationships and events. The sharing and sanctioning of others contributes to the emergence of beliefs, values, and codes of action by which the individual gradually evolves a sense of his own identity and role in life.

But the response tends to be conformist and highly responsive to the expectations and judgments of others, particularly peers. The grasp on one's own personal identity and capacity for autonomous judgment and decision-making is not yet secure enough to provide the basis for mature independence. In the multiple contexts of any individual's life experience, these expectations and value emphases can be variable and even conflicting. The individual must find some way of synthesizing and integrating these influences into a consistent, coherent pattern. The issue is resolved through compartmentalization or dissociation of frames of reference, or by creating a hierarchy of reference groups whose respective authorities tend to exercise a predominant role. Such individuals can be described as having significant beliefs and values by which they guide their actions and purposes, but these beliefs and values tend to be based on the authority of a significant other or on some form of valued group consensus. Depending on the quality of the individual's group involvements, the internalized value system may show contradictory values and beliefs, or express itself in the nonspecific, undifferentiated quality of such values and beliefs.

Authority is largely evaluated in terms of the personal qualities of the spokesperson for any given perspective; at the same time, socially legitimating or institutional contexts provide an important additional sanction. The individual looks to the sanction of such acknowledged authorities or properly designated spokespersons for some certification of his own inner coherence and meaning. Thus, authority remains external, even though the individual may accept responsibility for evaluating and choosing the sources of guidance.

By and large, membership in reference groups, in which face-to-face relationships predominate, provides a basis for identity formation and faith commitment. Such groups may be defined in terms of ethnic-familial ties, social class norms, regional loyalties, religious belief systems, peer values and pressures, sex role stereotypes, and so on. Moreover, in-group versus out-group relationships are often cast in stereotypical and prejudicial terms.

Moral evaluations tend to be based on a need to fulfill the expectations of significant others and to avoid conflict. This corresponds to Kohlberg's Stage 3 conventional morality, in which interpersonal conformity is a dominant motif. However, Fowler also observes that many adults at Stage 3 may also approximate Kohlberg's later conventional stage in which "law and order" predominate. The combination of Stage 3 faith and Stage 4 moral judgment is found more frequently among men, while that of Stage 3 faith and Stage 3 moral judgment is found more frequently among women.

The connection between the symbol and the symbolized no longer has the same literal-correspondence quality as before; it has attained a greater flexibility, with a capacity for metaphor and a more flexible affective experience of symbolic meaning. Images of God tend to be less physically anthropomorphic, and are based on personal qualities of God as friend, companion, comforter, guide, and so forth.

Stage 4: Individuating-Reflexive

The transition from Stage 3 may begin around the age of seventeen or eighteen, but a stable Stage 4 configuration is rarely established before the early twenties. For many adults, the transition comes much later.

Stage 4 is marked by the emergence of the self as a more independent entity; it has freed itself from dependence on significant others for its identity and autonomy. In a sense, the self stakes its claim to its own individual faith outlook. The individual becomes aware that his own faith view is different from that of others. The faith-knowing of this phase remains vulnerable to challenge and is open to change; its truth value and adequacy must be confirmed and justified.

The self attains a new capacity to stand apart; it is aware of its own unique ideology and is able to assume responsibility for it. The person's separation from the group is not necessarily individualistic, in the sense that he cuts himself off from interpersonal relationships or group memberships; but his sense of self and identity is no longer dependent on those relationships.

The need to maintain one's own sense of identity and faith orientation brings with it the development of a clear differentiation of one's self from others, of one's own perspectives from those of others. Often, thinking in this regard assumes an either/or, dichotomizing style. The individual's faith is more aware of the limits and interconnections of ideology, but it nonetheless aspires to a comprehensive system of beliefs. Abstract conceptualizations are brought to the surface of the belief system, but are more internally differentiated than before. The "penumbra of mystery" that surrounded central concepts, beliefs, and values in Stage 3 is no longer tolerated.

Acceptance of authority must be validated by internal processes. Such acceptance or rejection tends to be based on a complex evaluation of reality as experienced through the medium of one's own individual outlook. Authority is accepted or rejected to the extent that it fits or does not fit with the other elements of this outlook. The evaluation is not purely rational or intellectual; it also involves important emotional and motivational components.

The range of reference groups to which the individual feels some sense of identification, belonging, and participation tends to be broader. There is a better capacity for recognition and acceptance of the diversity of group interests, emphases, and values, as well as the capacity to take these divergent claims and values into account in shaping and evaluating one's own set of attitudes, beliefs, and values.

Moral judgments here are usually postconventional (Kohlberg's Stage 5). Even though the motivating intention is directed to an ideal of justice, moral judgments may still be based on group or class bias rather than on principle. Moral judgments may be relativistic or contextual, reflecting group-sanctioned prejudices or biases.

The symbolic function may be somewhat practical or pragmatic. Symbols and myths are useful to the extent that they can be translated into applicable and pragmatic concepts. The approach to the symbolic is strongly motivated by the need to seek explicit meaning, to gain internal consistency, and thereby to preserve the self's organization and ideological reference.

In psychoanalytic terms, the achievement of self-stability and cohesion is paralleled by other significant achievements, including the integration and structuring of drive derivatives with the relatively autonomous functions of the ego. Anxiety is organized on a signal level, which makes it manageable and permits the ego to utilize it in mobilizing ego resources. Intrapsychic dangers are no longer derived from the inner world of drives (although this source of psychic danger is never completely elimated), but derive more realistically from extrinsic sources and concerns. This allows for toleration of inner tensions and ambiguities without the need to find immediate resolution and integration in an all-embracing faith orientation or belief system. Faith-knowing can acknowledge the existence and of divergent faith traditions. It is able to grasp universal value validity orientations and beliefs through the multiple veils of particular religious expressions. Faith becomes a lived and vital source of strength and meaningful existence.

Stage 5: Paradoxical-Consolidative

While the effort of Stage 4 was directed to consolidating the inner structures and boundaries of the self and to delineating ideologies and faith orientations, Stage 5 moves in a somewhat different direction. Building on previous self-integration, the self seeks to extend the boundaries of self-awareness and to deepen the roots of its own identity. Fowler casts this dynamic in terms of a reclaiming and reworking of the past, an openness to deeper and more primitive aspects of one's own self, and a critical acceptance of the individual's social unconscious—that is, the myths, ideals, standards, and prejudices that have been incorporated into one's own sense of self and identity in relationship to significant reference groups, including social class, religious traditions, ethnic origins, national community, and so forth. In consequence, the individual's self-knowing becomes more complex and multidimensional, enhancing his capacity for mutual role-taking and empathic resonance with other individuals and groups.

The sense of truth and reality is increasingly complex and paradoxical. Truth is apprehended from multiple viewpoints; rather than experiencing a need to resolve or dissolve contradictions, ambiguities, and tensions, the individual is more able to maintain the diversity of perspectives as part and parcel of the character of truth. Consequently, faith-knowing becomes more complex even as it propels the integrating trends of earlier stages toward a more differentiated blend of reason and feeling, thinking and emotion, cognition and affection. This stage of faith development is rare at best, and is exclusively a phenomenon of adult life.

Thinking is in terms of formal operations, which are more exquisitely attuned to paradox and tension, able to embrace attitudinal polarities and to see many sides of an issue simultaneously. The individual is also more attuned to the elements of his own subjectivity as they play a role in his own thinking and judgment. Conviction about the validity of one's own point of view is often suspended in the interest of grasping the full impact of others' experience. The individual remains open to the potential modification of his own ideology, values, and beliefs, according to the degree of acceptance of other perspectives.

The acceptance of authoritative sources must pass certain critical tests implicit in the acceptance of multiple perspectives, of more comprehensive and mutual capacities for role-taking, and of an increased level of self-awareness and discriminating subjectivity. The acceptable sources of authority become more diffuse and complex, due to an increasing capacity for identification with and a sense of common purpose in relation to an expanded range of reference groups. The Stage 5 capacity for identification tends to reach beyond constricting boundaries of tribal, racial, economic, or ideological groupings. By implication, the individual experiences a more genuine, urgent commitment to the struggle for securing justice and recognition for all persons and groups, particularly those that are disadvantaged.

These concerns are immediately related to questions of moral judgment, which tends to be principled and relatively impervious to class or group biases, as might have been the case at Stage 4. Morality at this stage, then, is equivalent to that of Kohlberg's Stage 5 or 6, which implies a clearer understanding of the needs of justice and an imperative for righting wrongs.

A word of caution: it is not clear to what extent either Kohlberg's moral categories or the stages of faith-knowing developed by Fowler are relatively pure expressions of either moral capacity or the experience of faith. There are questions as to how much these formulations may have been influenced by other social and cultural considerations. Fowler, for example, regards a transition to the Stage 5 level as easier for people who have experienced disadvantage or some form of prejudice, or even oppression. Such individuals frequently advance to the Stage 5 level more easily and earlier than comparatively advantaged individuals. He argues that this should not be surprising since the capacity to survive and cope for such disadvantaged individuals depends in part on their ability to assume the perspective of more dominant, advantaged groups. It would also seem that compassion and empathy for the suffering and injustice done to others might be more readily available to those who have experienced similar vicissitudes in their own lives.

Caution is called for in interpreting such findings, however, since the extent to which these formulations may be contaminated by sociopolitical ideology is not at all clear. Certainly, this criticism has been leveled against Kohlberg's postconventional forms of morality, Stages 5 and 6 in his classification. The Stage 5 individual sees rules as necessary for maintaining social conventions and evaluates their worth in terms of their utility and promotion of individual well-being. For these individuals, the need for respecting individual autonomy has a primary place. In Stage 6, the stage of "individual principles," the emphasis is on abstract concepts of equity, universality, and justice. It has been pointed out, however, that these formulations contain a definite political slant in that individuals using different general philosophical principles—which would necessarily include political attitudes—would presumably score at different levels of moral development. Thus, a Burkean conservative would emphasize respect for authority and the maintenance of social order, and would presumably score at Kohlberg's Stage 4. Liberals embracing a Lockean view of society would express a contractual, legalistic orientation and would tend to score at Stage 5. And finally, radical students who have been socialized in terms of middle-class ethical and humanistic attitudes would express moral judgments in terms of in-dividual principles having a logically universal and consistent emphasis. Consequently, Kohlberg has been charged with transforming broad ideological stances into psychological categories (Rothman and Lichter 1982). It seems to me that this would inevitably raise parallel questions about Fowler's classifications, particularly about the extent to which so-cial and political attitudes of a relatively liberal stripe may have per-meated and contaminated his research. The implications for his un-derstanding and classification of faith-knowing consequently remain open to question.

In any case, the dialectical or paradoxical features of faith-knowing at this stage can find expression in a more intense, conflicted awareness of the demands of justice. The enlarged vision of truth and reality allows for a more telling recognition of partial truths and their constraints. Sym-bols, myths, and rituals achieve a new depth insofar as they are ap-prehended in the context of a more deeply appreciated sense of the com-plex reality to which they refer. The divisions, tensions, and antagonisms in the human community become all the more painful in the light of a deeper appreciation of shared needs and ideals. Caught in the tensions of these universalizing trends and the need to preserve its own integrity and identity, the self remains trapped in a paradoxical or divided phase. It must act out of conflicting loyalties, often finding itself constrained by its commitments to ideologies, beliefs, values, and identity. The analysis of faith development touches the relationship between faith and identity and the inherent limitations of ideology that serve as the focus of our consideration in Chapter 9.

Stage 6: Universalizing

Whereas the faith-knowing in Stage 5 remained paradoxical and open to multiple perspectives, Stage 6 moves on to a level of more unvi-ersal understanding and apprehension. Here, the imperatives of ab-solute love and justice, which have partially apprehended as guiding principles at Stage 5, are more thoroughly integrated, purposeful, and disciplined. Ideals and values become vital motivating forces.

There is a willingness to sacrifice oneself for principles of love and justice and in connection with the most lofty and universal, moral and religious principles. Individuals feel a sense of oneness or sharing with the intentionality of ultimate values and their source. The self seeks and finds the ground of its existence in its identification with its ultimate source of value: in the Christian perspective this ultimate source is God and, in its ultimate Christian implications, the divine Trinity. The synthesis of opposites is no longer experienced as paradoxical, but is viewed from the perspective of the transcendent actuality and value system. Social awareness tends to be universalizing, not merely in abstract terms but as a profound regard for the value and rights of all beings, perspectives, and ideologies. Commitment to ultimate value perspectives provides the fundamental framework for moral reasoning.

The lofty qualities of this level of faith development inspire idealized images of saintly self-abnegation, immolation, and devotion to the ultimate principles of love of God and neighbor and the search for justice. While these ideals provide an important context for considering the vicissitudes of faith and its development, some of the cautions I have urged earlier must also be kept in mind here. Although discrimination between the uniquely personalized, lofty moral and religious ideals of this level of faith and more pathological forms of deviation, which may involve pathological idealization and paranoid distortion (Meissner 1978, 1984), is difficult, to say the least, I would feel comfortable in maintaining this radical distinction, certainly in principle and hopefully in fact.

Fowler expresses some hesitation about his formulations regarding this advanced level of faith development. He comments that the individuals whom he has studied and who have apparently attained this Stage 6 development exhibit qualities that challenge the usual criteria of normalcy: heedless disregard for self-preservation, an over-intense commitment to transcendent moral and religious principles, and insistence on universalizing principles of justice that may run counter to more parochial interests. They also show a disregard for survival and security, a tendency to challenge existing standards of righteousness and prudence; and they often have utopian visions of universal human community that confront more limited, partial perceptions of group boundaries and pseudospecies. In their attempts to challenge established structures, their strategies of nonviolent sacrifice and suffering run counter to vested interests, pragmatism, and more mundane notions of realism and relevance. Fowler (1978) comments that it is little wonder that these individuals often become martyrs for the visions they incarnate. These deviant characteristics may also reflect degrees of unrealistic fanaticism and paranoid psychopathology.

Discussion

Mindful of the pitfalls that plague any attempt to translate highly abstract conceptual notions into empirical terms, and of my earlier cautions regarding possible extraconceptual contaminations from various ideological sources, it can still be said that Fowler's work represents a fundamental contribution to our understanding of the human experience of faith. His findings offer a strong basis for the view that the natural psychological correlates of faith, viewed even in terms of its most spiritually significant connotations, undergo a psychologically significant development as long as the adequate stimulus and relational contexts that are essential for human development are present.

The supernatural gift of faith, granted freely by God through his divine grace and presence, arises within the matrix of these same human correlates, and shapes its existence, as it were, from within the very structures and dispositions that faith development in its natural terms provides. Fowler's studies have clarified these dimensions of faith development and linked them with other patterns of psychological development, particularly the cognitive (Piaget) and moral (Kohlberg).

The spiritual gift of faith is both a grace and an effect of grace. Its permeation of the natural structures of faith takes place along the lines suggested in our analysis of grace (see Chapter 3). By the same token, the pattern of the emergence of faith would link up with the pattern of spiritual identity, discussed in Chapter 4.

The missing elements in the foregoing schema of the experience of faith and its development are particularly the dynamic and affective components of the faith experience. It is these aspects of the faith experience and of all human experience that are of special concern to psychoanalysis. Keeping in mind the complex currents of the analysis already considered, and with the ultimate objective of gaining coherence and integration in our overall understanding of this complex religious phenomenon, I now turn to the more specifically psychoanalytic aspects of our examination into the psychology of faith.

CHAPTER 8

Psychology and Faith

Regression in Faith

If faith endeavors to reach beyond reason, to go beyond the limits of infinite resignation, and to leap into the darkness of the absurd, there is in this impulse a deviation from the standards of reason. Reaching beyond the limits of logic and reason poses a problem. Is this deviation in a downward direction, i.e., a retreat to more primitive or less developed forms of thinking that might be found in primitive cultures or in children? If so, we could consider it a form of regression and seek its explanation in terms of wish-fulfillment and instinctive drives. This, I think, is the direction Freud (1927) chose in his analysis of religious beliefs; for him they were illusions whose power stemmed from the powerful wishes they were to gratify (Meissner 1984).

But the deviation may be in an upward direction, i.e., an advance beyond the limits of reasoned thought and the capacities of logical process to attain a unique and otherwise unattainable apperception of truth. As we saw in our discussion of faith and subjectivity (see Chapter 5), Kierkegaard (1941) points out that faith is unique in that the particular transcends the universal, whereas all other particulars are to be understood in terms of the universal. Faith escapes understanding precisely because it breaks out of the categories of reason. There is a similar problem with creative insight in science. Is intuition a form of regression, or is it a grasp of inherent intelligibility that lies beyond reasoning capacity? In science, the ultimate test is still based on evidence and reason; whatever intuition may provide must submit to the arbitration of experimental confirmation. But in faith, it is not so easy.

Regression need not imply pathology or impaired psychic functioning. It does imply a loosened organization of psychic functioning that unbinds psychic energies and permits them freer expression. There are many creative aspects of human activity that require a capacity to retreat from the confinement of strict logicality and to permit the emergence of more drive-dependent elements. This is presumably what happens in dreaming activity, and recent research suggests that it may be essential to the preservation of normal psychological functioning. This also seems to happen in the experience of artistic creativity: the artist regresses to allow unconscious energies and images a freedom of expression that he is then able to direct to new creative purposes. Kris (1952) has called this form of regression, aptly enough, "regression in the service of the ego." It is very likely that all truly creative thinking enjoys such a moment of regression by which it refreshes itself from the sources of its own unconscious energies.

As we shall see more fully later on, it is probable that something of this nature is to be found in faith. Faith dissociates itself from the resources of secondary process and, in so doing, reaches back to the most primitive levels of its experience and dynamic power, embracing them and finding in them a source of motivation. But this regression does not adequately characterize faith, for while faith reaches downward, it also reaches upward. Consequently, while unconscious, instinctive roots are identifiable in the process of faith, its organization is not drive-dependent, nor does it simply serve the purposes of wish-fulfillment. Therefore, faith has a regressive aspect and can be partially described in terms of unconscious dynamics and primary process organization (Freud 1900); but these express only fragments of it and do not characterize its most significant dimensions.

Thus, Kierkegaard is partially correct in his insistence on infinite resignation. Infantile wish-fulfillments must be effectively resigned before true faith becomes possible. Yet, it is part of the paradox of faith that as it progresses beyond finitude it simultaneously regresses to the most primitive level of that finitude. In resigning all wish-fulfillments, it revives and refreshes the most fundamental wishes and brings them to fulfillment. But wish-fulfillment is not the motive force in faith. There is a distinction between wish-fulfillment through drive-organization (primary process) and wish-fulfillment through faith. In the former, fulfilled wishes themselves provide the motive force. In the latter, the motive force comes from elsewhere.

The regressive moment in faith may in some aspects involve classic Freudian regression. It may also show some of the characteristics of regression in the service of the ego. But the ultimate characterization of regression in faith cannot be expressed in these terms alone, for in reaching back to and drawing upon basic instinctual forces, the regression also transforms and reorganizes them into a new synthetic integration. This reaching-back is both recuperative and restorative. At the same time, it constitutes a creative reemergence on a new level of psychic organization, which is neither drive-dependent nor dependent on secondary process, but is something totally different. As Erikson (1962:264) comments, "If this is partial regression, it is a regression which, in retracing firmly established pathways, returns to the present amplified and clarified."

Instinctual Bases of Faith

In its regressive phase, the process of faith touches and somehow embraces the fundamental instinctual forces of human nature. There is in this insight a rich psychology of human religious development, which we cannot fully develop here. Freud (1927:30) spoke of religious beliefs as follows:

> . . . we turn our attention to the psychical origin of religious ideas. These, which are given out as teachings, are not precipitates of experience or end-results of thinking: they are illusions, fulfillments of the oldest, strongest and most urgent wishes of mankind. The secret of their strength lies in the strength of those wishes.

And again (1927:31):

> Thus, we call a belief an illusion, when a wish-fulfillment is a prominent factor in its motivation, and in doing so we disregard its relations to reality, just as the illusion itself sets no store by verification.

Freud called religious beliefs illusions in order to bring to light the element of wish-fulfillment that he recognized in them. And thus his genius focused on what is probably the most significant single feature of the psychology of faith.

As Freud saw it, faith's motivation lies in the terrifying effects of infantile helplessness that arouses the need for protection through love. The continuance of such helplessness throughout life makes it necessary to seek a protective father. The benevolent rule of divine providence, the care of an omnipotent father, protects us in the face of life's dangers. While Freud's account was highly rationalistic and reductionistic, and did not reach much beyond wish-fulfillment, his fundamental insight has been extended in somewhat more sensitive analyses. The evolution of ego psychology and more recent developments in psychoanalytic thinking give us better resources for formulating it (Meissner 1984).

The fundamental element is narcissism, which plays a central role in the drama of childhood. The child's early narcissism, which gives him the feeling of self-centered omnipotence, is eroded gradually by two forces. The first is the child's unavoidable dependence on his parents for the satisfaction of his needs. The second is the clash between reality and the fantasies of omnipotence. Consequently, the elevated sense of self-esteem is reduced and reversed to esteem for an object. The high valuation placed on the parent gradually becomes associated with fears of abandonment and loss. The burden of childhood fears is eased by an evolving sense of trust (see below) and a belief that there will be one who cares and will be present.

The vicissitudes of childhood narcissism are basic to the psychology of loss and restitution. Rochlin (1965) has made some contributions to this understanding. He feels that the cycle of loss and restitution begins in early infancy and extends to the very end of life. Significant losses throughout life are often regarded not only as inevitable, but also as adventitious, painful, and primarily injurious to the individual's well-being. Personal deprivation produces an aftermath of loss that obscures the fact that losses, whether real or fantasied, serve as catalysts of change and bring into play the mechanisms of substitution and sublimation. And so losses play a critical role in psychic development, particularly in the human capacity for creativity. The losses man suffers are many: loss of love, limitations, deprivations, disappointments, frustrations, abandonment and loneliness, illness, and ultimately death. Central to all of these are a loss of a sense of well-being and a diminution of self-esteem.

The sense of loss and diminished self-esteem attack the fundamental narcissism at the root of our emotional lives. This narcissism is essential to our psychological well-being and any threat to it must be resisted. And so loss sets in motion restorative efforts by which the ego strives to recover the loss and reconstitute the sense of self-esteem. Self-esteem is a fragile but indispensable vessel, whose preservation requires care and constant effort in the face of the onslaughts of deprivation and loss (Rochlin 1965).

Our ultimate loss and most dreaded abandonment is death. We are unwilling to die; our death, taken as an end to our existence, is an affront to our fundamental narcissism. Religious belief restores to us the promise of life, beyond death and overcoming death.

Yet faith is more than this. In the context of loss and restitution, human faith answers to more than the loss and abandonment of death. Our inner sense of integrity and self-esteem demands a sense of meaningful completion to our existence, a sense of fulfillment to complement our own inner sense of esteem. As Martin Buber (1959) put it, our *I* calls out for an absolute relation to an eternal *Thou*.

I think that the exigency for faith is rooted in narcissism and responds profoundly to our deepest needs. The loss of personal meaning and the threat of meaninglessness lie at the heart of the dread that is rooted in existence. Faith's answer to these problems reverberates at many levels. It touches the unconscious, infantile dread of loss and fear of abandonment that are inherent in narcissism. At this level, then, faith is a wish-fulfillment—or perhaps better, wish-fulfillments. As Erikson (1962:112) writes, man "forgets that he achieved the capacity for *faith* by learning to overcome feelings of utter abandonment and mistrust."

Thus, faith is a response to the most basic human needs, including the fundamental instinctual needs derived from narcissism. Faith derives its strength from the motive power of these instinctive forces, its function transcends mere wish-fulfillment, and so the motive power of narcissism is integrated with other independent energies that are channelled into the creative and integrative commitment of faith.

Faith and Trust

Martin Buber (1961:1) distinguishes between two fundamental kinds of faith.

> There are two, and in the end only two, types of faith. To be sure there are very many contents of faith, but we only know faith itself in two basic forms. Both can be understood from the simple data of our life: the one from the fact that I trust someone, without being able to offer sufficient reasons for my trust in him; the other from the fact that, likewise without being able to give a sufficient reason, I acknowledge a thing to be true.

The lack of reasons is not a matter of defective intelligence, but rather flows from the relationship to the one trusted or the thing acknowledged as true. Believing is not a matter of rationality, but engages one's whole being; it is more than rationality and more than feeling. Buber goes on to say:

> The relationship of trust depends upon a state of contact, a contact of my entire being with the one in whom I trust, the relationship of acknowledging depends upon an act of acceptance, an acceptance by my entire being of that which I acknowledge to be true. (p. 8)

For Buber, the faith of trust is characteristically Jewish, and the faith of acknowledgment characteristically Christian. But the process of faith cannot be adequately conceived without embracing both trust and acknowledgment. The intellectualistic emphasis of Christian theology is worked out in the context of living trust in the revealing God. If the faith, which was born in the patriarchal migrations, took shape in the tradition of guidance and covenant and expressed itself as persevering trust in that guidance and covenant, the later doctrinal emphasis on acknowledgment is not abstracted from the psychological roots that vitalize all faith. As Buber himself comments (1961:35), the belief of the patriarchs was simple trust as Abraham trusted God, but "when anybody trusts someone he of course believes what the other says."

The implications of trust reach deep within the mind. The capacity for trust is an expression of one's whole self, it engages one's total being. As Buber observes (1961:40):

> But the realization of one's faith does not take place in a decision made at one definite moment which is decisive for the existence of him who makes the decision, but in the man's whole life, that is, in the actual totality of his relationships, not only towards God, but also to his appointed sphere in the world and to himself. A man does the works of God accordingly in proportion to the effectiveness of his faith in all things.

Faith is not, therefore, an isolated act standing apart from the context of the believer's life cycle, but a process that has a history and a genesis, and represents a fundamental disposition of human existence.

On the psychological side, Erikson (1959:64–65) has tried to illumine the continuities between faith and trust. He writes:

> The psychological observer must ask whether or not in any area under observation religion and tradition are living psychological forces creating the kind of faith or conviction which permeates a parent's personality and thus reinforces the child's basic trust . . . in the world's trustworthiness . . . . All religions have in common the periodical childlike surrender to a Provider or providers who can dispense earthly fortune as well as spiritual health; the demonstration of one's smallness and dependence through the medium of reduced posture and humble gesture; the admission in prayer and song of misdeeds, of misthoughts, and of evil intentions; the admission of inner division and the consequent appeal for inner unification by divine guidance; the need for clearer self-delineation and self-restriction; and finally, the insight that individual trust must become a common faith, individual mistrust a commonly formulated evil, while the individual's need for restoration must become part of the ritual practice of many, and must become a sign of the trustworthiness of the community.

Faith implies a capacity for trust, a receptivity and openness to God, a willingness to accept His Word. It involves a sense of confidence in His love and saving power. It also implies a sense of confidence in one's self and in one's capacity to make the necessary commitment to bridge the chasm between the security and self-reliance of reason and the absurdity and other-reliance of faith (Meissner 1966a).

The capacity to trust in any adult human being is not to be taken for granted. It is a precarious achievement that has undergone many vicissitudes. According to Erikson's schema, important, often decisive influences are brought to bear on the infant that contribute to the direction of his personality development. In the child's initial contacts with the world around him there is tension between basic trust and basic mistrust. With a growing sense of self as dissociated from surrounding objects, there is also a question of the quality of relations between self and objects. From the standpoint of inner development as well as that of physical nourishment, the most significant object in the child's environment is the mother, and the child's relationship to his environment is essentially oral. The child begins to resolve the primary crisis of trust versus mistrust through the feeding relation at the mother's breast (Erikson 1959, 1963).

The crisis of trust vs. mistrust is resolved in the total context of the child's relation to the mother rather than in the immediate feeding. At issue is whether the child can stand in a trusting relation to this source of warmth, affection, and physical assuagement. The outcome is largely dependent on the consistency and quality of the mother's response to the child. The degree of mutual satisfaction and fulfillment in this relationship determines the qualities of predictability and hopefulness in the child's orientation. Maternal warmth and love enable the child to entrust himself to her.

The resolution of this crisis is precarious, depending upon a host of complex variables that are derived from the mother's own personality. The mothering relation in general and breast-feeding contact in particular reflect the extent to which the mother has passed through her own crises and achieved maturity. Her own sense of identity as a person (a specifically female person), the extent of her sense of fulfillment in her feminine role as wife and mother, all contribute to the mutuality and fulfillment she is able to bring to her relationship with her child.

The environment also exerts an influence on the mother-child interaction. The mother's function within the family is not an isolated one. It requires love, support, and affection between husband and wife. In this sense, then, one must regard the events of the marriage bed, the family's economic stability, the security of its relationships, etc., as all having a bearing on the resolution of the crisis of trust. The important factor in this complex matrix of influences is the enduring quality of trust that they engender. A family argument does not destroy trust; it may, in fact, enrich it. But a perduring atmosphere of hostility and recrimination is incompatible with trust.

It is perhaps an oversimplification to say that trust begets trust, but that is the heart of the matter. Parental trust—especially maternal trust—provides the means through which the child may develop a trusting attitude to the world of objects, even though trust is never totally free of the seeds of mistrust. But it is also true that mistrust is never so absolute as to lie beyond the openness of trust.

Faith, then, rests on this basic disposition, for it is in faith that trust finds its unique expression. As Erikson (1962:255) observes, "The ratio and relation of basic trust to basic mistrust established during early infancy determines much of the individual's capacity for simple faith . . . ." Openness to and confidence in God, confidence in one's own trustworthiness before God in faith, trust in one's own sense of judgment and capacity for self-commitment in a faithful leap into the darkness of the absurd—these are impossible without basic truth. Faith, therefore, builds upon the infantile residues of basic trust, successfully developing them into a fundamental capacity of the mature adult personality.

Faith is, therefore, a recapitulation of infantile determinants, a reorganization, a reintegration, a synthetic process within the ego that summarizes and reasserts basic trust. But its assertion is not merely reassertion; it is a creative assertion of something beyond trust and far more significant. It returns to trust in order to go beyond it. There is something here akin to what Kierkegaard grasped in the infinite resignation—man resigns all finite goods in order to find them again in virtue of faith. He must also in a sense resign the imperfection and finitude of basic trust in order to reach beyond it and thereby recapture it more profoundly and more meaningfully in faith. The creative moment in faith is unique and beyond understanding. As Erikson (1962:264) has put it:

> But must we call it regression if man thus seeks again the earliest encounters of his trustful past in his efforts to reach a hoped for and eternal future? Or do religions partake of man's ability, even as he regresses, to recover creatively? At their creative best, religions retrace our earliest inner experiences, giving tangible form to vague evils, and reaching back to the earliest individual sources of trust; at the same time, they keep alive the common symbols of integrity distilled by the generations. If this is partial regression, it is a regression which, in retracing firmly established pathways, returns to the present amplified and clarified.

Faith and Fidelity

Implicit in the notion of faith is an element of perdurance and constancy, the assurance (to use a scriptural term, Hebrews 11:1) of God's continued faithfulness to His promises, a confidence in the finality and eternity of what one believes. There is a mutuality between the stability of one's belief and God's faithfulness, on the one hand, and the psychological dimension of fidelity, on the other. The commitment of faith is not transient and momentary, but a trusting commitment of one's total being in an absolute, perduring relation to God.

Erikson (1964) has provided an illuminating exploration of the psychology of fidelity. Fidelity is the particular ego-quality that emerges with and from adolescence. It is "the ability to sustain loyalties freely pledged in spite of the inevitable contradictions of value systems" (p. 125). Fidelity is a major component of the emerging sense of identity that receives its inspiration from confirming ideologies. Identity and fidelity are necessary though insufficient components of ethical strength. Youth selectively extends its fidelity to the conservation of what it feels to be true and uses its energy to correct or discard whatever has lost all regenerative significance for it. Each generation, then, must rediscover and regenerate the sources of its belief.

Cultural institutions provide the ideologies that shape the individual's sense of identity rejuvenate themselves at the same time with the energies of youthful commitment. Erikson (1962:22) speaks of an ideology as "an unconscious tendency underlying religious and scientific as well as political thought: the tendency at a given time to make facts amenable to ideas, and ideas to facts, in order to create a world image convincing enough to support the collective and individual sense of identity." Religion serves a cultural role, then, insofar as it provides an ideology for the emergent need to create so much a "world image" as a meaningful framework of existence. The religious ideology, if one may use this term, has a breadth and significance that surpass all others. It is no wonder that adolescents are preoccupied with a searching, even doubting, inquiry into religious beliefs.

The emergence of fidelity and the need for commitment require some degree of maturity and the development of specific capacities. This realignment, as it were, underlies and contributes to the ultimate self-definition of identity-formation. The formation of identity takes place in the intrapsychic realms, but is open on all sides to the extrapsychic realm of social and cultural interaction.

Adolescence is a period of peculiar sensitivity and vulnerability. The adolescent is confronted with powerful libidinal and aggressive drives, which create turmoil and disorder, and threaten the fragile sense of personal integrity. He or she is challenged to find new channels for expression and control of these powerful disruptive drives. The adolescent is beset by strong regressive pulls toward earlier developmental stages, and these too must be resisted. In addition, new social and cultural demands are made which reach far beyond the confines of the home, family, and neighborhood—the context of childhood perspectives. If the adolescent is to come through all of this and reach a new maturity which effectively turns from the things of childhood to the things of adulthood, it is essential that the ego develop a capacity to pledge and receive fidelity.

Faith is not the only source of fidelity, but it is an important one; it is more or less prototypical insofar as its scope and its assurance of truth and meaning reach beyond all the others. Faith, therefore, serves a culturally useful, psychological function. We have been referring to fidelity in terms of adolescence, but although fidelity has its greatest developmental significance in the adolescent stage, its importance is not limited to that stage. It is a continuing psychological necessity throughout the life cycle. Human life and existence demand meaning. The maintenance of identity requires continuing identification with significant institutions and meaningful commitment to convincing ideologies.

Thus, authentic faith has a psychological capacity to sustain the individual sense of identity. But beyond this dynamic and positive aspect there lies a danger. Commitment to an ideology tends to be exclusive, as ideologies themselves tend to be intolerant of each other. The danger in any commitment is overcommitment. The history of religious faith provides a rich legend of such overcommitments. The pity of it is that overcommitment, or overidentification, distorts the significance of the ideology that originally necessitated commitment and gave it strength and purpose. The outcome is not only a distortion of ideology but a fault in identity. The implicit incapacity of the ego provides a channel for the expression of (deneutralized) aggressive libidinal drives, which are legitimized in a sense by a perverted ideology. The result is a blend of sadism, sanctimoniousness, and moralism against which true religious faith must wage an endless struggle.

Such overcommitment, then, is inconsistent with true faith as well as with true identity. The essence of faith lies beyond fidelity, although it is impossible to express that essence except in terms of fidelity or in terms of trust. Fidelity is, after all, a finite good that—if we remain true to Kierkegaard's insight—must be resigned if we are to have faith. But beyond the resignation, absurdity and absolute relation become possible. The ability to pass beyond fidelity requires a strength of ego surpassing mere ideology. And paradoxically, to reach beyond fidelity is not to surrender it, but to find it again—enriched, more profound, more meaningful in virtue of faith.

Integrative Function of Faith

We have been concerned thus far with aspects of the psychological process of faith, each of which has rich implications for the psychic economy. I would now like to fit these considerations into a more general view of the function of faith within that same economy.

Faith is a dynamic process that involves and expresses man's total existence. It reaches back to the basic wishes and needs that characterize man's primary experiences and are subsumed into and unconsciously operative in his development. This reaching-back is both regressive and recapitulative, but it returns to infantile sources only to reorganize and revitalize them into a new psychic alignment. It finds power and creativity in the instinctual forces of fundamental narcissism and the dynamic cycle of loss and restitution. Thus, faith has its rich and powerful roots in the vital stratum of man's psychic structure.

On another, more complex level of psychic organization, faith functions as derivative from and as a dynamic extension of basic capacities that have emerged throughout the individual's developmental history. It requires and depends on, as well as enlarges and enriches, the basic sense of trust with which the infant emerges from his earliest experiences. The relation of basic trust and faith is both dynamic and reciprocal. Faith builds upon trust, but it also builds trust. Trust is always imperfect, carrying within it the shadow of mistrust, and so in all belief there is a shadow of disbelief, just as in all unbelief there is a shadow of belief. (The believer and unbeliever are closer to each other than they realize.) Faith is impossible without basic trust, but in faith, trust becomes more than it was and the shadow of mistrust is diminished (never abolished!). Whatever may have been the structure of trust in the psychic economy, it is altered and transformed by faith.

Faith embraces and builds upon man's inner need for fidelity and is, therefore, a phenomenon of psychological maturity. It must wait upon the emergence of fidelity and personal identity, which it then transforms. Thus fidelity is enlarged beyond adherence to an ideology in virtue of its relation to a personal absolute. In the process, identity itself is profoundly affected, since in faith we find the true validity of our existence.

Faith is a transforming process that touches all parts of the psychic structure, reorganizes them into a different pattern, and integrates them into a more mature functioning. Thus faith has an integrative function in the psychic economy. True faith is thereby restorative, recuperative, and effectively maturing.

We must immediately add that true faith rarely achieves all these teleological functions, or achieves them only partially. There are many ways in which to understand this impoverishment of faith. One can ask whether all believers really have faith. Kierkegaard was sure that few did. It is perhaps better to say that most have some minimal degree of faith—and even minimal faith can sustain and assuage in the face of personal tragedy and conflict. But the fullness of faith is rare; it requires great ego strength that few possess.

The integrative function of faith, therefore, is often impaired. But this should not blind us to the potentialities of faith in a psychological perspective. To the extent that faith's integrative function is realized, it enlarges and intensifies the sense of personal identity that is the hallmark of mature psychological adjustment. In faith, we more fully realize our psychological potentiality—and this in turn enlarges our capacity for autonomous, conflict-free function, for spontaneity, and for freedom for impulsive gratifications and restrictive compulsions.

Faith, whether individual or communal, is a dynamic, integrative, and therefore positively adaptive force in the psychic economy. It is not enough to think of it in merely defensive or restitutive terms. The process of faith draws its dynamic power of change from fundamental instinctual energies. But there is a question as to whether these energies are adequate for all the functions of faith we have considered. Faith requires creative energies that serve the ego as it reaches beyond the limits of defense, restitution, and adaptation through the veil of infinite resignation into the darkness of the absurd.

Faith and Grace

The process of faith, even within the limited purview of its psychology, is linked with many aspects of the theology of faith. Faith operates analytically in a sort of borderland where psychology fades into theology and vice versa, and the line between them is sometimes obscure.

The Christian theological tradition teaches that faith must be sustained and confirmed by the strength of God's grace. (See Section I, on the psychology of grace.) I shall not repeat these arguments here, but only reassert the conclusion, namely, that the action of divine grace can be adequately considered on the psychological level in specific energic and relational terms. Grace, therefore, operates to increase the ego's capacity to mobilize its inner resources and to perform effectively the ego-functions that underlie the regulation of instinctive forces, that reinforce the orientation to reality, that organize and direct the executive functions, and most significantly, carry on the dynamic processes of synthesis and integration within the ego itself, specifically contributing to the consolidation of the self and to its capacity for mature and meaningful relationships.

On these terms, then, the recuperative, restorative, and integrative functions of faith become more understandable. Faith requires and also creates basic trust and fidelity. If the ego's capacity for trust is impaired, the movement to faith is more difficult. But the energizing capacity of grace can shore up the ego's impairment and renew those basic sources of trust in and through faith. In doing so, grace and faith touch every stratum of the mind and affect all parts of the psychic structure.

In relating the process of faith to the intrapsychic economy and its object relational involvements, we are exploring the profound and enriching psychological impact of the action of grace. It changes, transforms, and reintegrates the psyche. Faith is only one aspect of the action of grace, however, and represents only a fragment of the economy of grace. It is one dimension of the "spiritual identity" that emerges under the action of grace operating through the synthetic capacities of the ego. The exploration of the psychology of faith is an exploration into some of the relationships between spiritual identity and the personal identity upon which it builds (Meissner 1966a).

A true psychology of grace embraces and integrates the most fundamental aspects of human psychological functioning. The psychology of faith relates to and derives from basic instinctual forces—yet its paradoxical openness to other sources of its transforming power ultimately leads us through the vagaries of psychological explanation to the mystery that must always lie at the heart of faith.

CHAPTER 9

Faith and Identity

The tangled web of influences linking the efforts of psychoanalytic inquiry to the perennial objects of theological speculation has no more perplexing or significant area of interaction than that of the psychological determinants of the experience of faith. Luther's most telling impact on the religious experience of the Christian world was precisely in the area of faith, and an exploration of Luther's faith experience may help us to penetrate more deeply into the connections between faith and identity.

Luther's religious odyssey, tortured and tormented as it was, can be seen as a conflicted and problematic search for the essence of a true faith. His *justificatio per solam fidem* was in one sense a resolution of that search, as well as a dialectical challenge, a call to arms in a conflict that tore asunder the unity of Europe. In some sense the torment of the Reformation can be seen as an externalization of Luther's own inner conflict—even though the wider conflict marshalled forces which Luther could not have even foreseen, much less controlled.

Luther's Quest

The real impact of Luther's greatness lies in the fact that what could be externalized of his own inner turmoil not only became the turmoil of history, but was also internally reflected in the religious consciousness and experience of countless millions—not only of his time and culture, but of other times and cultures as well.

We want to examine Luther's quest for faith from the vantage point of the interplay between psychoanalytic determinants and the more theologically relevant influence of grace, to examine this intertwining of divine and human action not from the point of view of its theological specifications, but rather from that of its dynamic significance within the human soul. From this viewpoint, Luther's struggle with his own conscience, his search for religious truth and solidarity, for a salvific experience that would quell his inner doubts and anguish, can be seen as taking place under the influence of divine grace.

Psychologically speaking, it remains a moot point whether Luther's struggle was ever satisfactorily resolved. If the case can be made that Luther achieved a sense of identity that provided sufficient meaning and purpose to still, at least in part, his inner doubts, conflicts, insecurities, and depressions, there is still a question as to whether he found under grace those rudiments of conviction and trust which might have provided him a peace beyond all understanding.

The Inner Turmoil

First let us trace some of the parameters of Luther's titanic struggle. Erikson has successfully elucidated some of the major dimensions of his conflicted early life. Our examination of this data is highly selective and strikes a slightly different note than that in Erikson's treatment.

Erikson (1962) remarks on the sense of criminality or abiding unconscious guilt that seemed to be a consistent element in Luther's inner life. He comments, "Luther all his life felt like some sort of criminal, and had to keep on justifying himself even after his revelation of the universal justification through faith had led him to strength, peace, and leadership" (p. 68). In some measure, of course, such an inner experience of guilt is prompted by the reverse logic which dictates that the punishment should somehow be proportioned to the crime. Thus, the innocent child falls victim to incomprehensible, absolutist adult consciences that are unable to distinguish between big sins and little sins.

Accordingly, little sins are punished with the severity due to major crimes, out of parental conviction that if little sins are not nipped in the bud and crushed with the full weight of parental wrath, they will grow into heinous crimes. Erikson's comment (1962:68) is to the point: "Criminals are thus often made; since the world treats such small matters as a sure sign of potential criminality, the children may feel confirmed in one of those negative identity fragments which under adverse circumstances can become the predominant identity element." Young Martin felt the primitive wrath of his father's troubled conscience. Psychologically speaking, we are well aware that the potential criminality that old Hans had to repress so rigorously was, in fact, within himself; it was a sense of evil and sinfulness that had to be crushed within, even as it had to be beaten out of his little son. And, if Erikson is correct in gauging that the resolution of Luther's crisis of faith brought him strength and leadership, it remains questionable whether it brought him real peace. If his father had beaten the sinfulness out of his son, he had also beaten into him a sense of evil that was not so easily discharged.

Luther was also haunted constantly by a readiness for judgment.

> Kierkegaard once said that Luther always spoke and acted as if lightning were about to strike behind him the next moment. He was referring, of course, to the mysterious thunderstorm considered the revelatory cause of Luther's decision to become a monk. Yet an excessive expectation of catastrophe, an all-too-anxious wish to be ready for the judgment, was part of Martin's world long before that thunderstorm, and it may have made that storm what it became. (Erikson 1962:59)

Luther was plagued by a constant fear of death, an expectation of sudden catastrophe—like the abiding, if unconscious, expectation the miner in his father's mines (if not his father himself) had of an unforeseen disaster that could thunder down upon his head.

Luther lived in the shadow of death, and his premonitions of it cast a dark shadow throughout his entire career. As Erikson (1962:83) comments:

> The counterpart of this waiting, however, is often a fear of an early death which would keep the vengeance from ripening into leadership; yet the young man often shows signs of precocious aging, of a melancholy wish for an early end, as if the anticipation of prospective deeds tired him . . . . A young genius has an implicit life plan to complete; caught by death before his time, he would be only a pathetic human fragment.

Young Martin grew to manhood with an overburdened sense of accountability, of impending judgment which made him feel called to render a total account of his life even before it was lived. He was haunted by a trepidation, an anxiety that prevented, or at least postponed, his own seizing of an identity before he had passed the test of acceptability.

He was raised in a context of belief—or, more accurately, of superstitious credulity—which was haunted by demons, devils, sorcerers, and witches, and this superstitious matrix provides a locus for externalizing his own unconscious impulses and malicious thoughts. His spiritual world was peopled with malicious forces and spirits whose evil purposes placed him in constant jeopardy. In this world, devils and potential disasters lurked at every turn. The potential for projection in such a magically spiritualized world of experience was very great. The fact that this was the common clay of spiritual reality in the world in which he lived did not diminish the intensity of his own inner guilt or his sense of precariousness and fragility.

Nonetheless, as Erikson suggests, these were not mere superstitions or primitive obsessions. They were also a form of collective mastery of the unknown, which provided a source of shared security in a world full of dangers. They gave the unfamiliar and the unknown a local habitation and a name. Thus, if young Martin was haunted by such dangers and insecurities, he was not the only one so haunted. It may be that such shared and commonly experienced projections provide an important starting point for the alleviation of otherwise unmanageable and unmasterable anxieties. We can also note that such relief is not simply offered in communal terms, but serves to alleviate inner intrapsychic dangers and insecurities as well.

Power and Victimhood

To put this overweening sense of criminality and sinfulness into proper perspective, we must realize that this inner turmoil was rooted in the internalizations which the young Luther acquired from his parents. Erikson (1962:73–74) focuses this issue in the following terms:

> Only a boy with a precocious, sensitive, and intense conscience could *care* about pleasing his father as much as Martin did, or would subject himself to a scrupulous and relentless form of self-criticism instead of balancing the outer pressure with inventive deviousness and defiance. Martin's reactions to his father's pressure are the beginnings of Luther's preoccupation with matters of individual conscience, a preoccupation which went far beyond the requirements of religion as then practiced and formulated. Martin took unto himself the ideological structure of his parents' consciences: he incorporated his father's suspicious severity, his mother's fear of sorcery, and their mutual concern about catastrophes to be avoided and high goals to be met. Later he rebelled: first against his father, to join the monastery; then against the Church, to found his own church—at which point, he succumbed to many of his father's original values. We can only surmise to what extent this outcome was prepared for in childhood by a cumulative rebelliousness and by an ever-so-clandestine hate (for our conscience, like the medieval god, knows everything and registers and counts everything).

Luther absorbed the aggressive, punitive aspects of his father's conscience, as well as the helpless, victimized aspects of his mother. He carried within himself both the brutal persecutor and the susceptible, suffering victim. As Erikson (1962:70) comments, "The double role of the mother as one of the powerless victims of the father's brutality and also as one of his dutiful assistants in meting out punishment to the children may well account for a peculiar split in the mother image. The mother was perhaps cruel only because she had to be, but the father because he wanted to be." We are poignantly reminded of another tortured son who suffered persecution at the hands of a rigidly sadistic father and a powerless, abetting mother: Daniel Paul Schreber, immortalized by Freud (1911). Schreber's experience of "soul-murder," remarkably akin to young Martin's beaten submission, laid the basis for those pathogenic introjects which were the substance of his paranoid psychosis (Meissner 1978). Luther's introjection of the brutal aggressor/persecutor in his father and the passive victim/abettor of the father's will in his mother provided the inner stuff of his own fragmented, burdened conscience.

Luther not only saw himself as the helpless victim of powerful authority figures—replacements for the punitive figure of his father—but also identified with that punitive power which sought to express itself against the powerless and helpless. Thus, when participants in the Peasants' Revolt looked to him as their leader, he repulsed them, saying, "No insurrection is ever right, no matter what the cause." Then, as Erikson (1962:235–236) notes,

> The peasants, as it were, quoted Martin back to Luther. He advised compromise, and he, Hans' son, found that he was being disobeyed, and ignored. He could forgive neither the peasants for this, nor later the Jews, whom he had hoped to convert with the help of the Scriptures where the Church had failed to do so. In 1525 he wrote his pamphlet *Against the Rotting and Murdering Hordes of Peasants,* suggesting both public and secret massacres in words which could adorn the gates of the police headquarters and concentration camps of our time. He promised rewards in heaven to those who risked their lives in subduing insurrection. One sentence indicates the full cycle taken by this once beaten-down and then disobedient son: "A rebel is not worth answering with arguments, for he does not accept them. The answer for such mouths is a fist that brings blood in the nose."

And Erikson adds, "Do we hear Hans beating the residue of a stubborn peasant out of his son?"

Martin's identification with the aggressive, brutal father is well established, since we know from his frequent outbursts in later life that he had his father's temper. Old Hans must have thought that he had beaten it out of little Martin. In fact, he did just the opposite. The psychological mechanisms for instilling hatred and violence in children are clearly delineated. The brutalizing impulses of the parent are introjected by the child and become a part of his own inner world, thus providing the material from which subsequent projections are elaborated. Erikson (1962:58) discusses this as follows:

> Here, I think, is the origin of Martin's doubt that the father, when he punishes you, is really guided by love and justice rather than by arbitrariness and malice. This early doubt later was projected on the Father in heaven with such violence that Martin's monastic teachers could not help noticing it. "God does not hate you, you hate him," one of them said; and it was clear that Martin, searching so desperately for his own justification, was also seeking a formula of eternal justice which would justify God as a judge.

Thus, the forbidding presence of old Hans and the anticipation of his punishment permeated the Luther family and intensified the ambivalent relationship between father and son. Young Martin's overwhelming dread and fear of his father burdened him with guilt and inadequacy, while a longing admiration of Hans caused an unsatisfied yearning for closeness and acceptance. As Erikson (1962:123) notes, "Where rebellion and deviousness are thus successfully undercut, and where, on the other hand, the father's alcoholic, sexual, and cruel self-indulgence obviously break through his moral mask, a child can only develop a precocious conscience, a precocious self-steering and eventually an obsessive mixture of obedience and rebelliousness."

The brutalizing, punitive figure of an old Hans became, in young Martin's mind, the prototype of the jealous, vengeful God whose loving care of his children was clouded by destructive malice, unforgiving judgment, and retribution. The face of the God to whom Luther looked for a profound experience of faith and trust became, in fact, the face of old Hans—a harsh, remorseless god. Again and again, Luther was led to repudiate God in tormented rebellion and to repudiate himself in obsessive melancholy. His later focus on figures such as the pope and the devil became paranoid, but these figures clearly represent a transference from the pervasive influence of old Hans, against whom Luther had defiantly rebelled, even as he had earlier submitted with self-effacing, compliant obedience.

Negative Identity

It was in the context of this inner struggle between defiance and compliance that Luther's struggle over what Erikson has called "negative identity" took place. The quest for total values could only be satisfied by the attainment of values that were completely foreign to everything that had been held up to him as desirable. Martin was inexorably caught up in this struggle between passive compliance and stubborn resistance. He complied with his father's wishes on one level, but repudiated his father's secular aspirations by embracing (prompted by the perils of a thunderstorm) traditional monasticism. But his resistance was not quelled even then. His fulfillment of the expectations of his religious superiors was challenged by his rebellious impulses as a crusading reformer. Erikson (1962:102) describes this phenomenon in the following terms:

> We will call all self-images, even those of a highly idealistic nature, which are diametrically opposed to the dominant values of an individual's upbringing, parts of a *negative identity*—meaning an identity which he has been warned *not* to become, which he can become only with a divided heart, but which he nevertheless finds himself compelled to become, protesting his wholeheartedness.

Or, as Erikson (1959:131) defines negative identity elsewhere, it is "an identity perversely based on all those identifications and roles, which, at critical stages of development, had been presented to the individual as most undesirable or dangerous, and yet as most real." It is important to note that the young Luther displayed the recalcitrant, rebellious, and provocative aspects which old Hans had successfully suppressed in himself. He was outwardly civil and compliant, but gave unbridled expression to his negative identity in the violence he unleashed toward his own family (Meissner 1978).

There was a further step to the shaping of Luther's identity. Erikson (1962:54) describes it in these terms:

> To these we must add the period of the completion of identity development at adolescence, which results in a massive glorification of some of the individual's constituent elements, and repudiation of others. In the life of a man like Luther (and in lesser ways in all lives), another screen is strongly suggested: the beginning of an artificial identity, the moment when life suddenly becomes biography. In many ways life began for Luther all over again when the world grabbed eagerly at his ninety-five theses, and forced him into the role of rebel, reformer, and spiritual dictator. Everything before that then became memorable only insofar as it helped him to rationalize his disobediences. Maybe this motivation is behind most attempts at historifying the past.

Consequently, if we can consider Luther's hammering the ninety-five theses to the Wittenberg cathedral door as symbolic, we can take it not only as an act of rebellion which resolved his own inner tensions and conflict, but also as a challenge and stimulus to which the troubled soul of Christian Europe responded. The reverberations of those hammer blows on the cathedral door in 1517 sent shock waves through the whole of Western Europe—reverberations which were not quieted until millions had lost their lives in centuries of religious wars and persecutions.

Conflict and Ideology

So it was that Luther's inner struggle resonated with the inner conflicts, suppressed hostilities, and ambivalences of many. The seeds of rebellion had lain dormant for centuries. Catholic Europe's inner unity had been weakened by many stresses and strains. The Church, influenced by new wealth and the spirit of the Renaissance, had become secularized. The papacy was embroiled in Italian and European politics, and when Luther visited Rome in his early monkish days, he encountered a shocking spectacle of deviousness, vanity, and corruption.

Closer to home, he launched his attack against a practice that become odious in the eyes of good Germans and was associated with the effrontery of the pope's Italian representatives, who must have seemed to the provincial Germans as agents of a foreign power. The money raised from the sale of indulgences was destined for the enrichment of the papacy. Certainly, the German princes who rallied to Luther's cause stood to gain, not merely financially by stemming the flow of German money to the papacy, but also by the confiscation of wealthy monastic properties and churches. For them, embracing Luther's cause not only served German patriotism, but also provided an opportunity for defying the power of the emperor and the pope.

Despite the many influences which contributed to the explosion,— historical, economic, social, and cultural—Luther was still the catalyst. His flamboyant, even sometimes violent, rhetoric fanned the flames and helped to focus latent rebellious attitudes which had long lain dormant in the German soul. His dramatic, defiant stance at Worms in 1521 became the watchword and battle cry of the Reformation: "Hier stehe ich. Ich kann nicht anders. Gott helfe mir. Amen." He provided an ideology which resolved the ambivalence of his own tortured conscience and took hold of the frustrated desires and fears of his contemporaries.

Thus, ideology is a powerfully constructive force for sustaining identity. Erikson (1962:22) defines it as "an unconscious tendency underlying religious and scientific as well as political thought: the tendency at a given time to make facts amenable to ideas, and ideas to facts, in order to create a world image convincing enough to support the collective and the individual sense of identity." Through the formation of an ideology—a system of beliefs and values—the group achieves its own proper identity, along with the coherence and solidarity that insure its persistence and effectiveness as a group. Without such an ideology, the group is nothing and has no inner life.

Only in terms of such an ideology can members attach themselves to the group with commitment and fidelity, thus sharing in the group's objectives and purposes. This is particularly true of religious ideologies, since they touch upon and preserve life's most profound purposes. Commitment and fidelity to an ideology provide strong support for the emerging sense of identity in adolescence, and preserve it in later stages of life.

But the blessings of ideology are not unmixed. Erikson (1959:58) points out some of the dangers:

> Ideologies seem to provide meaningful combinations of the oldest and the newest in a group's ideals. They thus channel the forceful earnestness, the sincere asceticism, and the eager indignation of youth toward that social frontier where the struggle between conservatism and radicalism is most alive. On that frontier, fanatic ideologists do their busy work and psychopathic leaders their dirty work; but there also, true leaders create significant solidarity. All ideologies ask for, as the prize for the promised possession of a future, uncompromising commitment to some absolute hierarchy of values and some rigid principles of conduct: ... it is in the totalism and exclusiveness of some ideologies that the superego is apt to regain its territory from identity: for when established identities become outworn or unfinished ones threaten to remain incomplete, special crises compel men to wage holy wars, by the cruelest means, against those who seem to question or threaten their unsafe ideological bases.

Judging by Luther's struggles with the enemies he proposed for himself—by his vituperative, vindictive tirades cast in terms of outrageous vulgarities and obscenities, and the paranoid cast of his lifelong struggles with the pope, the devil, and the Church of Rome—the ideology that he created and its theological rationalization did not quell the inner doubts and uncertainties, the conflictual torments which gnawed away at the foundations of his sense of truthfulness and purposefulness and provided a shifting foundation for his own inner sense of identity.

The Psychology of Faith

The problematic to which these considerations lead us is this: in Martin's tormented quest for true faith did he, in fact, achieve Luther's ideology with regard to the inner satisfaction of faith? Faith and ideology are not necessarily correlatives. But how do they differ? What does it mean to achieve an ideology without faith? Or to have faith without an ideology? Adherence to an ideology calls for a rudimentary commitment, a credulity and credence which make such adherence possible. But this need not yet be faith. The faith which we seek and which was the object of Martin's quest is a spiritual faith which derives from and expresses the deepest dimensions of trusting adherence and the sustaining, curative influence of divine grace.

Lynch (1973:9–10) takes up the question of the images by which we conceive of an experience of faith. He writes:

> The first is an imaging of faith as the most primary, the most elemental force in human nature; it is a force which *precedes* what we ordinarily call knowledge and all forms of specific knowing; this force is uneducated and needs education; it is educated by knowledge of every kind, by people of every degree, by irony but not by every irony; last of all it is formed and educated by Christ . . . . It is in this powerful, turbulent, primal form that we must first image faith, . . . but the first understanding of it . . . is that of a primal and broad force of belief, promise, and fidelity which—by its presence or absence, by its operation or collapse, by its goodness or fury, by its fidelities or treacheries—shapes (or misshapes) the welfare, shall I say the very existence, of men and women in life and society.

We must inquire whence comes this elemental force in terms of its psychological roots and derivatives.

In his study of faith, Martin Buber (1961) remarks that although there are many contents of faith, we really know faith in only two basic forms, one from the fact that I trust someone without necessarily being able to offer adequate reasons for that trust, and the other from the fact that I can acknowledge something to be true, again without being able to provide sufficient reason. Consequently, faith is not a matter of inadequate intelligence, but derives from the relationship to a trusted person or thing acknowledged as true. Believing is consequently not a matter of mere rationality, but engages one's whole being. Buber (1961:8) continues, "The relationship of trust depends on a state of contact, a contact of my entire being with the one in whom I trust, the relationship of acknowledging depends upon an act of acceptance, an acceptance by my entire being of that which I acknowledge to be true."

The process of faith embraces both trust and acknowledgment. Thus, the intellectualistic emphasis in Christian theology is elaborated in the context of living trust in the revealing God. Trust influences the deepest structures of the human mind. The capacity for trust expresses one's whole self and engages one's whole being. But as Buber has observed, faith is not realized in a single isolated decision; rather, it takes place in a person's whole life, in the totality of one's relationships not only to God but to one's world and to oneself.

The capacity of trust is implicit in faith. It represents a receptivity, an openness, a willingness to accept and integrate God's presence and his Word, as well as confidence in one's self and one's ability to make the necessary commitment of self, to bridge the chasm between the security and self-reliance of reason and the absurdity and other-reliance of faith.

This sense of trust, which is essential to other-reliance, begins to develop in early infancy, and forms the rudiments of faith. Lynch (1973:125) describes the process as follows:

> Perhaps we can say that it [faith] comes into force (which is better than saying that it comes into being) as soon as promises begin to be made to it. These promises need not always be spoken. I have said that most of the fundamental forms of faith are carved without words into the very structures of nature. The womb of the mother is a promise to the child. From earliest childhood faith becomes an increasingly active dialogue with promise. It is almost a dance of gestures between the mother and the child, a dance of offer, response, increasing complexity, testing, verification, misplacements, anticipations, overdemands, joys, cries, screams, withdrawals, renewals. There are so many steady, verified promises that there is a law of God: Honor thy father and thy mother. They are the makers and executors of promise.

The same can be said of the process of psychotherapy, which aims to bring faith, trust, and promise where they have never flourished or have been destroyed.

We can say simply that faith rests upon fundamental trust, for it is in faith that trust finds its unique expression. Erikson (1962:255) remarks, "The ratio and relation of basic trust to basic mistrust established during early infancy determines much of the individual's capacity for simple faith . . . ."

It was in terms of this inner struggle that Martin Luther wrought his greatest religious and theological accomplishment. Erikson (1962:257) observes:

> His basic contribution was a living reformulation of faith. This marks him as a theologian of the first order; it also indicates his struggle with the ontogenetically earliest and most basic problems of life. He saw as his life's work a new delineation of faith and will, of religion and law: for it is clear that organized religiosity, in circumstances where the faith in a world order is monopolized by religion, is the institution which tries to give dogmatic permanence to a reaffirmation of that basic trust—and a re-

newed victory over that basic mistrust—with which each human being emerges from early infancy. In this way organized religion cements the faith which will support future generations.

However, in order for true faith to remain, psychologically speaking, an elemental force in religious experience, it must maintain contact with its motivating infantile determinants. Thus, its trusting is a reaching back to those decisive moments of childhood trust. That reaching back is equivalently an unconscious regressive moment within the vitality of faith. But it is not merely a return, whether conscious or unconscious; it is a recapitulation, a reorganization, a reintegration, a synthetic process within the ego that summarizes and reasserts basic trust.

Moreover, Faith is a creative expression of something beyond trust and far more significant. The return to trust carries within it the seeds of its own capacity to transcend itself. This is similar to Kierkegaard's idea of infinite resignation—man resigns all finite goods in order to find them again in virtue of faith. The imperfection and finitude of basic trust must be resigned in order to recapture true faith more profoundly and more meaningfully.

Faith versus Ideology

All faith has a psychological capacity to sustain the individual sense of identity, but a risk is involved. The commitment to ideology tends to be exclusive, even as ideologies themselves tend to be intolerant of each other. The danger, of course, is overcommitment, and the history of religious faith is filled with such overcommitments. This results in a distortion of ideology as such, and brings about a defect in identity. From another perspective, a defect in identity can also underlie overcommitment. The ego's implicit incapacity provides a channel for the expression of deneutralized aggressive, libidinal drives, which are somehow legitimized by a perverted ideology. The outcome is a blend of sadism, sanctimoniousness, and hypermoralism against which true religious faith must wage an endless, unremitting struggle. Lynch's comments (1973:98–99) are to the point:

> It is the mark of an elite group to claim that it alone knows the meaning of words, it alone has the true faith, it alone is on the inside of things. If there are many forms of irony—many forms of language in which words say more than they seem or say the opposite of their seeming—this is the special irony of the elite, to declare that they alone are on the inside of words and things. This kind of irony is often used to create a sense of identity; it

marks people off from the everyday run of people . . . . It is clear that it is divisive. It does not *pass through* a lesser or the lower or the literal way; it is cabalistic and secret. It does not give any real power to the lower to move into the higher meaning. It does not want to move through the lower, but to transcend it. Secretly, therefore, it has no use for the human and is never really funny.

Such a distorted sense of exclusiveness, then, is inconsistent with true faith and ultimately with true identity. The essence of faith lies beyond fidelity, although it is impossible, in psychological terms, to translate that essence except in terms of fidelity or of basic trust. Fidelity is, after all, a finite good, which must (if we remain true to Kierkegaard's insight) be resigned if we are to have true faith. In this resignation, absurdity and absolute relation become possible. The ability to pass beyond fidelity thus requires a strength of the ego that surpasses mere ideology. Paradoxically, to reach beyond fidelity is not to surrender it, but to find it again; and in this refinding, it is enriched and deepened in virtue of the faith within which it is subsumed. (The capacity to transcend ideological commitments would be attained, presumably, in Fowler's Stages 5 and 6 of faith development. See Chapter 7.)

A question that concerns us here is whether Luther's tormented inner struggle was ever able to reach the level of ideological commitment, or even further, to reach the expanses of true faith. Erikson's treatment of Luther's psychological development seems to imply that it did. But the evidence is not conclusive, and there are ample reasons to suppose that Luther remained tormented and troubled to the very end. Doubts remain, and many people—particularly religious antagonists— have been quick to point them out and make of them what they will. Almost twenty years before Erikson's treatment of Luther was written, Erich Fromm provided his own analysis of the economic, social, and cultural factors which joined with Luther's rebellion to create the onslaught of the Reformation. Fromm (1965:96–97) focused on the contradiction between Luther's torment and the self-justification of his appeal to faith. He writes:

> Luther's doctrine of faith as an indubitable subjective experience of one's own salvation may at first glance strike one as an extreme contradiction to the intense feeling of doubt which was characteristic for his personality and his teachings up to 1518. Yet, psychologically, this change from doubt to certainty, far from being contradictory, has a causal relation. We must remember what has been said about the nature of this doubt: it was not the rational doubt which is rooted in the freedom of thinking and which dares to question established views. It was the irrational doubt which springs from the isolation and powerlessness of an individual whose attitude

toward the world is one of anxiety and hatred . . . . The compulsive quest for certainty, as we find with Luther, is not the expression of genuine faith, but is rooted in the need to conquer the unbearable doubt. Luther's solution is one which we find present in many individuals today, who do not think in theological terms: namely, to find certainty by the elimination of the isolated individual self, by becoming an instrument in the hands of an overwhelmingly strong power outside of the individual. For Luther this power was God and in unqualified submission he sought certainty. But although he thus succeeded in silencing his doubts to some extent, they never really disappeared; up to his last day he had attacks of doubt which he had to conquer by renewed efforts toward submission. Psychologically, faith has two entirely different meanings. It can be the expression of an inner relatedness to mankind and affirmation of life; or it can be a reaction formation against a fundamental feeling of doubt, rooted in the isolation of the individual and his negative attitude toward life. Luther's faith had that compensatory quality.

The question of Luther's resolution of the inner struggle remains unanswered. I do not intend to settle that question nor to pass judgment on Luther, but rather to elucidate the role of faith in such an anguished search. To better envision faith's role in this fateful process, I would like to focus here on the function of faith in the psychic economy.

Beyond Ideology

Faith is a dynamic process that embraces and expresses man's total existence. The emergence of faith must wait upon the emergence of fidelity and a sense of personal identity. But even as it touches them, it transforms them. Fidelity becomes more than an adherence to an ideology; it is enlarged and enriched in meaning and purposefulness. Moreover, identity itself is affected, since in faith man finds his authentic validity. Faith transforms and touches all parts of the psychic structure, reorganizing and integrating them into a more mature, effective pattern.

Faith serves an integrative function in the psychic economy. But although true faith is restorative, recuperative, and maturing, it rarely performs all these functions, or it performs them only partially. There are many causes for the impoverishment of faith. As a process, it endures many vicissitudes and rarely if ever survives them unimpaired. I would like to suggest here that the failure of faith is somewhat correlative to the distortion of ideology. In Luther's case, there were both ideological rebellion and adherence to a new, personally more meaningful ideology—particularly in his reassuring notion of justification without works. The defects in ideological commitment can extend from degrees of overcommitment, through those of undercommitment, to the ranges of ideological rebellion and rejection of commitment.

What I suggest here is that the distortion of ideology, whether by excess or defect, can result in the formation of a "false self." This notion of a false self was introduced by Winnicott (1965) and has implications that should be examined in relation to the problem of identity and identity formation. A related problem is that of the exclusivity of ideologies and the pressures exerted by ideological groups, which demand unquestioning adherence to and compliance with their particular ideologies. Such commitments tend to set themselves off against other ideologies which are decried as heretical, dangerous, and evil (Meissner 1978).

The fragile identity which commits itself unquestioningly to such an ideology does so out of a sense of compliance and a need to overcome, compensate for, and defend against the inner sense of weakness, inadequacy, and powerlessness. In such circumstances, adherence to an ideology does not heal these inner wounds; it leaves the inner sense of fragile identity little better off than before. Nonetheless, a false sense of identity can arise around a false self-configuration that derives its strength and stability from compliant adherence to its own ideology and from the approval given it by the group with which it shares that ideology. One variant of this false-self organization attaches itself to a group ideology, thereby stabilizing its fragmented, fragile sense of identity. Another variant corresponds to what Erikson describes as "negative identity"— one formed and sustained in rejection of and rebellion against a proposed ideology. It is a false self rooted in defiance rather than compliance. These are both variations on the theme of despair. (See the discussion of Kierkegaard's notion of despair and the pathology of faith in Chapter 5.)

This formulation comes strikingly close to those Erikson uses to describe the links between ideology and identity in the positive, constructive frame of reference that he intends for them. One useful way to discriminate and test the difference is that, in the measure to which identity fails or becomes distorted, and the false-self organization takes its place, there is a corresponding need for enemies. In other words, the false self is built upon defensive introjects, which can be sustained and defended only in terms of corresponding projections which view opposing ideologies and commitments as threats to the in-group and the self. The extent of prejudice, bigotry, and conflict among nations, races, and classes assures us that this is the basic stuff of human experience—and may, in fact, be universal.

If we undertake to schematize this view of the connection between identity and faith—with the risk that the schema may be interpreted as a simplification—the distortions of ideology, which we have been discussing, can be linked to the formation of a false identity as a component of a false-self organization. On the other hand, the constructive expression of ideology to which Erikson (1959) addresses himself can be linked with the emergence of a sense of personal identity, which involves a configuration which "gradually integrates constitutional givens, idiosyncratic libidinal needs, favorite capacities, significant identification, effective defenses, successful sublimations, and consistent roles" (p. 116).

Faith and Spiritual Identity

The entrance of faith into this process adds a new and different dimension. As Luther himself commented, a man without spirituality becomes his own exterior. We have described the exteriority of compliance and adherence in terms of a false-self organization. Faith, however, leads the process of identity formation to transcend itself. It is the elemental force of faith, dynamized and motivated by the power of grace, which elicits and elaborates a spiritual identity. The spiritual identity builds upon and perfects personal identity—*gratia perficit naturam.*

Faith is only one dimension of that spiritual identity which emerges under the action of grace through and with the ego's synthetic capacities. This action repairs, heals, and supports the underlying identity within which it functions and expresses itself. The exploration of the psychology of faith is an exploration into some of the relationships that exist between spiritual identity, so conceived, and the personal identity upon which it builds and which, in building, it enriches and transforms.

The basic question is this: can a true sense of identity—transcending the vicissitudes of ideology and loyalties partially conceived and exclusively pledged—be achieved and sustained without the elemental motivating power of faith, generated and energized by the persistent influence of grace? Or can the claims of ideology, the pledging of human loyalties, provide only partial solutions for the fragmentations and diffusions that afflict humanity?

We further note that faith takes place in relation to a community of believers and to institutionalized religions. These provide a context of social integration by which the faith of a given community is rejuvenated and replenished from the faith of the individual. Even if the faith of the community so enforces the faith of the individual, the relationship is nonetheless precarious. Faith is essentially a dynamic process, but the institution of faith is cast in static, dogmatic formulae and repetitious ritual and cult. The vitality of the process and the renewed significance of the objects of faith must be related.

The personal act of belief and what is grasped in the act of belief are distinguishable but inseparable. *Fides qua* and *fides quae creditur* form a totality. Belief is always belief in something. The process cannot be cast simply in dogmatic terms, since its very nature is radical openness. It is always an intentional, existential act. The complexities of the relationship between faith as act of belief and faith as content of belief belong to a theology of faith rather than to its psychology; yet it is reasonable to insist that the reaffirmation of trust, the enrichment of fidelity, and the clarification of identity are stabilized by a participation in the shared meaning of communal beliefs.

We must bear in mind that we stand at an intricate, problematic intersection of the problems of psychopathology, psychic health and identity formation, and the restorative, transforming action of grace. The elements of faith involve a complex interplay of these multiple factors. The case of Luther and his dramatic religious experience provides us with a study of the powerful actions of grace stirring within a tormented soul. We cannot judge the outcome of Luther's struggle, nor can we absolve him of primitive hatred and persecutory anxiety.

Like the unremitting furies, the devils never left Martin alone. They were buried deep within his heart and soul. Psychologically speaking, they were embedded within the complex or pathogenic introjects which came from the brutal, primitive image of old Hans and the victimized vulnerability of Martin's mother. Around these pathogenic introjects was organized a false self based upon those elements of the repressed parental conscience, which young Martin had internalized and which had become his own.

I would like to suggest that powerful, grace-filled forces were unleashed in Martin's soul, drawing him toward a greater freedom, a greater integrity, more secure, creative autonomy. His first attempts at rebellion came with his religious conversion, but he succeeded merely in substituting one false self for another. For his compliance to the secular tyranny of his father, he substituted another which placed him in subservience to a spiritual tyranny. The struggle of submission and defiance had been moved from the exterior realm to the interior realm.

The second rebellion exchanged one spiritual ideology for another. It exchanged the ideology of obediential compliance to God's all-powerful will, which required the satisfaction of that will through continuing good works (an enterprise which Martin felt was beyond him because of the evil contamination from within) for the security and assurance of an ideology of justification through simple faith. If Martin was able in each rebellion and at each stage of the struggle to win some greater degree of freedom, he was probably never able to free himself from the torments and evils that possessed his heart. This suggests to us that the power of faith in the greatest souls may not be limited by dogmatic rigidities and ideological persuasion.

PART 2

HOPE

CHAPTER 10

The Theology of Hope

Post-Vatican II developments in theological reflection, and in psychological reflection and interest, have focused on hope as a central aspect of integrating human experience. Theologians have approached hope as an essential and dynamic element in religious motivation. Concurrently, concern over the role and function of hope in human psychological functioning has also been growing. Psychotherapists have begun to take into account the place of hope in the therapeutic process as well as the influence of hopelessness on various forms of psychopathology (Sipe 1970).

I hope to draw together some of the threads of these approaches in this reflection, but I wish also to establish a specific focus. In the continuing dialogue between theology and the psychological sciences an effort at integrating theological actualities with psychological realities constitutes an important development. The theological and religious dimension of our experience has particular relevance for our intrapsychic functioning and growth. Theologically conceived processes and their effects need to be conceptualized and their specific correlates on the intrapsychic level need to be formulated and clarified. The present discussion, then, can be placed in conjunction with the preceding efforts to articulate certain of these issues and interrelated processes. (See the preceding Sections 1 and 2 on grace and faith.)

The consideration of hope is particularly relevant for our attempts to integrate both the psychological and the theological dimensions of human existence and experience. Hope has been traditionally regarded as a central element in Christian belief and in the living of Christian life. It is hope that brings vitality and strength to man's religious convictions. But contemporary developments have brought the theology of hope even closer to human concerns. The hopes generated through Christian belief and practice are being focused not in some distant and ultimate eschatological realm, but in the world as we know it. The new eschatology to which Christian hope directs itself is a creative and militant eschatology. Its objective is to bring about change in the world so that the Christian vision of justice and charity may begin to be realized in this world— rather than in the next. As Metz (1969:94) puts it:

> How does the Church realize its mission to work for the future of the world? It cannot be by pure contemplation, since contemplation by definition relates to what has already become existent and to what actually exists. The future which the Church hopes for is not yet here, but is *emerging* and *arising (entstehend)*. Therefore, the hope which the church sets in itself and in the world should be creative and militant. In other words, Christian hope should realize itself in a creative and militant eschatology.

As the purpose and objectives of Christian hope come closer to this world and its embrace extends to our human hopes, the conceptual gap between the theology of hope and its inner workings in the human psyche becomes narrower. The theological virtue of hope—rooted in faith and sustained by the action of grace—originates and finds expression within our psychological organization and structure. If we cannot see it in human and specifically psychological terms, it remains disembodied and unreal. An eschatology that is at once realized and creative in terms of the immediate Christianization of the world gives to the virtue of hope an immediacy and a functionality that it never had before. Moreover, our understanding of hope in its this-worldly function cannot be satisfactory unless we understand its role within man himself.

I should emphasize at the beginning of this undertaking that the psychology of hope is not at all well established. That is part of its fascination. Rather than a body of established facts and formulations on which to build, we have only scattered observations that provide little more than an initial understanding. We are, therefore, undertaking an exploration—with all the interest of what lies ahead to be discovered.

Traditional approach

The traditional approach to the theology of hope left it very much in the realm of the objective. Hope was treated as a supernatural, infused, theological virtue. The emphasis was placed on the object of hope—God himself. What predominated in the development of this theology was the consideration that our attainment of God was beyond our natural capacities. The gap between finite and infinite, between man and God, could only be bridged with supernatural assistance. The effect this supernaturally infused virtue had on man was seen in terms of the metaphysics of act and habit. Hope was thus an ontological modification of the human will through grace that made it possible for man to direct himself to the future but (humanly) unattainable goal of eternal life. The expectation of eternal life and the means to attain it rested on trust and confidence in the promises of God.

The traditional approach emphasized the other-worldly basis of hope. Its focus lay beyond death, with man's ultimate goal and salvation. Hopes on this side of the grave were considered merely natural, with the implication that the Christian life of hope had nothing to do with such hopes.

There was likewise little room within this framework for a psychology of hope. The traditional approach concentrated on preserving a separation between the intrapsychic mechanisms and the operation of supernatural virtues—presumably to keep the supernatural virtues uncontaminated by natural processes, in a general effort to underline the distinction between natural processes and processes motivated by grace. Only gradually did important theological principles come into sharper focus, giving rise, inevitably to tensions within the theological perspective.

The understanding of grace as operating not as an extrinsic force in moving the will, but as an inner influence working in and through our psychic potentialities, raised serious questions about the nature and function of the action of God's supernatural grace. If grace transcended nature as the traditional approach emphasized, it was also immanently operative only in terms of and through the natural capacities of the human psychic structure. Given this more natural perspective, a full understanding of hope could not be satisfied with a merely ontological explanation in terms of acts, habits, and potencies. There was also a need to understand the psychological implications of hope and to formulate its influence in psychologically meaningful terms.

Recent approaches

Contemporary thinking about the theology of hope is rooted in the thinking of Ernest Bloch (1970). Bloch's thought has moved away from the existentialist finitude of Heidegger with its theological extrapolation of Bultmannian demythologization. Heidegger's translation of an eschatological perspective into existentialist terms served to achieve relevance at the expense of human horizons. Bloch attempts to open those perspectives beyond the limits of man's finitude; he does so by basing his thinking on hope. For Bloch, man is caught *"zwischen zwei Zeiten"*—between two ages of human experience, a phase of human development between the past that was and the future that is not yet. Man is thus forced to live in a condition of radical expectation and anticipation.

In such a view hope becomes central to our existence. We are essentially creatures who hope, who fantasize, who imagine and dream the future, and who strive to attain it. To be human is to be *unterwegs*, to be "on the way" to something different, something better. It is to be *homo viator*. Marcel (1962:153) had observed that "perhaps a stable order can only be established on earth if man always remains acutely conscious that his condition is that of traveler . . . " Man's face is always pointed toward a destination beyond, and it is hope that leads him.

Though hope builds on fantasy and desire, it is more than these. It is a source of creative strength—not merely in the expression of wishes, but in the attainment of realities. Bloch (1970:69–70) writes:

> And yet we here, suffering and benighted, can hope far afield. If it remains strong enough, if it is pure and undistinctly aware of itself, hope will not fail us. For the human soul encompasses all things, even the beyond that is not yet. The soul alone is what we want, and thinking serves it. It is the sole space of thought, the content of its language, and its object—an object scattered all over the world, concealed in the darkness of the lived moment, promised in the form of the absolute question. And because that which is cannot be conceived any more, only reconceived and reduced to a matter of the soul; because good wishes, as they can be fathers to the thought, can also become fathers to things, which alone are truthful; because of this eventually unfactual, antimundane, world-dividing homogeneity of thought and of *not-being, not-yet-being*, the *creative* concept deals now only with the constitutive fantasies that are inaccessible or transcendent, if not indeed the "metaphysics" forbidden by Kant.

Hope directs the traveler's footsteps neither in the path of despair nor into the presumptive quiet of overconfidence. It rests not on its being or its possession of being, but on its beginning to be. It places a demand and an expectation. It cannot satisfy itself with the confidence of possession since it does not yet possess. It cannot despair because its emptiness looks forward to a fulfillment that is not yet. The expectation of hope lies in the *yet*; its demand derives from the *not*. It is a state of unfulfillment that looks forward to fulfillment.

In his major work, *The Principle of Hope*, Bloch places hope at the very heart of our religious experience: "Where there is hope there is religion." The religious impulse is a questing for something that is beyond itself. Our questing has in it an antistatic element that in its very restlessness reveals the truth. An openness pervades us as experiencing subjects and the world of our experience and belief. This anthropological view of our religious dimension presupposes both a *Deus absconditus*—a hidden God toward whom our hopes are drawn—and a *homo absconditus*—a subject whose creative power remains hidden yet present in promise.

Bloch views our condition as a form of utopian latency in which a dynamic openness to the realization of creative possibility lies at the root of our religious impulse. The inner instinct of dynamic and creative intentionality must reach out beyond ourselves to engender creative possibility in our world as well as in the object of our belief. Bloch writes (1970:210):

> The kingdom is outwardness, not only inwardness; it is order, not only freedom—essentially it is the order of a subjectivity to which objectivity is no longer something extraneous, and so the objectivity that still surrounds man as nature must be understood and honored in whatever part of it has not appeared as yet. Thus hope, which has been at work in religion and has now rid itself of illusions, of hypostases, of myths, intends through the idea of the kingdom that a utopian light shine on the border of the objective possibility as it shines in the subjective one. To a religious intentionality the germ is also on the move without. The light in the stable of Bethlehem and the light of the star that stood still above it are one and the same.

Thus for Bloch, the key to our existence lies in our hope for the future—for hope fires the human spirit in the present and unveils the ultimate meaning of our existence. Through hope we are open to the future, and this futurity is basic to Bloch's ontology of "not-yet-being." Man's radical hopefulness releases him from the prison of finitude in which Heidegger had locked him. Entering the theological dialogue, this view of man's hopeful openness has helped to underscore the radical element of hope inherent in Christian eschatology. Christian hope rests on a revelation of promise and directs itself toward a reality not yet realized. Hope contradicts the reality that we know and looks to the future for the ultimate resolution of good and evil. But such hope is not mere utopian idealism, because that future and its promise have already entered history in the person of Christ. Thus, hope is rooted in confidence about God's promises, a confidence that assumes a dynamic ontology of history in which the future-orientation of man's existence makes the horizon of new possibilities real.

Moltmann's theology of hope takes its point of departure from this basic perspective. The promise of Christian eschatology has contributed continuing vitality and meaning to the Christian religious experience. Without hope in the future, belief and religious commitment would perish. In his *Theology of Hope*, Moltmann (1967) regards revelation as an event of promise that excites hope in man's religious response. In the Old Testament, God's revealing words are words of promise. God reveals himself as the power that guarantees the future—"God before us"—drawing men on in belief and hope. God's word is not merely God revealing His truth; it is God giving his word, his promissory word that guarantees His commitment to a future reality. Marcel long ago commented that the antithesis to hope is capitulation to fate. Confrontation with inexorable and immutable events over which man has no control leads to despair. Hope lives in the expectation and confidence that new possibilities can be attained and that the patterns of life and social process can be changed.

Hope, therefore, insists on the possibility and availability of meaningful change as well as the radical human freedom to effect it. Hope is rooted in freedom, the basic human freedom to do, to change, to direct, to make the promise of the future a living reality. As Gustafson (1970:536–37) has written:

> Hope assumes that freedom exists: freedom to become what one now is not, freedom to change not only the course of one's life, but the course of the social history of which one is a part. Hope can be passive, or it can be active. Passive hope sits and sits, expecting other persons or other groups, or some great interruptions in history from a power within or beyond it, to fulfill man's expectations. Active hope moves to perform the possible, to fulfill purposes, intentions, convictions, that are shaped in part by the object of hope.

Thus, the Christian is summoned by God's promises not to repose tranquilly in the present order, but to strive restlessly for something more. The eschatological vision cannot rest content with what is, but must stretch forward and strain for what is not yet. This is the tension of history—the inner tension that gives rise to those acts of creative responsibility by which we transform our world and move it toward the future.

Moltmann, relying on Bloch's anthropology, sees the future to which the word of God calls us as carrying with it a freedom that transcends present conflicts and limitations. But that future must be attained through responsible action that initiates the realization of what is not yet and thus breaks through the bondage of the present. We cannot escape into the future. We can attain it only by responsibly facing the tensions of the present and thus opening ourselves to an enrichment of experience and freedom. The political, social, and even personal alienation afflicting modern man, which seeks unbridled freedom as a way of avoiding personal and social responsibility, has access only to the past and the present, not to the future.

The future, of course, is not what is, but what will be, and thus a matter of the objective conditions of possibility, but not merely these. For its realization requires subjective grounds of possibility as well. Our affective experience of reality accounts for the internal, intrapsychic dynamics that make us want to change reality, to shape it to fit our future. To affirm the future, means taking responsibility for reality and committing ourselves to meaningful action. Without believing hope, the subjective conditions for realizing the promised future are lacking.

The complex of relationships and structures that makes up the social system has its objective dimension; but it is also a human construction permeated with meaning. It originates in human concerns and shared goals and purposes. Faced with the massive character of social reality, we can easily forget that we are agents of social process and that the social structure is an extension of our own purpose and intent. The social system is an open process, an unfinished project. The theologians of hope, following Bloch's Marxist emphasis on social change, have stressed the link between hope and social and political responsibility. Christian hope is hope for this world—not merely for the Christian in this world, but for the world in which the Christian exists. Hope thus points to a responsibility that is realistic and even militant. God's promise of fidelity draws us to achieve a responsible grasp on the future. The future is not a random process of unpredictable events filled with the primitive dread of chance, but a process of fuller freedom and control directed and made attainable by our responsible action.

This fresh emphasis on hope has created a new sensibility: a "passion for the possible," as Metz puts it. Man's consciousness of the past fades and his sensitivity and appetite for the future grows. Metz (1967:171) puts it in these terms:

> The relationship to the past takes on more and more a purely aesthetic romantic or archaic character or it depends on a purely historical interest which simply confirms that the past is over and done with. This modern consciousness has a purely historical relationship to the past, but an existential relation to the future. It frees man from a tyranny of a history concerned only with origins, and turns him towards a history conceived with ends.

We no longer need approach the world as an imposed destiny; the subjective sense of possibility engendered through hope transforms it into the material in which the objective possibility is realized through responsible action. We can transform the world and make it the setting for our historical actuality. Thus, Christian eschatology has little room for passivity and boredom. It is, rather, productive and militant. Eschatological faith and temporal engagement embrace and infuse each other with a common hope.

The theological perspective, then, is spelled out in terms of eschatological possibilities and worldly commitments—worldly in the political and social sense. But it is the subjective sense of possibility that I wish to emphasize here as most relevant to the psychological perspective as well as to the realization of hope within the self. The eschatology of Christian hope is not limited to the world; rather, it is primarily personalized and personally realized.

Hope is engendered in the first instance within the psyche, in the inner world, before it can be projected to the external world of political and social realities. The eschatological vision must be focused within the heart and mind, as a sense of the possibility and fulfillment of the self, if it is to find its primary and most meaningful realization. This is where Christian hope and creative eschatology converge. Supernatural hope and the human experience of hopefulness come to a common focus in this meeting of God's word of promise and man's yearning for fulfillment.

CHAPTER 11

The Psychology of Hope

More than a score of years ago, Karl Menninger (1959) addressed himself to the subject of hope. He felt that hope was of central importance to the practice of psychiatry at all levels, but that we knew so little about hope and its workings in the human psyche that any scientific analysis of it was out of the question. In the intervening years we have learned more about hope—enough perhaps to permit the beginnings of an analysis, but little more than that. We must content ourselves with tentative explorations.

Psychodynamics

For all of that, the notion of hope is not vague or indefinite; it is rather specific, in fact. Part of my effort here is to specify the concept of hope and to clarify our understanding of the conditions that elicit and encourage it. The first and most important characteristic of hope is that it is realistic: it seeks, imagines, and finds the real. This realistic direction of hope is fundamental to understanding its psychology. Hope imagines the real, in Buber's phrase, and it does not give up such imagining. But the real it imagines is the real that is not yet—that it grasps, however, as possible and attainable.

This aspect of hope was grasped by Marcel (1962) in his pioneering work. He put it in the context of man's capacity to work—to employ himself in the bringing about of real effects in his world. He wrote:

> To be at work, on the other hand, is to be possessed by the real in such a way that we no longer know exactly whether it is we who are fashioning it,

or it which fashions us. In any case, difficult as it is to form a perfectly intelligible idea of its operation, we can say that it involves the reciprocal movement by which man and reality embrace each other, which is none the less effective in the artist and the scholar than in the artisan, for instance, or the labourer. All that varies is the manner in which the real is present to man, or correlatively, the manner by which man is present to the real . . . . The unemployed or the man without hope of whom I spoke just now is not only someone who no longer gives anything, he is someone who has lost the power of animating the world into which he feels he has been thrown, and where he is superfluous. But this animating power should not be understood in a purely subjectivistic sense, like the faculty of making fantastic shadows move across a lifeless screen: the power of animating is the power of using to the full, or, to go more deeply, of lending ourselves, that is to say of allowing ourselves to be used to the full, of offering ourselves in some way to those *kairoi*, or life-giving opportunities, which the being, who is really available (*disponible*), discovers all around him like so many switches controlling the inexhaustible current flowing through our universe.

The real, however, is not merely metaphysical; it is primarily toward real objects and real persons that hope directs itself. Hope is, therefore, an act of mutuality, an act of shared imagination, of *imagining with*. To lose hope is to lose the capacity for shared imagination, hope is an act that builds and is sustained by community. Through it we are able to align ourselves with social structures and can come to depend on one other. In the following section, I examine the mutuality and dependence that obtain in the child's first meaningful object relation, the relation to the mother. It is here that the rudiments of hope are acquired. In addition, I explore the stirrings of hope in the mutuality of the therapeutic relation.

Another important aspect of hope is its relation to desire—or, in other terms, wishing and wish-fulfillment. The link is a strong one. Part of the capacity to hope is to identify and recognize one's wishes. As William Lynch (1965:24) puts it: "When I cannot wish, I am moving toward despair." Yet, if hope is rooted in wish-fulfillment and desire, it is not limited to these instinctual aspects. If hope reaches backward to the sources of instinctually based desires, it also must reach forward to attain realizable goals. It is the function of hope, therefore, to integrate wishes and impulses for gratification with real possibilities.

Hope is not merely a vehicle for the expression of wishful fantasies or a defense against feelings of depression or despair, but an adaptive resource for effective and realistic coping (Korner 1970). Desire is the expression of wishfulness; it does not translate itself into real terms without the intervention of effective and purposeful action and intention. This is exactly the difference that separates wishing and its associated desires from hope. It is equivalent to what Marcel (1960) called "the prophetic function of hope." He comments:

> The man who has hopes of the coming of the world in which justice will be paramount does not confine himself to saying that such a world is infinitely to be preferred to an unjust world—he proclaims that this world *shall come* into existence; in this lies the prophetic nature of hope. But by this, too, we may see more clearly in what courage, which is the driving force behind hope, truly consists. (p. 178)

The prophetic emphasis in hope has nothing to do with fantasies of wishful desire; it is prophetic precisely insofar as it proclaims a reality, though one not yet achieved. Thus, the line between desire and hope, however thin it may be, is as significant as the line between fantasy and reality. It is hope that translates realizable fantasy into attainable reality. This "prophetic" function of hope represents a major aspect of the integrative capacity of the healthily functioning ego, which Freud saw as mediating and integrating the demands of our instinctual drives and wishes with the limits and demands of external reality. A major modality of this function is exercised through hope.

The interplay among wish, fantasy and desire, and their integration with purposeful activity takes place at the heart of any creative work. Hope thus shares in part in the ego's capacity to regress constructively. In so doing, it enables the ego to recapture the sources of imaginative potentiality and creativity. It serves the ego's adaptive purposes by focusing and integrating instinctual derivatives with real possibilities. Thus, hope is liberalizing: it frees and channels our creative and imaginative capacities by distinguishing what it is within our power to accomplish and what is not. Thus, hope channels wishful desire into a capacity for willing. For willing entails purposeful intention and a capacity for the translation of intention into execution. Desire issues in wishful fantasy; willing issues in directed and purposeful action. Willing is the exercise of will, which Erikson (1964:119) defines as "the unbroken determination to exercise free choice as well as self-restraint . . . " And he adds:

> *To will* does not mean to be willful, but rather to gain gradually the power of increased judgment and decision in the application of drive. Man must learn to will what can be, to renounce as not worth willing what cannot be, and to believe he willed what is inevitable. (p. 118)

I shall return to the question of the relation between hope and freedom at a later point.

Hope, therefore, demands a sense of the possible, while hopelessness means being ruled by a sense of the impossible. Without this sense
of being able to set and attain goals, there is no movement, no action, no
motivation. Stotland (1969) has gathered much of the relevant experimental and clinical evidence and related it to the functioning of
hope. He concludes that accomplishment, achievement, or the attaining
of future goals is impossible without hope, without the conviction that
such goals can really be reached. Motivation in this approach is a joint
function of the perceived probability of attaining the goal and of the perceived value of the goal. This is where hope plays its part in the
motivational process. When hope, the perceived probability of attaining
the goal, is high, affective commitment and motivation are increased.
Conversely, when the perceived probability of attaining the goal is low,
motivation sinks, and the outcome is liable to be anxiety or depression.

Thus, hopefulness must to some degree be learned through experience. We have to learn the conditions of objective possibility imposed by the structure of reality as well as the limits of subjective
possibility. But in addition, we need the reinforcement of experienced
success in seeking and achieving anticipated goals. The rudiments of
these basic experiences reach back to early levels of childhood experience, as we shall see, but they continue to contribute to the development of a sense of competence and capacity in adult experience. Sustaining a sense of the possible depends on a perception of the goal as
attainable in relation to one's own potentialities and in relation to objective conditions. If goals seem difficult or remote, hope tends to diminish.
The degree of difficulty against which different individuals can maintain
their hopefulness varies considerably. Certain persons become hopeless
in the face of minimal difficulty; others strive hopefully in the face of
often overwhelming odds. The capacity to maintain a sense of the
possibility of even difficult goals may be an index of available ego
strength.

The real strength of hope lies in its capacity to set and acknowledge
its own limits. Hope finds its strength in maintaining a sense of what is
really possible in the world of human limitations. It is only when expectations exceed the limits of the possible that hopelessness arises. As
Lynch (1965:47) expresses it:

> There is nothing as strong as hope when it knows how to limit itself. Its
> first victory was to discover that it was a relative idea, related to help, and
> could cast off the burden of being an absolute. Now it discovers, with
> relief, that its range is not absolute. The human world must be divided be-
> tween hope and hopelessness. Since there are many things that are hope-
> less for man, hopelessness is a fact. This is a second reduction in the bur-

den of hope. The important thing is not to think that all things can be hoped for, but to keep the hopelessness out of hope.

Insofar as hope fails to adapt itself to the limits of the real and the really possible, it ceases to be hope, enters the realm of the wishful, and immerses itself in hopelessness. The reasons for this are complex, as we shall see, but the essential dynamic involves a wishing for the impossible that brings on hopelessness. The impossible may mean what is impossible for this specific individual, for the possible is always defined in terms of a particular individual and his unique capacities and limitations. To lose sight of this fundamental fact is to run the risk of infecting hope with hopelessness.

I should like to add a further word about wishing, lest it be relegated to the realm of wishful fantasy. To do so would be to underestimate its importance and to devalue it unduly. The capacity to wish is a basic human resource; it lies at the root of our creative potential. Human creativity depends in large measure on the capacity to entertain wishes and desires, even beyond the limits of what is apparently possible. Only by the exercise of this imaginative capacity can we reach out to the limits of the real and expand our awareness of the extent of real possibilities. But if wishes are to become anything more than wishful fantasy, they must come into engagement with reality.

One of the basic elements in human hopefulness is the individual's willingness to take responsibility for his wishing. Only thus does wishful fantasy have the chance to become creative imagination and thus open the way to realization. If the wishing subject takes responsibility for his wishes, he then accepts them as either mere fantasy or as translatable into reality. When individuals do not take responsibility for their wishes, they tend to place the blame for their failure to realize them on others, to retreat from the responsibility of translating their own wishes into reality, as well as from the realization that what is wished for is either within the realizable limits of their personal capacities or—in the case of impossible wishes—beyond those limits. When one is able to vacate responsibility, the door is open for the entrance of hopelessness—one is no longer able, in Lynch's excellent phrase, "to keep the hopelessness out of hope."

Development

If hope is a resource and a strength by which we strive for meaningful goals, it is not merely a given of the personality, a sort of constititutional foundation on the basis of which the personality functions. It has a history and a course of development, and is subject to the vicissitudes of development as well as to the uncertainties of the resolution of psychosexual and psychosocial crises. Hopefulness is a developmental achievement, and in its achievement it becomes a resource for further adaptive functioning and coping.

The development of hopefulness begins at the beginning of life. Erikson has remarked that hope is the earliest and most indispensable strength that inheres in the very fact of being alive. Hope is, therefore, a basic quality of experience that marks the first strata of the infant's interchange with the world. The primary focus of that initial interchange lies in the interaction between the child and the mothering figure. At first, the process is predominantly physiological. The infant's inner states of physiological disequilibrium and need are met by the mother's ministering, feeding, caring responses. The critical variables involve the infant's capacity to express its inner states and issue the appropriate cues, and the mother's capacity to read and respond to these cues. Thus, in a healthy mothering situation a pattern of mutual responsiveness and sensitivity is set up between mother and child that enables the child to build a sense of trust and reliance on the availability and responsiveness of the mother and on his own assured inner capacity for regulating distressing inner states.

The process is complex and delicate, but its essential elements pertain to the mutual regulation and responsiveness that emerge between mother and child. The central constituent in the inception of the process is the mother's innate capacity to respond with appropriate mothering activity to the cues emitted by the child. To do this she has to respond in terms of the uniqueness of the child more than according to her own inner perceptions or needs. Children differ quite strikingly from the moment of birth. Some are more active and demanding, some less. A mother may achieve greater success in responding to one child than to another. This is partly a function of her personality, partly a function of her flexibility in providing mothering activities. Where this process is successful, the conditions for trust and hope are engendered. As Erikson (1964:116) has written:

> Hope relies for its beginnings on the new being's first encounter with *trustworthy maternal persons,* who respond to his need for *intake* and *contact* with warm and calming envelopment and provide food both pleasurable to ingest and easy to digest, and who prevent experience of the kind which may regularly bring too little too late. This is far from being a merely instinctive, or merely instinctual matter. Biological motherhood needs at least three links with social experience: the mother's past experience of being mothered; a conception of motherhood shared with trustworthy

contemporary surroundings; and an all-enveloping world-image tying past, present, and future into a convincing pattern of providence. Only thus can mothers provide.

The element of trust enables the child to establish confidence in the needed and vital other; the element of hope lets the child reach beyond that primary relationship. The child's future growth critically depends on the emerging capacity to separate himself out from a secure union with his primary objects. His capacity to do so depends in part on the assurance that in the process of separating he does not lose the support he needs in relation with the object. Mahler (1968, 1975) has described this process in terms of separation and individuation. The child must be able to separate from the maternal matrix in order to establish and achieve his own relative independence and individuality.

The child's emerging capacity for hope depends on this ability to renounce prior dependencies and attachments in order to commit himself to future possibilities. Separation, renunciation and the turning toward future potentialities are pertinent at every stage of the life cycle. The process depends on a succesful dialectic between the negative and the positive, between renunciation and anticipation, between the past and the future. A generally positive resolution of this dialectic enables the child to grow in hope even as he develops an ever greater capacity for renunciation, toleration of disappointment, and delay for gratification in the interest of larger or more distant hopes.

Perhaps one of the most difficult things to accept is the realization that human hope is not simple or unified; rather, these hopes are multiple and riddled with ambivalence and conflict. No single hope or set of hopes can ever be completely fulfilled since by their very nature they run counter to other hopes. To the extent that we are unable to allow our ambivalence to find some level of integration with this multiplicity of hopes, hope becomes a staunch bulwark for repressed omnipotent wishes. The acceptance of reality as mature adults carries with it the recognition that many of our most private hopes are irreconcilable and often inherently destructive, not only of other hopes and wishes we might cherish ourselves, but even of the hopes and wishes of others. These multiple, disparate, and conflicted hopes must be woven into a more or less coherent and reasonably synthesized pattern if we are to achieve developmental integration. This requires the working through of disappointments, the resolution of past losses and griefs, the surrender of infantile omnipotence and its related frustration. Such a synthesis ultimately requires the recognition and acceptance of the limitations and imperfections of human existence and the unavoidable ambivalence of human relatedness.

Thus, the process of growth in hope entails a continuing dialectic of renunciation of the past and an affirmation of the future. As the child develops, he is constantly verging on new possibilities and new capacities—driven in part by the pace of organic maturation with its stock of new powers and new capacities but, even more importantly, prompted by new levels of psychological awareness and interaction with the environment. In order to grasp to these new possibilities, the growing child must be able to surrender the gratification and security of his present status and reach out toward the uncertainty of what is not yet. The ability to do so rests on carrying along as one's own inner possession the early successes in trusting and hoping. As Erikson (1969:154–155) puts it:

> At the beginning when the mother is truly the matrix of survival, we can learn to trust the world and to develop the basic ingredient of all vitality: hope. Having tasted our mother's body with mouth and senses, we remain part of it and yet also become strong enough to part from it. Our first firmament is the mother's face, shining above the goodness of nourishment; and only the study of universal mythology and of the deepest mental pathology can give us an inkling of the sinister rages and the confused imagery which that early trust must help us to contain before we can emerge from the maternal matrix. Those moods and that confusion must often be lived through again in adolescence—and this especially in passionate youths beset with a sense of sin—when the original trauma of separation from the mother's body is repeated in the necessity to leave "home"— which, as we have seen, may include motherland, mother tongue, mother religion.

From a psychodynamic perspective, this reaching forth toward the future entails a capacity to renounce dependence and attachment to present realities. This is a basic law of development for groups, institutions, and political entities no less than for the internal growth of organisms. And it applies equally to psychological development. In human development, the motive force of change is hope, which promises future goals in return for surrendering attachment to present conditions. Rochlin (1965) has developed the concept on the basis of Freud's insight into the relationship between renunciation and substitution—losses of all sorts are followed by attempts at restitution.

Freud (1908:145) has written: "Actually, we can never give anything up; we only exchange one thing for another. What appears to be a renunciation is really the formation of a substitute or surrogate." The loss of anything that we value—whether it be a beloved person, a possession, a skill, a pet, or even our own sense of resilience as we advance through life—sets off the operation of psychological mechanisms that mitigate the sense of loss by the appropriation of substitutes. The underlying force behind the interplay of loss and restitution is primarily libidinal. Libido restores its loss by seeking new objects for its cathexis, a process that may be adaptive or not. Psychotic processes are a form of restitutive effort, but they are clearly maladaptive. The psychotic directs his restitutive effort to the erection of an inner world of fantasy within which he withdraws to ward off the pain of potential and actual loss in his ambivalently charged relations with real objects.

Hope is what determines the success of this restitutive effort in reaching reality rather than fantasy. The adaptive effort to deal with losses that injure the self requires an ego response that intervenes in the libidinal economy and directs it to real restitutive objects. Left to itself, the libido will respond to loss by following the principle of pleasure and immediacy of gratification—thus leading in the direction of cathecting inner (hallucinatory) objects. A return to the real world requires the modification of this process by the reality principle. It is hope that makes this return possible by redirecting psychic energies toward real possibilities and locating the potential for restitutive gratification in the real order. Thus hope becomes the principle that directs the process of psychological growth toward increasing inner stability and more adequate interaction and integration with real objects. The child's growth must be nurtured by the real promise of increasingly more adequate functioning and attainment, and ultimately by the possibility of mature adult role status. The child's emerging identity thus functions as a beacon to draw him on. Hope makes it possible for the child at each step of the process to relinquish the achieved actuality of development with its attendant gratifications and to reach out for the anticipated possibility of greater development and adaptive integration.

One of the central issues in development is the giving up of dependence on parental figures and the achievement of mature autonomy. The libidinal roots of dependency conflicts are basically oral and lie embedded in the most primitive roots of the childhood experience. The basic question is whether the growing child can separate from the parent, in whatever manner and extent is appropriate to his age and stage of development, without incurring the sense of abandonment that would expose him to the destructive impact of inner impulses and rages. We have suggested the role of hope in making that separation and transition possible. The child must increasingly integrate oral needs and their derivatives into the functioning personality. These oral needs permeate the primitive experiences of interaction between mother and child from which hope takes its origin. But at the same time oral libidinal needs themselves cannot be integrated with the needs of the developing personality without the presence of a perduring sense of hopefulness.

The residual effects of oral needs and impulses find their integration in the emerging personality in a variety of ways. We often describe oral characters as needing to be given to and taken care of, clinging, demanding. Such characters are often pervaded by infantile fears of loss and abandonment—of being left or lost, of being denied and deprived. Such fears can be combined with aggressive impulses to get for oneself by depriving others—a pattern we describe as oral sadism. Many such patients have a large depressive component in their personalities that leaves them feeling empty and worthless. They counter such painful feelings by making others feel empty and worthless—often by subtle criticism, undercutting, and verbal attacks. But oral needs can also express themselves more positively in the form of giving and receiving. Even in the best functioning personalities, oral needs reveal a residual element from that primitive period when we were utterly dependent on powerful providers. They express themselves in our hopeful as well as our hopeless states and desires.

At each stage of development the resolution of conflicts between wishes to remain dependent on powerful providers and the inner impulse toward greater independence and autonomy requires the exercise and direction of hope. The child of two years of age cannot tolerate even brief separations from this protecting and supporting mother without some realistic sense of her anticipated return. When the separation is permeated with a sense of loss, separation anxiety overwhelms the child. Adolescents cannot leave behind their childlike dependence on parents without some realistic sense of their own potential to function as adults. Fears of loss and abandonment destroy the sense of future possibility and lead the adolescent to a defensive posture of dependency. Hope is thus the ego's capacity to imagine and retain a sense of future real possibility in the face of infantile fears of loss and abandonment. At each stage of the developmental process, the need to master developmental tasks, the capacity to tolerate painful affects of depression and anxiety, the potential for relinquishing passive dependencies for more active and autonomous positions—which are essential to the successful accomplishment of the developmental process—all hinge on the capacity to envision in realisitic and realizable terms the availability of future desired states of existence and functioning.

CHAPTER 12

The Psychopathology of Hope

It was Nietzsche, in his consummate cynicism, who remarked that "Hope is the worst of all evils, for it prolongs the torment of man." But as any psychiatrist knows well, man's hopefulness is not his torment; it is rather hopelessness that torments his soul. Man loses hope by way of defect; he withdraws from it through a failure to wish, to desire, to ambition or to plan. He also becomes hopeless by way of excess, by clinging to excessive expectations beyond the limits of what is realistically possible. It is this burden of omnipotent expectations, not hope, that prolongs man's torment.

A healthy sense of hopefulness is clearly not the same as the euphoric or manic repression that accompanies loss and despair. In contrast to such manic denial, hope is based on the capacity for mourning and on an accumulation of successful experiences of mourning. Hope emerges out of the matrix of disappointment, disillusionment, and despair through the successful acceptance of and integration of loss. Springing out of such loss, hope is an essential part of the ego's restitutive effort to recover what has been lost and to set its face toward a brighter future. Hope, therefore, is an essential component of the restitutive aspect of the loss complex (Rochlin 1965).

The sense of hopelessness that pervades so many forms of psychopathology is permeated by a sense of the impossible. The hopeless person feels caught in a prison from which there is no escape. We can recognize this radical loss of hope in the depressed, withdrawn, and apathetic states of seriously disturbed patients and, at less intense levels, in the similar conditions of neurotic patients. We can recognize a failure or distortion of the capacity for spontaneous willing in the compulsive behavior of the obsessional, as well as the loss of purposeful restraint in narcissistic and impulse disorders. Hopelessness embraces a sense of futility. What needs to be done seems to stand beyond one's capacity to perform or achieve. The patient is trapped and checkmated at every turn, and his watchword is "I can't!"

In his hopelessness the patient presumes that he possesses no inner resources to solve problems or fulfill wishes—or, at least, that his inner resources are completely inadequate. Feeling frustrated and inadequate, he may expect or demand that others do things for him. He may be unwilling to try, but at the same time be angered and resentful that others do not respond to or satisfy his wishes. In his sense of frustrated entitlement, he may blame others for his failures and become enraged at their inability to satisfy his expectations. The shifting of blame and responsibility away from oneself and onto others is often accompanied by the projection of malignant and evil intent on others, a process that can become openly paranoid.

This hopelessness grows out of the perception of oneself as unworthy, inadequate, unacceptable, valueless—a perception that reflects a persistent and resistant introject derived from the internalization of the punitive and hostilely aggressive parent. This internalization gives the child a sense of inner evil and destructiveness, and subsumes the instinctually derived impulses of hateful destructiveness and infantile wishes to hurt and damage. This internalized destructiveness builds up a negative sense of self that permeates the rest of the individual's life and remains stubbornly resistant to any alteration by the influence of reality factors. One often sees clinically depressed patients who persistently maintain this view of themselves as worthless and devalued in the face of a lack of confirming evidence, and not infrequently in the face of overwhelming evidence to the contrary. The inner sense of evil means that the individual cannot perform good acts, cannot set useful goals, has no right to hope or strive, for what it produces must bear the stamp of its origin: worthlessness and evil.

Role of the Superego

This pattern of internal organization has been described in psychoanalytic terms by the functioning of a primitive and punitive superego which functions in a harsh, critical, and devaluing manner as the agency of internal self-deprecation. Through the superego infantile sadism and hostile destructiveness are directed against the self, leading to depression, guilt, and self-devaluation. This may may affect the individual's behavior as well, so that the internal dictates of the superego are lived out in a variety of forms of self-defeating and self-destructive activity. It is as if the superego's claim of worthlessness and evil serves as a mandate, which is then acted out—a self-fulfilling prophecy of self-defeat and self-degradation. This process is an operative mechanism in many forms of mental disturbance and mental illness. The severity of the self-destructive wishes may reach the point of suicidal wishes and action. In seriously sick and psychotic patients, the power and destructiveness of these instinctually derived forces are often overwhelming.

The activity of the superego is at the root of what Lynch (1965) has called the absolutizing instinct. It arises out of the developmental failure to achieve a capacity to tolerate and resolve ambivalence, one of the important tasks that the child must accomplish in relation to the important figures upon whom he is dependent. He must be able to accept the hateful feelings and destructive wishes he bears toward those he also loves. The primary figures for the child, of course, are the powerful parents. If he were to give vent to his angry and hateful feelings toward them, he would run the risk of loss of love, abandonment, rejection, and even punitive retaliation. These issues are resolved in the separation-individuation process. The parents must help the child to tolerate and resolve his hostile and destructive wishes and help him grow to realize that his aggressive impulses and wishes are not intolerable or evil.

Where this resolution does not take place, the child learns to absolutize, to cling to simple and simplistic ways of thinking and feeling of his relations with other people. If he loves, he can find no room for negative feelings; if he is angered, he can find no room for love. He treats these feelings as though they were absolute and exclusive. Since, in fact, there is no significant human relation that perdures over a significant period without ambivalence, the absolutizing tendency works considerable havoc in interpersonal relations. The inability to tolerate negative affects is dealt with by the internalization of aggression, as I have suggested. The outcome is an increase of the severity and destructiveness of the superego and the intensification of self-punitive and self-devaluating processes. Positive and loving feelings toward the significant objects are preserved at the cost of punishing and devaluing the self.

The splitting of the two sides of the ambivalence and the absoluting process was described by Freud (1917) in his *Mourning and Melancholia*. In considering ambivalence toward a lost love object, Freud uncovered the introjective mechanisms that led to his understanding of the superego. When the loved person dies, for example, the mourner may feel a sense of guilt or worthlessness in addition to grief. The negative feelings toward the dead person are submerged, and the good aspects of the dead person and positive feelings toward him are put in the ascendancy. *Nil de mortuis nisi bonum.* Negative and hostile feelings, particularly any angry and destructive wishes for the person's death, are out of place. The absolutizing conscience demands this, but it is impossible. So the mourning may continue for months and years in an attempt to deny, avoid, repress the negative aspects of the ambivalence. The mourner continues to punish himself for the anger and destructive wishes that he cannot tolerate or accept in himself.

Hopelessness

Hopelessness is related to the individual's subjective estimate of the probability of achieving certain goals (Melges and Bowlby 1969). Plans and goals seem to be out of joint. Goals may be sought and striven for long after any realistic expectation of their fulfillment is past. Plans may be restricted merely to immediate short-term goals to the exclusion of long-term ones. The expectation of hope is that plans of action will reach and achieve anticipated goals. Hopelessness expects failure; planning is futile and meaningless. The disjunction of plans and goals and the feeling of hopelessness are most characteristically found in depressed patients who are overwhelmed with a sense of purposelessness and futility.

The depressive patient believes that his skills and capacities are inadequate to achieve the goals he has proposed for himself, that his failure is due to his own inner inadequacy, and that his previous attainments are meaningless. He harbors a sense of helplessness, of dependency on others for any success or gratification, and of being foredoomed to futility in any exercise of his own resources. His incentive is lost; he sees no recourse but to give up. The depressive patient does not surrender his goals, particularly the continuing and long-range ones. Rather, he despairs because of the disparity between his aspirations and achievements and because he senses the unattainability of his goals. The experience of frustration, far from extinguishing long-term goals and aspirations, causes the depressive patient to cling to a future that is thwarted and frustrated. The patient believes he can reach his goals only through his own capacities and skills but he also believes that his resources simply do not measure up to the task.

The picture for the sociopath is somewhat different. The sociopath believes that his own capacities and plans have little to do with his attainment of future goals. He sees others as sabotaging his attempts to reach his goals, and thus as being to blame for his frustrated lot. Any attempt to set goals that would be perduring or long-range is foredoomed to failure. The sociopath thus finds himself in a chronic state of hopelessness that permits little future orientation. He escapes this feeling of futility by seeking his rewards and gratification in the present, with little regard for the future. The more distant and future any given goal, the less realizable does it seem to him. He sees his future as out of his own hands and in the control of others who are basically hostile and not to be trusted. The depressive patient takes responsibility for setting and attaining goals, but he devalues his own inner resources to achieve them. The sociopath on the other hand, does not accept this responsibility. He places the responsibility elsewhere and satisfies his feelings of entitlement by taking his gratification from the present without regard to long-term effects or consequences. A similar shift is seen in paranoid patients who blame the hostility of others for their own failure or inadequacy.

A particular manifestation of hopelessness is boredom, which carries within itself a sense of purposelessness and of the meaninglessness of things. It is the death of wishing. Though it may mask itself with hypomanic flourishes—forms of pseudowishfulness and pseudohopefulness—boredom is substantially a withdrawal of cathexis from things and objects in the environment. This withdrawal and the cessation of wishing are essentially narcissistic. For boredom is an expression of entitlement that places the responsibility for stimulation, interest, attraction, and involvement on other agents besides oneself. It represents a disappointment with the world, a reaction to the denial of expectations, a falling out of love with reality. Its withdrawal of interest and involvement covers an implicit hostility expressed in a devaluing disregard for what lies beyond the boundaries of the self. Boredom is an expression of the deeper resentment that the world has not done for me what I can only do for myself. In an excellent phrase, Marcel calls this a "narcissism of nothingness."

Hope can also be connected, negatively, with destructiveness or sadism in a variety of ways. The engendering of hope that is doomed to failure and disappointment inevitably has its sadistic aspects. But the mere expression of hopefulness can serve as a vehicle for sadistic elements insofar as it implicitly places demands upon the other to fulfill one's expectations—demands that may be extremely difficult, painful, or impossible to fulfill. But such hopes, insofar as they withdraw from the range of realistic expectations, would have to be regarded as false hopes, and thereby withdrawn from the influence of the ego into the conflictual turmoil of the id and its impulses.

CHAPTER 13

The Psychotherapy of Hopelessness

Our discussion of the functions and the dysfunctions of hoping and hopefulness comes to a particularly vital focus in the psychotherapeutic process. It has been my experience, and that of others who work with psychologically impaired patients, that the achievement of a hopeful attitude is a central ingredient in any therapeutic success (Boris 1976). I have found this to be true even in the case of healthier analytic patients. To lend some clarity and depth to the synthetic views I have been discussing, I want to focus now on the human process of psychotherapy.

Study of the psychotherapeutic process over may years has returned again and again to a common motif, namely, the importance of gaining and sustaining a sense of hopefulness in the treatment of psychiatric patients. Some years ago, for example, Martin (1949) had discussed the role of reassurance in psychotherapy. I would regard reassurance in this context as being equivalent to the engendering of a sense of hopefulness in the patient. Martin distinguishes several forms of reassurance: (a) false reassurance, (b) superficial or defensive reassurance, and (c) basic reassurance. False reassurance often takes the form of expressions of confidence, faith, encouragement, and support in response to the patient's attitudes of self-devaluation and self-hatred. While this approach can be understood as part of a countertransference reaction, the patient more often than not continues to maintain his sense of self-devaluation and self-disparagement even more strongly. Defense reassurance takes the form of an effort on the part of the therapist to restore a failing neurotic defense when some of the underlying anxiety, depression, or other pathological affect begins to show itself. This sort of "back-to-normal" superficiality often goes unacknowledged and may serve as a rationale for short-term therapeutic interventions. That form of reassurance which is most realistic and most helpful is basic reassurance. This more therapeutically productive form of reassurance expresses itself in the therapist's humane and understanding approach; in his affective involvement with and acceptance of the patient; in his ability to maintain a sense of discrimination between the patient's pathological conflicts and symptoms and the more mature, constructive, and healthy part of the patient that has the capacity of entering into a meaningful and collaborative therapeutic alliance and engaging with the therapist in the work of the therapy.

A report of a quarter of a century of research on psychotherapy summarized this body of experience with the statement that the beneficial results of psychotherapy seemed to include as one of the important components an activation of the patient's expectations of improvement. As a rule, greater therapeutic improvement was found when the patient was able to attribute his improvement in some degree to his own efforts rather than to some outside agent, when he saw himself as in control of his environment rather than controlled by it (Frank 1976).

In other writings on this subject, Frank (1974a) has placed the emphasis on the importance of the restoration of the patient's morale. Most patients suffering from neurotic difficulties experience a state of demoralization, which begins with some form of emotional or affective distress that they cannot understand, or with failures in the tasks of ordinary living. Such experiences can shatter an individual's self-confidence, resulting in an inability to master one's own thoughts or feelings, a loss of control, depression, guilt or shame, anxiety, and feelings of hopelessness and helplessness. Frank argues that whatever the specific results of various therapeutic approaches, all forms of psychotherapy bring relief by raising the level of the patient's morale. Regardless of diagnosis, symptoms of anxiety and depression, which are the major manifestations of demoralization, are likely to show some therapeutic improvement, which, in turn, brings with it a subjective sense of increased self-reliance, self-confidence, and independence. The patient experiences this improvement to the degree that he can see himself as controlling his own life and destiny rather than being controlled by external forces. Thus, a central element in the therapeutic effectiveness of all forms of psychotherapy is that they strive toward mobilizing the patient's resources and eliciting a sense of hopefulness about dealing with his difficulties.

If the psychotherapeutic situation is geared to the generation of hope, we should note that hope is not possible in a vacuum. It requires a meaningful integration of the individual within real human relationships. We develop hope from others even as we derive help from them. The initial roots of hopefulness are laid down in the mutual regulation and responsiveness between child and mother (Boris 1976). The generation of hope requires such trusting dependence on another human being, and so the therapeutic context requires real contact between two persons. Patients find countless ways to avoid the reality of the therapist, but in the analytic model therapy and the successful generation of hope demand a real relationship between therapist and patient. In the analytic model, the process requires a therapeutic alliance as a central constituent of the analytic situation in order to make the work of the analysis possible. It is likewise the basis of hope.

When the patient discovers that his disappointment, hopelessness, and despair can be shared with another empathic and understanding person, hope springs into being. The sharing of such painful and vulnerable feelings opens the way to a deeper relation to another human being that draws the patient away from alienation and isolation.

The therapeutic process takes place through the medium of language, the expression of inner thoughts, feelings, associations, observations. The patient's commitment to this process within the doctor-patient relationship is an engagement in a time-limited process that works itself out step-by-step in a slow, gradual exploration of the patient's inner life and experience. At each step of the process the patient must commit himself to and engage in the reality of the next step and in the reality of the process. This gradual reality-limited process runs counter to the implicit expectation that underlies his hopelessness, an all-or-none expectation that says implicitly: "If what I need to accomplish cannot be accomplished all at once—and now—it cannot be accomplished at all! So what's the use?" The patient's hopelessness can offer many objections to the efficacy of the process, but engagement in it sets the stage for a process of immersion in reality, which is never all-or-nothing and which involves the frustration of working through many complex elements piece-by-piece. The therapeutic process both builds and requires a capacity to tolerate the postponement of satisfying results. Hopelessness does not want to take a limited next step and to keep on taking next steps; it wishes to leap to the final result. Therein lies its impossibility. Only in taking the next step does the patient achieve a sense of the possible.

This sense of the possible is central to the process. Patients must gain a sense of what is possible and what is not. Healthy and mature persons learn this discrimination, and they learn to live within its limits. We have legs, but not wings. We can walk, but not fly. The hopeless patient does not accept that discrimination and has not learned to live with it. One of my patients was a very intelligent and gifted young man who continued to live his young adult life in terms of his adolescent dreams of glory. His academic career was strikingly successful, but when he began to experience disappointments and was no longer able to meet his own idealistic expectations, both in his work and in establishing a meaningful heterosexual relationship, he became suicidally depressed. As his narcissism and his elaborate expectations became clearer, we both began to realize that he would have to modify this excessive expectation in favor of a more realistic direction. I commented one day, "You know, you seem to want to fly; most of us have to content ourselves with walking." "I know," he replied, "but the trouble is, God damn it, that part of me still insists on flying!"

This young man, for all his capabilities and attainments in academic life, had allowed himself to become paralyzed in a state of diffuse equilibrium and lack of commitment to adult roles and functions. He could not determine on a career—nor could he settle on a satisfactory mate—even though there were many available candidates. On the instinctual side, he was trapped in incestuous ties of dependency on his mother and frightened by oedipal concerns over aggressive competition with his rather authoritarian father. As he neared the end of his schooling and the necessity for decision, these inner conflicts intensified. To avoid them, he clung to his infantile narcissism and omnipotence, but in so doing found himself unable to satisfy these excessive expectations and responded with overpowering feelings of hopelessness. Therapy for this young man was a process of self-discovery, of finding his own real power and limits, his capacities and incapacities, as a child begins to discover himself in his increasing ability to separate from his mother.

For this young man, as for so many others, learning to recognize and tolerate ambivalence was a central part of the therapeutic process. In his idealism, for example, he had set himself the ideal of a pure and sexless love with a woman who combined great beauty with noble apirations and intelligence. When his love objects failed to meet this high standard, he could not tolerate his anger and disappointment. Instead of being angry at these women, he experienced depression. In his altruism, as well, he expected everyone he worked with to be high-minded and selfless, as he tried to be himself. His expectations were continually being disappointed, but again he could not manage the inner sense of disappointed rage. It issued instead in a vague sense of resentment and alientation from a society where people acted for their own interests, in utopian wishes for an idealized social and political order, and in a wish to withdraw from any participation in the real world that surrounded him. Clinically, he presented the symptoms of Erikson's (1959) "identity diffusion."

The toleration of ambivalence and the capacity to resolve it are one of the essential tasks of healthy development. The tendency to absolutize and idealize reflects an underlying intolerance of ambivalence and a loss of hope. Love and hate, however, are staples of human life and experience; they inhere in any meaningful human relation. The therapist can help the patient come to recognize and accept these unacceptable emotions by allowing them to be worked out within the therapy relationship. The phenomenon of transference thus becomes central for the working through of ambivalence, permitting the patient to work through the developmental achievement that he could not resolve with his real parents. When this is attained, the patient can begin to live with a certain degree of uncertainty; he is not compelled to respond to life in terms of absolutes; at the same time, the role of magical expectations and demands begins to diminish. Reality is uncertain and real relations are ambivalent; with increasing tolerance for ambivalence, the patient gains an increasing tolerance for and contact with reality.

The relation with the therapist provides the reality for this resolution. Through it the patient begins to turn from sickness toward health, from alienation toward social involvement, from narcissism toward realism, and from hopelessness toward hope. The achievement is not always easy or accomplished without considerable effort. One of my analytic patients came to analysis with an inner conviction that his entering into treatment was a hopeless gesture that would only conclusively prove his inadequacy and the impossibility of any meaningful help for his anxiety and depression. From the first moments of our involvement, he responded to me as a critical, controlling, punishing, judging authority figure. His response was fear, severe anxiety, a feeling of helplessness and hopelessness, and the wish to fight back in an angry, recalcitrant manner. It took many months of careful clarification and interpretation and repeated opportunities to test out his fearful and hostile anticipations within the therapeutic relation before he could sufficiently set aside his subjectively determined perceptions to begin to recognize the reality of my person and of his relation to me. Only when he was able to appreciate the transference elements in his response—derived from an insecure, controlling, overly possessive, and intrusive mother—could he begin to see that the fears and expectations had been generated from within and that these anticipations distorted not only his perception of his relation to me, but also many other relations and situations in his life. Only when the fantasies derived from an infantile level of experience were clarified and separated out could this otherwise intelligent and capable young man begin to deal with reality. The contact with reality started a process that gave him renewed hope and a sense of the possibility of things and of himself. Lynch (1965:170) has described this process admirably:

To put the matter as simply as possible: The patient begins to feel, after the travail of work and grace, that the doctor is on his side. Until that moment the doctor has been a judge, a punisher, hostile, a threatening giant, an enemy with whom to contend. He is the law in all its objectivity and exteriority. He is the symbol of all the exterior and interior giants before whom we seem helpless. He is omnipotent with an omnipotence that forbids interior growth, action and equality. The agonies of the sick before such images are incalculable and without hope .... The first insights into the possibility of mutuality are remarkable in their effects. This transfiguration is the object of all the hopes of the sick and the well. Now that one point of reality is transformed, the whole of reality is transformed with it. The doctor, who was the enemy, is now seen in his actual role of a helper: as a result half of the pain vanishes, because the pain had been a construct of hopelessness. The patient had felt the constant need to be alert; but now he enters a new and creative passivity that acts almost without acting, because it now wishes *with* and not *against,* and is felt to be wished *with* by another.

In therapy, the patient must find not only a basis for hope in the reality of his relation with the therapist, but also sufficient trust in the therapist and in the process to enable him to delay his wish and to continue to work toward therapeutic goals. Patients often come to the treatment process with magical expectations of cure or with peremptory demands for instant relief from their anxiety or depression. The beginning of hope for them is synonymous with the willingness to wait, to tolerate the unavoidable delay, and to set their sights on distant goals for which they are willing to work. In accepting these limits of the reality and possibility of the therapeutic process, they are beginning to surrender mere wishfulness and willfulness and are becoming more attuned to and accepting of reality: the reality of themselves, of the limitations of the treatment situation, and perhaps most significantly of the limitations and lack of omnipotence of the therapist.

One of the formulae that Freud originated for describing the therapeutic process was that of making the unconscious conscious. He thus underlined an essential aspect of the therapeutic process that contributes to the evolution of hope. The neurotic symptoms with which patients are afflicted—depressions, anxieties, phobias, etc.—are unconsciously derived and consequently overwhelm the patients. They cannot understand what is happening to them and feel they are being afflicted by alien forces over which they have no control. One young woman came to treatment with desperate feelings of depression and anxiety. She felt worthless and frustrated—unhappy with her work and with her heterosexual relations. She felt helpless, unable to see any reason for these desperate and depressed feelings. It did not take very long for us to discover in her history a most malignant and devaluing relation with a hostile and probably schizophrenic mother and a rather distant and uncaring father. When she became aware of the nature of this relation, it became possible for her to look at what she was experiencing in realistic terms as anger directed toward a frustrating and hostile mother. It then became possible for her to deal with that anger and to do something about it.

The bringing of such pathogenic unconscious material to consciousness has important consequences for the patient. It means that what he is experiencing is not an affliction by nameless and uncontrollable forces. It has meaning, it has an identifiable source, it serves specific purposes, and it relates to specific contexts, objects, and behaviors. But even more significantly, beyond the real context in which the problem becomes located, the patient comes to realize that what he is dealing with is his own thoughts and feelings and that these are, after all, within his capacity to control and direct. He is not a helpless victim. He is capable of determining how he wishes to evaluate and respond to the distressing and difficult situations that confront him. His symptoms have meaning as unconsciously determined ways of dealing with painful conflicts, but he has available to him other options and more effective ways of dealing with these conflicts, if he so chooses. Bringing unconscious elements into the light of awareness brings them into contact with reality and draws them into the orbit of real possibility. This opens the way from unconsciously determined hopelessness to hopefulness based on the awareness of real possibility.

While the therapeutic process serves to induce, even as it builds on, hope, the patient is often not willing to surrender his hopelessness. Patients may repudiate hope and maintain considerable conflict about allowing themselves the luxury of hoping. As French (1963) observed, the repudiation of hope may be a central and highly significant resistance. The emergence of hope brings with it a revitalizing of the traumatic experiences that undermined hope in the past. When the patient begins to hope and to take his hopes seriously as really possible, he must assume the responsibility for doing something about them. Often the associated trauma relates to the fears of separation, loss, and abandonment that were aroused in the child's early attempts to separate from and function more independently of his protective and supportive parents. The hopeful anticipation of the possibility of functioning on one's own makes the essential developmental separation from the maternal matrix possible, but the failure to resolve ambivalence can impede the process. The same problem can arise in therapy where the patient's incipient hopefulness can be overridden by his unresolved ambivalence. Moreover, certain patients may cling to a regressive and narcissistic position that a more hopeful and realistic stance would require them to surrender. In any number of relatively depressed patients, one sees a persistent clinging to the inner conviction of specialness. The young man mentioned above clung quite stubbornly to the conviction that he was so unusual and special a case that even psychoanalysis could not cure him. There is a special inner gratification that is overlayed by feelings of depression and worthlessness in clinging to a hopeless and helpless position. This narcissistic entrenchment can provide a powerful resistance and challenge the limits of therapeutic skill and possibility. The patient must come to see that he is clinging to an infantile position and that he can find a better and more effective way. He must also see that he has it in his power to choose between these courses.

Thus, the psychotherapy of hopelessness is a slow and painful process of coming to grips with reality—both the reality outside oneself and the reality within oneself. As Lynch (1965:191) has remarked: " . . . the fact is that reality is healing for those who are without hope, and it is the separation from reality that causes despair. It is all the forms of separation that cause all the degrees of hopelessness. It is all the degrees of contact that give us the degrees of hope." The therapeutic process seeks its objectives by exploring and resolving the pain and rage of separation and by bringing to bear all the forms of contact with the real: contact with the reality of self in inner unconscious feelings and thoughts, contact with inner fantasies and instinctually colored imaginings, contact with the therapist with all its inherent feelings of love and inner rage, contact with the reality of one's own limited capacity and potentiality, contact with the reality of one's meaningful relations with other human beings with all the pain and satisfaction they entail. Only to the extent that therapy achieves these contacts and resolves their latent uncertainties and ambivalences does it engender hope that sustains and perdures.

In rounding off these comments on the psychotherapy of hopelessness, I would like to quote a passage from Marcel's *Homo Viator*. As Marcel saw so well, it is the essence of man to be a *viator*, to be on the way toward a goal beyond himself, and the essence of that is hope. To be able to hope, to be able to accept the limits of self and reality, to be able to look to the future with realistic anticipation and purposeful striving— this is what it means to be human. Marcel (1962:211–212) comments:

To sum up, I should say that the mode of thought . . . . can be conceived either as a perverse but fascinating game, or at a deeper level and more truly, as the end of a process of auto-destruction which is going on within a doomed society, within a humanity which has broken, or thinks it has broken, its ontological moorings. However this may be, it is nothing but a pure and simple imposture to claim to hold up as some unheard-of metaphysical promotion or as a triumph of pure lucidity the really blinding gesture by which all that humanity has ever acquired is swept away and we are thrust headlong into the dungeon, itself a sham, of a Narcissism of nothingness, where we are left with no other resource but to wonder tirelessly at our courage, our pride and our stubbornness in denying both God and the being full of weakness and hope which in spite of everything and for ever—we are.

To the degree that we offer our patients the possibility of becoming truly human, we offer them the rudiments of hope—the sense of real, human possibility.

CHAPTER 14

Hope and Faith

My effort here has been to draw together an understanding of hope that derives from contemporary theological perspectives as well as from the understanding of psychological process as embodied in the course of development and in the concrete experience of the clinical therapeutic encounter. The parallels between the more contemporary theological formulations and psychodynamic understandings are ready and easy— so much so that Christian hope growing out of a creative eschatology and embedded in real human experience finds its immediate counterparts in the therapeutic concerns for reality testing and the achievement of real human relatedness. In these terms, one could personalize the theological formulations and thus translate them into perfectly applicable psychological terms, or one could theologize the psychological formulations and readily apply them to eschatological concerns. The parallels and the areas of potential ovelap, however, do not violate the essential distinction and differential focus of the respective areas of discourse.

To bring these approaches to a focus, the concept of humanization or "hominization" serves rather well. It was Teilhard de Chardin who first enunciated the themes of the sanctification of human endeavor and the humanization of Christian endeavor as rudimentary to Christian spirituality. This "making human" is the intent and objective of Christian theology and spirituality as well as the implicit goal and purpose of therapeutic endeavors. To make human is to give hope and a sense of human reality and possibility. Speaking from an eschatological perspective, Metz (1969:76–77) has given expression to this purposeful intent:

Must it [faith] not first accept the hominized world as part of its own historical development and in accepting it overcome it? No other way is open today. The hominized world still lies more before us than behind us. Man is changing more and more from an observer of the world to its shaper. His view of the world is its transformation . . . . The hominization of the world must not be left to the ideologies, it must be taken hold of in hope as a burden and a task. Everything we have tried to say was concerned to show that faith is able to do this task. In the hominized world, which ultimately Christian faith itself will have made historically possible, man moves in an incomparable way into the center of the world. This anthropocentricity does not mean that man's experience of God is radically obscured, but that ultimately a greater immediacy is given to the experience of the numinous: we encounter God as the transcendent mystery of the unity and richness of human life, which is constantly lost in the pluralism of its areas of experience; finally, as the God whose nearness seeks to reveal itself in our encounter with our brother. Thus faith has a genuine future in the hominized world—less obvious, it is true, less apparent, but more inescapable than ever.

There is an inner link, a mutual reciprocity that flows between religious hope and faith and the roots of human hopefulness. We have seen that, developmentally, hope is first rooted in the basic sense of trust that evolves between mother and child. The confidence the child accrues by virtue of the supportive protectiveness of that relationship, with its mutual regulation and acceptance, allows him to respond to the enlarging possibility of his awareness of himself and his capacities. This basic sense of the possible allows him to separate himself from the maternal matrix without overwhelming fears of loss or abandonment. This incipient hope also leads to unavoidable conflicts of will between the child's emerging self-will and the imposed will of parents and adults. Hope gives rise to purposeful intention and the capacity to will. The conflict is one of willingness and willfulness, of the capacity to shape ends and purposes in conjunction with or, if need be, in opposition to other ends and purposes. The conflict of grace and God's predestining will vis-à-vis man's free will was, at its psychological root, an expression of just such an inner human conflict. Implicitly it tended to envision willing as willfulness rather than as willingness, as though the expression of individual will were somehow inevitably placed in opposition to an omnipotent paternal will.

Yet, as Erikson (1959) has observed, if religious belief in its lesser moments trades off of infantile fears, doubts and wishes, in its better moments it performs an invaluable, if not essential, function in human life and adaptation, giving concerted expression to man's mature need for a meaningful context of belief that can sustain human hopes and vitalize human existence. Individual hope is sustained and the meaningfulness of human life and activity is confirmed by the communal hope found in institutionalized religion.This function is served by all forms of religious creed and practice, by orthodoxy and orthopraxy alike. In an analogous sense, the religious community provides the same sort of sustaining, hope-embodying matrix as does the maternal matrix, which allows for the infant to find support and confirmation of his own inner possibility and meaning. It is no accident that churches are "mothers" and undertake to sustain the hope of their children.

Faith, whether individual or communal, is a dynamic, integrative, and therefore positively adaptive force in the psychic economy. It is not enough to think of it in merely defensive or restitutive terms. There is no question that the process of faith draws its dynamic power of change from fundamental instinctual energies; the question is whether they are adequate to serve all the functions of faith we have considered. The cycle of loss, restitution and adaptation serves the defensive and restitutive aspects of psychic functioning involved in faith. But, in order for the ego to reach beyond those limits, faith also requires creative energies that serve its creative and integrative capacities.

The creative energies required to sustain faith and give it purposeful existence pertain to the operation of hope. Hope sustains faith and gives it life. Hope is the creative and sustaining expression of the operation of grace in the human psyche, and is to that extent grace-derived and grace-dependent. Grace thereby serves psychologically as an inner source of energic potential that enables the functioning ego to direct its capacities to realistic and adaptive goals.

I am not concerned in making this formulation with the priorities of grace and nature. I see them as correlative and not opposed—*gratia perficit naturam*. If the ontology of supernatural reality requires supernatural specificity—so be it. My concern here is with an understanding of the workings and function of grace within the human psychic apparatus. The effects of grace can sustain man's hopefulness or even bring it to life. Man's innate hopefulness offers a ground for the receptivity to sustaining power of grace (Meissner 1964). Psychologically, grace and nature become indistinguishable. In ontological terms, there is a tendency—historically embedded—to think of grace as divine action and nature as receptive potency. I would rather think of it in more personal—if psychological—terms. The more radically I am able to accept love from another person, the more fully do I come into possession and awareness of my own individuality and identity. So it is with grace: the more fully receptive man is to the action of grace, the more fully is he capable of the free realization and expression of his own reality and capacity.

The effect of grace, then, must be seen in terms of its capacity to make free and to make human. Metz (1969:49) has written:

> But grace is freedom, it bestows upon things the scarcely measured depths of their own being. It calls things out of their sinful alienation into their own. It calls the world into its perfect worldliness. *Gratia perficit naturam*— this is true also of the "consecration of the world" by grace. It seals the world within the deepest worldliness, it gives, in a supreme way, the world to itself, bestowing on it an unexpectedly rich existence of its own. Grace perfects the true worldliness of the world.

This world is not first of all the world of things; it is man himself, and his worldliness is his humanness. Grace, then, summons and enables man to hope, to become the active creator and shaper of his own reality—the reality both of his inner world and by extension of the external, surrounding world in which he moves and breathes.

Thus, hope is an elemental strength and capacity of the human ego that derives its strength from many basic sources, including infantile experience and residues within the mature personality. It is sustained by and sustains common hopes that are embedded in systems and institutions of belief—uniquely and particularly in religious beliefs and institutions. And it remains open to the sustaining and strengthening potential of grace that flows from a loving and supportive divine initiative. Man's capacity to hope is the clearest example of the creative and sustaining potential of grace, for it uniquely embraces man's capacity to wish, to mobilize energies from instinctively based resources, and the ego's basic capacity to will the future. And this, after all, is what is uniquely human—to look into the future and to will it. To be a *homo viator* is the essence of man's humanity as well as the essence of his belief.

Toward an Understanding of Religious Values

The Place of Values

Values as Psychological

Values as Cultural

Ethical Identity

The Place of Religious Values

Alienation and the Crisis of Values

CHAPTER 15

The Place of Values

In the contemporary setting of radical cultural change, there is no concept more central or more essential to an understanding of cultural and religious change than the notion of value. Concern over the place and function of values in contemporary society reflects our uneasiness before the shifting value-systems that constitute the cultural matrix of our personal existence. Perhaps nowhere in this flux of values and value-orientations is the impact on personal experience felt more acutely and self-consciously than in the realm of evolving religious values. The ferment set off and reflected by Vatican Council II has stirred the consciousness not only of the Catholic community, but of the whole Christian world. We have entered a new era of shifting religious values marked by increasing democratization of the structure of the Catholic Church, a decline in religious vocations, a swing toward secularization, liberalized sexual attitudes and mores, and a whole range of fundamental religious attitudes that bear a new and different cast. Yet the pattern of change that arouses our anxieties is no less than the dawning awareness that our understanding of what contributes to and determines these changes is fragmentary and inadequate.

Both the changes in cultural values and the difficulties we experience in bringing the resources of scientific discipline to bear in coping with these changes confront us with a situation of some urgency. Cultural change is a dynamic process that is continually active and operative. It is a group phenomenon, multidetermined and constantly adaptive. The role of values in this cultural context is primary, for values represent the most significant locus at which the cultural matrix touches the individual member of society.

Values in Social Science

The concept of value has been largely the property of anthropology although its origins lie in the philosophical literature. Cultural anthropology has used the term value in a broad sense, almost synonymous with the concept of culture itself. The value concept reflects and synthesizes those aspects of the culture that are more or less goal directed (Belshaw 1959). While culture as such embraces aspects of technology and material substance lying beyond the notion of value, there remains a set of attitudes, beliefs, and significances that, in fact, define the pattern by which individuals within the culture adapt to and are involved in its more material aspects.

Linton (1945:111–12) remarks that "A value may be defined as any element, common to a series of situations, which is capable of evoking a covert response in the individual." And the covert response is itself an attitude. There is, then, a link between the value-system endogenous to any culture and the covert responses of the participating member of the society. The society, therefore, maintains control over the individual by both external and internal means. The external means are exercised through the structures of the legal apparatus and less formally through the instruments of mass communication and the infinitely broader and more significant determinants of public opinion and acceptance. But there are also internal means—the internalized norms of individual behavior that are in some sense generated and maintained by cultural processes, but that at the same time structure the internal frame of reference of the individual and serve as the valuative determinants of his behavior.

It is not obvious, of course, that anthropological and individual values are synonymous. The values that originate by reason of cultural processes cannot simply be reduced to the values of the participating subjects of the culture. Nor can the values of participating subjects be identified with the cultural values to which they are exposed. The processes by which cultural values evolve are continually at work, continually interacting with the intrapsychic processes through which individual values are generated. The area of overlap is often great and is probably extended in proportion to the generality and uniformity of the value-system within the culture. Here the value-systems of subcultural groupings and the heterogeneity of value-systems in a pluralistic society complicate the issues. But within these complex areas of interaction it is clear that the individual must achieve a certain degree of cultural conformity in order to attain an acceptable level of adaptation. The community demands it.

The issues, then, become issues of the degree of acceptable deviation from culturally established norms. The deviant is branded as criminal or mentally disturbed if he exceeds the level of tolerance of the community. At least one aspect of the community's anxiety is related to the implicit threat to culturally embedded values. There may be other aspects as well. It is interesting to speculate on the extent to which the community is able to tolerate deviant behavior that does not challenge cultural values. As Erikson (1963) has suggested, the homogeneous culture of the Sioux deals with its deviant members by assigning them a secondary role. They are labelled as clowns, prostitutes, artists, or *berdaches*. And they are maintained in these roles while being subjected to the ridicule and degradation other members of the society must use in order to suppress their own unconscious deviant wishes. But primitive systems do not attack the stricken individual. They regard his deviation as the work of evil spirits, not as the product of personal motivation. In our more complex and sophisticated culture, the mechanisms are more elaborate but serve the same ends—at greater cost perhaps to the deviant member.

Values in Anthropology and Sociology

The evolution of the notion of values in the anthropological context as major determinants of group and individual behavior has found a complementary development in sociology (Adler 1956). The sociological and the anthropological conceptions converge on a common awareness of the function of values, even though they retain their distinctive concerns and enjoy a rich heterogeneity of formulations within them. The sociological process, cast in terms of group action, works itself out in relation to a set of beliefs, norms, and ideals that constitute the group value-system. The sociological perspective and the anthropological perspective are thereby complementary, just as social action, group process, and cultural norms are reciprocally related. Whether approached from the aspect of culture or from the aspect of group process, the value-system remains a central focus.

Clearly, the complex processes operating through social structures contribute greatly to the formulation and vitality of the sociocultural value-system. Indeed, the social sciences can barely record the complex interactions and significations of these processes. If we envision the value-system of a social organization not as a static property but, as a dynamically evolving process, then the value-system at any point in its evolution represents and derives from variables that depend on economic, political, religious, sociological, and cultural functions.

Individual Values

These processes are, in fact, poorly understood. This reflects, in part, their complexity, but also the lack of a central integrating concept of the value-function. The value-system at the social level remains an abstraction, even as the social organization itself is conceptually constructed. The sociocultural value-system derives in a complex way from the value-orientation of individuals. Thus, the objective and subjective are ultimately related and interdependent.

The primary reality of the value-system resides in the subjectivity of the human person wherever it is generated as an intrapsychic reality by the individual; but its generation is not a solipsistic phenomenon. The individual value-function operates within a richly determined and complex context of influences. The direction of influence in the developmental setting runs downhill, as it were, from prior societal investments in value structures to the emerging individual psyche. The latter enters this interaction innocent of all values.

As the process continues, however, the relations become considerably more complex. Values are not merely assimilated; they are formed. The formation rests upon creatively autonomous processes within the individual psyche. Piaget's considerations of assimilation and accommodation are perhaps relevant here. The injection of an autonomous element into value formation adds another aspect to the evolutionary character of the sociocultural value-system. The system of group values rests upon the formational processes of individuals, which operate continually and uniquely in the respective participating members of the group. The individual, then, contributes to a progressive modification of his own value-system, and derivatively to the value-system at work in the culture at large.

Values and Psychic Function

We have seen that the ultimate locus of value-formation and the primary level of organization of the value-system reside in the human psyche. The place of values as a functional aspect of human personality, however, is by no means secure. There has not yet emerged any systematic attempt to articulate the psychology of values. Implicit in such a theory of value is any number of sticky issues. It is apparent that values are at once a consciously held and, within limits, articulable aspect of the personality. Yet they are simultaneously the vehicle of individual beliefs and the dictates of conscience. Values therefore open out onto a highly organized level of personality function in which ethical demands and prohibitions play an important part. In psychoanalytic terms, then: the value-system seems to serve as a functional system with close relations to both ego- and superego-functions. Behind the issue of value formation as part of the psychic organization, the complex and fluid interaction of ego and superego would seem to demand clarification.

It seems safe, and perhaps more significant, to suggest that the value-system has a decisive impact on our affective development. The psychic structure must be seen in its integral totality. One of the essential insights of the psychological perspective is that the highest levels of psychic functioning are derivative from, dependent on, and reciprocally interactive with the fundamental, affective, and instinctual roots of human existence. The value-system represents an organized system that serves an integrative and directive function within the mental apparatus, thus indicating a high level of psychic activity. Yet values have their roots in the basic driving forces of human nature, namely, narcissism, aggression, libido, and the basic instincts that provide the motive power of life. Their understanding requires a careful elaboration of this relationship, just as the understanding of ego-functions in general cannot stand alone.

Ethical Relevance

In this analysis, we can begin to bring into focus certain of the fundamental problems that touch on the inner meaning of basic ethical concerns. Values are rational and authentic, or they are irrational and inauthentic. It is only in relation to an evolved psychology of values, however, that it becomes possible to clarify the bases of choice so that authentic values can be recognized and realized. The authenticity of the value-system rests on a mature and integral psychological foundation which bears scrutiny, whereas inauthentic values are rooted in unconscious fear, guilt, and infantile anxieties and wishes.

It is important, at this juncture, that we see clearly the role of an emerging psychology of values as an effort to understand the nature of value-formation and function. Its object is values, authentic as well as inauthentic, ethical as well as nonethical, religious as well as irreligious. The scientific interest is neutral; it makes no value judgments. Its conclusions, however, need not be neutral. If it exposes the infantile roots of inauthentic values, the relation remains neutral. If, however, it concludes that such infantilism underlies immature, conflictual, and neurotic behavior, the conclusion strains credulity if it claims neutrality.

The distinction between authentic and inauthentic is paralleled by another distinction between values that are expressive and those that are repressive. Expressive values flow from the totality of our psychic need and are correlative with it. Only those values that express our fundamental needs at all strata of our existence in some integral fashion can be regarded as authentic. Unquestionably, the biological and instinctual dimension is vital and significant, but an authentic system of values cannot express this dimension of human existence (the id) without at the same time expressing the more complex intellectual and moral levels of the mental apparatus (ego and superego). Authentic values, then, imply a certain integrality that is correlative with the spontaneity and autonomy of psychic functioning.

Values can be repressive as well. They are particularly so when they serve the demands of a harsh or severe superego. But repression—or better, the repressive aspect of values—is not synonymous with lack of authenticity. Insofar as the value-system in some degree serves the purposes of instinctual renunciation, it is repressive. It can also be authentic and serve the same ends. There is also no question that cultural values can be repressive in the sense that they repress the free expression of autonomous personality out of false motives of fear and taboo. The same repressive morality in the individual distorts the authenticity of the value-system by a kind of sphincter morality that reflects the inner imbalance of personality. Neurotic guilt can only stem from an inauthentic and repressive value-structure.

Value-Theory and Ethics

One must be careful to strike a balance in working out the relations between value-theory and ethics. The balance is delicate and too easily thrown out of kilter. A recent propagandizing book (Feur 1955:30) had this to say:

> The values of a free society are the expressions of an unthwarted emotional foundation. Potential feelings of affection are liberated from warping, constricting social forms. The creative imagination then conceives social relations in which emotional lives can grow to fullness, with minimal frustration and defeat. Happiness liberates human affections and energies through its own emotion, and all authentic values share in this liberation.

To add balance to this formulation, we would have to add that authentic values cannot be achieved in the face of completely unthwarted emotion, that they imply and express some form of social constraint, and finally that authentic values not only liberate human affections and energies but also serve the construction of psychic structure and the diversion of instinctual energy to constructive and positive enterprises.

Needless to say, the balance is difficult to attain and maintain without an integral theory of value-function. The development of such a theory is the work of science, psychological and social. The further question is whether the theory is to become normative, whether it is itself to represent a scientifically derived value. It is not the place of science to issue axiological directives. The relation between value propositions and indicative statements of fact is complex. Certainly, normative statements must be kept distinct from descriptive statements, even though descriptive and theoretical statements can validly be made about the psychological processes involved in either. As Hartmann (1960:51–52) has remarked:

> The relevant difference is rather between the empirical study of actual valuations, their study in the context of psychology or social science, on the one hand, and the decision on what "ought" to be valued, on the other. The concept of moral value has to be demarcated from the concept of those mental acts by which these values are set or realized.

The decision as to what "ought" to be valued is an ethical one. One must respect the autonomy of ethics as a specific and separate discipline. The issue is inevitably raised, however, regarding the relation of psychology and ethics. It is not enough to say that psychology makes descriptive statements and ethics makes normative statements. The matter is more complex, for psychology and the other social sciences make affirmative statements that are scientifically relevant and at the same time implicitly evaluative.

Sexuality

An area where this problem becomes more or less critical is in relation to human sexuality. Human sexual response is the object of the most intense psychological and ethical concern. The theory of values cannot be divorced from a theory of sexuality, any more than the functioning value-system can operate in isolation from the motive power of libido. The broader implications of sexuality are intimately involved in the emergence and integration of the mature adult personality. Further, a mature and authentic value-system is a correlative of this sense of identity. Such a value-system is highly relevant to the individual's attitudes toward and participation in sexual activity. Sexual behavior is, in fact, the vehicle for some of the most significant aspects of the value-system.

From the point of view of ethics, the ethical system contributes specific normative statements that set the standards for sexual behavior.

We are concerned on one level with the manner in which such prescriptive statements become incorporated into the cultural and individual value-systems. But on another level, we are concerned with the question of the extent to which social science contributes to the ethical decision. Can the norm of mature personality development and autonomous adaptation serve as a standard for judging ethical matters? Or are the grounds of ethical decision quite independent?

Ethical Neutrality

The role of values for the social sciences and psychology is something else again. It raises ethical issues. The exercise of Weberian ethical neutrality remains a scientific ideal, subserving scientific objectivity. The ideal is no less applicable in the social sciences than in any other. This, of course, represents a major value for the functioning of scientific method. However, it applies primarily at the investigative, research, heurisitc, and theoretical levels. The social sciences are being drawn more and more into the areas of social action and planning, and into the areas of application of scientific understanding, where objectivity and neutrality are less pertinent, and evaluative judgment comes into greater prominence. The value-system inherent in the discipline and the value-system of the individual scientist thus begin to shape the decisions and directions by which science is applied to personal and social problems. The psychologist will take a stand against mental illness, the sociologist against anomie. But is there anything in the investigative and theoretical approaches of these sciences that dictates these value-decisions, or are they based on nonscientific determinants of valuation?

Whatever the answers, the question itself brings us to the fringes of scientific concern where science encounters fundamentally ethical concerns. At this level the need for a meeting ground between the scientific and the humanistic disciplines becomes acute. The one area of concern they share is that of values.

Particularly significant in this regard is the social and personal function of religion. Religion or religions are the social repositories of specific value-systems. Part of the social science study of religion entails the examination of religious values, which may or may not be embedded in a moral code, but which inevitably underlie religious behavior and cult. The religious influence is unquestionably one of the most important determinants of cultural and personal values. As a social structure, organized religion not only influences the value-system, but is continually interacting in the cultural matrix with forces that cause it continuously to adapt, modify, clarify, and reinterpret the value-system that is its unique and traditional inspiration.

CHAPTER 16

Values as Psychological

Since it seems clear that the location of the value-system is in the human psyche, it is essential that the primary meaning of value be established in relation to the structure and function of the psychic apparatus. We are therefore directing attention specifically to a clarification of the concept of value from a psychological perspective. The analysis undertaken here is not intended in any exclusive sense, but is proposed as a more or less tentative formulation aimed at further elaboration of the psychic mechanisms involved in the development and structure of values. The intention is thus integrative and focuses on one aspect of an admittedly complex question.

The initial problem which presents itself in the theoretical approach to values is the problem of definition. The literature is overburdened with a bewildering melange of definitions and approaches, most of which focus on and illumine one or other aspect of the valuing process or its derivatives.

Components of Values

The first group of approaches to values share a tendency to reduce the value process to behavioral terms (Morris 1949, 1956). Dewey (1939) was the original proponent of this view, more or less equating values with behavioral choices. A more elaborate formulation stresses the goal-oriented quality of the choice situation and thus regards values as emerging from preferential decisions that are expressed for certain "end-states," as well as "ends-in-view" that help to realize these end-states (Woodruff 1942; Woodruff and DiVesta 1948). One can say that values pertain to what is desirable in the sense that what one values one also sees as desirable, but the valuing is somehow antecedent to the desirability and, in fact, determines it. The decisive quality of values and value-judgments, moreover, is not that of a "wish," but of an "ought."

The distinction between the feeling of liking and the feeling of obligation is expressed by Kluckhohn (1962:396) in similar terms:

> A value is not just a preference but is a preference which is felt and/or considered to be justified—"morally" or by reasoning or by aesthetic judgments, usually by two or all three of these. Even if a value remains implicit, behavior with reference to this *conception* indicates an undertone of the desirable—not just the desired. The desirable is what is felt or thought proper to want.

The attempt is to bring the note of obligation within the purview of the *desirable*. As Barton (1962:65) commented:

> The conception of values as any and all preferences tends to go with the conception of values as implicit and manifested by observable choices in behavior. The conception of values as standards which we feel are justified, to which people *should* adhere, focuses attention on verbal statements, and particularly on verbalizations which distinguish internal feelings of "ought" from those of "liking". The "sense of obligation" or "sense of value" is what distinguishes "normative values" in this sense from "mere preferences".

While these latter authors are in agreement that the definition of value must include the sense of obligation, it is questionable that the *desirable* is adequate to encompass this sense. There is a qualitative gap between what is desirable and what is obligatory. If an object or action is "proper to want," it does not yet impose any obligation on the one who wants.

Another group of definitions points up the relationship between values and needs. Values in these terms are defined generically as needs or need-satisfying and are given a biological basis (Mace 1953; Maslow 1954, 1955). Thus, Maslow (1959) sees biologically determined constitutional differences as preferences in the ways in which an individual relates to himself, his culture, and his environment. These preferences are such as to generate values. The entire hierarchy of values is a response to basic needs and is ultimately subordinated to the ultimate goal-values of self-actualization. Other authors speak of values as organized in terms of the need for fulfillment of individual capacities (Goldstein 1959) or even of the need for productive love of oneself and others (Fromm 1947).

As Weisskopf (1959) astutely observed, such formulations already contain an implicit value-judgment. There is little room for doubt that valuation, as a psychological process, responds to basic needs at all levels of personality organization. But values are psychologically distinct from needs, in the first place, and not all needs can be regarded as giving rise to values. Thus, the basic nutritional need and its attendant sensations of hunger may give rise to specific forms of behavior calculated to satisfy the need, may create appetitive behavior with its physiological components, may intensify the desirability of certain edible objects, and may reinforce the wish-aspects of the organism's psychological state—but none of this constitutes or gives rise to the value process.

Other theories have focused on the motivational aspect of values. Here we can place Gordon Allport and the other originators of the *Study of Values* (Allport et al. 1951; Cantril and Allport 1933; Vernon and Allport 1931), who were essentially following the older view of Spranger (1928). Allport sees values as beliefs upon which the individual acts by preference. Thus, values serve the function of directing cognition and motivating behavior. Besides the obvious difficulty that values do not always motivate (e.g., impulsive behavior), there would seem to be a residual distinction between values and beliefs. Here again, the two are closely related: beliefs of various kinds do embody and express values. But beliefs, whether religious or political or whatever, connote commitment to a cognitional system or understanding or conviction about something. The emphasis is primarily cognitional and implies cognitive assent. While values may be embedded in a system of beliefs (Tolman's (1962) belief-value matrix), the belief organization of itself makes no commitment to a course of action and does not include any implication of obligation. As Kluckhohn (1962:432) puts it: "Values differ from ideas and beliefs by the feeling which attaches to values and by the commitment to action in situations involving possible alternatives. If you are committed to act on a belief, then there is a value element involved."

Another important group of theories has emphasized the cognitive aspect of values. Smith (1963), for example, refers to values as "conceptions of the desirable that are relevant to selective behavior." Such conceptions may serve as standards of behavior that have the capacity to generate motivation. Smith's formulation, however, suffers from the limitation that its object need be no more than the object of choice of any kind. While it is presumably correct to say that the value as such is primarily conceptual, it is a concept that embraces more than desirability or preferability. A value is somehow normative—and normativity embraces desirability, but also goes beyond it. If values are not normative, they are meaningless as standards of behavior.

Perhaps the most significant attempt to crystallize the concept of value has come from Kluckhohn and his associates (1962). Their formulation comes closest of any of the available conceptions to this study's concept of value. According to these authors, "A value is a conception, explicit or implicit, distinctive of an individual or characteristic of a group, of the desirable which influences selection from available modes, means and ends of action" (p. 395). The value is, then, a code or standard that enjoys persistence through time and serves to organize a system of action. As a conception, values are not directly observable but can be inferred or abstracted from behavioral events, i.e., preferential behavior. Values are, however, experiential events capable of introspective and reflective identification. This point touches upon a basic methodological issue, which remains pertinent to the psychology of values, namely, that values are not only inferable from behavior, but that other direct evidences are available (Meissner 1966b, 1966c).

Values, then, are fundamentally ideas that formulate action commitments. They are thus distinct from sentiment, emotion, drives, needs, motives—but not divorced from them. They are consistently associated with elements of approval and disapproval. They deal with "justified preference," which Kluckhohn uses to include moral and aesthetic aspects. They are not always consciously or explicitly operative, but may function implicitly. They may be thus inferable from behavior and not actually introspected. They are, however, always introspectable. Moreover—and this is a most significant point—values can always be verbalized; they are capable of abstraction and rationalization. It is this aspect of value that clearly distinguishes it from mere preferences, instincts, needs, attitudes, and sentiments.

The proper object of value is characterized as the "desirable." But, as Kluckhohn clearly intends, the object of values is not only what is desired or desirable, but what ought to be desired. The formula has some weakness here, since, as I have hinted before, the relation between values and the desirable is ambiguous. Desirability introduces the motivational component to the notion of value. Here Kluckhohn distinguishes between cathexis, as a short-term, limited, and impulse-related affective state, and value as a long-term, broader focusing of impulses in terms of wider, more permanent goals. Values thus define the limits of permissible impulse satisfaction in relation to personal goals and cultural requirements. They may be regarded as serving an integrative function in the psychic economy, organizing affective and conceptual functions in the service of action. As Kluckhohn (1962:425) indicates, "Values may be defined as that aspect of motivation which is referable to standards, personal or cultural, that do not arise solely out of immediate tensions or situations."

One can argue, of course, that what is valued is always desirable in some sense. Even in the case of negative values, the object may be desirable and rejected as a result of a value-judgment, but one can reasonably argue that the value is really dealing with the desirable, even in rejecting it. "Desirable" has clearly different connotations in these respective uses. But the subject-predicate relation of value-desirable is not adequate to define the concept of value. The logical relation would also define pleasure, love, and more. To close the definition, one must also be able to say that the desirable is valuable. Here it is clear that not all desirable things or objects are valued. Someone who impulsively snatches a piece of candy is acting in reference to a desirable (and, in fact, desired) object, but this action has nothing to do with values.

Values are action-oriented; they operate in situations where the individual has the option of selecting one course of action out of a variety of real alternatives, i.e., those that are possible, rather than the realistic. Selection of a very difficult goal may require extraordinary efforts that we might regard as "unrealistic," yet they are still in the realm of possibility, and may reflect the individual's values. The available courses of action may be real in that sense, but may not be alternative. The compulsive, for example, may follow a real course of action, but his neurosis may preclude real selection (he is *not* free) so that his courses of action are not real alternatives. Values, therefore, would not be operative. Values are substantially operative only in such preferential behavior in which an actual selection is made among real alternatives on the basis of normative concepts.

Recapitulation

What follows is a capitulation of the elements of the complex notion of value that would seem useful for further theorizing.

(1) Values are *intrapsychic* and *nonobservable*. They can be introspected and experienced. This neither considers nor excludes the sociocultural aspect of values. However one interprets or understands cultural values, they must be derivative from individual values. This is true even though individual values are preceded by cultural values. This will become an important point for considerations of interactions of culture and personality, and interactions of cultural and individual value-systems, since it is precisely the idiosyncratic character of individual values that makes change in cultural values possible.

(2) Values are *perdurable,* a more or less permanent aspect of psychic organization, unlike many of the psychic mechanisms with which values are allied (emotions, attitudes, sentiments, etc.). They have a long

developmental history, and an elaborate root-system reaching into the most primitive levels of the mind; they share in the by and large permanent cast of the personality—at all stages of the life cycle. This does not mean that individual values cannot change. The mechanisms and conditions of such change are not well understood, but if change does occur, it would seem to require significant insight and motivation. This has been a problem in therapy from the beginning. Also, the mechanisms of cultural value change are poorly understood. This characteristic of the values or value-system justifies consideration of values as a structural aspect of the psychic apparatus, and we can properly speak of value-structure as a more or less perduring cognitive organization underlying the multiple functions of value-judgments. Specifically, they are classifiable as structures of secondary autonomy as defined by Hartmann (1939) and Rapaport (1960).

(3) Values are *intentional* structures. They are, therefore, concepts, ideas. The intentionality of values is clearly unacceptable to behavioristically oriented approaches to valuation, both because of the inherent difficulties in definition and because of the implications of the notion that general ideas, goals, and purposes can influence the course of behavior. The further implication of the conceptual nature of values is that they are both *verbalizable* and *rationalizable.* Values can be formulated and articulated, they can be expressed and communicated, discussed, argued, and debated. They can be supported with reasons, integrated with beliefs, buttressed with the accoutrements of intelligence and reason. It is in terms of this dimension of values that the interaction of personal value-systems and philosophical or religious value-orientations can take place.

The role of ethics in this regard deserves some comment. The science of ethics or moral philosophy is (or ought to be) a realistically based and empirical study of the foundation and sources of the moral obligations in terms of which human life is ordered. Further, the ethical argument reaches a conclusion that is expressed in terms of obligation. Ethics, then, is a science that formulates values. It is quite distinct from the psychology of values, which concerns itself with the formation and structure of values and does not, strictly speaking, arrive at any "ought" conclusions. Psychology does not formulate values. It is well to keep the distinction between the conceptual processes involved in ethics and those of valuation clear. The former is an objective, affect-independent reasoning process; the latter is a subjective, affect-involved and personally committing cognitive process.

(4) Values are *explicit* or *implicit.* They are neither fully conscious nor unconscious. They are rarely explicit and conscious at the moment of selection, but they are capable of explication. Rather than regarding im-

plicit values as unconscious, we should regard them as preconscious elements of the mental topography.

(5) Values are *action-oriented*. They operate in contexts in which a specific course of action is being selected or in which available means or approaches to a course of action are being considered. The value-system operates specifically at the level of decision, presumably secondarily influencing the level of action as well, but only actually influencing behavior in the decision process. The decision as such directs the course of individual action and may also direct the actions of other individuals on the social level.

The point should also be made that not all human actions are value-related. The individual agent may be acting on a nondecisional basis (impulsive behavior, compulsive behavior, drug states, certain organic states, including psychomotor epilepsy, etc.), in which case his behavior is independent of the value-system. One may also suspend the decision process in the carrying out of routine activities, but can, at any point, interrupt these activities by subjecting them to decisional organization and, in some instances, valuation. The former kind of nondecisional action is more resistant to decision and/or value. On a decisional level, moreover, the individual may decide upon a course of action that is consistent with the value standard, or he may decide to follow a course of action that violates it. Thus, we can speak of action as value-independent (nondecisional) or as value-dependent. Both of these categorizations might also be subdivided on a positive-negative basis as follows:

Independent: positively—action resistant to valuation
negatively—actions not related to values but potentially relatable
Dependent: positively—actions congruent with valuation
negatively—actions incongruent with valuation

Value-dependent actions are always the result of a positive decision.

(6) Values are *goal-oriented*. The decisional process in value-dependent situations involves a reference to objectives, purposes, ends, and goals. This telic dimension of the value-system has a channelling effect insofar as it organizes or tends to organize the various drive-derivative aspects of personality and directs them toward specific goals. The goals in question enjoy varying degrees of importance, breadth, and extent of influence, and are determined by personal and cultural influences. The perdurability of values is an important consideration here. In consequence, not all goal-directed behavior can be said to be value-dependent. Preferential behavior of all kinds can be related to specific goals

(satisfaction, tension-reduction), but valuation and preferential behavior are not coextensive.

(7) Values are *biologically derived*. This point, touching on the relationship between values and biological needs, is a slippery one, but nonetheless valid. Values are undoubtedly important dimensions of personality organization. But the mental apparatus, even in its highly organized and elaborate forms of structure, is not divorced from the vital stratum of the mind. The value system, then, is built upon a biological substratum that is continually active. The value-structure is both a response to fundamental needs of the organism and a directive influence toward goal-satisfactions that meet and correspond to these needs. The specific needs in question are not the primary biologically dependent needs of the organism for food, sleep, sex, etc., which derive from the total organization of the human organism as a biopsychological entity, but the needs of the total organism for self-actualization (Maslow) or self-productive love (Fromm), for example. They are, therefore, not independent of basically biological forces.

Hence, values, in some poorly defined and as yet ill-understood fashion, serve an adaptational function. They are, on the one hand, derivative from primary instinctual forces and biologically determined needs of the organism, and on the other hand, they operate to organize and integrate the capacities of the organism for higher-order goal-directed behavior that satisfies fundamental needs of the total organism.

(8) Values are *motivational*. They are not directly and of themselves sources of motivation, but they often serve an organizational and directive function in the channelling of energies. Kluckhohn (1962:425) comments, for example, that "value may be defined as that aspect of motivation which is referable to standards, personal or cultural, that do not arise solely out of immediate tensions or situations."

Specifically, values are operative in the integration of cognitive and affective dimensions of the personality. This important dimension of values has been underlined by the use of the term "desirable" in defining values. But the investment of objects with energy implied in the notion of cathexis is not value-dependent unless the cathexis is directed and channelled in cognitional and decisional fashion, in terms of more or less long-term goals. Values, therefore, set limits on impulse gratification of all kinds in relation to an organized system of personal and cultural goals and standards. Further, and most importantly, they organize, direct, and integrate these same impulses, whether libidinal or aggressive, to adaptational ends.

The intrapsychic value-system, therefore, is an adaptive structure in the more elaborative levels of the mental apparatus, but it has close ties with the fundamental driving forces of human nature that derive from more primitive, energic levels of the mental organization. If we are to regard values, then, as concepts, we must also add that they are concepts that have a dynamic function in the mental economy, and that their distinctive characteristic is that they are related to more primary, affective, and motivational forces of the psychic.

(9) Values are *selective* or *decisional.* I would only add to what has already been said that there may be some question about conformity to accepted values already established culturally. Action may be determined by values without an actual decision process being immediately related to it. Thus, values can be implicit, but they are always capable of explicitation. But, is the individual's participation in the cultural value-system always dependent on a decisional process in the individual?

The value-system certainly has a developmental history that parallels psychic development as well as the enculturation of the personality. The emerging individual does not make, and is really not capable of making, decisions about available directions of development until he evolves a personal decision-making capacity. He then becomes gradually capable of injecting himself into the complex interaction of developmental influences, giving the whole the stamp of his own individuality. This is very close to Erikson's concept of identity-formation as an active, dynamic intervention of the ego in a self-determining synthetic process. Value-formation, as I see it, must involve such a personal decisional moment at some point in the developmental history. The process is obviously subject to all degrees of organization. The failure of the process is correlative to the failure of personality integration. Utterly conforming behavior, therefore, without decisional involvement—even if it is consistent with the value-system and orientation indigenous to the culture— must be regarded as value-consistent behavior, without being value-dependent. Whether such a situation is really possible is another question.

(10) Values are *normative.* This is perhaps the most central note of the concept of value. The normative includes the notion of obligation. As normative concepts, values impose or propose an obligation. "Obligation" and its correlative "ought" are strong words. Needless to say, values do not always impose the strongest sense of obligation. Values, rather, share in degrees of "requiredness" that place a demand on the person at almost any level of intensity (Vivas 1963). Many values are better expressed by a "should" than an "ought".

It is not at all clear where the normative or required aspect of value stems from. I do not believe that the understanding of this aspect of values will be captured in any simplified formula. The forces at work are multiple and include psychological, social, and cultural factors. There is also the pertinent issue of what Vivas (1963) calls the "ontic status of value," the reality of values antecedent to our discovery of them.

Values and Psychic Organization

We have conceptualized values as conscious or preconscious structural elements in the mental apparatus. This, along with their relation to judgmental functions, means that values can be regarded as complex psychic structures which involve and operate in terms of ego-capacities and functions. The development of value-structures is a vital part of the understanding of ego-development. Further, we can suggest that values share in the derivation of other ego-structures from pregenital levels of development.

Moreover, insofar as values are inherently normative, they are in some sense dependent on or reflect superego functions. As Brierley (1947) commented, "psycho-analysis shows that personal morality is the result of superego development through which cultural standards are individualized and operate as mental controls of instinct." How ego and superego collaborate in the formation of values and in the operation of the value function is not at all clear. The question involves complex metapsychological considerations that touch on some of the most fundamental issues in the understanding of psychic structure. The issues involved are related not simply to problems of ego-formation and superego-formation but to the organization of their respective structural systems. The potential for often severe psychopathology lies behind the failure to achieve this important level of psychic integration, particularly in the areas of narcissistic transformation and in the establishment of a firm and consistent sense of identity. As Jacobson (1964:139–40) has commented:

> The maturity and consistency of superego standards and ego goals, and the consistent influence of the moral system on the goals of the ego are, indeed, an indispensable prerequisite for the ego's ability to build up not only a coherent, effective defense structure but also a hierarchic organization of the different personal relations, ego identifications, ego interests, and ego functions. Since severely conflicting scales of values are inevitably reflected in dangerous discordances within the ego, superego and ego may indeed defeat each other's purposes by irreconcilable contradictions, which interfere with the development of superego and ego autonomy, with the ego's mastery of reality, its control of the id, and its adaptation to the object world.

From a psychoanalytic perspective, the understanding of value formation and value structure can be cast in terms of the integration of ego and superego functions, as well as their corresponding identifications. The understanding of such integrations has been limited by the fact that psychoanalysis primarily deals with contexts in which these functions are separated or divided in more or less pathological ways. The fundamental understanding of the superego and its functions arose in the context of exploring depressive, obsessional, and paranoid conditions. Despite this negative focus, there has also emerged an understanding of the superego which is more benign and contributes positive elements to the organization and stabilization of personality structure (Schafer 1960). It is this more positive aspect of the superego, derived from crucial internalizations, that offers the potentiality for more stabilizing integrations with ego structures. In a theory of conflicting and divided structures, psychoanalysis has had difficulty in coming to terms with such areas of integrated functioning and structure, but the recent emergence of a more articulated psychology of the self may provide the vehicle for further theoretical advance in this field.

The integration of ego and superego is enhanced by the gradual achievement of superego autonomy. Superego autonomy implies the capacity of the superego to function independently of drive influences and drive derivatives. The development of a relatively autonomous superego depends on the quality of internalizations, particularly introjections and identifications, that have taken place in the growing child's inner world. Where introjections have been based on essentially positive and constructive object relations and do not carry within them an excessive burden of ambivalence, and where identifications have not been contaminated by introjective components that carry within them the unresolved and pathological residues of narcissism, aggression, and libidinal conflicts, the potentiality for the development of a relatively conflict-free and autonomous superego is available (Meissner 1978). Ticho (1972:219) has described such a superego in the following terms:

> An autonomous superego is consistent, impersonal, tolerant, accepting, and guided by abstract principles. Therefore we can say that the more impersonal the individual's superego, the more of a person he will be. The autonomous superego is neither too afraid of the drives nor too strongly influenced by social anxiety. But we do not assume that the mature superego is independent of the ego. Hartmann and Loewenstein point out that "the further evolution of the superego does not diminish the developing ego's influence, but tends to increase it." Thus begins an increasing collaboration between ego and superego.

A central focus for the realization and expression of superego autonomy is the area of value formation and value systems. The achievement of superego autonomy requires the modification and substantial integration of the narcissistic issues related to the formation of the ego ideal. The ego ideal remains one of the most important structures for the establishing of a mature and adaptive personality. The early narcissistic and infantile aspects of the ego ideal must be progressively modified in the direction of less extreme, more realistic, and less potentially pathological expression. The most important sector within which such resolution takes place and is achieved is the individual's value system. Jacobson (1964:129–30) has pointed out the importance of superego integration and the attainment of superego autonomy for the establishment of value systems. She writes:

> Tremendously increasing the endopsychic tensions, the superego develops into an autonomous central system for the regulation of the libidinal and aggressive cathexes of the self representations, independent of the outside world. It assumes an eminent part in the entire psychic economy. By gaining control of the course and modes of the discharge processes, it exercises an enormous influence over our emotional and thought processes and our actions. However, the development of our concepts of value does not end with the establishment of a superego, even though our moral self evaluation remains predominantly a superego function.
>
> The maturation of the ego and of critical judgment considerably modifies our concepts of value and our actions. Leading to an acceptance of what is realistic and reasonable, it accomplishes at least a partial victory of the reality principle, not only over the pleasure principle, but also over exaggerated "idealism" and thus over the superego. Only then do the superego functions work with more neutralized energy. In fact, the final maturation of both the ego and superego sets in only after the tempest of instinctual conflicts during adolescence has subsided. Then we observe a gradual moderation of youthful idealism and illusions, leading to the setting up of more reasonable goals and to a further development of moral judgment: of the ability to test and to evaluate the outside and inside reality correctly, reasonably, and with greater moral tolerance, and to act according to such judgment.

The value system, therefore, provides an internalized regulatory and directive way for individual personality to organize and direct its activity. It is thus the repository of narcissism—but a narcissism purged and modulated so as to find its place in the limits and constraints of reality and thus become a vital force in the achievement of more mature personality functioning and meaningful living.

One can also cast the problem in a developmental perspective. Where do values become operative in personality functioning? What aspects of the psychic organization at various stages of development are pertinent for understanding the formation of values? I would suggest that the developmental phase most closely related to value-formation is adolescence. Value-formation in a sense parallels and reflects the personality organization. Vivas (1963:61–62), in fact, speaks of personality as "an integration of values" whose "growth is a growth in the values men recognize and from which they select some for espousal." The vicissitudes of value-formation, then, are the vicissitudes of personality—in all its structural complexity and vital dynamism. As Jacobson (1964:142) adds:

> The history of such patients reveals that the internalization of such confusing parental attitudes at an early infantile stage may result in lasting contradictions in a person's unconscious and conscious sets of values; this not only may affect the establishment of stable personal relations with sufficient object constancy, and hence of consistent superego and ego identifications; it also predisposes the child to identity problems which may gain a dangerous momentum during adolescence and extend into the life of the adult.

If this chapter has failed to achieve a definition of value, it has at least articulated a concept of value. This concept is essentially a psychological one that may give us access to a partial understanding of value-function in the psychic economy. It has, however, other dimensions that lie beyond our present scope. We must keep both our concepts and our minds open to the possibilities of fuller understanding as other perspectives—social, cultural, economic, religious—can be brought to bear on the problem. At least, the examination of the concept of value makes it clear that the problem of value is relevant to the concerns of psychoanalysis. We may hope, then, that an analytic theory of value can be developed that will serve the purposes of further integration and understanding.

CHAPTER 17

Values as Cultural

It is apparent, given this emphasis on the psychological structure and function of value-systems, particularly in terms of their impact on the individual personality, that the intrapsychic aspect of value, though quite valid and substantive in itself, cannot remain an isolated consideration. While the structure of values can be defined in terms of intrapsychic functions, it nonetheless turns its face to the outer world, initiating and modifying itself by continuing dialogue with a preexisting climate of values. The value-system of the individual is both created and assimilated from the surrounding culture.

Since the world of value works on both psychological and cultural levels, the understanding of value as an integrative concept must embrace both these aspects. Our concern here is with values at the cultural level. Our interest is not so much definitional as heuristic. Clarification of the notion of cultural values will serve to deepen our understanding of the reciprocal interplay between cultural and individual value-systems.

Views on Culture

The first approach to the notion of culture is somewhat bewildering. One is overwhelmed by the diversity of opinions and viewpoints. Culture is learned behavior or an abstraction from, and therefore *not*, behavior. Culture consists of both mental events or ideas, and of things and events in the external world. It exists in people's minds, in the anthropologist's mind, and independently of either of these (White 1959). The classic definition was that provided by E. B. Tylor (1874:1). He defined culture as "that complex whole which includes knowledge, belief, art, morals, law, custom, and any other capabilities and habits acquired by man as a member of society." The emphasis of this early definition was on certain abstractions from the results of human behavior—knowledge, art, law, etc. Anthropology was not concerned with behavior as such—this was the province of psychology or sociology—but with abstract propositions about kinship systems, religious beliefs, legal codes, etc., which could be studied and described with little reference to the people involved. Moreover, anthropology was the science of culture as a generic phenomenon, not the study of particular cultures. The effect of this early view was to define anthropology as an independent science with its own proper object; but it also removed it from its rather obvious behavioral roots.

As Spiro (1951) pointed out, Tylor's definition carried an inherent dualism. It pointed to culture as a "complex whole," but at the same time a whole that was acquired by man as a member of society. In the study of cultural evolution in abstract terms, this latter aspect could be pretty much ignored. But in the more concrete work of field study of a given society, what was its "culture" to be? Was it to be that society's social heritage, the "complex whole" that can be thought of as independent of or antecedent to its acquisition by the members of the society? Or was it to be identified with the behavior of the members of the society by which they acquire and express their social patterns?

The obvious need to refine these concepts for purposes of analysis and interpretation led to a diversity of conceptions. The various approaches have been conveniently categorized as cultural realism, cultural idealism, and cultural nominalism (Spiro 1951). Cultural realism maintains that culture does not exist in the organism, that it cannot be identified with behavior, but that it has independent existence in a realm of its own—the realm of the superorganic (Kroeber 1917). The mass of culture and its constitutive elements (values included) "have a persistence and can be conceived as going on their slowly changing way 'above' or outside the societies that support them" (Kroeber 1948:254). The corollary of cultural realism is cultural determinism. People act in certain ways because their culture so determines, so that behavior is the organism's response to cultural stimuli. Human beings are thus merely instruments for the expression of culture (White 1948). An inherent fallacy of the realist position has been pointed out, namely, that if culture is superorganic with its own ontological realm of operation, how can it influence behavior? (Spiro 1951).

Cultural idealism views culture as consisting of ideal norms or patterns. Culture in this view is not to be identified with behavior, nor is it something external to the organism with its own independent existence. It exists as an idea or set of ideas in the mind of man. White (1959) suggests that behind this approach is the notion that ideas are basic and primary, and that they can initiate behavior that will produce the trappings of culture. But the ideas themselves need explaining, and although culture does indeed involve ideas, it also involves a complex of other mental acts, patterns of behavior, and objects.

Many idealists speak of culture as consisting of abstractions, though what the abstractions are is not clear. Thus, Kroeber and Kluckhohn (1952) describe culture as a form or pattern or way. Cultural traits are "ideal types" because the trait is never expressed in precisely the same way. The trait is, therefore, an abstraction—a conception that has the reality of an idea in the mind. Cultural idealists are logically compelled to hold that material objects are not culture, and that the concept of material culture is fallacious (White 1959). The confusion in the ideal-abstract formulation is basically between the concept of culture, which is a logical construct in the mind of the anthropologist, and the actual existential culture in the real order (Bidney 1954).

The third basic position is that of cultural nominalism, which denies all ontological standing to the concept of culture. It is neither a superorganic reality nor an idea in the human mind. It is rather a logical construct, abstracted from human behavior, and thus exists nowhere else but in the mind of the investigator. But the construct must have some relevance to the culture it describes. The real culture embraces all the behavioral configurations in the society which have a range and variation. The culture construct must establish "the mode of the finite series of variations which are included within each of the real culture patterns" (Linton 1945:45). Thus, the real culture, as far as the observer is concerned, is the actual behavior of the members of the society. Hence, the culture of any society, as abstracted and recorded, is a logical construct in the anthropologist's mind (Spiro 1951).

The nominalist approach to culture is in greatest favor currently and seems to represent a methodologically more sophisticated theory. Strictly speaking, this approach precludes any meaningful conception of cultural determinism. Constructs do not determine behavior. But many self-professed nominalists speak loosely of cultural influence or determination and thus slip unwittingly into cultural realism. As Spiro (1951:25) remarked, "One suspects that despite the methodological sophistication involved in the nominalistic theory, the nominalists are dissatisfied with their own formulations and, unwittingly, allow a superorganicist conception of culture to enter into their thinking." The problem is one that anthropological theorists share with other disciplines dealing with human behavior. It is extremely difficult to maintain a methodologically "pure" position in the face of methodologically "impure" evidence. One winds up either by outlawing methodologically

unacceptable evidence, which may be more significant, or by con-
taminating methods, often surreptitiously (Meissner 1958). Thus, learning theorists who professed a rigidly behaviorist and operationist
methodology found themselves introducing phenomenological elements unsystematically. Not only were such elements introduced, but
the theory could not survive without them. One wonders whether back-
sliding into cultural realism and concepts of cultural determinism does
not have a similar survival value in the present context as well.

Values in Culture

We must remember that cultural values share in these conceptual
ambiguities. Values somehow preexist the individual; the individual
assimilates the values resident in his culture. But the scientific mentality
finds it difficult to accept the superorganic perspective. Besides, if enculturation implies only the assimilation of a previously existing culture,
we are hard pressed to say how it is that culture exists at all or how culture ever began. Culture must have its source and its residence in man,
but in such a way that its existence depends on the existence of the
group, and not on the existence of any particular individual.

While the realists run into logical difficulties, the idealists and
nominalists run into other problems. Culture, with its inherent value-
systems, has a directive or normative aspect that leads the members of
the social system to behave in a certain way because they feel that they
ought to behave in that way. The realist conception of something behind
behavior directing it is perfectly consistent with this aspect of culture.
But the nominalist approach does not explain this dynamic aspect at all.
The idealist approach conceives of culture as ideal norms of how people
ought to behave. This serves to identify, but not to explain, the normative elements since it makes a dynamic element static and deprives it of
compelling force by insisting that there is no necessary correspondence
between these ideal norms and actual behavior (Spiro 1951). Values,
therefore, are conceivable in an otherwise unacceptable approach, and
are inconceivable in otherwise acceptable approaches.

The key issue is whether culture is going to be regarded as behavior
or as abstraction from behavior. White (1959) tries to pick his way
among these ambiguities. He points to the class of things and events that
consist of or are dependent on symboling. These are *symbolates,* and they
can be considered in many different contexts: in their relationship to
human organisms, the context is "somatic;" in their relationship to other
similar symbolates, rather than in relation to human organisms, the context is "extrasomatic." White (1959:231) goes on to say:

When things and events dependent on symboling are considered and interpreted in terms of their relationship to human organisms, i.e., in a somatic context, they may properly be called *human behavior*, and the science, *psychology*. When things and events dependent on symboling are considered and interpreted in an extrasomatic context, i.e., in terms of their relationship to one another rather than to human organisms, we may call them *culture*, and the science, *culturology*.

Culture, in this view, is merely symbolates considered extrasomatically. Values, then, are a subset of the class of symbolates which can be regarded somatically or extrasomatically. However regarded, it involves the same set of events. By inference, therefore, the cultural and the psychological approaches to values are talking about the same reality.

Culture and Personality

The consideration of values has been carried on at both the cultural and the psychological levels in relative independence. Under the impetus of interpersonal interests stimulated largely by Sullivan, however, there has grown up a culture-and-personality literature of some importance. The anthropological interest in this area came from Benedict, Mead, Linton, and LaBarre. The more psychiatric interest was found in Kardiner, Fromm, and Erikson. These overlapping interests stemmed from an appreciation that the character of the individual personality was somehow shaped by the culture in which he lived. It is interesting that most of the early thinking was governed by a basically psychoanalytic model of the biologically given, instinct-based organism, which undergoes cultural modification and socialization as the result of interaction with other culturally formed persons.

Conceptually, there was difficulty in formulating ideas about culture and personality in such a way as to maintain their autonomy, while at the same time developing the understanding of their continuity and interaction. Thus, Laswell (1939:538), trying to expand the interpersonal frame of reference, could offer some working definitions:

"Personality" is the term used to refer to the way a person acts toward other persons. "Culture" is the term used to refer to the way that the members of a group act in relation to one another and to other groups. A "group" is composed of persons. A "person" is an individual who identifies himself with others.

A sense of group identity and interaction is inherent in the concept of culture, and the context of cultural exchange defines and establishes the individual personality. This tendency to continuity of definition results in the conception of culture as a system that operates to maintain a pattern of subjective events by a process of dynamic equilibrium in which distortion or interference at one point in the system activates adaptive mechanisms in other parts of the sytem to restore balance. The personality is articulated within the more general cultural system as a specific subsystem, geared to maintaining a certain degree of internal consistency. At the same time, the personality is dynamically responsive to alterations in other (personal) subsystems that may impose adaptive demands on it. The study of personality consisted in an analysis of the totality of component relationships and situations within the culture and the interaction between cultures. The conceptual models, as Kluckhohn and Mowrer (1944) suggested, were more in terms of "culture *in* personality" and "personality *in* culture" than "culture and personality."

These authors, in their elaborate systematizing attempt, displayed the complexities of variation and continuity involved in dealing with these problems. "Any consideration of 'personality *in* culture' must be carried on within the framework of a complex conceptual scheme which explicitly recognizes instead of tacitly excluding a number of classes of determinants" (p. 1). Personality is the individual's social stimulus value—any attempt to describe an individual's personality must be based specifically on the regularities in stimulus value which the individual has for others. They distinguish the *determinants* of personality, the "classes of forces which may be abstracted out as influencing social stimulus value," from its *components*, "those facets of the social stimulus value of the individual as an integrate in action which may be regarded as produced primarily by one or another of the classes or determinants" (p. 3). The determinants are described in quantitative (universal, communal, role, idiosyncratic) are qualitative (biological, physical-environmental, social, cultural) terms. Thus, cultural determinants may be universal (incest taboo), communal (traditions, manners), role-related (doctor, father), and idiosyncratic.

The complexity of the undertaking is apparent. The culture-and-personality investigations concentrate on trying to describe and characterize certain cultural configurations and establishing certain related personality types. The link was conceived in terms of cultural determinism, but among the multiple influences special emphasis was given to early childhood interpersonal relations. The enterprise has enjoyed limited success and has been severely criticized for its methods and for the logic of its approach. For example, Lindesmith and Strauss (1950) have challenged these studies on grounds of circularity of proof, immunity to negative evidence, confusion between fact and the investigator's interpretations of fact, inadequate evaluation of the investigator's influence on the situation and the data, and the operation of Western biases and "projective systems."

The role of infant experience has been a crucial area of investigation in attempts to bridge the gap between preexisting culture and the developing personality. Under the strong influence of psychoanalytic theory, the predominant character-forming influence of the infant disciplines (nursing, weaning, mothering, bowel-and-bladder training, etc.) has been emphasized. But the evidence is not as good as one might wish, carrying with it a setting of anthropomorphism and unsupported assumption (Orlansky 1949). There is general agreement, of course, that the assumption of the significance of early learning is quite valid, but what precisely is learned and how it influences later development are still unsettled issues.

If we ask how the cultural value-system relates to and influences the individual value-system, we are equivalently asking about the relation of a set of symbolates regarded extrasomatically to another set of symbolates regarded somatically (cf. White 1959). If we are really to make sense out of our question, we must cast the question in one modality or the other. We must regard the value-system of the culture (society) somatically, or we must regard the individual value-system extrasomatically. Changing the context of consideration, moreover, does not change the symbolates, the value-systems; the reality of the individual value-system is that of an individual psychic structure as a major component of the real person. The reality of the cultural value-system, on the other hand, is nothing other than the reality of individual value-systems, but these individual systems demonstrate common elements than can be abstracted and logically constructed as a value-system of the group. Thus, the objective reality of the symbolates is unaffected by our constructions. The question of the influence of cultural value-systems is equivalently a question about the impact on one individual value-system (regarded somatically) of another individual value-system or value-systems (regarded somatically) that can be regarded as sharing a determinable set of value elements. The multiplicity of value-systems involved is determined by reference to the culture of a specific group, whether family, town, state, country, or whatever grouping is in question.

Culture and Values

The interaction of personality and culture makes it apparent that they are dependent on and related to the same set of real events. The development of human personality and human culture, both phylogenetically and ontogenetically, runs a parallel course. As Hallowell (1960:360) points out:

> Along with a greater diversification in the forms of social structure that characterize *Home sapiens*, we are confronted with a change in their underlying dynamics. At this more advanced stage, societies function as *moral* orders. It is this fact that gives us the major key to the kind of psychological transformation that occurred.
>
> The functioning of a social system as a moral order implies a capacity for self-objectification, self-identification, and appraisal of one's own conduct, as well as that of others, with reference to socially recognized and sanctioned standards of behavior. Without a psychological level of organization that permits the exercise of these functions, moral responsibility for conduct could not exist, nor could any social structure function as a moral order.

This capacity depends on the development of ego-functions as well as on the capacity for symbolic projection of experience in terms that are meaningful and intelligible to other individuals. Culture and the organization of society required the evaluation of a new principle of symbolic interaction, which itself derived from the prior development of a capacity for extrinsic symbolic representation (Spiro 1951). As Hallowell (1960:366) puts it, "extrinsic symbolic systems, functioning through vocal, graphic, plastic, gestural or other media, make it possible for groups of human beings to share a common world of meanings."

While the existence of culture depends directly on the capacity for shared meaning through extrinsic symbolic representation, cultural participation requires and reflects the integration of the individual's own personality, with its own capacity for intrinsic symbolic representation. Enculturation involves the frustration of unsocialized drives and instincts that clamor for satisfaction and cannot tolerate delay, and requires some adjustment, often symbolic in nature, involving a host of unconscious symbolic mechanisms of repression, displacement, condensation, projection, sublimation, identification, etc. (Spiro 1951). These mechanisms originate as unconscious infantile responses, but become in time the typically human defense mechanisms of interpersonal adjustment and intrapersonal integration. The acquisition of culture and the development of personality, then, are really the same process.

The values by which the individual regulates his behavior are a major form of symbolic representation. As Spiro (1951:34) indicates, "Behavior, though perceived as a series of responses, is always based on a system of values. From the tremendous number of potential, and equally effective, responses to any given stimulus, only a limited number are actually chosen, and the selection of the few from the many implies a principle of selection—that is, a system of values, articulated as ideal norms, according to which the choices are made." Value-related behavior is associated with a feeling of rightness or wrongness that is part of the cultural heritage. As Hallowell (1950:169) puts it, man's emotional nature "becomes structuralized in such a way that anxiety, guilt and depression become indices to the integrative level reached by the personal adjustments of the individual in relation to the symbolically expressed and mediated norms of his society."

The pattern of structuralization and integration is unique to each individual and enjoys a wide range of diversity within any cultural grouping. The cultural heritage of any one person is different from that of any other in the society (Spiro 1951) since the child is principally exposed to the culture of the family rather than to that of a society. Given the diversity of family cultures, there is a further distortion in the development of the personal cultural heritage of an individual. The necessary incorporation of values is a personal response—not merely an assimilation of preexisting cultural givens, but a symbolically mediated learning process in which multiple adaptive mechanisms play a role in the integrative process of personality formation. The evolving personality, therefore, selects and adapts a personal culture out of the cultural heritage presented him by his parents, family, and society. And, as Spiro (1951:42) says, "it is not the cultural heritage of a given generation, but its culture, that becomes the cultural heritage of the succeeding generation."

The value-system of each individual personality is also something unique and distinctive of that individual. But the uniqueness of its integration does not violate its capacity for shared meaning or the familial or communal aspects of its symbolic integration. Herein lies the solution of the unique sharing of the individual in the communal system of values which makes social life possible.

The Notion of Cultural Values

In order to clarify the notion of value in this cultural context, we need to establish a set of relations between the ideas of culture, symbol, and value. We can follow here the lines of thinking laid down by Parsons and Shils (1962).

Culture, taken as a whole, represents the universe of meaningful products of the symbolizing activity of a society. The elements of culture are transmitted by learning or by cultural diffusion between societies. Symbols embody the meaningful aspects of the multiple ways of orienting and acting that characterize the social system. The symbols, therefore, become controlling elements of the system, since they are not internal to but outside it, functioning as objects of orientation that often take the forms of graphic or plastic representation. The ways of orienting in a society become learnable and transmissible by reason of this symbolic aspect.

Symbols, then, are ways of orienting embodied in and controlled by symbolic objects. The society elaborates a variety of symbol systems to express and organize the primary ways of orienting. Systems of beliefs and ideas enjoy a cognitive primacy; systems of expressive and appreciative symbols have an emotional or cathetic primacy. Other symbol systems, however, have an evaluative primacy. They embody normative standards that refer to the resolution of conflicts, solving of problems, and the organization and direction of action (goal-related). They represent a synthesis of cognitive and affective-cathectic elements through which the acting individual is committed to action in terms of a balance of consequences and implications that conform to the imperatives of a larger social (interactional) system of normative orientation. Parsons and Shils (1962:171–72) point out that the value-standards

> are not logical deductions from systems of beliefs or manifestations of systems of expressive symbols, nor do they derive from cognitive or appreciative standards. They depend in part on such systems, but they draw on all the elements of cognitive, cathectic, and evaluative selection from the alternatives of action. The important alternatives, (which define the problems of action) emerge for the actor only when he, armed with his cognitive and cathectic symbols and standards, directly confronts the relevant situation with all its functional exigencies. As he develops general methods for making choices among these alternatives, he thereby gains a new set of super-ordinate standards. These are moral value standards.

Values, therefore, are symbols of normative orientation. They serve an organizing and integrating function at the levels of both personal and community action. They are the means by which the individual's choices among the alternatives of action are integrated, within the limits of variability, with the symbolic orientations of the society. Insofar as the integration is successful, the conditions for social interaction and the integrity of the social system are maintained and the individual functions in a socialized or encultured manner.

The value-system is a significant symbolic system and a vital aspect of culture. It shares the ambiguities of conceptualization and definition which are inherent in the concept of culture. Whatever the approach to value, whether it is conceived as purely conceptual and abstract or whether it is regarded as consisting of actual preferences and actions, the concept of value carries with it the implication of worth and worthwhileness. This intrinsically normative aspect of the value-system eliminates merely preferential behavior from the value-perspective, although preferential behavior, since much of it is value-dependent, seems a perfectly legitimate starting-point for the study of cultural values. Thus, current usage is generally agreed that values involve reference to normative standards of action that they are intrinsically goal-oriented. Belshaw (1959:560) concludes:

> One cannot conceive of a value without an expression of the goal envisaged. Thus a moral precept, for example, is important because it expresses a goal; if it did not relate to behavior in this way, it would have no significance as a value. Thus a significant element in the anthropological treatment of value so far is that it purports to elucidate goals.

Some of the implications of the cultural concept of value in terms of value-orientation have been well displayed by Kluckhohn and Strodtbeck (1961). They define value-orientations (cultural values) as "complex but definitely patterned (rank-ordered) principles, resulting from the transactional interplay of three analytically distinguishable elements of the evaluative process—the cognitive, the affective, and the directive elements—which give order and direction to the ever-flowing stream of human acts and thoughts as these related to the solution of 'common human' problems." What emerges here is the normative and directive character of the value-system, which underlines the basically selective nature of the value process. Directiveness is a fundamental biologically derived property in that the organism has selective dispositions to react differentially to heterogeneous aspects of the stimulus field. Where human behavior is instinctively based, it is inherently directed; where it is *not* instinct-bound, the range of directive influences is expanded. As Hartmann (1948) has pointed out, the functions served by instinct in lower animals are served by more complex forms of integration at the human level.

Thus, cognitive and cathectic elements are caused of behavior, but they are incapable of achieving the guiding and integrating function that is inherent in the directive aspects of the value-system. The value-system does, in fact, derive the content of its existential and normative assumptions from cognitive and affective elements. If it were not for the level of human capacity for intellection and affection, the value-system by which man transcends the instinctual could not exist. At the same time, however, while the value-system transcends the instinctual, it is dependent on and derivative from that which it transcends. As Kluckhohn and Strodtbeck (1961:9) observe:

> Any given value system of human beings has both a content and a direction which derive from biologically given capacities and predispositions

but are not instinct bound, but it is the directive aspect which is the most crucial for the understanding of both the integration of the total value-system and its continuity through time.

Variations and Variability in Values

As we have observed, the objective reality of values is that of its existence as intrapsychic structure within individual personalities. It is the symbolic dimension of shared meanings that makes if possible to abstract a common normative orientation in the social system and refer to it as the value-system of that social group. This abstractive procedure, along with its concomitant reification of the resulting construct, often leads us to ignore the range of variation in the actual valuings on which the cultural value-system is based.

As soon as we direct attention away from the abstraction toward actual social groupings, variation becomes apparent. Variant subgroups in the culture have a diversity of values, so that the culture itself can be understood in terms of a dominant value-orientation that is continually in interaction with constituent and variant value-orientations. The existence of variant values, however, need not be seen only as deviations from a dominant cultural ethos. Such values may also serve a primary function in the maintenance of the sytem. Thus, Hyman (1953) has demonstrated a different set of values in regard to education and socioeconomic advancement among low classes from those in middle and upper classes. Here is a clear case of divergent subcultural values; but how is this divergence to be regarded? One can regard lower class values either as deviant and therefore as creating strain in the social system, or as part of a pattern of systematic variation in which their variation serves to stabilize and maintain the whole system.

No value-system can be completely consistent. There are inevitably difficulties in fitting the value-system to the demands of the real society or personality. An inconsistent value-system, or a forced articulation of the social system with the value-system produces strain. The society responds by adopting various adaptive mechanisms calculated to reduce the strain and achieve some degree of functional integration. A compromise evolves between "functional imperatives" (Parsons and Shils 1962) of the concrete situation and the dominant value patterns of the society. The society may establish a priority ranking among the dominant values, so that a gradation in tolerance for deviant values and deviant action is established. The degree of tolerance will be smaller in authoritarian organizations as a rule, since they will tend to seek as broad a pattern of conformity to the predominant value-system as is possible. The society may confine divergent values to special contexts and roles, thereby isolating the bearers of divergent values and limiting disintegrative effects on the predominant system. Thus, deviation from the normal can be defined as pathological and thereby isolated, or it may be accepted as normal and ascribed to a special role in the society. The Siberian shaman, for example, seems to represent a class of privileged status that is achieved by passing through a stage of frank psychosis (Ackerknecht 1943). Shamans are respected, honored, and severely circumscribed, and thereby successfully integrated into the overall system.

Whether it is more accurate to regard such examples as deviations or as expressions of the range of permissable variation is a moot question. The alternatives are relevant to the understanding of values, since behind them lies the question of whether the value is to be conceived of as an ideal norm that behavior approaches in varying degrees so that one's behavior either conforms or deviates (black-and-white), or whether the values, in fact, represents a range of permissible behaviors. An interesting example is Stouffer's (1949) study of role conflict. On the assumption that in any authoritarian situation conformity will depend on the compatibility between ruler and the dominant values of those who must obey, Stouffer found that the range of approved acts for authorities and students showed almost complete identity in some students, no overlap in others, and differing ranges with some degree of overlap in still others. He concluded that the range of approved or permissible behavior as perceived by a given individual is important for the analysis of what constitutes the social norm.

> In essay writing in this field it is common and convenient to think of a social norm as a point, or at least as a very narrow band on either side of a point. This probably is quite unrealistic as to most of our social behavior. And it may be precisely the ranges of permissible behavior which most need examination, if we are to make progress in this realm which is so central in social science. For it may be the very existence of some flexibiity or social slippage—but not too much—which makes behavior in groups possible. (p. 717)

It should be pointed out, in addition, that what is relevant to the cultural value-system in terms of conformity and deviation, in terms of value-conflict and strain, and in terms of value orientation and the conception of values as representing ranges of permissible behavior, is also relevant to the personal value-system. The participation of the individual in the values of the culture is conditioned by his own inner valuing processes, which are a function of his own unique personality, and which may demonstrate any degree of "deviation" from the cultural pattern. The result is conflict and strain, which call forth adaptive and integrative mechanisms. Cultural mechanisms operate to lessen the degree of social strain and preserve the integrity of the social system. Personal mechanisms operate to minimize intrapsychic conflict and preserve the integrality of the personality. Here, too, we need not think of such mechanisms as being required except beyond a certain range of personally permissible and acceptable behaviors.

Values as Integrative

As we have seen, values are a form of symbolic activity that require the emergence of self-objectivation and identification and the capacity for participating in shared meaning with others. These capacities underlie the development of human personality and establish the possibility of culture.

Values, then, are more or less permanent symbolic structures within the intrapsychic economy. Their functions are involved at the level of symbolic expression and require the capacity for abstraction, intellection, and the communication, transmission, and sharing of meaning. The value-system must, therefore, be considered as implicating ego-structure. It is, moreover, normative and directive, and therefore integrative on both psychological and social levels. We can suggest, in the light of all that has gone before, that the concept of value is not only consistent but congruent with the more or less heuristic notion previously elaborated on psychological grounds. What we have added in this present consideration is the cultural aspect, i.e., that values are also symbolic systems capable of shared meaning and abstraction.

This understanding of the role and structure of values is consistent with the nature of culture and symbolic structures as forms of transitional phenomena (Meissner 1978). Values are a point of integration of subjective derivatives of the individual's inner world with the prior communally asserted and symbolically shared systems of evaluative significance that are the common heritage of a society, a group, or even a religious tradition. They thus partake of the nature of illusory experience that is the hallmark of such transitional existence. Values, understood in this connection, are the primary locus for the validity and value of the life of illusion that Freud sought to destroy, and for which Pfister pleaded (Freud and Meng 1963; Meissner 1984b). Freud sought to destroy the illusory values of faith without reason, and to replace them with the values of reason without faith. The present argument, following the lead of Pfister, would opt for a mediating alternative, the values of faith and reason, of *fides quaerens intellectum*.

CHAPTER 18

Ethical Identity

The integration of internal psychic structural systems with meaningful social realities and shared symbolic reference systems—as these have been articulated in the preceding consideration—sets the stage for reflecting on the appropriate place of these systems in the human personality. A convenient point of transition is provided by Erikson's (1959, 1963) notion of identity.

The concept of identity has not yet found its definitive place in psychoanalytic theory. Erikson's attempt to articulate this notion as an aspect of ego psychology is clearly inadequate, even in terms of his own discussion. Identity embraces aspects of instinctual functioning, ego organization, and superego vicissitudes in a complex understanding, integrating them in a supraordinate synthesis that embraces higher-order facets of internal psychic organization, variations in patterns of object-related interactions, and complex individual-societal influences. Since the understanding of values we have been developing embraces the same empirical ground, we are now approaching, in theoretical terms, the area of overlap and integration between complex personality systems and the influence of values and value-orientations.

My purpose here is simply to trace the evolution of value dimensions in Erikson's thought. Its progressive development makes increasingly explicit the ethical relevance of the concept of identity and leads to provocative questions about the relationship among the complexities of identity formation, the influence of culturally embedded value-systems, and the role of religious values. Without presuming to ascribe these ideas to Erikson himself, I want simply to explore what his formulations imply about this dark frontier of religious and psychological thinking.

The Life Cycle

Erikson's major contribution came with the publication of his *Childhood and Society* (1963), in which he laid out a program of ego development that reached from birth to death: the individual passed through the phases of the life cycle by meeting and resolving a series of developmental psychosocial crises. In the earliest stage of infancy, at the mother's breast, the child developed either a sense of basic trust or a sense of mistrust. In later infancy, the child had to achieve a sense of autonomy or, failing that, he would be left with some degree of shame and doubt. In early childhood the child developed a sense of initiative, hopefully without guilt. In latency the issue was a sense of industry without a sense of inferiority. The adolescent crisis was the crystallization of the residues of preceding crises into a more or less definitive sense of personal identity, as opposed to a diffusion of identity and a confusion of roles. For the young adult the question was the development of a sense of intimacy rather than isolation. For the older adult the issue was generativity, as a concern for establishing and guiding the next generation. And finally, in the twilight of life, the crisis to be resolved was that of ego integrity in the face of ultimate despair.

These eight phases of the life cycle with their respective crises accomplished several things. First, they made it clear that ego development was open-ended and never finished. The child's capacity to resolve successfully any one developmental crisis depended on the degree of resolution of the preceding crises, and laid the foundation for engaging in the next developmental crisis. Second, they clarified the relation between the various phases of development and previous phases of libidinal development. The latter had been the basic contribution of earlier efforts of psychoanalysis. But Erikson's developmental schema explained better how earlier libidinal developmental residues were carried along in the course of growth and were built into later developmental efforts of the ego. Psychoanalysis had previously lacked the conceptual tools to deal with this problem, particularly in regard to the postadolescent phases of the life cycle. Finally, Erikson's treatment of these crises as specifically psychosocial showed that the development of the ego was not merely a matter of the intrapsychic vicissitudes of inner psychic energies. It was that, certainly, but it was also a matter of the interaction and "mutual regulation" between the developing human organism and significant persons in its environment. Even more strikingly, it was a matter of the mutual regulation evolving between the growing child and the culture and traditions of his society.

Development is seen as a process of complex interaction between maturational, intrapsychic, and extrapsychic processes. The child is born with fragmentary drives, libidinal and aggressive. The development of these patterns of drives depends on the process that guides parental responses. The outcome, even when expressed in cooperative achievements and inventive specializations, ties the individual to the traditions and institutions of childhood, and exposes him to the autocracy of conscience, the inner voice of self-regulation. One of the deepest conflicts in life is the hate for the parent who serves as the model for development of the superego—the organ of moral tradition. Inconstancy in parental morality produces a suspiciousness and evasiveness which when linked with the absolute quality of the superego makes "moral" man a potential danger to his own ego and to his fellow men. The formation of the superego requires a submergence of infantile rage leading sometimes to a self-righteous intolerance or moralism that, inhibits rather than encourages initiative in others. In turn, the initiative of "moral" man can break through the boundaries of self-restriction (conscience) and permit him to do to others what he would never permit to be done to himself.

The Ethical Dimension

Ethical concern runs as a slender thread through the entire schema. Erikson sees adolescence as a traditional psychosocial stage between childhood and adulthood. The individual must pass from the morality learned by the child to the ethics of the adult. The adolescent mind, then, is prone to ideology, where the outlines of what is best and most valuable can be most clearly delineated. There is danger in harnessing human ideals to such overriding ideologies, whatever they may be—communist, capitalist, religious, etc. The young adult, emerging from the quest for identity, is ready for intimacy: the capacity to commit himself to concrete partnerships and affiliations, and to develop the ethical strength to abide by such commitments regardless of personal sacrifice. The adult phase is dominated by the ethics of generativity—regulated by what is required to promote and guide the emergence of the coming generation to the fullness of its own identity.

In Erikson's view, all institutions codify the ethics of generative succession. This extends beyond the demands of genitality as such. Even where spiritual tradition advances the renunciation of the right to procreation, there is a care for creatures of this world and for the charity which meets, as it transcends, this world. Man's ethical character ultimately rests on the extended period of his infantile dependency. Only thus does he develop that dependence on himself by which he becomes dependable: his conscience. Only when he becomes thoroughly dependable in fundamental values of truth and justice can he become independent and so pass on and develop tradition. Thus, the development and handing on of tradition is contingent on the development of the individual. And the ethics of generativity are ultimately contingent on the development of ethicality in individuals: the ethical sense of individuals builds and extends the traditions and values to be passed on. Erikson encapsulates this insight into the relation of adult integrity and infantile trust by saying that children will not normally fear life if their elders have integrity enough not to fear death.

It is difficult to escape the realization that values are a crucial part of each stage of the life cycle and its correlative psychosocial crisis. Each such crisis creates a specific set of important human values that become vital for the progressive development of the individual personality and provide the groundwork for the individual's participation in the world of shared human experience. The acquisition of basic trust, the sense of one's own trustworthiness and the trustworthiness of significant others, implies the internalization of a set of fundamental values which are rudimentary in any form of meaningful human sharing and communication. The failure to acquire basic trust is reflected in the deep-seated impairment of many of our most severely disturbed patients. This failure of internalized value is accompanied by developmental failures and structural deficiencies in the organization of personality and places a severe impediment to any meaningful human sharing. Such patients are narcissistically crippled and show little capacity for love.

Religion and Trust

Erikson's next major effort came with the appearance of *Young Man Luther* in 1958, where he studied the manner in which one great historical figure resolved the crises of late adolescence and young adulthood. It is significant that Luther is a religious reformer. It is in a way inevitable that the ethical concern carry the inquiring psychoanalyst to the threshold of religion. Erikson (1959:64) had written: "The psychological observer must ask whether or not in any area under observation religion and tradition are living psychological forces creating the kind of faith and conviction which permeates a parent's personality and thus reinforces the child's basic trust in the world's trustworthiness." All religions share the childlike surrender to a beneficient deity who dispenses blessings and graces, and are based on the insight that individual trust must become a common faith and individual mistrust a common evil; that the need for restoration must become part of a common ritual and thus a sign of trustworthiness in the community. Religion, then, assumes an important function in preserving the societal matrix within which individual trust and the ethical sense of identity are generated and can be passed on to succeeding generations.

Ethical Sense and Virtue

Subsequently, in his *Insight and Responsibility* (1964), Erikson became more explicit and specific about the centrality of ethical dynamism in his thought. He wrote (1965:45):

> . . . that the collective life of mankind, in all its historical lawfulness, is fed by the energies and images of successive generations; and that each generation brings to human fate an inescapable conflict between its ethical and rational aims and its infantile fixations. The conflict helps drive man toward the astonishing things he does—and it can be his undoing. It is a condition of man's humanity—and the prime cause of his bottomless inhumanity. For whenever and wherever man abandons his ethical position, he does so only at the cost of massive regressions endangering the very safeguard of his nature.

Man's basic ethical sense was in turn contingent on the inner strengths that supported and sustained it.

Erikson turned his attention to the concept of virtue, reminiscent of the traditional notion, but enriched by the deeper understanding provided by his basic psychoanalytic perspective. What is that "virtue" that goes out of a man when he loses strength, and what is that strength that he acquires when he achieves that spirited quality without which "his moralities become mere moralism and his ethics feeble goodness"? Virtue, he answers, is that human quality of strength which the ego develops from generation to generation. The virtues he selects for analysis are hope, will, purpose, competence, fidelity, love, care, and wisdom. The astute reader will note that Erikson has selected eight virtues, and the inference that they are correlated with the eight stages of the life cycle is on target. The developmental phases provide the source of these basic strengths which belong to ego maturity. And these virtues in turn provide the ethical identity and value which alone preserve the integrity of human life—in individual egos as well as in the sequence of generations.

Erikson draws a distinction between morality and ethics. Moral rules are based on a primitive level of development. They are derived from fear, a response to threats of abandonment, punishment, exposure, or the inner threat of guilt, shame, or isolation. Ethical rules, however, are based on ideals to be striven for. The moral sense and the ethical sense are different in their development and in their psychodynamics. This does not mean, however, that the primitive morality of fear and retribution can be bypassed developmentally. Every major step in the comprehension of the good in one's cultural universe is related to another stage of individual growth.

The Golden Rule

Erikson derives a principle from this sense of ethics which he puts in terms of his reformulation of the Golden Rule: "Truly worthwhile acts enhance a mutuality between the doer and the other—a mutuality which strengthens the doer even as it strengthens the other" (1964:233). This is an extension of Freud's theory of genitality, in which the strivings of sexuality and love point to the mutual activation of the potency and potentialities of each partner. A man is more of a man to the extent that he is able to make a woman more of a woman, and vice versa.

Erikson's version of the Golden Rule encapsulates his concept of an adult ethical sense. We must grow beyond childhood, which provides the moral basis of identity, and beyond the ideology of youth, to reach the adult ethical maturity which alone can guarantee to coming generations the opportunity to experience and internalize the full cycle of humanity and ethicality. The danger of any ideology or value system that chooses to remain juvenile is that it absolves itself of responsibility for generational concerns and thereby advocates an abortive sense of identity. Only through authentic ethicality can we transcend the limits of our own individuality. It is the ethical sense that is the mark of the adult as it subsumes areas of responsibility, competition, and libidinal investment and thus transforms the moralism of childhood and the ideological conviction of youth. Thus, Erikson writes (1968:259–60):

> Moralities sooner or later outlive themselves, ethics never: this is what the need for identity and for fidelity, reborn with each generation, seems to point to. Morality in the moralistic sense can be shown to be predicated on superstitions and irrational inner mechanisms which, in fact, ever again undermine the ethical fiber of generations; but old morality is expendable only where new and more universal ethics prevail. This is the wisdom that the words of many religions have tried to convey to man . . . . The overriding issue is the creation not of a new ideology but of a universal ethics growing out of a universal technological civilization. This can be achieved only by men and women who are neither ideological youths nor moralistic old men, but who know that from generation to generation the test of what you produce is the *care* it inspires.

The Ethics of Generativity

Gandhi's Truth (1969) was an attempt to study in the matrix of personal development, culture, and history the flowering and fulfillment of that generativity and care that marks the fullness of adulthood—even as the Luther book had sought out the elements of identity and fidelity. Even more, it was a search for the ethical core that formed the inner dynamism of Gandhi's life and work: the Satyagraha, the "truth force." The inquiry did not stop at the threshold of ethicality but carried over into the realm where the ethical merges with the religious and the religious expresses itself in ethical terms. Gandhi was certainly a political man; but he was also a religious man. The logic of his life carried a conviction of truth based on a divine covenant transcending all parental prohibitions and "moralities." He dared to stand, naked and unprotected by any conventionalities, between absolute evil and absolute truth.

The religious person is one who confronts ultimate realities and ultimate facts. Religiosity is a striving for ethical clarity in the face of the one fact that gives all humanity a shared identity: a consciousness of death and the love of all men as equally mortal. Between the morbid adolescent consciousness of death and the imminent certainty of death in old age there must be a period of consolidation that lends credence to the illusion that classes, nations, or churches can provide a security or certainty superior to the fact of death. The illusion finds support in the signs of procreative and productive capacity. Religious ritual offers regular ceremonial confrontations which try both to reveal and to conceal the fact of death through the security of dogma. Religious men and women gather into priesthoods and religious orders to serve as the crafters of ritual, pledging poverty and chastity to become living bridges to an eventual clarity of existence, or at least to provide a sense of consolation which makes it possible to produce, create, and serve without despair in the face of death. "Craftsmanship, however, tends to become crafty, and all ritualization and consolidation leads eventually to rigidity, hypocrisy, and vanity. This, in turn, is felt with deep indignation and passionate concern by those men who are the true *homines religiosi* of their age" (Erikson 1969:195).

Moralism and dogmatism tend to bring the fanatic religionist to split himself into a harsh judge and a wicked sinner, to grant himself the right to view others and treat them as no better than the worst in himself. Adult moralism is easily subverted to moral vindictiveness. There is a violence inherent in the moral sense. We violate children and arouse them to an inner rage when we keep from them the guidance and support they need to develop fully. Nonviolence means more than the preservation of another's physical inviolacy; it means the protection of his essence as a developing person and personality. Erikson (1969:251) writes:

> Nonviolence, inward and outward, can become a true force only where ethics replaces moralism. And ethics, to me, is marked by an insightful assent to human values, whereas moralism is blind obedience; and ethics is transmitted with informed persuasion, rather than enforced with absolute interdicts.

Gandhi's truth is at once a statement of the ethics of nonviolence and a statement of the ethics of generativity. Under the Babul tree, Gandhi announced: "That line of action is alone justice which does not harm either party to a dispute" (1964:239). One cannot find a way to avoid physical and moral harm to another person without caring for the development and growth to maturity of that other, and without surrendering the impulse to violence. If the other is a child, the care is that of one generation for another. If the other is an adult, it is for his achievement of identity and ethical maturity, so that he too might reach and carry on the fullness of humanity and generative care.

Religion and Identity

The fullness of the life cycle elicits concerns for the transcendence of our individuality and identity. Great religions offer a traditional wisdom which is directed to ultimate individuation, while remaining true and responsible to the culture in which they live. They seek transcendence by renunciation, yet maintain an ethical concern for the things of this world. A religion is measured by the meaning it provides to shape the next generation as well as the opportunity to grow to meet ultimate questions with clarity and strength. From the stages of life evolve those basic strengths which give life to human institutions. Institutions falter and fail without them; but

> without the spirit of institutions pervading the patterns of care and love, instruction and training, no strength could emerge from the sequence of generations. Psychosocial strength, we conclude, depends on a total process which regulates individual life cycles, the sequence of generations, and the structure of society simultaneously: for all three have evolved together. (Erikson 1968:141)

One might wonder how the inner dynamism of psychoanalysis leads to an insistence on man's ethical sense as integral to his nature and development, or how that same dynamism leads to the threshold oᵢ man's religious spirit and belief. Erikson's genius is that he has been able to embrace the fundamental insights of psychoanalysis and integrate them into a higher and broader view of man without doing violence to the inner truth of those basic insights. He has brought into focus within a psychoanalytic perspective the complex aspects of our reality as socially embedded and culturally related. Psychoanalytic man is no longer a creature closed within his own psychic structure and wholly caught up in the inner vicissitudes of drives and instincts. Under Erikson's molding, he has become a creature open to and involved in the social processes around him in a pattern of continual interaction and mutual regulation that persists to the end of the life cycle.

CHAPTER 19

The Place of Religious Values

The Nature of Religious Values

Values lie at the heart of any religious belief system or tradition, particularly the more developed ones. The value system is a central component of the essential message that the religious system attempts to communicate to its members. At the same time, however, they are rarely specifically expressed as such. They may be transmitted through a more or less explicit system of morality, but they are more often embedded in a context of doctrine and belief which constitutes the shared tradition of the religious group, or they are expressed through religious cult and ritual, making the acceptance of the value system the touchstone for membership in the community of believers.

The values may be derived from a scriptural tradition, such as the Old and New Testaments, the Torah and Talmud, or the Buddhist scriptures, or they may be articulated in terms of the teachings of religious figures, whether of the founder of the sect or of his followers. The basic schema of Christian values is found in the teachings of Christ, but is also expanded and embellished in the writings of the apostles, St. Paul, the evangelists, the patristic literature, the writings of the saints, and the long theological reflection on the data of revelation.

The tradition proposes ideals as guides for the good Christian life. The figure of Christ is the primary embodiment of such ideals, and the imitation of Christ is the dominant motif of the long tradition of Christian asceticism. Freud (1921:134) was not slow to note this point. He commented:

It is otherwise in the Catholic Church. Every Christian loves Christ as his ideal and feels himself united with all other Christians by the tie of identification. But the Church requires more of him. He has also to identify himself with Christ and love all other Christians as Christ loved them. At both points, therefore, the Church requires that the position of the libido which is given by group formation should be supplemented. Identification has to be added where object-choice has taken place, and object love where there is identification. This addition evidently goes beyond the constitution of the group.

The central issue in the imitation, however, is a focus on specific ideals and values that are embodied and symbolized in the life and teaching of Christ. These values reflect the Christian ideal of what it means to be a Christian and to live the essence of that belief. Insofar as the believer becomes Christ-like, he has effectively internalized those values and approximates to some degree their realization in his daily life, as did the saints, who are endorsed as the heroes of the Christian ideal.

As a cultural possession of the religious group, the value-system, in fact, preexists the believer. The believer is born into a culture that is permeated by the inherent value system. As the believer comes to live within his culture and its values, that culture—and particularly the value-system it embraces—takes root in him. Religious values, like cultural values in general, cannot be understood without embracing both the realm of inner subjective experience (the psychological realm) and the contexts of shared and communicated meaning and value (the cultural level). The understanding of religious values, then, requires an intelligent grasp of both realms and their mutual interaction and interpenetration. The participation of the believer in his religious belief system involves both assimilating preexistent values that carry the stamp of the inner life of the religion and shaping new values through a spontaneous and internally derived creative impulse. With regard to the communication of adolescent values, Erikson (1964:126) comments:

> But here we enter the domain of ethical values. Identity and fidelity are necessary for ethical strength, but they do not provide it in themselves. It is for adult man to provide content for the ready loyalty of youth, and worthy objects for its need to repudiate. As cultures, through graded training, enter into the fiber of young individuals, they also absorb into their life-blood the rejuvenative power of youth. Adolescence is thus a vital regenerator in the process of social evolution; for youth selectively offers its loyalties and energies to the conservation of that which feels true to them and to the correct or destruction of that which has lost its regenerative significance.

While religious values in any religious tradition enjoy a degree of continuity through history, there is nonetheless a continuing process of modification, development of the value-system in response to the influences from the social and cultural matrix within which the religious tradition flourishes. Religious values, in this sense, share the same characteristics of variation and variability that characterize all cultural values, and they are subject to the same modifying forces. The first commandment of the Christian tradition, for example, the love of God and the love of one's neighbor, remains a persistent theme that has not altered in its impact or validity through all the Christian millenia. However, the notions of what it might mean to love God, or the practical implications of what it means to love one's neighbor, may undergo significant modification from time to time in the course of history. By the same token, the sacredess and sacramental character of marriage has been consistently maintained throughout the long history of Christian teaching and practice. Yet, at the same time, there has been a considerable evolution in the manner in which the church and the Christian community regulate the maintenance of that sacramental bond. Even within recent memory there has been a demonstrable shift in the attitudes of the Christian community toward the permanent or indissoluble character of the marriage bond. In the modern context, there is a much more ready acceptance of divorce and a broadening of what is to be regarded as the legitimate basis for the dissolution of such a bond.

The question of the variability and evolution of values within a religious tradition is connected with the broader question of changes within the religious tradition itself. Values are frequently more directly articulated within the moral teaching of the tradition which expresses guidelines, ideals and directives for the shaping of behavior. Here again, both continuity and change are involved. Basic moral propositions, for example, good is to be done and evil avoided, remain fixed. So too, the commandments remain unalterable within the Christian doctrinal structure. These immutable precepts are generally cast at a more universal level of abstraction that allows for considerable interpretation and requires the use of moral judgment in making practical applications. More specific moral positions, however, display a much greater degree of mutability. If we recall for a moment the considerable modification of moral attitudes toward contraception in recent decades within the Christian churches, it seems clear that practical moral imperatives are susceptible to considerable modification from the social and cultural environment in which they operate.

By the same token, the broader doctrinal context of such values also undergoes significant evolution. The concept at issue here is the evolution of dogma. The theological argument rages on whether the doctrinal teaching of a given religious tradition does, in fact, evolve or, if one admits such evolution, in what sense the doctrine can be said to evolve and in what sense not. It seems sufficiently clear, however, from this theological debate that doctrinal concepts do undergo sufficient modification to give rise to such an argument, even though the essence of the teaching remains unaltered.

Moreover, it is equally evident that our understanding of religious doctrines changes from one stage of man's historical development to the next, and even from one level of his developed consciousness to the next. In this more subjective sense, the evolution of doctrine is more a matter of fact than of inference. This is particularly important to the understanding of religious values, since, as I have argued, religious values, in common with the broader range of cultural values, incorporate subjective influences which cannot be reduced to merely objective terms, but which nonetheless are integrated with the objective elements of cultural expression. What this understanding does is to put more emphasis on things like the context of understanding, the human process of affective involvement and reaction, the subjective components of man's evaluative capacity, and the inevitable role of human subjectivity and freedom of choice in the expression and shaping of all values.

In other words, we are dealing here with the realm of transitional phenomena in which the value system as a form of extrasomatic shared cultural symbolization is entered into and experienced by each individual as a subjectively grasped part of his own personality while being shared in and endorsed as the common possession of many. It is through the sharing and participating on the part of the group of believers that the value system as such maintains its validity and its consensual endorsement.

Religious Values as Internalized

While values as such may have a communal existence as the common possession of the religious tradition and the believing community, they do not become functional until they become an operative part of the individual believer's inner psychic world by means of internalization. The whole question of value formation is exceedingly complex and fraught with difficult theoretical issues, but a mainstay of the psychoanalytic understanding of value formation is that it is related in a significant degree to the processes of internalization that contribute through the course of development to the building and shaping of the personality in a more general sense. The religious value system, as we have noted, in some sense preexists the child as a common and historically embedded symbolic possession of the religious community. How then does the child come to gain possession of this value system, not merely as a cognitively grasped and acknowledged body of value propositions but more specifically as a lived and integrated part of his own psychic organization?

We can go back for a moment, in our attempt to understand this process, to some of Freud's original formulations regarding the ways in which children shape the development of their personality through internalizations. One of Freud's most central considerations was his notion of how the superego came about as a significant structural component of the child's functioning psyche.

Freud's formulations on the question of identification came in 1923 with the publication of *The Ego and the Id*. His emphasis is on the essential role of identification in the development of the ego. To begin with, the giving up of infantile sexual objects results in an alteration in the structure of the ego. The character of the ego evolves as object-cathexes are replaced by identifications. The alteration of the ego is such that it draws more and more of the libido to itself as an internal love object. The transformation of object-libido into narcissistic libido is equivalent to a desexualization of libidinal energy. Thus, ego extends its control over the instinctual forces of the id.

Identification then assumes a developmental role in which it is a primary mechanism for the origin of these changes in the ego structures which derive from relations with significant others. The early identifications are the most important and the most lasting. Early identifications with the parents issue into the complex relationships of the oedipal situation. The resolution of this complex of identifications is decisive for the organization of the individual character. As Freud (1923:34) remarks:

> The broad general outcome of the sexual phase dominated by the Oedipus Complex may, therefore, be taken to be the forming of a precipitate in the ego, consisting of these two identifications in some way united with each other. Then modification of the ego retains its special position; it confronts the other contents of the ego as an ego-ideal or superego.

As the ego progresses in development, it gains in strength and becomes more resistant to such influences. But the process of identification remains operative. Ultimately, Freud conceived of human character formation as resting genetically on a complex of identifications. Fundamentally, the identification with parental agencies gave rise to the superego, but there were added to this further identifications with the parents of later periods, identifications with other influential figures, identifications formed as precipitates of abandoned object-relations.

As Freud envisioned and applied identification, it took the form of a common mechanism internally related to instinctual needs through which a more permanent and more highly organized psychic structure was erected as a result of the vicissitudes of these instincts. The gradual broadening of Freud's concept from the status of a substitute for abandoned object-cathexes to the sharing of common qualities was extended in the neo-Freudian literature to imitation of admired or respected models, to group adherence, to acceptance of a cause, or to any close sympathetic or unifying action with other persons.

Sanford (1955) describes identification as a process in which "the individual may be observed to respond to the behavior of other people or objects by imitating in fantasy or in reality the same behavior himself." Classes of behavior between a subject and a model are imitation learning, prohibition learning, identification with the aggressor, and vicarious affective experience. Imitation may be the behavioral offshoot of an identification, but imitation may occur without any identification. Imitation and identification provide two major ways in which patterns of social behavior are adopted from models. According to Parsons and Shils (1962), imitation assumes that the other is a model only for a specific pattern of learned behavior, whereas identification implies a model for general orientation to behavior. It is obvious that general orientations can generate specific patterns of behavior, but that they need not. Prohibition learning, adopting the prohibitions of parents and parental substitutes, is a part of superego formation and involves identification. Identification with the aggressor was originally proposed by Anna Freud, who saw it as a means by which the developing ego mastered the anxiety from an outside threat. She proposed it as a fairly common stage in the normal development of the superego. It serves to transform the threat of the passive position into a more active assault on external objects. Finally, vicarious affective experience refers to a variety of forms of positive or negative affect which are experienced in consequence of identification with a model.

These various forms of identification, have a common connotation in that they represent attempts by the ego to modify itself in relation to a model—in Freud's terms, the shadow of the object falls on the ego. Identification with a model may serve not only to reduce anxiety over anticipated aggression; it may also serve more positive adaptive ends as a means to obtain certain goals or gratifications. The model may be perceived as capable of achieving certain rewards or objectives, and the desire for these same goals may induce the subject to adopt some of the characteristics of the perceived model. As Freud (1921:108) commented:

> Identification . . . may arise with every new perception of a common quality shared with some other person who is not an object of the sexual instinct. The more important this common quality is, the more successful may this partial identification become, and it may then represent the beginning of a new tie.

More recent applications of the concept of identification point to its centrality in socialization. It is generally agreed that identification with adult models is an essential mechanism in the socialization of the child. Much of the knowledge required for cultural participation is passed on from generation to generation in this way. Acquired patterns of social behavior are taken over from established social models. Since imitation is the vehicle for acquiring specific elements of culture, and identification pertains to the acquisition of more generalized patterns of orientation, the latter's most important role in the socialization process is the development of an acceptance of adult values and value-orientations. Attachment to the social object creates a sensitivity, not only to the object's behavior, but to his attitudes, beliefs, and values, for it is these that characterize the object as a person. The subject seeks not merely to have what the model has, or to do what the model does; he seeks to be what the model is.

When we appeal to identification, we are appealing to a mechanism which aims at making the subject like an object. The little girl aims at becoming like her mother; the group member aims at becoming like the leader. It is not always clear what constitutes this likeness, but it is probably safe to say that the likeness is different for different contexts of identification. The identification of the child is on the straightforward level of behavior. The girl acts like her mother. It is immediately apparent that mere similarity of mannerism or action does not satisfy more adult needs to identify. Adult identification extends beyond action and mere imitation to a level at which the internal psychic organization of the subject begins to approximate that of the other. Adult identification has to do with the reorganization of the internal modulation of behavior so that it approximates the internal regulators of the object of identification. The subject becomes internally like the object when he has internalized its intrinsic norms. These norms then produce by way of secondary effect a congruence of attitudes, beliefs, and behavior. The essential dimension of identification, implicit in many of the more sophisticated contexts in which it plays a role, is congruence of value-systems. The individual becomes identified with a group by internalizing the group evaluative symbols and norms so that these norms become a functional and integral part of his own personal value-system.

Identification has additional significance since it provides a basis for further motivation to accept still more social discipline. The needs it fosters for approval and esteem are essential for the functioning of the social system, and the ability of the society to gratify them is a measure of the success of the system in internalizing common patterns of value-orientation.

The relevance of all of this to ongoing group processes has been increasingly appreciated in recent years. Socialization has its primary analogue in childhood development, but the process is continuing and extends to adult adaptations, to social life and culture. Culture is never static. It is a dynamic process which requires constant assimilation and adaptation in its participants.

The original Freudian analysis was cast in terms of the relation between the group members and the leader. This analysis is more consistent with totalitarian groups, where the concentration of total authority is extreme. In more democratic group structures, however, identification continues to play a primary, although more diversified, role. In such group structures, the individual identifies primarily with the group rather than with a leader. Here again the sense of solidarity both reflects and promotes identification. The individual chooses and internalizes a certain selection of the constituent group values, and thereby identifies himself with the group, gaining a sense of community with it. This basic sense of community is then consolidated by identification with significant figures in the group, whether it be the leader or particularly influential members.

The complex of identifications answers very basic needs for recognition, acceptance, esteem, and belonging, and also bring about an alteration in the ego of the identified person. We can conceptualize this alteration in terms of the value-systems and identity, which bear an intimate relation to the problem of character. The whole complex of character, values, identity, and identification is interwoven in complicated ways which reinforce the impression of their mutual dependence. While identification is the common mechanism, these elements all point to more or less permanent structural formations in the personality, and account for the general disposition to act consistently in terms of persistent standards and style.

The value-system is an autonomous structure in the ego (Hartmann's secondary autonomy), which is built, in part, out of elements assimilated by identification. Adult identifications pertain less to matters of style than to matters of standard. They are concerned less with the manner of action than with the basic values and orientations incarnated in the model. Identification with the group is almost exclusively of this latter kind. Identification with significant persons is often an amalgam of other elements, but it can also reflect the assimilation of values on many fronts and from many directions. These internalized precipitates of external relations demand synthesis into an integral psychic system. The work of integration is a form of active intervention of the ego through its own synthetic function. The value-system is never to be regarded wholly as a precipitate of acquisitions from outside; it represents, in addition, a synthetic organization produced actively and creatively by the further intervention of the ego.

At its highest level of inner regulation and structural integration, the ego has at its disposal a self-created system of values that both provides a stable integration of intrapsychic processes and reflects the ego's reciprocal interaction with a sociocultural matrix (Meissner 1970, 1971). It is at this level of value integration that ego and superego reach maximal congruity. Superego elements are reprocessed selectively through identification and integrated as ego elements. Such depersonified superego constituents become the building blocks of the value-system, which provides the ego with its most important structural regulatory constituents. In the construction of the value system, the ego achieves a level of function in which the integration of id, superego, and reality is increasingly realized. As Jacobson (1964:130) writes:

> The maturation of the ego and of critical judgments considerably modifies our concepts of value and our actions. Leading to an acceptance of what is realistic and reasonable, it accomplishes at least a partial victory of the reality principle, not only over the pleasure principle, but also over exaggerated 'idealism' and thus over the superego. Only then do the superego functions work with more neutralized energy. In fact, the final maturation of both the ego and the superego sets in only after the tempest of instinctual conflicts during adolescence has subsided. Then we observe a gradual moderation of youthful idealism and illusions, leading to the setting up of more reasonable goals and to a further development of moral judgment: of the ability to test and to evaluate the outside and inside reality correctly, reasonably and with greater moral tolerance, and to act according to such judgment.

It is important in conceptualizing these processes to remember that such identifications carry out their structuralizing effects, particularly on the level of value formation, by a selective inner construction modeled after elements found in introjects, objects, or social structures. The ego's individual value system is a unique and autonomous product of the personality. Value formation, therefore, builds itself out of a matrix of value orientations from many sources, as well as providing a medium for the transformation of instinctual derivatives. It is determined, in part, by all of these multiple influences, but not completely. It is a process of creative self-synthesis that builds a uniquely autonomous and personalized structure within the ego. It is thus the epitome of identification structuralization (Meissner 1981).

As is the case with most value formation, the internalization of values is less a matter of what is preached than of what is authentically lived and practiced. While religious values inhere in the life and practices of a religious community, the critical internalizations by which values are assimilated in the inner life of the growing child are more specifically embodied in the significant relationships that constitute the immediate fabric of the child's life.

We are talking here primarily about the child's family, and particularly about the most powerful, influential, and significant objects of the child's growing years, his parents. The quality of the child's internalized religious values is, in large measure, influenced by the manner in which the parents themselves realize and live out these same values. In a family context where religious values are expressed in repressive terms of prohibition or of threats, the balance will shift toward the predominance of superego components so that unresolved aggressive elements become distilled in the child's sense of value and permeate his ethical and moral outlook. Such repressive and prohibitive attitudes have all too frequently characterized parents' efforts to educate their children in the ways of morality and religion. In such contexts, the child is instilled with an abiding spirit of self-doubt which carries with it a burden of guilt and insecurity, and may often result in pathological forms of depression or obsessional ritualism. Thus, a harsh, rigid, and punitive superego may hold sway over the individual's inner life and correspondingly give rise to a value-system which is itself rigid, harsh, extreme, forcing the individual to the excess of either obsessional compliance or destructive rebellion.

However, where the course of development allows for a more normal and adaptive integration of the superego and the internalization of parental images on which it rests, the quality of the child's introjections comes to be considerably less ambivalent, less laden with the residues of aggressive conflicts, and open to the emergence of meaningful identifications. Such nonambivalent and constructive identifications do not entail either submission to or violent overthrow of the parental value system. Without these pathologically determinative forces at work, the child identifies readily with the more realistic, balanced, and tolerant dimensions of the parents' own inherent values; moreover, he finds room to assimilate parental values more spontaneously and creatively in a manner open to the possibility of selecting, reshaping, reformulating, and integrating a value system which is uniquely and personally his own.

There is an important principle of proportionality at work in all of this. Where the parental values reflect pathological dimensions and are determined by instinctual forces—whether libidinal, narcissistic or aggressive—the internalizations through which the child passes in his developmental program are forced into certain stereotypical molds more or less imposed on him by such pathological aspects of the parents' own values. For example, parents who approach the parenting interaction with unresolved narcissistic needs that mar their capacity for empathy and appropriate valuing of the child, create a pressure that powerfully influences the child's psychic development. The child is forced into a defensive position requiring certain narcissistic, libidinal, and aggressive adjustments.

Such influences cannot help but affect the quality and nature of the child's internalizations, giving them a more conflictual, defensive, and pathological cast. Such internalizations in turn help the child's emerging value-system along pathological lines. In these circumstances of developmental determination and pathological pressure, the creative capacity of the child to select and integrate a value-system more directly expressive of the constructive aspects of his own inherent nature is correspondingly limited.

By way of contrast, where the child is loved, respected, and cherished in nonambivalent ways, where his parents are able to value and support his individuality, while tolerating his increasing separateness and uniqueness, then the child will be able to shape a value-system inherently and characteristically his own. I do not mean, of course, that the child's value-system is going to be something that is totally unique and idiosyncratic. Rather, what is in question is the child's capacity to accept and integrate the values by which his parents live, the beliefs by which they guide their lives, and the symbols, traditions, and beliefs of their community as a possession inherently his own, rather than as an acquisition imposed on him as a result of coercive pressures, however subtle they may be.

In proportion as the child internalizes value systems because of constructive identifications rather than pathogenic and defensively based introjections, the role of the superego shifts from that of an aggressively, even pathologically punitive force in the psychic economy to that of a realistic and effectively integrated arbiter of ethical conduct. The functioning of the superego, then, is shifted from the infantile and heteronomous level in which parental prohibition, the motivating force of guilt, and the fear of punishment predominate, to the autonomous level, where principles, purposes, and values determine ethical choice and moral behavior.

To its historical, and often continuing, discredit, religious education has not always helped the child grow in to a more autonomous and adaptive internalization of religious values. Religious teaching has often been overburdened with an emphasis on sinfulness and guilt, leaving a constant impression on the child's mind of looming punishment. The assimilation of such attitudes, often reinforced by the more implicit and subtle forms of identification with such morally prohibiting and guilt-ridden objects—no matter how caring and loving these objects may otherwise be—gives rise in the child to an internalized burden of guilt, doubt, shame, and the fear of punishment that can in the long run, only undermine the child's own native impulse toward more authentic and realistic values. It was precisely against such infantile and pathogenic forms of religious value-orientation that Freud found it necessary to launch his attack. It is unfortunate that Freud was unable to see beyond this pathological expression of religion to envision the powerfully formative influence that religious convictions might offer for the shaping of more maturely functional and adaptive value-systems.

Religious Values and Identity

In a previous part of this discussion (pp. 000–000) I have emphasized the inherent value dimension of the psychoanalytic notion of identity, particularly as it is formulated by Erikson. Psychoanalysts have since developed further the connection between values, as inherent structural components of the psychic organization, and the sense of identity. Recent contributions have tended to emphasize their intrinsic connectedness and to recast the identity notion more specifically in value terms. For example, in his recent pioneering work on the psychology of the self in psychoanalysis, John Gedo (1979:xi) has moved the concept of value into a central position in his understanding of the self-organization. He writes:

> The central concept around which my tentative revision of psychoanalytic psychology is built is that of human personality as a hierarchy of personal aims. The infant's biological needs constitute the earliest of these goals; by the end of the second year of life, these have been supplemented by a variety of subjective wishes; the entire hierarchy, in both conscious and unconscious aspects, will form the person's primary identity, or, as I would prefer to call it, the "self-organization". The formation of the self-organi-

zation and its later transformations, especially through the acquisition of systems of values, should be viewed in epigenetic terms as the core of personality development.

The importance of the articulation and stability of value systems in the formation of personality and in the maintenance of an effective sense of personal identity was recognized by Jacobson (1964). The developmental period in which the emergence and shaping of value systems reached its crescendo was adolescence. Jacobson (1964:176) wrote:

> The adolescent is thus confronted with the complex and confusing task of toning down the idealized sexually prohibitive parental images, of reconciling them with realistic concepts of sexually active and increasingly permissive parents, and at the same time of building up new sets of moral and ethical standards based on a firm re-establishment of the incest taboo. We realize that this presupposes significant changes in the content and qualities of the ego ideal and superego—changes which are not merely the result of identification processes but which . . . eventually gain strong reinforcement from new structure formations in the maturing and increasingly autonomous ego.

The adolescent development is thus a process of gradually reworking and reshaping both ego and superego structures in the interest of achieving their greater autonomy and in setting in motion an increasing process of integration toward progressively more adaptive and realistic value systems. The evolution of adolescent values follows the inclination to idealize, even idolize, and consequently identify with new adult objects who may offer more adaptive solutions to adolescent conflicts than parents. The adolescent tendency to affiliate with a variety of social, athletic, cultural, political, or even religious groups provides a continuing source of new ideas and ideals which correspond to the adolescent's need for new criteria of behavior and new cultural and moral norms. The fresh current of identifications allows for a gradual reduction of the impact of earlier introjections and fosters the establishment of increasing ego and superego autonomy. This carries with it an increasing liberation not only from external constraining influences, parental, social, and cultural, but also from the outmoded defensive pressures derived from a relatively infantile superego.

In late adolescence, the balance shifts explicitly from the modification and management of superego pressures toward a greater emphasis on the shaping of moral values and value-systems. Jacobson (1964:185–86) writes in this regard:

However, in late adolescence there occurs a slow but unmistakable shift of power to the ego, whose gain of strength manifests itself in its increasing influence on id and superego, causing a partial reversal of the situation. The ego now plays as it were the role of an active mediator. It employs the adolescent's worldly strivings and his identifications with realistic images of his parents and other "grown-ups" as aids for the toning down and readjustment of the superego and its moral codes, but then conversely calls on the latter for assistance in restricting the id and in developing mature ego goals and adult achievement standards. The ego's contribution to the restructuring of ego ideal and superego, and to the concomitant curbing of the adolescent's excessive instinctual and narcissistic expectations, slowly bridges the gaps and contradictions between his moral and worldly trends. In increasingly close collaboration, superego and ego thus gradually build up new sets of values which provide him with realistic goals and with consistent moral and other directives for the future.

In the context of the increasing collaboration and integration between ego and superego functions, the ego ideal also undergoes a gradual modification. Originating in early narcissistic internalizations, it continues to play a significant role in later modifications of the more explicitly personalized ideals which are gradually developed out of the increasing autonomy of both ego and superego during and after adolescence. Increasingly, aspects of the ego ideal come to be the common possession of both the ego and the superego systems operating in integrated conjunction. As Jacobson (1964:187) observes:

> In fact, the final stages in the development of the ego ideal demonstrate beautifully the hierarchic reorganization and final integration of different—earlier and later—value concepts, arising from both systems, into a new coherent structural and functional unit. At the same time we must realize that this reconstruction of the ego ideal can proceed only in conjunction and close interrelationships with the remodeling of the entire superego system and of its directive, enforcing, and critical functions, and with a corresponding growth of the ego's capacity for critical and self-critical moral and intellectual judgment.

In his seminal treatment of identity, Erikson (1959:113) had stated:

> *Identity formation*, finally, begins where the usefulness of identification ends. It arises from the selective repudiation and mutual assimilation of childhood identifications, and their absorption in a new configuration, which in turn is dependent on the process by which a *society* (often through sub-societies) *identifies the young individual*, recognizing him as somebody who had to become the way he is, and who, being the way he is, is taken for granted.

It would perhaps be more precise to say that identity formation is founded on more selective, differentiated, constructive, realistic, relatively autonomous, and adaptive identifications. In other words, identity formation becomes possible when the more defensive, drive-impregnated, less realistic, and less adaptive forms of introjection have been replaced by meaningful identifications (Meissner 1971, 1972, 1981).

From a theoretical point of view, it is difficult to draw a line at which the identificatory process runs out and the process of identity formation takes over (Meissner 1972). However, it seems safe to say that the process of identity formation is continuous with the inherent dynamism of identification and expresses the creative, self-shaping, dimension that characterizes the identificatory process and which culminates in the consolidation of a mature sense of identity.

The successful formation of identity, however, also depends on the establishment of constructive and satisfying relationships with important groups within the individual's social environment. The influence of such group relations and identifications continues to play a significant role throughout the entire course of the life cycle. Such group involvements can be the source of significant identifications and may provide a meaningful frame of reference within which the individual articulates a set of ideals which determine the pattern of his living. By the same token, such group relationships and identifications serve to define the individual's social role, and correspondingly dictate certain expectations of behavior.

The internal integration of ego and superego functions together with the consequent articulation of realistic value systems does not always mesh smoothly with the extrinsic patterns of identification and relating. The roots of psychopathology can be found both in the inner framework of failures of structural development and in the external failures of social involvement and mutual acceptance. Jacobson (1964: 197) comments:

> In some of our patients, however, the group identifications and group relations may be in sharp conflict with each other, so that their reconciliation and integration may present extraordinary problems. Such persons usually manifest conspicuous identity conflicts. Their narcissistic attitudes and behavior, rapid emotional vacillation, inconsistency and changeability of their scales of value, and the dependency of their opinions on their current environment, or their opposition to the latter, frequently show at first glance that these persons suffer from protracted adolescent problems.

It is clear that religious belief systems form one of the most significant cultural influences in the shaping and sustaining of value-systems. Cultural groupings and social structures of various kinds offer to the emerging adolesent the resources of a context of belonging within which values can be assimilated and evolved. As Erikson (1964:125) observes, "Cultures, societies, religions offer the adolescent the nourishment of some truth in rites and rituals of confirmation as a member of a totem, a clan, or a faith, a nation or a class, which henceforth is to be his super-family."

An aspect of the impact religious belief systems have has been expressed by Erikson (1964:152–53) in his analysis of hope as one of the primary human strengths. He writes:

> Human strength, then, depends on a total process which regulates at the same time the *sequence of generations* and the *structure of society*. The ego is the regulator of this process in the individual.
>
> To use, once more, hope as an example: the emergence of this vital quality can be seen as defined by three co-ordinates: the relation of the mother's motherhood to her own past childhood; the mother-child relation itself; and the relation of both to institutions providing faith in procreation .... At the same time, however, the adults entrusted with the maintenance of an infant's hope need some societal confirmation and restoration of hope, whether it is offered by religious rituals or inspired and informed advice, or both. Once given, this reassurance is reflected in the gradual transformation of the small individual's generalized hopefulness into a faith related to the predominant assumptions concerning the order of the universe. And as he grows up, he will not only become ready to transmit such faith (in the form of hope) to his progeny, but he will also contribute to the preservation or change of those institutions which preserve a tradition of faith.
>
> What begins as hope in the individual infant is in its mature form faith, a sense of superior certainty not essentially dependent on evidence of reason, except where these forms of self-verification become part of a way of life binding technology, science, and new sources of identity into a coherent world-image. It is obvious that for the longest period of known history religion has monopolized the traditional formulation and the ritual restoration of faith. It has shrewdly played into man's most child-like needs .... This has led to the interpretation that religion exploits, for the sake of its own political establishment, the most infantile strivings in man. This it undoubtedly does. Yet at the height of its historical function it has played another, corresponding role, namely that of giving concerted expression to adult man's need to provide the young and the weak with a world-image sustaining hope.

We are in a position at this point, I think, to draw together the threads of our previous argument. The establishment of a mature sense of identity derives from core processes of internalization. Moreover, an essential dimension of such identifications, at the highest level of the hierarchical organization of the individual self, pertains particularly to the internalization of values which are subsequently selectively modified into value systems that form the core of the individual's identity. Given these two processes, we can conclude, I believe, that the forming and maintaining of religious values is an essential contributing force in the origin and sustaining of personal identity.

A recent contribution to our conceptualization of these matters was made by the philosopher of religion, Donald Evans (1979). The development of the concept of value as we have been proposing it in these pages is translated in Evans' terms into the notion of "attitude-virtues." Following a paradigm established by Erikson in terms of developmental crises, Evans pictures human growth in values as a constant struggle between such attitude-virtues and their conflicting attitude-vices. He describes them in the following terms (1979:14):

> The attitudes which we will consider have a *moral* significance as well as a religious relevance. They are moral virtues. A moral virtue is a pervasive, unifying stance which is an integral part of a person's fulfillment as a human being, and which influences his actions in each and every situation, especially his dealings with other human beings, where it helps to promote their fulfillment. A moral vice is a pervasive stance which frustrates human fulfillment in oneself and others. Both a virtue and a vice shape a person's conduct. The virtue gives it a distinctive life-affirming tone, whereas the vice gives it a characteristic life-denying tone.

Such "virtues" or "vices" should not be regarded merely as dispositions to certain patterns of external behavior, a view of morality that might think of it as a set of rules for regulating social behavior, reducing conflict, and fostering cooperation. Certainly, the values we are concerned with do influence external behavior, but they are also embedded in the individual personality's organization, style of behavior, and inner spirit of life-affirmation or denial. Since values in this sense exercise such an internally pervasive influence, their scope cannot be restricted to certain patterns of behavior which may most clearly express it; rather, they exercise an influence on all of the individual's behavior and actions. As Evans (1979:15) notes, "In general, it is not so much a way of behaving as a way of being in the world." Thus, while values and value-systems serve as the regulators and implicit directive components of much of human behavior, they are nonetheless concerned with the prior and more significant question of what kind of person the individual ought to be. Thus, an "ethic of being" takes precedence over an "ethic of doing" in this approach. In their broadest implication, therefore, such moral virtues not only contain an ethical concern, but also have a degree of religious relevance insofar as the religious value-system to which they relate concerns itself in precisely the same way not only with how man should behave in order to be morally good, but also with how he should be as a human person.

Thus, these values or virtues are related to and involve specifically religious attitudes, which are connected with and reflective of more general religious beliefs. In this sense, then, the schema of values rests on foundations that are established during the course of the individual's developmental history, and perhaps most pertinently and forcefully in the early stages of that experience, as I have suggested above. These provide the building blocks for the emergence of a sense of identity that is cast in terms of these value components. Evans (1979:161) states this connection in the following terms:

> The foundations are similar to what Christians have called "faith" (trust, humility, self-acceptance, self-commitment) and "works" (responsibility). Such foundations bring a firm sense of one's own identity. This is a prerequisite for risking oneself in the venture of friendliness and, more generally, for moving out of the various kinds of self-preoccupation into friendliness, concern, and contemplation. Responsibility is especially important in establishing a sense of one's own competent reliability. If responsibility is lacking, one may want or intend to live the life of love, but actually living it will not be possible.

The attainment of such values is at the same time the achievement of a capacity for significant interaction with other people. This process, following the basic paradigm provided in Erikson's account of epigenetic development, is linked with the developmental vicissitudes of emerging bodily needs and capacities. Thus, the process by which values develop and emerge in the human personality is natural, not in the sense of inevitable organic growth, but in the sense that values flow out of the natural developmental process by which the human personality moves toward increasing structuralization, stabilization, and sense of identity. Where the life- and self-affirming forces, both in the individual and in the others with whom he relates, are operating effectively, this process of natural growth in values takes place automatically. However, the sources of distortion of this natural growth process are multiple, complex and well-known to students of psychopathology.

A further question has to do with the integration of value-systems, both as core elements of a sense of identity, in Erikson's terms, and in their relation to religious experience. Evans' statement (1979:172) of this connection deserves to be quoted. He writes:

> Morality has to do not only with how we treat other people but also with what one ought to be as a person. To view a pervasive stance as a moral virtue is to consider it not only as it is expressed toward other people but also

as it constitutes a part of human fulfillment. A conception of human fulfillment depends on a value-laden view of human nature, a normative anthropology in which a certain way of life is morally commended. Insofar as the attitude-virtues are selected on the basis that they are the stances needed for human fulfillment, morality is prior to religion. That is, normative anthropology is prior to religious beliefs. I first ask what stances are constituents of human fulfillment and then find that they imply various religious beliefs. It is clear that if different stances had been selected as constituents of human fulfillment different cosmic convictions would have been implied.

One can add to this that most of the world's major religions embrace a core of values which carry within them this positive life-affirming force and consequently can serve both as the basis for the achievement of moral maturity and as powerful unifying and stabilizing forces in the attainment of personality growth and development. It must be acknowledged, however, that this benign and positively productive aspect of religious values and belief systems is not universal. Even in the great religions—the traditions of Judaism, Christianity, Buddhism and Islam, for example—pathological elements have been included that can exercise a destructive effect on human development. There are also myriad forms of cultic deviation in which irrational and pathological elements seem to exercise unrestrained sway. Such pathological elements can contribute to the undermining of values, to the development of what Evans (1979) has called "attitude-vices," and consequently must be regarded as malignant influences.

Erikson also points out that the religious influence is neither total nor exclusive in the cultural effort toward shaping and maintaining values, since other social structures and cultural forces also play significant roles. The point to emphasize here is that religious influences can and often do play a powerful role in shaping and maintaining individual identity by shaping and determining specific values. Participation in the common belief system of a religious community carries with it the implication of accepting and internalizing a value system vital to that religious tradition.

I have attempted elsewhere in this work to articulate a concept of spiritual identity. Spiritual identity parallels and originates from the notion of personal identity. Central to it is a value-system with particular moral components and religiously based spiritual traits. These traits represent significant internal achievements, as well as the integration of meaningful values nourished within the religious group. The achievement of such spiritual identity must be regarded, then, as the internalization of the most central and powerful values and ideals of that belief system.

It should be noted that in this context the values which are thus shaped, communicated, and internalized are specifically religious in that they derive from the tenets of the belief system and are sustained by the continuing faith of both the individual and the religious community. We need only emphasize that it is through a sharing in the belief and value systems of the religious group that important developmental achievements are realized, through which the individual can gain in the most mature and adaptive manner a stabilization, a consolidation, and even— in specifically religious or theological terms—an elevated sense of identity.

Values and Grace

We can elaborate the notion of spiritual identity by turning to a more traditional analysis, involving awareness and acceptance of spiritual values derived from a prior acceptance of a supernatural order of existence. The basic disposition to such an acceptance comes through faith (see pp. 151–207). There is in addition a maximal development of the basic strengths of temperance, fortitude, justice, and prudence. Thus, the full complement of the natural virtues is crowned by the theological virtues of faith, hope, and charity. In short, spiritual identity in the fullness of its development stands for the full flowering of Christian virtue and saintliness.

Spiritual identity is dependent on grace for its growth and achievement. Without grace, it is not possible. Spiritual identity is related to psychological qualities of a distinctly different order from the qualities associated with personal identity. This does not mean that there cannot be a tremendous area of overlap between these respective identities. It is difficult, if not impossible, to conceive of a man motivated by supernatural charity not being at the same time capable of trust and of intimate relations with his fellow men. But it remains true that without grace supernatural charity is not possible and although it presumes intimacy, it involves much more. Further, it is not enough merely to indicate that spiritual identity encompasses the Christian virtues. Our understanding of the Christian virtues must also be set down in psychological terms.

It is important to stress, from the psychological point of view, that the achievement of spiritual identity, to whatever degree this is realized in the individual person, is an achievement of the ego itself. Grace does not change us, but it gives us the power to change ourselves. If the development of the virtues is to have any meaning psychologically, it must be in terms of the synthetic activity of the ego. Their development implies growth and integration within the ego and, in consequence, in the organization of the self as well.

The achievement of spiritual identity implies a right ordering of behavior and internal impulses and the integration of psychic energies under the direction and control of the ego. This is akin to what theologians have referred to as "ordered concupiscence." The rebelliousness of man's lower nature through disordered concupiscence is one of the unfortunate consequences of original sin. But the effect of grace is to reestablish the control of our higher nature and bring about an internal integration. This is achieved psychologically through the establishment and maintenance of ego-control over the energies of the instinctive part of our psychic structure. Consequently, both spiritual identity and personal identity imply such ego-integration.

It should be evident, from the terms of this partial analysis, that there is a kind of reciprocal relationship between personal identity on the natural level and spiritual identity on the supernatural, when we are speaking of spiritual identity as a psychological reality. Obviously, the life of grace involves much more than a change in our psychological organization. But it is precisely this latter that we are concerned with here, and not the whole gamut of theologically relevant effects, which are the proper matter of a theology of grace. In psychological terms, then, spiritual identity builds upon personal identity, as grace builds upon nature. There are two consequences of this relationship. First, the degree of spiritual identity which a man can achieve is limited by, or related to, the degree of prior personal identity he has achieved. Second, spiritual identity is in some sense perfective of personal identity.

An explanation of these propositions makes their relationship more clear. If spiritual identity is dependent on the capacity of the ego to exercise its synthetic function autonomously, then the extent to which the ego has achieved a sense of identity is a measure of that capacity. Therefore, the more mature ego is more autonomous, more in control of the energies at its disposal, and so more capable of bringing about the self-modifications motivated through grace.

Spiritual identity is perfective of personal identity in the sense that the effect of the added energizing activity of grace is to enable the ego to function more perfectly, due to the greater energy resources at its disposal. Furthermore, the structures and functions associated with spiritual identity are identical with the structures and functions associated with personal identity, but raised to a higher level of activity. This underlines the point I have already made, that grace is operating in and through ego functions (see pp. 00–00). The increase of energy which the ego can channel into these functions underlies the capacity of the ego to form a spiritual identity.

In terms of our previous analysis, then, the core of this spiritual identity resides in a set of values and value-orientations that are specifically spiritual in significance and direction. The value-system which is thus internalized is religious in origin, intention, and direction. The ultimate action of grace, therefore, in psychological terms, can be spelled out specifically in relation to the formation, maintenance, consolidation, and deepening of this value schema within the psychic organization. This means the achievement of increasing degrees of ego and superego autonomy and integration, and the synthesis and elaboration of a progressively deepening and spiritually meaningful sense of identity.

CHAPTER 20

Alienation and the Crisis of Values

The Context of Alienation

The problem of alienation has exceedingly broad implications not only for modern psychiatry, but for society as a whole, particularly for the religious dimensions of modern life. The implications are especially relevant to individual religious conviction and belief, and even more to a vitality of institutional religious affiliation. It was the existentialists, beginning with Kierkegaard, who, in our own time, have called attention to the growing sense of alienation, which implies not merely a disturbance of significant relationships with other human beings, but a profound disturbance of man's relatedness with his environment and with the historical structures that undergird his experience of himself.

Psychiatric concern over the last several years has focused increasingly on the problems of loneliness, estrangement, and isolation. Psychoanalytic thinking has shifted its emphasis from forms of psychopathology rooted in the disturbance of instinctual life to forms that have more to do with the impairment of object relations. Considerably more attention is paid these days to character defects of a narcissistic, depressive, or schizoid variety. A significant portion of the patients seen these days show certain schizoid features—detachment, poor capacity for object relations, isolated and withdrawn affect, intellectualizing defenses, etc.

Central to the alienation syndrome is the rejection of, or the conflict over, social values. This syndrome, as we have already noted, lies at the interface between the individual and social processes, and raises a problem in differential diagnosis. It is usually described in terms of inner psychic dysfuntion, for example, some form of character pathology, or in terms of its narcissistic or depressive aspects.

But the associated estrangement reflects a more basic rejection of values which the society embodies and implicitly requires that an individual accept. Rejection of these values may leave one in a relatively valueless vacuum, or actively fostering divergent values in opposition to those prevailing in the surrounding culture. Or an inner conflict may arise between partially accepted values of the general culture and partially accepted contrary values.

The rebellious aspect of the alienation syndrome is characterized by the formulation or acceptance of a deviant set of values, often in conjunction with a group of like-minded individuals. This seems to be an important part of the formation of various religious cults or pseudocults that reflect varying degrees of psychopathology (Meissner 1984a). The term "deviant" in this context does not have the connotation of better or worse, but simply emphasizes that the values of the subgroup stand somehow in opposition to the general culture. Such value-oriented subgroupings are alienated from the larger social group, but may be quite unified within themselves. This allows the alienated individual to achieve a compensatory sense of belonging, which is, in fact, a significant part of the motivation behind adolescent gangs and the youth movement in general. The value deviance can be expressed in almost any aspect of behavior—clothing, hairstyles, sexual mores, language, expression of values, attitudes, beliefs, etc.

The important dimension of this value divergence is not so much the formation of new, meaningful values but the rejection, and, in the rebellious extreme, the overthrow of preexisting values. Alienated groups seize on any ideology or any formulation of divergent attitudes to express their rejection. Often in the service of frustrated and impotent rage, the objective seems to be to find the most extreme form of articulation of values and to flout prevailing social values. The most extreme forms of a belief system that strain the bounds of credibility may be embraced and often fly in the face of established fact with fanatic adherence. There is also a need to challenge and confront social institutions and practices on all levels.

Approaches to Alienation

As a result of the emergence and development of analytic ego psychology in recent decades, the relation between man's intrapsychic life and the familial, social, and cultural contexts in which he develops and functions has undergone a profound reconsideration. In this more extended understanding of man's psychic development and structure, it has become possible to rethink neo-Freudian contributions and to integrate them meaningfully with the main body of analytic understanding. Horney (1950) related the problem of alienation to the disparity between the idealized self and the real self. Because of his failure to measure up to the ideal, the neurotic hates himself—hates his own limitations and inadequacies. This self-hate expresses itself in relentless demands on oneself, repeated self-accusations, self-devaluation, forms of self-torment, and self-destructive behavior. In its extreme forms, such alienation can take the form of amnesias and states of loss of reality-sense and depersonalization. But more often, alienation can take the form of a feeling of numbness and remoteness. The individual tends to become impersonal in all his dealings. He loses a sense of responsibility for himself and for the direction of his life and activity. His continual feeling of disappointment with himself and with his interaction with his environment leads to a gradual disowning of his real self and a retreat into an ineffectual style of life. One of the serious questions that confront us is the extent to which this pattern of life experience is emerging as a cultural type. The line between psychopathology and cultural adaptation becomes thin and highly permeable. Alienation in its many guises and *formes frustres* may have permeated our society to such an extent that it can no longer be regarded as deviant or pathological in the usual sense.

Riesman (1950) made the argument in his *The Lonely Crowd* that the isolated, lonely, and alienated character type is endemic in our society and that the trends in that direction have been increasing with time. Camus' stranger is the contemporary alienated man who wanders through his world a stranger to those he seeks to know or pretends to love—he wanders in a continual state of homelessness and diffuseness, without any sense of conviction, as if he were a stranger in a foreign land, unable to communicate with his fellows and doomed to wander in quiet despair and lonely frustration (Camus 1946).

The problem of alienation, therefore, becomes a middle ground on which psychiatric concern for intrapsychic dynamics mingles with and to some extent overlaps with the concern of more social approaches to human behavior. Alienation is always *from* something that is around and outside the individual. One of the most valuable insights of modern social science has been the discovery that patterns of deviant behavior are not merely the product of disordered intrapsychic processes or impediments of development, although these play an unquestioned and critical role; but that the organization of social structures and social processes within which the individual functions has a determining influence on the patterns of adaptation.

Robert Merton cast this process in terms of the interplay of culturally defined goals and institutionalized norms. Cultural goals consist of the legitimate objectives held out to all the members of a society for which they can and should strive. But these are integrated in varying degrees according to a hierarchial system of values embedded in the culture and its institutions. The institutionalized norms operate to define, and regulate the acceptable or available modes of striving for these goals. These two cultural elements (goals and norms) vary independently of each other and may receive different degrees of emphasis in any given social structure. At some levels of social organization, the culturally defined goals may be considerably more available than in other segments—although the goals are held out to each segment of the society as equally valid and desirable. Thus, where culturally defined goals function without the institutionalized means for their attainment, they set up a situation of continual frustration and cultural estrangement.

In the analysis of adaptation of these cultural elements, Merton (1957) has provided a typology which describes the ways in which individuals can respond to them. These patterns may vary in different social contexts or in reference to different culturally determined goals. Individuals can *conform* by accepting both the cultural goals and the existing institutionalized means. This insures the stability and continuity of the social structure and its basic values. A second pattern of adaptation is *innovation,* in which the individual has assimilated the cultural emphasis on the goal, but has not equivalently internalized the institutional norms governing the means for its attainment. Individuals may thus make use of effective but institutionally prescribed means for attaining the desired goals. Merton uses the example of sharp business practices or organized crime as deviant means for attaining the culturally acceptable goals of financial success. In this modality the failure to accept or abide by institutionalized means offering the promise of financial success, combined with the relative unavailability of such means, create pressures which tend to reinforce deviant patterns of behavior.

The third pattern is *ritualism.* This pattern involves the scaling down of cultural objectives to meet the relative capacity one enjoys within the societal structure. This response is more characteristic of a middle-class orientation which emphasizes adherence to institutionalized norms much more than lower class attitudes do. Anxiety is avoided by retreating from competitive struggle for achievement and rigidly adhering to established social mores. The fourth pattern is that of *retreatism,* which involves the rejection of both cultural goals and institutionalized means.

These people are in the society but not of it. They are the social dropouts—the vagabonds, tramps, hippies, drunks, and drug addicts (Frederick 1972).

The last pattern of adapting to social pressures is *rebellion*. Rebellious individuals not only reject the existing social structure and its values, but actively seek to overthrow it and to replace it with an entirely new social structure in which cultural standards would be significantly modified and the emphasis placed on merit, effort, and reward. The rebellious individual is caught up in diffuse feelings of hate, envy, and rage. He has a continual sense of impotent hostility—an inner anger that cannot be adequately expressed or relieved. The rebel regards the norms and standards of contemporary society as arbitrary and meaningless.

These patterns of adaptation represent responses to anomie in the social structure. As originally proposed by Durkheim, the concept of anomie had more to do with a relative lack of social norms. The subjective aspect of this concept has since been extended to include a sense of purposelessness and isolation. Corresponding to this psychological dimension of anomie is a social dimension which refers to a breakdown in cultural organization. As Merton (1957:162–63) puts it,

> Anomie is then conceived as a breakdown in the cultural structure, occurring particularly when there is an acute disjunction between the cultural norms and goals and the socially structured capacities of members of the group to act in accord with them. In this conception, cultural values may help to produce behavior which is at odds with the mandates of the values themselves.
>
> On this view, the social structure strains the cultural values, making action in accord with them readily possible for those occupying certain statuses with the society and difficult or impossible for others. The social structure acts as a barrier or as an open door to the acting out of cultural mandates. When the cultural and social structure are malintegrated, the first calling for behavior and attitudes which the second precludes, there is a strain toward the breakdown of the norms, toward normlessness.

The questions of alienation and anomie are actually two faces of the same problem. Social anomie produces and is reflected in a psychological anomie on the individual level. This latter is what I have been describing as alienation.

The Alienation Syndrome

The interrelation between social anomie and psychological alienation is complex. The cultural disparity involved in anomie has its psychological counterpart in the disorganization and inner conflicts of values within the individual. The basic question is how intrapsychic and social processes influence each other in the complex business of value formation and value change. Merton has suggested that the organization of our contemporary culture, with its emphasis on material wealth and competitiveness, creates a certain strain toward anomie. The shift of cultural emphasis from the satisfactions involved in competitive effort to an almost exclusive concern with the outcome—in terms of measurable criteria of wealth and power—tends to create a stress on the regulatory structures and an attenuation of institutional controls. Cultural and personal values are undermined and calculations of personal advantage and risks of punishment become the main regulatory resource. This social strain toward anomie can be paralleled by a failure of internalization processes and a regression from internalized sources of inner regulation to a more primitive reliance on external rewards and punishments, on directives and prohibitions of external authorities. The social strain toward anomie is paralleled by an inner strain toward extremes of conformity or rebellion.

I would like to try to focus on a specific constellation of features reflected in the patterns of retreatism and rebellion described in Merton's analysis of anomie. The alienation syndrome has been described primarily within the adolescent and postadolescent group, but I think it has wider application than that. The elements of the syndrome include a basic sense of loneliness—the feeling that one somehow does not belong, is not a part of things, not in the mainstream of life and interests that surrounds one. There is a sense of estrangement and a chronic sense of frustration. The alienated person carries with him a continual sense of opposition between his own wishes and desires and the wishes and desires of those around him—with the additional feeling that his wishes, desires, and ambitions are actively being denied by others. He lives in a chronic state of disappointment—others are continually letting him down, disappointing his expectations, frustrating his designs, pressuring him to conform to their wishes and desires. His disappointment and chronic frustration produce an inner state of continual and unrelenting anger that serves to isolate him further and to put him in a condition of estrangement. Occasionally, the anger erupts in destructive outbursts that leave him even less satisfied and further disappointed.

An important element in the syndrome is the alienated person's sense of continuing frustration. He carries within him a chronic despair—a sense of hopelessness and helplessness which he sees as unremitting. When this sense of hopelessness dominates the picture, alienation tends to take the drop-out, give-up form of retreatism. The individual may resort to any number of pathological forms of behavior to alleviate his sense of inner frustration—including alcohol, drugs, or other forms of escape. Much of what we have seen over the years in the skid-row phenomenon and much of what we are seeing on the contemporary drug scene has this quality of frustrated retreatism. When the sense of frustrated rage dominates the picture, however, we are much more likely to see its manifestations in rebellious behavior of one kind or other. The sense of helplessness and the sense of smoldering rage can easily coexist in the same individual—so that the helpless victim may find himself striking out in impotent rage from time to time.

The loneliness that is characteristic of the alienation syndrome is a deep loneliness. It is not the same as the sort of acute and temporary loneliness that is produced by the loss of significant objects. Rather, it is a deep-seated loneliness that the individual carries with him as a part of his inner conviction about himself and the world. It is akin to the experience of existential dread that Kierkegaard placed at the center of the existential concern—it is the loneliness of self-assertion, self-determination, and the assumption of the ultimate responsibility for the exercise of freedom and choice. As we shall see, that inner dread has a more clinically relevant context, but patients will go to extremes in their efforts to escape from this inner anxiety. The list includes alcoholism, drug addiction, hypochondriasis, compulsive behaviors, masturbation, suicidal gestures, etc. Often such deviant forms of behavior are attempts to get significant others concerned and involved—but the failure of the significant other to respond in a manner that satisfies the individual's expectations leads to further frustration, rage, and disappointment.

One of the basic questions I wish to raise concerns the formation of divergent values. The capacity to reformulate and revitalize values is essential to the continuing flexibility, strength, and vitality of any social system. The formation of divergent or deviant values can have a constructive impact on the social system, or it can have a decidedly destructive impact. Thus, there is an inherent ambiguity about alienation. Is it an expression of psychopathology, or does it carry the potential for growth and the revitalization of social values? Are the elements of the alienation syndrome, as I have described them, a form of pathological failure to mature or the product of inner conflicts—or are they a necessary byproduct of a dialectic of deviance and revolt that the reformulation of social values requires? It is not so easy to disentagle these elements. They may be closely intertwined and one has to examine each individual case carefully in order to gain some approach to resolution. The extremes of rebellious alienation are rarely met. Rarely does one see the naked wish to overthrow and destroy—without an accompanying ideology and a wish to replace what is rejected with something better.

Adolescent Alienation

Alienation is a familiar part of the picture presented by adolescents in our culture. Adolescence is a developmental period of regressive disorganization followed, one hopes, by a progressive reorganization of the personality. This progression allows the child to pass through the physical and inner psychic changes that are required for him to approach his definitive role and position in adult society. But the adolescent is on the outside looking in. He will be able to integrate himself with the adult world only by forming himself to fit adult roles and by demonstrating to the adult community that he is ready and able to fulfill them. A sense of estrangement is embedded in the adolescent experience in our culture (Berman 1970).

Deutsch (1967) has pointed out the frequency of depressive affects in adolescents. For many, adolescence is a traumatic period where they are confronted by the demands of reality, performance standards, adult competition for positions, awards, etc., that is often intense, and by an increasing realization of their own limitations. A crucial aspect of the child's capacity to adapt is related to the issue of narcissism. Promising children often come to the adolescent challenge with narcissistic dreams of accomplishment and glory, dreams that may have been fostered and prolonged by their parents' own frustrated expectations,—most often those of the mother. Thus, infantile narcissism, with its dreams, expectations, and sense of entitlement, is often prolonged into adolescence, and the inevitable disappointment becomes traumatic.

To this basically narcissistic picture, alienated adolescents bring an added feature. Narcissistic investment from the mother tends to undermine the position of the father as a model for identification. The mother's disappointment is often intensified and magnified by the failure of the father to measure up to her standards. The father is thus devalued. The child who is caught up in this process must, therfore, devalue his father in order to share his mother's dream and to gain her approval. He, too, devalues and rejects his father, especially during adolescence. At a deeper level, this resentment against the father is often due to the fact that the father was too weak to protect him from an often ambivalent dependence on his mother, as well as from an incestuous involvement with her. The rejection extends to the entire world of adults and their standards and institutions.

Thus, the boy stands on the threshold of a world of adult standards and expectations, but it is his father's world. The devaluation of the father and the struggle against identification with him leads to a rejection of all social commitments, values, conventional roles, responsibilities, and many of the forms of emotional relatedness with others that form the normal fabric of society. A similar problem confronts the adolescent girl. If she idealizes her father excessively, she runs the risk of devaluing and despising her mother, with an intensification of her penis envy and an impairment of a meaningful and constructive identification with her mother. She thus tends to reject and rebel against any conventional forms of feminine role or status and strives for more masculine competitiveness and accomplishments. The rebellious expression of these aspects is discernible in some of the more extreme elements of the feminist movement.

It is useful to realize that in large measure the process of alienation may serve some important developmental functions. One of the questions that the apparent increase in manifest alienation raises is the extent to which social and cultural conditions require that the forms of alienation take the patterns of expression that they do. Alienation is a feature of all adolescent development, but the reorganization of inner structures, defenses, values, and patterns of identification can be compressed into maladaptive and even pathological molds. This developmental perspective is expressed by Berman (1970:250) in the following terms:

> The process of identification facilitates adaptation during childhood. Its characteristics will determine how the adolescent will cope with change. When adolescence is reached, childhood identifications must undergo radical revision because of the strength of the sexual drive and the need to master it. Alienation is a mental process serving to achieve this necessary physical and psychic distance from parents and society. It is a defense against painful ideas and affects associated with the disruption of cathexis to the past relationships. The process also supports the establishment of genital primacy, new object relation, and a firm sense of self.

In the normal course of things, such adaptive alienation is not extreme and is resolved into functional adult patterns of identification. The extremes of alienation, however, distort the growth process and make adaptive resolutions more precarious.

Deutsch (1967) has noted that many of these alienated adolescents come from upper-middle-class families. The idealized world of academic or professional success is often held up to children in such families, but as reflected in the parent's dream. The alienated adolescent protests specifically against that world. To realize the dream, to achieve success, to join the establishment, is to become like his parents, embracing and endorsing what he feels he must reject and devalue. The alienated adolescent thus becomes a paradox of our society: often

brilliant, talented, sensitive, perceptive, and imaginative, but also emo-
tionally empty, isolated, lonely, estranged.

Such feelings can be seen in their more flamboyant forms in many
public expressions, but they are also the common coin of many apparently well-adjusted and well-functioning adolescents. Feelings of loneliness and isolation are endemic among them. The more narcissistic
adolescent may seek others out in order to gain their admiration; the
alienated adolescent prefers to isolate himself and often rejects attempts
to interfere with his isolation. Many adolescents seek relief from these
feelings in group activities, motivated by a need for group acceptance
and approval—so-called "peer-group pressures." Pot-smoking has this
quality almost universally; it is a minor form of escape, but it also has the
connotations of sharing a group experience and gaining transient relief
from the intolerable feelings of loneliness. It also symbolizes a shared
antiestablishment, anticultural position—a rejection of what the adult
world holds up as a standard of acceptability. This was all displayed in
striking ways in the "hippie" movement (Williams 1970), as it is more
recently in "punk" styles of clothes and hairdo.

Again I would like to emphasize the rejection of values in this form
of adolescent alienation. There is a strong need to seek out and embrace
the direct antithesis of what the parents value and stand for. Such adolescents reject success, accomplishment, and achievement as well as adult
standards of behavior, dress, appearance, and even language. The use of
obscenities in the common discourse of adolescents in increasingly
familiar. They complain about the "unreasonable" attitudes of adults.
They resent any infringement of their freedom, any restriction or control. They feel a need to emphasize their sense of estrangement. It is important for maintaining their own sense of separateness and selfhood for
them to exaggerate their differences from their parents. The adolescent
seeks to immerse himself in a subculture or counterculture. The need for
difference may express underlying psychopathology. Giovacchini
(1968:654) has noted:

> The degree of difference required may, however, be proportional to the
> severity of psychopathology. It is conceivable that better structured egos
> can feel their individuality without having to be flamboyantly different or
> adopting standards that are the antithesis of all contemporary cultural
> standards.

The failure to achieve a meaningful and effective value-system and subculture that are different from those of their parents leaves these adolescents with feelings of depression and misery, low self-esteem, and an im-
poverished sense of their own identity.

Alienation and Dissent

The problem and the paradox of alienation are acutely focused in the use of social protest and frankly revolutionary violence. Revolution and the use of violence in the service of revolution are obviously nothing new—but they have taken on new social implications in our own time. The threat of violence has become a familiar refrain from all sorts of disaffected and dissatisfied subcultural groups. We hear it currently with vehement insistence from terrorist groups.

The first important consideration is that we live in a culture that sanctions violence as a means of conflict resolution. We approve of some forms of violence and disapprove of others. Our best heroes are those who are the toughest and capable of the greatest violence. Of course, we rationalize the violence of our heroes—they are violent only in the service of justice and the protection of the weak and innocent. As a nation, we use a similar rationale for our participation in the violence and destruction of war. The violence of the enemy is evil and without justice—while our own violence is found to be just and good. The psychology of legitimate violence requires our being able to attribute evil intentions and motives to the enemy. Because they are violent, we are forced to be violent also—and because their violence is evil, our violence must be good. The inevitable conclusion is that if I can find a justification, if I can convince myself that what I oppose is unjust or evil, I am thereby justified in using violence to destroy it. This is precisely the rhetoric and rationale of terrorists and "freedom fighters."

We must be clear about the role of protest and dissent in social processes. The process of dissent, protest, challenge, and innovation is an essential part of human progress at all levels. It is also an essential ingredient of individual human psychological development. It is inherent in many forms of intellectual and scientific progress, and is a necessary channel by which social structures correct intrinsic defects and adapt to changing conditions of life. The principle of dissent is essential to the democratic political process. The democratic principle is not only based on the right of the minority to have a point of view different from that of the majority; it also includes both the political necessity that the minority be free to persuade the majority to accept its point of view. There are two important elements necessary to preserve this basic aspect of the democratic process: there must be willingness and courage on the part of those who dissent to express their view and to persuade others to accept it, and the majority must safeguard the means by which effective dissent can be expressed. Both the minority and the majority have an interest in the expression and effective channeling of dissent.

Behind such currents of discontent and dissatisfaction there often lies a strong ideologically colored commitment to a form of utopian idealism. Erikson (1964) has taught us that ideological commitment is a necessary ingredient in the growth of youth to maturity. But ideology can be put at the service of inner growth and the confirmation of cultural integration, or at the service of infantile needs and the dynamisms of alienation (Meissner 1978). Social idealism has served as guiding inspiration for human social and political aspirations for centuries. But utopian ideals can represent the prolongation of infantile narcissism and wishes to have unconditional love, protection, care, and freedom from those powerful sources which represent the omnipotent parents. It may also represent the opposite and equally unrealizable wish to obtain such omnipotence for oneself.

For many of today's more fanatical revolutionaries, the utopian wish must be responded to and fulfilled immediately—without delay, planning, consideration, reflection, or questioning. They have no patience for the slow process of cultural change, they cannot wait for the plodding deliberation and interaction of positions and interests that constitute the political process, they demonstrate little capacity for toleration of delay and postponement of gratification of their wishes.

The frustration and denial of such pressing inner demands and the deeper narcissistic expectations that so often lie beneath them, lead to a sense of inner disappointment and rage and its sometimes violent expression. There is increasing evidence to suggest that much of the violent confrontation that seems so frequent these days is produced by a relatively small group of alienated individuals who are acting out their infantile needs and wishes in immature ways—lashing out with destructive rage without any constructive plan or purpose. There is no doubt that deeply unconscious, irrational, and infantile wishes are frequently rationalized under the guise of social idealism, and that the frustration of such wishes lies at the heart of the pressure for violent social reorganization. But the analysis of inner psychodynamics does not explain away or substitute for social change.

Thus, the problem of alienation can be viewed from more than one perspective. Is it a problem of the alienation of the young and the underprivileged from society? This is the perspective that a psychiatric point of view would emphasize. Or is it a problem of the alienation of society from some of its important subgroupings? This is the perspective that includes ultraindividual and societal concerns. Unfortunately, the inner and the outer perspectives tend to reinforce each other, as culture and personality interact and are mutually influential. Social alienation creates the conditions for and provokes psychological alienation—and psychological alienation brings life and inner conviction to the conditions of social malaise. Our efforts to treat or resolve the one cannot be divorced realistically from our efforts to deal effectively with the other.

The alienation syndrome presents modern psychiatric thinking with a different form of psychopathology. It brings the interface between the individual and his culture into the center of the picture. It impresses on us the importance of the cultural integration of the individual for his psychic development—and vice versa. Alienation does not merely imply a disparity between individual values and social values—a form of social estrangement—but it also implies an internal estrangement from one's self. It refers to the manner in which the individual ego experiences its own self—and by extension, the social reality in which he lives (Bychowski 1967).

I have proposed in this consideration that the basic alienation is the alienation from parental objects. The patterns of alienation in more adult and social contexts reflect this basic developmental alienation. The basic ambivalence of these early object relationships leads to the internalization of alienated aspects of the parental objects. These internalized objects form the nucleus of the child's developing personality—and in the ambivalent context of parental withdrawal from the child, the internal object takes on qualities of an undesirable and unlovable self. Such an alienated self is an outcast, from parental intimacy in the first instance and from social belonging in the second instance. The internalized object thus colors the individual's entire perception of his world and the important relationships in it. We must ask ourselves in what manner the structure and organization of social processes respond to this inner alienation to validate the alienated person's projection of dissatisfaction and feelings of injustice and deprivation.

Religious Alienation

Alienation can take place in specifically religious terms as well. Alienation in religious terms expresses itself particularly in the form of conflict over religious values, or, in its more rebellious expression, in the formulation or acceptance of a divergent set of religious beliefs and values. The phenomenon of the grouping of like-minded individuals to embrace a set of deviant beliefs and values is familiar in the process of cult formation. The organization of such cults and the unification of individuals within them allow for the compensatory sense of belonging that is so essential in providing the matrix for the deviant individual to find a functional sense of identity and communal context. The formation of a system of beliefs and values unique to the deviant cult also provides a vehicle for expressing the rejection of more traditional values and feelings of frustration and impotent rage.

The typology provided by Merton (1957) for describing the varieties of adaptation to culturally determined goals has its application in the discussion of religious alienation as well. The acceptance of religious value-systems and of the existing institutionalized means for implementing and expressing such values is a form of *conformity*. Conforming individuals, consequently, are those who continue the values and beliefs of the religious tradition, tend to accept these values as an integral part of their own religious lives and orientations, and find in them a sufficient basis for forming and maintaining their inherent sense of identity. Such individuals are not conflicted about religious values and are thus able to shape their own identities in a manner congruent with the preexisting expectations and value-orientation of the religious community.

It is worth commenting in this regard that conformity can also serve as a vehicle for pathological adaptation and can thus reflect an imbalance in the individual's value-orientation and in the structuring of his value-system. Intrinsic to the notion of value-formation, as described above (pp. 257–265), is the dynamic process through which values are internalized in a manner which is selective and adaptive, and which calls into play the synthetic and creative capacities of the individual personality. Value-formation in its optimal sense, then, is never merely a matter of internalizing an external set of values. Where such a process occurs, the internalization takes place through a form of introjection that reflects underlying conflictual and defensive needs and leaves a residue of pathology in the value-system. The internalization of values ideally takes place through identifications by which the creative force of the personality finds room for expression. The conforming individual runs the risk of defensively retreating from this degree of individuality and opting for the security of clinging to preestablished and accepted values. The exercise of values and the commitments they imply require a degree of freedom that to such personalities is threatening, often terrifying. They choose a philosophy of better safe than sorry, a strategy of minimum risk. The price is the impoverishment of themselves as human beings, a loss of freedom, and the acceptance of a constraint on their own personal self-fulfillment. Their integration of religious values becomes life-denying rather than life-affirming.

The second mode of adaptation is that of *innovation*. In the religious context, innovators are those individuals who have assimilated the value-system, but have not successfully internalized the institutional norms and means for its realization. They may thereby use deviant approaches for attaining stated ideals or implementing certain values which are relatively unacceptable to the religious group, though nonetheless effective. The founders of religious orders fit this description, as do church leaders who initiate new forms of ministry or new institutional means for carrying out apostolic and charitable works. Such innovations may also find expression in a variety of splinter movements which deviate from the primary religious body in discipline, practice, liturgy—matters which do not immediately pertain to questions of belief and value. Such groups may in some sense be schismatic, but tend not to be heretical. Groups that insist on earlier forms of worship—so-called traditionalists—or groups that introduce new patterns of religious practice, like some of the charismatic groups, may fall under this grouping.

Ritualism expresses itself in toning down the demands of ideals and values, particularly moral values, in the interest of expediency or of making as few waves as possible. Merton has emphasized the middle-class character of this mode of adaptation. The value-system is maintained more or less as an abstract system of norms and directives, but is disengaged from practical concerns and is thus prevented from exercising any meaningful effect in the life of the believer. This orientation toward the religious value-system is in all probability characteristic of the vast majority of churchgoers. For such individuals there is no contradiction in espousing the values of universal brotherhood and equality while at the same time exercising outright prejudice; or of embracing the values of honesty and integrity in all one's dealings, while at the same time engaging in dishonest business practices.

Retreatism also has its form of expression in the religious sphere. Such individuals ultimately reject both the religious value-system itself and any of the institutionalized means to its achievement or expression. They withdraw their allegiance from the religious value-system, while at the same time abandoning any participation in the ongoing life of the religious community. They withdraw from any participation in the life of the religious group, or any share in its sacramental or liturgical life, and usually from any share in its more human and social life as well.

The last of Merton's modes of cultural adaptation is that of *rebellion*. Religious rebellion is perhaps the most significant and important expression of religious alienation. Such individuals not only reject the religious value-system and the belief system corresponding to it, but they actively seek to reject, overthrow, and replace the preexisting religious value-system with an entirely new social structure, a new set of religious beliefs and orientations, and consequently, a new and different system of religious values.

The primary expression of religious rebellion, as we have seen, is in the formation of cults and sects, both of which may be regarded as deviant religious expressions existing in a relatively intense degree of tension with the surrounding sociocultural environment. The sect is a form of schismatic movement that has separated itself from the previously existing institution. The cult, in contrast, does not enjoy this tie with the previously existing religious body, but often is imported from an alien religious context, or may arise through independent innovation than schism. In this sense, the cult represents something innovative in relationship to the previously existing religious movements in any given cultural context. The cult thus generally bases itself on a claim to some new revelation or religious insight which justifies its existence and reinforces its claim to be religiously and often culturally unique.

In a basic sense, the cult phenomenon expresses a general tendency in human religious experience and in the formation of religious groups. In psychological terms, the cult phenomenon can be found in all forms of organized religious experience in the tendency to form subdivisions or factions organized around divergent or deviant elements of belief that may be at variance with or even in opposition to the belief system of the religious group. Internal tensions in the religious group do not always arise strictly on the basis of the system of beliefs or values. Such variation may concern matters of ritual or liturgy, deviations in various forms of religious practice, and even other matters of churchly discipline. The deviant grouping, however, will usually not be regarded as a cult or sect unless significant aspects of the belief system or value-system are brought into question.

In terms of the problem of religious alienation and the related conflicts of values, a problem arises in psychological terms regarding the extent to which such deviant religious subgroupings may become channels for the expression of psychopathology. The question itself is controversial, but I think it is possible to reach some degree of consensus regarding the role of psychopathology in religious cults. In the analysis of religious subgroupings, the phenomenon of the "mote-beam" projection is familiar enough. Religious adherents are not slow to seek out the mote in their neighbor's eye, while they remain blind to the beam in their own. Realizing the generality of aspects of the cult phenomenon helps to avoid such "mote-beam" distortions.

Pruyser (1977) has recently discussed a number of aspects of cultic belief that reflect varying degrees of psychopathology. One such neurotic feature of religious movements is the sacrifice of intellect. In many cultic contexts there is a demand for blind and unquestioning faith, often in seemingly undeserving objects that strain the bounds of credibility. Unquestioning adherence is given to cult leaders who hardly give any evidence of meriting it by their own personal gifts or characteristics, and who must consequently be invested with an idealized aura in order for the believer to maintain the integrity of his belief system. Even within the charismatic movement, large numbers of Christians profess to witness expressions of the activity of the Holy Spirit in acts of meaningless babbling or fits, as if to deny that the spirit of love possessed any intelligence or reason. Tendencies toward archaism or fundamentalism even in the more established churches express an inclination to pose a dichotomy between faith and reason.

In addition to the sacrifice of intellect, in more pathological forms of religious belief there is often a subtle form of thought control which expresses and masks an underlying authoritarianism which leads to the surrender of freedom. There is regressive surrender of ego controls and responsibility that expresses itself in various forms of impulsive emotionality and a projective tendency to attribute such impulses to the influence of the good spirit on one side, or of the evil on the other.

We can readily recognize in these attitudes the characteristics of the authoritarian personality (Adorno et al. 1950). The study of this type began in the attempt to understand anti-Semitic attitudes, but it was soon extended to a description of a style of personality that expresses itself in multiple forms of prejudice, ethnocentricity, and conflicts over power, dependence and aggression. The sacrifice of intellect, the surrender of freedom, the retreat from responsibility by submission to the power and influence of the cult leader, the frequent repression of aggressive impulses and their projectionn onto a hostile environment outside of the cult, are all characteristics consistent with the authoritarian personality. I would suggest that similar basic conflicts may operate in many members of religious cults.

One aspect of cult involvement that is of particular interest is fanaticism which involves both commitment—that is, the intensity of emotional attachment to the group or to the leader—and the modification of the belief system characteristic of the cult group. There are normal degrees of each of these elements, but if one or the other becomes disproportionate, it is then a question of fanaticism. The degree of fanaticism demanded of its members can vary within any religious group or movement, and to a significant degree its level tends to be proportional to the extent to which the cult phenomenon is operative in that group.

Of particular interest to psychoanalysts is the degree to which pathological narcissism has a role in the formation of cults. It is characteristic of religious cults that they set themselves apart as somehow elite or exclusive, in opposition to outsiders, who are often regarded as hostile and judged harshly. This claim for special status and elitism appeals particularly to individuals suffering from feelings of shame and inferiority, which reflect underlying narcissistic personality defects. The organizing and sustaining of this elite status calls into play paranoid mechanisms by which undesirable or feared qualities are projected out-side of the group, and, correspondingly, qualities of self-enhancement and idealized aggrandisement are attributed to the group. Participation in the cult thereby often provides a special form of relief for inner feelings of inadequacy, powerlessness, emptiness, meaninglessness, or anomie. With regard to such idealization, Kohut (1976:389) has com-mented:

> ... The idealization of a group model protects the individual member of the group against certain states of narcissistic disequilibrium which are ex-perienced as envy, jealousy, and rage. If these narcissistic tensions remain undischarged, they are exquisitely painful; if, however, they are dis-charged (through actions especially motivated by narcissistic rage), then they are socially dangerous .... If the imago of the leader ... has been securely included in the member's idealized superego and has thus become a part of the self, then he can disregard contemporary com-petitors, they are not a threat to his own narcissistic security, and he can avoid suffering the painful narcissistic injuries which the comparison with the actual rivals for the goals of his narcissistic strivings might inflict on him.

One of the major characteristics of the cult phenomenon is that it presents to the potential convert a charismatic leader with whom the believer can identify and idealize. The experience of attachment to the leader undoubtedly has both libidinal and hysterical components, but these also reflect important narcissistic dynamics as well. The leader's presentation of himself to the believer as an object for idealization ob-viously responds to profound inner needs in the believer. In terms of the dynamics of religious alienation, we can suggest that these narcissistic needs may be replacing the role of the more traditional value-system in absorbing narcissistic cathexis and maintaining narcissistic equilibrium.

To a certain extent, this consideration takes us onto familiar ground. In Freud's (1921) work on the psychology of groups, he placed the em-phasis on the nature of the relationship to the leader as a central compo-nent of the process of group formation. In Freud's analysis, the iden-tification with the leader based itself on a modification of aim-inhibited sexual love. This attachment led to a form of idealization of the leader-object, a state of mind that Freud compared to being in love. Consequen-tly, the idealized object was introjected and came to take the place of the individual's ego ideal. As he put it, "A number of individuals ... have substituted one and the same object for their ego-ideal, and consequen-tly have identified themselves with one another in their ego" (p. 116). In the more pathological forms of cult organization, the cult leader often tends to exploit this narcissistic attachment—not infrequently for his own personal aggrandizement or enrichment. The dynamics of this process have also been described in terms of the narcissistic transferences (Kohut 1971), so that the variants of these transference forms can be recognized easily in the context of group processes. It would perhaps not be entirely accurate to conclude that all members of such cults were suffering from severe narcissistic defects, but to the extent that such transparently narcissistic vicissitudes enter into and characterize cult formation and organization, we can conclude that narcissistic issues are central to the pathology of such deviant cultic expressions.

There seems to be a certain amount of evidence to suggest that the degree of psychopathology and emotional distress is higher in cult converts. They manifest higher scores on measures of neurotic distress than normal controls, and also have higher incidences of psychiatric difficulties as manifested in a higher percentage of hospitalizations for emotional problems or of seeking out psychiatric assistance (Galanter et al. 1979). Members of the Unification Church ("Moonies") have been found to show higher degrees of preconversion than of postconversion distress. The greatest improvement seems to be observed by those who experienced the greatest commitment to the movement. Similar findings have been documented in members of Eastern religious cults (Galanter and Buckley 1978). Other studies of these groups have compared the strong proselytizing activity and pressures for commitment within such groups to brainwashing (Ungerleider and Wellisch 1979).

We can conclude, therefore, that the group ethos and the commitment by conversion offer the new member the opportunity for an integration of his life experience that can provide a new sense of belonging and meaningfulness, that alters the participant's sense of self. Such cult participants show a relatively "strong ideological hunger" (Lifton 1956) which cult membership satisfies, at the same time as it provides significant relief from the individual's inner turmoil and conflict. Cult adherents generally find greater emotional relief and stability in cult membership than those who drop out, and they are more readily able to identify with the cult leader, thus minimizing any sense of submission that acceptance of the leader and cult membership might otherwise imply (Ungerleider and Wellisch 1979). Since participation in the cult and acceptance of active cult membership carry with them by implication the acceptance of the inherent value-system of the cult, and since the newly integrated values become a source of new internal integration in terms of which the individual's sense of self is in some degree consolidated and stabilized, cult adherence carries with it the potential for resolving often severe and paralyzing inner conflicts and turmoil, particularly those that pertain to or derive from an unresolved conflict in values and value orientations.

Thus, one of the main impulses toward conversion and adherence to the cult ideology is specifically the consolidation and reinforcement of this sense of identity. In this sense, the religious belief system—insofar as it involves significant projective elements and an elaboration of them in the form of a paranoid construction (Meissner 1978)—offers the psychological context for the maintenance of the individual believer's internal introjective organization around which he shapes a sense of self. Consequently, adherence to such a religious belief system, however deviant, is important for sustaining inner cohesiveness and identity, and these needs may have greater intrinsic motivational power than any libidinal or narcissistic components.

Religious adherence in general and particularly the often fanatic and pathological adherence of cult members offers another vantage point for our understanding of these powerful forces of the human personality. Something similar can be said about the phenomenon of psychotic conviction and adherence to delusional beliefs. The most powerful and convincing aspect, at least subjectively, for such patients may well be that the delusional system is in important ways required for maintaining a sense of inner self-coherence and some semblance of self-organization.

Such a need is not necessarily to be regarded as pathological, as Freud might have seen it. In fact, the search for meaning, purpose, acceptance, and a sense of belonging is a basic quest that no human being can avoid. Consequently, to the extent that religious systems respond to such basic human needs, they may be providing one of the most important functions in the sustaining of human life. While the emphasis in this discussion of religious alienation falls on its more pathological dimensions, it should be remembered that these same processes and mechanisms—which I have described elsewhere in terms of the mechanisms of the paranoid process (Meissner 1978)—have an inherent potential for human growth and strength; they often provide in highly meaningful ways the vehicle for positive and constructive adaptation and for the maintenance of a more positive and constructive sense of identity.

Recapitulation

The contexts and manifestations of alienation are many. One can find aspects of the alienation syndrome in many forms of psychopathology and in many social classes. From a purely psychiatric viewpoint, one can focus on the pathological aspects. Were we to concentrate on this aspect alone, I think we would be ignoring the crucial aspect of the condition we are dealing with.

Each of these contexts of alienation manifests either a direct conflict in values or a situation in which the institutionalized means for attaining cultural values are limited or denied. The distinguishing element in the alienation syndrome is the impaired capacity for the integration of personal and cultural values. However, the attempt to resolve such conflicts—and thereby to resolve the inner psychic distress attendant upon them—can take either an autoplastic or an alloplastic course. The individual may seek conformity with and resignation to the external situation. If one adopted a traditional psychiatric perspective, one would focus on the inner conflict and address one's therapeutic efforts toward the dynamics of depression and/or narcissism. But it may also be quite reasonable and realistic to adopt an alloplastic alternative. There may, in fact, be something wrong with the world of adult values that the adolescent is being asked to embrace, over and above the pathological aspect involving the devaluation and rejection of his father. There may be something that can and should be done about economic inequities and circumstances of poverty. There may be a situation of injustice and violation of human rights in racial prejudice. There may be a real need for change in the church's attitudes and modes of functioning vis-à-vis the world. If that is so, the psychiatric resolution that does not take the possibility and even the necessity of social change into account is inadequate.

The next obvious point to be made is that perhaps the alienation and conflict of values that we have been discussing carry within them a potential for constructive change. What can be viewed from one perspective as pathological may from another perspective serve as a necessary prelude to meaningful social reorganization and structural change, particularly in the formation and implementation of values. Are we being confronted with the paradoxical problem that what presents itself from one perspective as identifiable psychopathology is from another perspective a necessary process in social progress?

The New Romanticism

My interest in discussing the alienation syndrome has been not only to try to make clear the nature of the processes involved, but also to try to discern the constructive and restitutive potential that it may contain. This concern has relevance not only for our understanding of and reaction to the activities of alienated social groups, but for our understanding of how to deal with such patients in a therapeutic and religious context.

In reconstructing this material, I have become increasingly impressed with the similarities in spirit and the nature of the basic problem between contemporary alienation and the romantic movement. Alienation has become in a sense the new romanticism. The romantic movement was rooted in a deep disillusionment and sense of estrangement. It had in it as well the seeds of discontent and frustrated rage that boiled over into a revolution that shook the continent of Europe. The disillusionment of Goethe developed into the despair of Chateaubriand. The sentimentalism and melancholy of preromanticism reflected the spirit of the prerevolutionary bourgeoisie, even as the pessimism and apathy of the emigré literature reflected the life of the postrevolutionary aristocracy. The romantic mood after the fall of Napoleon became the common possession of all Europe, particularly the upper and educated classes.

The common complaint was that the conventional society could not respond to or meet the individual's spiritual needs. Life became meaningless; there was a yearning for fulfillment that would never be attained; desire was useless; all striving and struggle were pointless. The romantic atmosphere was full of disenchantment, disappointed hopes, frustrated desires. As Hauser (1970) has put it:

> Nothing is worth being desired, all striving and fighting are useless; the only sensible action is suicide. And the absolute separation of the internal and external world, of the poetry and prose of life, the solitude, the contempt for the world and the misanthropy, the unreal, abstract, desperately egoistic existence, which the romantic natures of the new century lead, is already suicide. (Vol. 3:189)

This sense of estrangement was compounded by a contempt for social norms that was expressed in the antagonism to philistinism, the contempt for the rigid and unimaginatively soulless life of the bourgeoisie, and the struggle against everything mature, serene, secure, traditional, or conventional. The shift in values embraced the basic principle that what was youthful and new was intrinsically better than what was older and traditional. The idea was particularly opposed to classicism, but was also alien to most previous cultural attitudes. It was only in the establishment of the romantic movement that the young became the natural representatives of creativity and progress. And with this basic principle came the accompanying emphasis on spontaneity and freedom from artistic restraints as the criteria of creativity and originality.

Of all the romantic heroes, it is perhaps Byron who best typifies the qualities of romantic alienation. The Byronic romantic ideal is the proud and lonely hero marked by destiny. He is an eternally homeless wanderer, marked with an unsociable nature and afflicted by the incompatible claims of individual morality and the conventions of society. Before Byron, the romantic estrangement had been tinged with guilt and placed in an uncertain relation to the social order. In Byron's hands, however, the estrangement was transformed into an open and unhesitating mutiny. It became a self-righteous and self-pitying indictment of man. Isolation developed into a cult of solitude, and the loss of faith in the old ideals was transformed into anarchic individualism. His heroes enjoy the torment of abandonment and self-destructive despair. The sense of abandonment rings through these opening lines of *Prometheus:*

> Titan! to whose immortal eyes
> The sufferings of mortality,
> Seen in their sad reality,
> Were not as things that gods despise;
> What was thy pity's recompense?
> A silent suffering, and intense;
> The rock, the vulture, and the chain,
> All that the proud can feel of pain,
> The agony they do not show,
> The suffocating sense of woe,
> Which speaks but in its loneliness,
> And then is jealous lest the sky
> Should have a listener, nor will sigh
> Until its voice is echoless.

It is in *Manfred* perhaps more clearly than anywhere else that Byron expresses the profound alienation that marked the romantic spirit. The hero cries out:

> My pangs shall find a voice. From ,my youth upwards
> My spirit walked not with the souls of men,
> Nor looked upon the earth with human eyes;
> The thirst of their ambition was not mine,
> The aim of their existence was not mine;
> My joys, my griefs, my passions, and my powers,
> Made me a stranger:

The sense of guilt, despair, and self-condemnation is part of this profound estrangement. Manfred in proud contempt tells the old abbot:

> Old man! There is no power in holy men,
> Nor charm in prayer, nor purifying form
> Of Penitence, nor outward look, nor fast,
> Nor agony—nor, greater than all these,
> The innate tortures of that deep despair,
> Which is remorse without the fear of hell,
> But all in all sufficient to itself

Would make a hell of heaven—can exorcise
From out the unbounded spirit the quick sense
Of its own sins, wrongs, sufferance, and revenge
Upon itself; there is not future pang
Can deal that justice on the self-condemned
He deals on his own soul.

Proud despair and splendid isolation are mingled in Manfred—a disdain of the common herd, with which he mingles only to lead. "The lion is alone, and so am I." The good abbot can see the tragedy of this profound alienation:

This should have been a noble creature: he
Hath all the energy which would have made
A goodly frame of glorious elements,
Had they been wisely mingled; as it is,
It is an awful chaos—light and darkness,
And mind and dust, and passions and pure thoughts
Mixed, and contending without end or order—
All dormant and destructive; he will perish,
And yet he must not.

It seems to me that Byron, through the mouth of his hero, Manfred, expresses much that we find at the root of contemporary alienation. I find myself often moved to think the same thoughts as did the wise old abbot when I think of the alienated patients I have known.

But where in this lies the creative potential that might be turned to productive and progressive uses? The romantic hero, in turning away from society and the values of his culture, was able to turn within himself. He found in his own subjectivity the resources for a new synthesis. The problem posed by the European romantics—the alienation of the individual from society and the essential loneliness and isolation of modern man—was cast by the great Russian thinkers in terms of the problem of human freedom. No one has wrestled with this problem more intensely than Dostoevsky. It is the central problem for Raskolnikov, for Ivan Karamazov, for the hero of the underground. They all struggle with the threat of absolute freedom, which to the Russian mind becomes lawless chaos. Dostoevsky's heroes depict the unending struggle against the demons that cause man to become estranged from society and to revolt against the community of his fellowmen.

Freedom was the central problem for the romantics as well, and for their philosophical contemporaries. For the romantic, freedom was the victory of the individual over convention; it represented the courage to disregard and transcend the moral and aesthetic prejudices and standards of the age. In the person of Raskolnikov, we are forced to face the absolutizing of the problem; to what extent is freedom a value in itself, regardless of the deeds it creates and the consequences it elicits? Human freedom has a destructive potential as well as a creative and constructive one. The romantic model serves us well here, because the romantic hero was not merely a rebel against his society; he was also a man of ideals and inner strengths. As Bernbaum (1948) has written about Byron:

> The key to an understanding of Byron's peculiar place in the Romantic Movement lies, I believe, in the words quoted above, "his august conceptions of man, and his contemptuous opinions of men." Man is an idea or an ideal; men are what they are. Although Byron seems to sneer at everything, he admired, as much as any Romantic, whatever was really true, good, and beautiful.

The romantic solution dictates a return to inner individuality and subjectivity as to a basic resource for renewed strength and creative adaptations. In this sense, every effective course of treatment becomes a romantic quest. Doctor and patient are caught up in a quest for those inner sources of strength and purposefulness that will enable the patient to become a more resourceful, responsible, and functional adult. In the process, the patient must surrender the pseudoromantic vision of himself as either the victim of destructive external forces or as a frustrated romantic hero. The combat with dragons and demons must become an internal conflict and a struggle against the residues of the infantile past. The patient cannot recover his inner sources of creative potential unless he is able to accept his own realistic limitations. He cannot become human unless he is willing to surrender his wish to be superhuman. Only by discovering his weakness can be uncover his inner strength.

The patient becomes capable of facing the real challenges, rewards, and dangers of human existence only when he renounces the struggles and anxieties of childhood. But to renounce that struggle, with its implications of absolute victory or absolute defeat, is to renounce the dreams of omnipotence and the despair of frustrated narcissistic expectations. Only in so doing can he allow himself to become responsive to the central ambiguities and uncertainties of human action and experience. It requires a certain tragic sense of life to experience and accept victory in defeat and defeat in victory, pain in pleasure and pleasure in pain, loss in every new growth and growth in human loss, the renunciation that is required for each new gratification and the gratification in meaningful renunciation. As Roy Schafer (1970:285) has written:

> The person with a tragic sense of life knows the renunciations that are mingled with the conditions of gratification, the necessity to act in ig-

norance and bear the fear and guilt of action, the burden of unanswerable questions and incomprehensible afflictions, the probability of suffering while learning or changing, and the frequency with which it is true that only in the greatest adversity do men realize themselves most fully.

The strength of the romantic derived from a faith that the world of reality could become better than they found it to be. The romantics scorned and rejected the real world, a world of evil, ugliness, and human wretchedness. Human inhumanity and the disregard for human suffering and misery moved them to indignation and rage. This was the mood and attitude of Byron: a rebellious withdrawal from the evil and meanness of the world into a noble solitude. The alienation of the romantics did not end in despair. They looked forward to and held out the ideal of a better world. The evils of grinding poverty and cruel war had brutalized man and the inroads of industrialism had mechanized, standardized, dehumanized, and crushed the human spirit. But the romantic dream held out the promise and the possibility of something better for mankind, the possibility of a free and humane human life.

The romantic vision was inspired by hope—no ordinary hope, but a hope that was deep and strong. Wordsworth would write:

> ... whether we be young or old,
> Our destiny, our being's heart and home,
> Is with infinitude, and only there;
> With hope it is, hope than can never die,
> Effort, and expectation,and desire,
> And something evermore about to be.
>
> (*The Prelude*, VI, 603–608)

Such hope is not a utopian idealism of unattainable expectations. It is a hope for what is real and attainable, a hope that can accept the limitations of life, the ambiguities of human existence, and the inevitability of disappointments. It is the infantile ideal that harbors omnipotent expectations and leaves no room for failure. Real hope can accept the possibility of attainment only insofar as it also can accept the possibility of disappointment (Meissner 1973).

Conclusion

I have been dealing in this chapter with an increasingly common form of psychopathology—the alienation syndrome. I have discussed the aspects of depression, narcissism, and aggression that form essential aspects of the syndrome. I have tried to stress the essential dimension of alienation, the disparity between individual and social (and religious) values, and the rejection and rebellion against social structures. The alienated individual is not merely angry, disappointed, frustrated, and lonely; he is also estranged from the society in which he lives, from himself, from his church, and from his God.

In considering the destructive aspects of alienation, we should not overlook its creative potential. The disparity of individual and social values is an essential and integral part of the social process and necessary for the continuing growth and adaptation in human culture and social existence. In dealing with alienated patients, psychiatrists and religious ministers cannot concern themselves with the resolution of inner conflict to the detriment or undermining of individuality and positive difference. It is in the unique individuality of each human being that his resource for meaningful social contribution lies. However, only to the extent to which the individual becomes authentically free—free from enmeshment in inner conflicts, from infantile impediments and struggles with the projected demons of his own intrapsychic world—can he utilize and constructively direct that inner potentiality.

The therapeutic task, therefore, on both an individual and a religious level, is to oppose and eliminate what is infantile and destructive, but at the same time to respect and respond to the ideal. If we destroy the ideal and the faith and hope that engender it, we destroy something precious in itself and crucial to our own betterment and survival. The crucial question that confronts our society and our religious commitment at the present hour is whether we can eliminate, reject, control, or cure the residues of infantile rage and resentment without at the same time destroying the ideals, values, faith, and hope that are the lifeblood of society.

REFERENCES

Ackerknecht, E.H. 1943. "Psychopathology, Primitive Medicine and Primitive Culture," *Bulletin of the History of Medicine* 14:30–67.

Adler, R. 1956. "The Value Concept in Sociology," *American Journal of Sociology* 62:272–79.

Adorno, T.W., E. Frenkel-Brunswick, D.J. Levinson, and R.N. Sanford. 1950. *The Authoritarian Personality.* New York: Harper.

Allport, G.W., et al. 1951. *A Study of Values,* revised ed. Boston: Houghton Mifflin.

Balint, M. 1948. "On Genital Love," in *Primary Love and Psychoanalytic Technique.* London: Tavistock, 1959, 109–20.

Barton, A.H. 1962. "Measuring the Values of Individuals," in *Review of Recent Research Bearing on Religious and Character Formations. Religious Education* (Suppl.), 62–97.

Baum, G. 1966. "Vatican II's Constitution on Revelation: History and Interpretation." *Theological Studies* 28:51–75.

Baum, G. 1969. *Faith and Doctrine: A Contemporary View.* New York: Paulist Press.

Belshaw, C.S. 1959. "The Identification of Values in Anthropology." *American Journal of Sociology* 64:555–62.

Berger, K. 1968. "Grace. I. Biblical," in K. Rahner, S.J., et al., eds., *Sacramentum Mundi* 2:409–12. New York: Herder and Herder.

Berman, S. 1970. "Alienation: An Essential Process of the Psychology of Adolescence." *Journal of the American Academy of Child Psychiatry* 9:233–50.

Bernbaum, E., ed. 1948. *Anthology of Romanticism,* 3rd ed. New York: Ronald.

Bidney, D. 1954. "Review of Culture: A Critical Review of Concepts and Definitions by Kroeber and Kluckhohn." *American Journal of Sociology* 59:488–89.

Bloch, E. 1970. *Man on His Own: Essays in the Philosophy of Religion.* New York: Herder and Herder.

Boris, H.N. 1976. "On Hope: Its Nature and Psychotherapy." *International Review of Psycho-Analysis* 3:139–50.

Bretall, R., ed. 1946. *A Kierkegaard Anthology.* Princeton: Princeton University Press.

Brierley M. 1947. "Notes on Psychoanalysis and Integrative Living." *International Journal of Psycho-Analysis* 28:57–105.

Buber, M. 1959. *I and Thou.* New York: Charles Scribner's Sons.

Buber, M. 1961. *Two Types of Faith.* New York: Harper and Row.

Bychowski, G. 1967. "The Archaic Object and Alienation." *International Journal of Psycho-Analysis* 48:384–93.

Camus, A. 1946. *The Stranger.* New York: Knopf.

Cantril, H., and G.W. Allport. 1933. "Recent Applications of the *Study of Values.*" *Journal of Abnormal and Social Psychology* 28:259–73.

Colburn, F. 1970. "The Theology of Grace: Present Trends and Future Directions." *Theological Studies* 31:692–711.

Collins, J. 1953. *The Mind of Kierkegaard.* Chicago: Henry Regnery.

Deutsch, H. 1942. "Some Forms of Emotional Disturbance and Their Relationship to Schizophrenia," in *Neuroses and Character Types.* New York: International Universities Press, 1965.

Deutsch, H. 1967. *Selected Problems of Adolescence.* New York: International Universities Press.

Dewey, J. 1939. *Theory of Valuation.* Chicago: University of Chicago Press.

Edwards, P. 1971. "Kierkegaard and the 'Truth' of Christianity." *Philosophy* 46:89–108.

Erikson, E.H. 1959. *Identity and the Life Cycle.* New York: International Universities Press. Psychological Issues, Monograph 1.

Erikson, E.H. 1962. *Young Man Luther.* New York: Norton.

Erikson, E.H. 1963. *Childhood and Society.* 2nd ed. New York: Norton.

Erikson, E.H. 1964. *Insight and Responsibility.* New York: Norton.

Erikson, E.H. 1968. *Identity: Youth and Crisis.* New York: Norton.

Erikson, E.H. 1969. *Gandhi's Truth: On the Origins of Militant Non-Violence.* New York: Norton.

Evans, D. 1979. *Struggle and Fulfillment: The Inner Dynamics of Religion and Morality.* New York: Collins.

Feuer, L.S. 1955. *Psychoanalysis and Ethics.* Springfield, Ill: Thomas.

Fowler, J.W. 1974. "Faith, Liberation and Human Development." *The Foundation,* 79. Atlanta: Gammon Theological Seminary.

Fowler, J.W. 1976. "Stages in Faith: The Structural-Developmental Approach, in: T.C. Hennessey, ed., *Values and Moral Development.* New York: Paulist Press, 173–211.

Fowler, J.W., and S. Keen. 1978. *Life Maps: Conversations on the Journey of Faith.* Waco: Word Books.

Fowler, J.W. 1981. *Stages of Faith: The Psychology of Human Development and the Quest for Meaning.* New York: Harper and Row.

Frank, J.D. 1974a. "Psychotherapy: The Restoration of Morale." *American Journal of Psychiatry* 131:271–74.

Frank, J.D. 1974b. "Therapeutic Components of Psychotherapy." *Journal of Nervous and Mental Diseases* 159:325–42.

Fransen, P. 1962. *Divine Grace and Man.* New York: Mentor-Omega Books, 1965.

Fransen, P. 1964. "Towards a psychology of divine grace," in W. Birmingham and J.E. Cunneen, eds., *Cross Currents of Psychiatry and Catholic Morality.* New York: Pantheon, 31–61.

Fransen, P.F. 1969. *The New Life of Grace.* New York: Desclee.

French, T.M. 1963. "Hope and Repudiation of Hope in Psychoanalytic Therapy." *International Journal of Psycho-Analysis* 44:304–16.

Freud, S. 1900. "The Interpretation of dreams." *Standard Edition,* 4 and 5. London: Hogarth, 1958.

Freud, S. 1908. "Creative Writers and Day-dreaming." *Standard Edition,* 9:141–53. London: Hogarth, 1959.

Freud, S. 1911. "Psychoanalytic Notes on an Autobiographical Account of a Case of Paranoia (Dementia Paranoides). *Standard Edition,* 12:1–82. London: Hogarth, 1958.

Freud, S. 1917. "Mourning and Melancholia." *Standard Edition,* 14: 237–60. London: Hogarth, 1957.

Gesell, A. 1947. *The Child From Five to Ten.* New York: Harper.

Greenacre, P. 1970. "Youth, Growth and Violence." *The Psychoanalytic Study of the Child* 25:340–59.

Greenberg, J.R., and S.A. Mitchell. 1983. *Object Relations in Psychoanalytic Theory.* Cambridge: Harvard University Press.

Grolnick, S. A. 1978. "Dreams and Dreaming as Transitional Phenomena," in S.A. Grolnick and L. Barkin, eds., *Between Fantasy and Reality: The Transitional Object,* New York: Aronson, 213–31.

Gustafson, J.M. 1970. "The Conditions of Hope: Reflections on Human Experience." *Continuum* 7:535–45.

Hallowell, A.I. 1950. "Personality Structure and the Evolution of Man." *American Anthropologist* 52:159–73.

Hallowell, A.I. 1960. "Behavioral Evolution and the Emergence of the Self," in S. Tax, *Evolution after Darwin.* Chicago: University of Chicago Press, 309–71.

Hartmann, H. 1939. *Ego Psychology and the Problem of Adaptation.* New York: International Universities Press, 1958.

Hartmann, H. 1948. "Comments on the Psychoanalytic Theory of Instinctual Drives," in *Essays on Ego Psychology.* New York: International Universities Press, 69–89.

Hartmann, H. 1960. *Psychoanalysis and Moral Values.* New York: International Universities Press.

Hauser, A. 1970. *The Social History of Art.* New York: Vintage Books.

Holt, R.R. 1967. "The Primary Process," in R.R. Holt, ed., *Motives and Thoughts: Psychoanalytic Essays in Honor of David Rapaport.* New York: International Universities Press, 345–83.

Horney, K. 1950. *Neurosis and Human Growth.* New York: Norton.

Hyman, H.H. 1953. "The Value System of Different Classes: A Social Psychological Contribution to the Analysis of Stratification," in R. Bendix and S.M. Lipset, eds., *Class, Status, and Power.* Glencoe, Ill.: Free Press, 426–42.

Jacobson, E. 1964. *The Self and the Object World.* New York: International Universities Press.

Keniston, K. 1965. *The Uncommitted: Alienated Youth in American Society.* New York: Harcourt, Brace Jovanovich.

Kernberg, O.F. 1976. *Object Relations Theory and Clinical Psychoanalysis.* New York: Aronson.

Kernberg, O.F. 1977. "Boundaries and Structure in Love Relations. *Journal of the American Psychoanalytic Association* 25:81–114.

Kierkegaard, S. 1834–55. *The Journals of Soren Kierkegaard,* ed. A. Dru. New York: Oxford University Press, 1938.

Kierkegaard, S. 1984a. *Either/Or.* 2 vols. New York: Doubleday, 1959.

Kierkegaard, S. 1843b. *Fear and Trembling.* New York: Doubleday, 1954.

Kierkegaard, S. 1846. *Concluding Unscientific Postscript.* Princeton: Princeton University Press, 1941.

Kierkegaard, S. 1849. *The Sickness unto Death.* New York: Doubleday, 1954.

Kluckhohn, C., and O.H. Mowrer. 1944. "Culture and Personality: A Conceptual Scheme." *American Anthropologist* 46:1–29.

Kluckhohn, C., et al. 1962. "Values and Value-Orientations in the Theory of Action: An Exploration in Definition and Classification," in T. Parsons, and E.A. Shils, eds., *Toward a General Theory of Action.* New York: Harper and Row, 388–433.

Kluckhohn, F.R., and F.L. Strodtbeck. 1961. *Variations in Value Orientations.* Evanston, Ill.: Peterson.

Kohlberg, L. 1969. "Stage and Sequence: The Cognitive Developmental Approach to Socialization," in D.A. Goslin, ed., *Handbook of Socialization Theory and Research.* Chicago: Rand-McNally, 347–480.

Kohlberg, L. 1972. "Continuities and Discontinuities in Childhood and Adult Moral Development Revisited," in P.B. Baltes, and K.W. Schaie, eds., *Life-Span Developmental Psychology: Research and Theory.* New York: Academic Press.

Kohlberg, L., and C. Gilligan. 1971. "The Adolescent as a Philosopher: The Discovery of the Self in a Postconventional World." *Daedalus* 100:1063.

Kohut, H. 1971. *The Analysis of the Self.* New York: International Universities Press.

Kohut, H. 1976. "Creativeness, Charisma, Group Psychology: Reflections on the Self-Analysis of Freud," in J.E. Gedo and G.H. Pollock, eds., *Freud: The Fusion of Science and Humanism.* Psychological Issues, Monograph 34/35. New York: International Universities Press, 379–425.

Korner, I.M. 1970. "Hope as a Method of Coping." *Journal of Consulting and Clinical Psychology* 34:134–39.

Kris, E. 1952. *Psychoanalytic Explorations in Art.* New York: International Universities Press.

Kroeber, A.L. 1917. "The Superorganic." *American Anthropologist* 19:163–213.

Kroeber, A.L. 1948. *Anthropology.* New York: Harcourt.

Kroeber, A.L., and C. Kluckhohn. 1952. "Culture: A Critical Review of Concepts and Definitions." *Papers of the Peabody Museum of American Archaeology and Ethnology,* Harvard Univeristy, 47(1):1–223.

Lasswell, H.D. 1939. "Person, Personality, Group Culture." *Psychiatry* 2:533–61.

Lichtenstein, H. 1970. "Changing Implications of the Concept of Psychosexual Development: An Inquiry concerning the Validity of Classical Psychoanalytic Assumptions concerning Sexuality." *Journal of the American Psychoanalytic Association* 18:300–18.

Lickona, T., ed. 1976. *Moral Development and Behavior: Theory, Research, and Social Issues.* New York: Holt, Rinehart and Winston, 34–35.

Lifton, R.J. 1956. *Thought Reform and the Psychology of Totalism.* New York: Norton.

Lindesmith, A.R., and A.L. Strauss. 1950. "A Critique of Culture-Personality writings." *American Sociological Review* 15:587–600.

Linton, R. 1945. *The Cultural Background of Personality.* New York: Appleton-Century.

Loewald, H.W. 1978. *Psychoanalysis and the History of the Individual.* New Haven: Yale University Press.

Lonergan, S.J., B.J.F. 1972. *Method in Theology.* New York: Herder and Herder.

Lowenfeld, H. and Y. Lowenfeld. 1970. "Permissive Society and the Superego: Some Current Thoughts about Freud's Cultural Concepts." *Psychoanalytic Quarterly* 39:590–608.

Lynch, S.J., W.F. 1965. *Images of Hope.* Baltimore: Helicon.

Mace, C.A. 1953. "Homeostasis, Needs and Values." *British Journal of Psychology* 44:200–210.

Mahler, M.S. 1968. *On Human Symbiosis and the Vicissitudes of Individuation.* New York: International Universities Press.

Mahler, M.S., F. Pine, and A. Bergman. 1975. *The Psychological Birth of the Human Infant.* New York: Basic Books.

Marcel, G. 1960. *The Mystery of Being. II. Faith and Reality.* Chicago: Regnery.

Marcel, G. 1962. *Homo Viator: Introduction to a Metaphysics of Hope.* New York: Harper and Row.

Martin, A.R. 1949. "Reassurance in Therapy." *American Journal of Psychoanalysis* 9:17–29.

Maslow, A.H. 1954. *Motivation and Personality.* New York: Harper and Row.

Malsow, A.H. 1955. "Deficiency Motivation and Growth Motivation." In M.R. Jones, ed., *Nebraska Symposium on Motivation.* Lincoln: University of Nebraska Press, 1–31.

Maslow, A.H. 1959. "Psychological Data and Value Theory." In A.H. Maslow, ed., *New Knowledge in Human Values.* New York: Harper and Row, 119–36.

McDargh, J. 1983. *Psychoanalytic Object Relations Theory and the Study of Religion. On Faith and the Imagining of God.* Lanham, Md.: University Press of America.

Meissner, S.J., W.W. 1958. "Nonconstructural Aspects of Psychological Constructs. *Psychological Review* 65:143–50.

Meissner, S.J., W.W. 1963–1964. "Psychological Notes on the *Spiritual Exercises.*" *Woodstock Letters* 92:349–66; 93:31–58, 165–91.

Meissner, S.J., W.W. 1966a. *Foundations for a Psychology of Grace.* New York: Paulist Press.

Meissner, S.J., W.W. 1966b. "The Implications of Experience for Psychological Theory." *Philosophy and Phenomenological Research* 26:503–28.

Meissner, S.J., W.W. 1966c. "The Operational Principle and Meaning in Psychoanalysis." *Psychoanalytic Quarterly* 35:233–55.

Meissner, S.J., W.W. 1970. "Notes toward a Theory of Values: The Place of Values." *Journal of Religion and Health* 9:233–49.

Meissner, S.J., W.W. 1971. "Notes on Identification. II. Clarification of Related Concepts." *Psychoanalytic Quarterly* 40:227-302.

Meissner, S.J., W.W. 1972. "Notes on Identification. III. The Concept of Identification." *Psychoanalytic Quarterly* 41:224-60.

Meissner, S.J., W.W. 1973. "Notes on the Psychology of Hope." *Journal of Religion and Health* 12:7-29, 120-39.

Meissner, S.J., W.W. 1974. "Portrait of a Rebel as a Young Man." *International Journal of Psychoanalytic Psychotherapy* 3:456-82.

Meissner, S.J., W.W. 1977. "The Psychology of Religious Experience." *Communio* 36-59.

Meissner, S.J., W.W. 1978a. *The Paranoid Process.* New York: Aronson.

Meissner, S.J., W.W. 1978b. "Psychoanalytic Aspects of Religious Experience." *The Annual of Psychoanalysis* 6:103-41.

Meissner, S.J., W.W. 1979. "Internalization and Object Relations." *Journal of the American Psychoanalytic Association* 27:345-60.

Meissner, S.J., W.W. 1980. "The Problem of Internalization and Structure Formation." *International Journal of Psycho-Analysis* 61:237-48.

Meissner, S.J., W.W. 1981. *Internalization in Psychoanalysis.* Psychological Issues, Monograph 50. New York: International Universities Press.

Meissner, S.J., W.W. 1984a. "The Cult Phenomenon: Psychoanalytic Perspective." *The Psychoanalytic Study of Society* 10:91-111.

Meissner, S.J., W.W. 1984b. *Psychoanalysis and Religious Experience.* New Haven: Yale University Press.

Melges, F.Y., and J. Bowlby. 1969. "Types of Hopelessness in Psychopathological Process." *Archives of General Psychiatry* 20:690-99.

Meng, H., and E.L. Freud, eds. 1963. *Psychoanalysis and Faith: The Letters of Sigmund Freud and Oskar Pfister.* New York: Basic Books.

Menninger, K. 1959. "Hope." *American Journal of Psychiatry* 116:481-91.

Merton, R.K. 1957. *Social Theory and Social Structure.* New York: Free Press.

Metz, J.B. 1967. "Creative Hope." *Cross Currents* 17:171-79.

Metz, J.B. 1969. *Theology of the World.* New York: Herder and Herder.

Modell, A.H. 1968. *Object Love and Reality.* New York: International Universities Press.

Moltman, J. 1967. *Theology of Hope.* New York: Harper and Row.

Morris, C.W. 1949. "Axiology as the Science of Preferential Behavior." In R. Lepley ed., *Value: A Co-operative Inquiry.* New York: Columbia University Press, 211-22.

Morris, C.W. 1956. *Varieties of Human Value.* Chicago: University of Chicago Press.

Mouroux, J. 1954. *The Christian Experience.* New York: Sheed and Ward.

Nicholi, A.M. 1970. "Campus Disorders: A Problem of Adult Leadership." *American Journal of Psychiatry* 127:424-29.

Niebuhr, H.R. 1941. *The Meaning of Revelation.* New York: Macmillan Paperbacks.

Niebuhr, H.R. 1960. *Radical Monotheism and Western Culture.* New York: Harper and Row.

Niebuhr, H.R. 1963. *The Responsible Self: An Essay in Christian Moral Philosophy.* New York: Harper and Row.

Niebuhr, R.R. 1972. *Experiential Religion*. New York: Harper and Row.

Orlansky, H. 1949. "Infant Care and Personality. *Psychological Bulletin* 40:1–48.

Parsons, T., and E.A. Shils, eds. 1962. *Toward a General Theory of Action*. New York: Harper and Row.

Pfister, O. 1928. "Die Illusion einer Zukunft." *Imago* 14:149–84.

Piaget, J. 1977. *The Essential Piaget: An Interpretive Reference and Guide*, eds. H.E. Gruber and J.J. Vonèche. New York: Basic Books.

Pruyser, P.W. 1977. "The Seamy Side of Current Religious Beliefs." *Bulletin of the Menninger Clinic* 41:329–48.

Rahner, S.J., K. 1965. "Concerning the Relationship between Nature and Grace." *Theological Investigations* 1:297–318. Baltimore: Helicon.

Rahner, S.J., K. 1968. "Grace: II. Theological. B. Systematic." In K. Rahner, S.J., et al., eds., *Sacramentum Mundi* 2:415–22. New York: Herder and Herder.

Rahner, K., and H. Vorgrimler. 1965. *Theological Dictionary*, ed. C. Ernst; transl. R. Strachan. New York: Herder and Herder.

Rapaport, D. 1960. *The Structure of Psychoanalytic Theory*. Psychological Issues, Monograph 6. New York: International Universities Press.

Rickaby, S.J., J. 1923. *The Spiritual Exercises of St. Ignatius Loyola*. London: Burns, Oates and Washbourne.

Ricoeur, P. 1970. *Freud and Philosophy*. New Haven: Yale University Press.

Riesman, D. 1950. *The Lonely Crowd*. New Haven: Yale University Press.

Rizzuto, A.M. 1979. *The Birth of the Living God*. Chicago: University of Chicago Press.

Rochlin, G. 1965. *Griefs and Discontents: The Forces of Change*. Boston: Little, Brown.

Rothman, S., and S.R. Lichter. 1982. *Roots of Radicalism*. New York: Oxford University Press.

Sanford, N. 1955. "The Dynamics of Identification." *Psychological Review* 62:106–18.

Schafer, R. 1960. "The Loving and Beloved Superego in Freud's Structural Theory." *The Psychoanalytic Study of the Child* 15:163–88.

Schafer, R. 1970. "The Psychoanalytic View of Reality." *International Journal of Psychoanalysis* 51:279–97.

Schafer, R. 1976. *A New Language for Psychoanalysis*. New Haven: Yale University Press.

Sipe, A.W.R. 1970. *Hope: Psychiatry's Commitment*. New York: Brunner/Mazel.

Smith, M.B. 1963. "Personal Values in the Study of Lives." In R.W. White, ed., *The Study of Lives*. New York: Atherton Press, 325–47

Smith, W.C. 1979. *Faith and Belief*. Princeton: Princeton University Press.

Spiro, M.E. 1951. "Culture and Personality: The Natural History of a False Dichotomy." *Psychiatry* 14:19–46.

Spranger, E. 1928. *Types of Men*. Halle: Niemezis.

Stotland, E. 1969. *The Psychology of Hope*. San Francisco: Jossey-Bass.

Ticho, E. 1972. "The Development of Superego Autonomy. *Psychoanalytic Review* 59(2):217–33.

Tolman, E.C. 1962. "A Psychological Model." In Parsons and Shils, eds. (1962), 279–361.

Tylor, E.B. 1874. *Primitive Culture*. Chicago: Brentano.

Ungerleider, J.T., and D.K. Wellisch. 1979. "Coercive Persuasion (Brainwashing), Religious Cults, and Deprogramming." *American Journal of Psychiatry* 136:279–82.

Vergote, A. 1969. *The Religious Man*. Dayton, Ohio: Pflaum.

Vernon, P.E., and G.W. Allport. 1931. "A Test for Personal Values." *Journal of Abnormal and Social Psychology* 26:233–48.

Vivas, E. 1963. *The Moral Life and the Ethical Life*. Chicago: Regnery.

Weisskopf, W.A. 1959. "Comment." In A.H. Maslow, ed., (1959), *New Knowledge in Human Values* 199–223.

White, L.A. 1948. "Man's Control over Civilization." *Scientific Monthly* 66:235–47.

White, L.A. 1959. "The Concept of Culture." *American Anthropologist* 61:227–51.

White, R.W. 1963. *Ego and Reality in Psychoanalytic Theory*. Psychological Issues, Monograph 11. New York: International Universities Press.

Williams, F.S. 1970. "Alienation of Youth as Reflected in the Hippie Movement." *Journal of the American Academy of Child Psychiatry* 9:251–63.

Winnicott, D.W. 1960. "Ego Distortion in Terms of True and False Self." In *The Maturational Process and the Facilitating Environment*. New York: International Universities Press, 1965.

Winnicott, D.W. 1971. *Playing and Reality*. New York: Basic Books.

Woodruff, A.D. 1942. "Personal Values and the Direction of Behavior. *School Review* 50:32–42.

Woodruff, A.D., and F.J. DiVesta. 1948. "The Relationship between Values, Concepts and Attitudes." *Education and Psychological Measurements* 8:645–59.